ANDREY BELY

STUDIES OF THE HARRIMAN INSTITUTE

The W. Averell Harriman Institute for Advanced Study of the Soviet Union, Columbia University, sponsors the *Studies of the Harriman Institute* in the belief that their publication contributes to scholarly research and public understanding. In this way the Institute, while not necessarily endorsing their conclusions, is pleased to make available the results of some of the research conducted under its auspices. A list of the *Studies* appears at the back of this book.

ANDREY BELY

SPIRIT OF SYMBOLISM

Edited by

John E. Malmstad

Cornell University Press

Ithaca and London

First published 1987 by Cornell University Press.
International Standard Book Number 0-8014-1984-0
Library of Congress Catalog Card Number 86-29095
Printed in the United States of America
*Librarians: Library of Congress cataloging information
appears on the last page of the book.*

In memory of
Klavdiya Nikolaevna Bugaeva

Contents

Preface

Turn-of-the-century Russia is gradually becoming familiar to us. Yet it is still a remote world that defies easy interpretation, perhaps because its culture is a richness of contradictions and extremes. No figure of the time better exemplifies its paradoxes—its mood of "cheerful apocalypse," to borrow Hermann Broch's characterization of prewar Vienna—than the man who was born in 1880 as Boris Nikolaevich Bugaev but who is known to us as Andrey Bely. Among the Russian Symbolists who served as shock troops of modernism were many striking and innovative writers and personalities. Even in such company Bely stands out. A writer of versatility and lavish gifts, he cast a critical eye on received standards of truth and value in every area of intellectual endeavor, subjected nineteenth-century modes of writing prose, poetry, and criticism to a penetrating and comprehensive critique, and longed for a radical transformation not only of society but of life itself. His visionary maximalism is quintessentially typical of the age. Like his fellow creative spirits—writers, artists, composers, and choreographers—he transformed every area he touched. His experiments and innovations became part of the sensibility of every important Russian writer in the generation that followed.

When Bely died in 1934, Boris Pasternak wrote a panegyrical obituary that appeared in *Izvestiya* (January 9, 1934) above his signature and those of Boris Pil'nyak and Grigory Sannikov. They called Bely the "most remarkable [*zamechatel'neishii*] writer of our age," one whose name would stand among those of the greatest writers not only of Russia but of the world. They found Bely's achievement "more perfect" than Marcel Proust's, and even referred to James Joyce as Bely's "literary pupil." A judgment no less questionable declared Bely the creator of a "huge literary school," in which they presumably included themselves. (It was his prose that was clearly uppermost in their minds.) Now, Bely is argua-

9

bly *the* major Russian writer of this century, but his influence, in all but
the most elusive sense of the word, is hard to pinpoint. To be sure,
Viktor Shklovsky wrote in 1929 that the "new Russian literature" of the
1920s would have been inconceivable without Bely's earliest works ("Ornamental'naya proza," in *O teorii prozy*). Marina Tsvetaeva, Il'ya Eren-
burg, Evgeny Zamyatin, and others expressed similar opinions. It would
be absurd to deny the impact of Bely on Russian literature, and it is
difficult to imagine how twentieth-century Russian prose or poetry—by
Zamyatin, say, or Pil'nyak, Andrey Platonov, Vladimir Nabokov,
Tsvetaeva, and Pasternak—would have looked without him. But the fact
is that such writers as Zamyatin and Aleksey Remizov exerted more
palpable influence on Soviet literature of the 1920s than did Bely. He
never really created a "school," although a number of writers clung to
his coattails for a time. That is not to say, as some critics have done, that
Bely's work represents a dead end, but rather to insist on his powerful
eccentricity. He was an "experimental" writer in ways few others would
ever have dreamed of risking. His narrative and linguistic quests were
fundamentally inimitable (if superficially imitatable), so closely were
they bound to his idiosyncratic world view. One senses, too, that his
hesitations and failures were as essential to his identity as were his indu-
bitable successes. It is unreasonable to expect that Bely could have resolved all the tensions and contradictions of so varied and daring an
oeuvre. But it is precisely those irresolutions that might have shaped the
future of Russian prose had it been allowed to grow organically after the
Revolution. Bely's writings were a powerful force that might have liber-
ated Russian literature from the past once and for all. Liberation was
not, however, what the postrevolutionary cultural authorities had in
mind.

   In Bely's case, the hasty neglect and overdue revival traditionally experienced by many great writers was complicated by the special ways in
which Soviet literature developed. The final volume of his memoirs
appeared after his death, as did his study of Nikolay Gogol. Along with
Valery Bryusov and Aleksandr Blok, he figured in the 1937 volume of
Literary Heritage (*Literaturnoe nasledstvo*), devoted to Russian Symbolism.
Thereafter, only a tiny volume of verse came out during that strange
year of "phony war," 1940, when in a weird outburst of relative liber-
alism the works of several previously suppressed writers, such as Fedor
Sologub and Anna Akhmatova, were allowed into print. For the remainder of Stalin's life, Bely's name was passed over in silence; then at
last it resurfaced, along with those of many of the best Russian writers of
the century. It was not until 1966, however, that any of his writings was
reprinted: a volume of selected verse; and since then the only work of
his to be published in his homeland has been *Petersburg,* which many
readers place on a short list of the greatest novels of the century. Even

Petersburg is apparently considered insufficiently noteworthy to be kept in print. Meanwhile, scholars in the West have been discovering Bely, and the enterprising Fink Verlag of Munich has issued reprints and new editions of all his major works. Yet a proper edition of his literary heritage—almost fifty individual volumes and hundreds of articles—still remains an immense project for the future.

Literary studies move centripetally: the more commentary that is written on a particular author or problem, the more inevitably will be written. This observation seems to hold for Bely at the moment: over the last decade or so, specialized studies have appeared in English, French, German, Italian, and other Western languages in increasing numbers. Yet, with the exception of Konstantin Mochul'sky, whose 1955 monograph is now seriously out of date and marred by numerous errors of fact, no one has ventured a work addressing all areas of Bely's work—fiction, verse, memoirs, critical and theoretical writings. The sheer immensity of his output has been a deterrent. With the selective opening of his archives in the Soviet Union, a new generation of Bely scholars has begun to realize how much remains to be investigated before anything like a definitive critical study can even be attempted, much less the kind of biography English readers have come to expect for the great figures of their literature. In the meantime, John Elsworth's fine brief biography, *Andrey Bely* (1972), can be recommended.

The centenary of Bely's birth in 1980 passed virtually unmarked in Russia, as did the fiftieth anniversary of his death in 1984. Again, scholars in the West tried to fill some of the gap with a book of centenary papers and a conference in Bergamo. In the second week of June 1984 I convened a small symposium under the auspices of the Harriman Institute of Columbia University. Each essay was submitted well in advance, read by all the participants, and then subjected to intensive commentary and discussion over a five-day period. I decided not to invite highly specialized papers on a variety of narrow topics in favor of long essays surveying Bely's major works in all genres, summarizing the present state of research, reassessing critical approaches, or offering fresh readings of major works. The essays naturally vary in tone and emphasis, partly because of the state of Bely studies and the fluctuating fortunes of criticism (or lack of it). The late novels, the poetry, and the memoirs, for instance, have attracted far less critical attention than *Petersburg* and therefore warranted more general treatment. Still, the resulting essays do constitute a kind of collective monograph.

The kind of controversy that surrounded Bely from his first appearance in print until his death reappeared during our symposium and made for lively exchanges. Some of our disagreements could be traced to Bely's terminology: when he uses the word "religion," for example, he surely does not mean a particular form of doctrinal allegiance, but rather a general form of human cultural activity, of which all religions are instances. Therefore, when he talks about the religious nature of art, people are bound to disagree about his meaning. The same problem arises with such terms as "metaphysics," "the transcendent," and "faith." Some of Bely's contemporaries, notably Vyacheslav Ivanov and Nikolay Berdyaev, accused him of utterly lacking any "idealist" (i.e., metaphysical) dimension. Bely heatedly denied the allegation, but the question remains open. The participants in the symposium kept returning to it, often with strong differences of opinion between those who saw a holistic Bely and those who saw a far more schizophrenic figure who desperately wished to believe in the transcendent and at times convinced himself of its existence, but who achieved the most satisfactory aesthetic results when conviction clashed with doubt. The issue cannot be laid to rest here. Aware of Bely's habit of seeming to change the question every time his critics thought they had found the answer, we agreed to disagree; but it seems that this issue will certainly be one of the major areas of investigation in any future study of Bely that goes beyond the formal.

The metaphysical is touched on, in one way or another, in each of the essays in this volume. But the main emphasis falls elsewhere.

Roger Keys surveys Bely's most experimental prose works, the little-studied "symphonies." Early Symbolist doctrine, which Bely helped to form, insisted that there was no division between art and theurgy. By making claims far beyond those usually advanced for fiction or poetry, it created obvious aesthetic problems, which Keys examines, focusing on the implications for narrative strategies.

The spirit of the times was marked by a turning toward the cosmos. Yet scholars of Bely (like those of Yeats in the recent past) have often been embarrassed by his fascination with the occult and the esoteric, which he approached just as seriously as more "acceptable" philosophical traditions. Bely himself saw no conflict here. Nor does Maria Carlson, who probes the impact of Bely's wide reading in these areas on his first novel, *The Silver Dove,* his monument to the spiritual questing of his Symbolist contemporaries. "As above, so below": this occult idea of correspondence informs the novel in ways never before suspected, including Bely's patterning of its many levels according to the horoscope of its hero.

The interpenetration of the immanent and the transcendent can also be seen in *Petersburg.* But Robert A. Maguire and I have chosen to examine *Petersburg*'s multidimensional world against the background of two important articles Bely wrote at the same time he was working on the novel. Read together with the novel, the articles shed new light on it, especially its argument with Nietzsche. As all the essays in this volume show, however, Bely's nonfictional writings may guide us but we must not consider them prescriptions. Bely himself was the masterful chronicler of the human insistence on allegorizing experience into rigid forms cut off from life and destructive of it. Critics must be wary of falling into certainty when dealing with any of his works, especially one as complex as *Petersburg*.

Vladimir E. Alexandrov deals with the autobiographical imperative in the novels of Bely's middle period. The subjective impulse is important in all phases of Bely's career, but it became a central concern after he discovered Rudolf Steiner's anthroposophy. Alexandrov engages the question of Bely's interest in this esoteric doctrine. He shows how it is refracted in these works, how its eclecticism complemented Bely's own voracious ability to absorb the most varied influences, and how it buttressed and helped systematize views he had long held.

Bely's late period, from 1923 to his death, remains enigmatic and controversial. The works he produced then have always been greeted with reservation or rejected outright by even his most fervent admirers, who have difficulty seeing in them any connection with what went before. John Elsworth frankly notes all the doubts that have been voiced about the late novels, but he shows that in them, especially in *Masks*, Bely was seeking new ways of expressing what Carlyle calls "visible infinities." Bely had always been fascinated by the idea of a dynamic growth in the inner and outer worlds of thought and nature, but had never explored it so deeply or tied it so closely to the ethical dimension as in his last novels. Like Joyce in *Finnegans Wake,* he may have made impossible demands on his readers, but Elsworth points to the consistent system that underlies such a novel as *Masks*. He makes a persuasive case (as does Bely's widow in her memoirs, which still await a translator) for our need to catch up with Bely and to approach these works from Bely's premises, instead of testing them against preconceptions. Perhaps no one now speaks their language, but we can learn to do so if we try, instead of dismissing them out of hand as unreadable.

In his account of the memoirs on which Bely worked in the last decade of his life, Lazar Fleishman examines the "persistence of memory," with all its Daliesque overtones. He shows that these most criticized and least studied of Bely's works must be seen in a polemical context, for he wrote them at a time when disinterestedness was impossible: issues, values, even lives were being fought for. Fleishman is concerned with literary history, but he does not ignore the complications that arise when we remember that the memoirist, like the autobiographer, is a uniquely multiple figure—writer, narrator, and subject in one—and writing *now* about *then*.

It may well be that prose, both fiction and memoirs, best conveyed Bely's permeable sense of a world drenched in childhood memories and nightmares and skewed by fantasy. Yet he is a major poet too. That side of his work has scarcely been touched by serious criticism. This imbalance, oddly enough, characterizes the study of Russian Symbolism in general, even though it was a poetic movement above all. (Clearly Symbolism and poetry go in tandem, given Symbolism's strong antimimetic base.) G. S. Smith examines Bely's work in verse theory and assesses his contributions to its development in Russia. Even more important, he ventures into an area that has proved daunting to critics as he guides us through the labyrinth of Bely's poetry, where titles often refer not to clearly defined works but to a complex temporal process, and where the work's shape, far more than that of most poetry, is determined by the standpoint of the reader.

Bely sought to establish a theoretical basis for Symbolism in his critical writings, and often achieved it in his fiction and poetry as well. As we read him we are constantly reminded of Goethe's statement that "there is a delicate form of the empirical which identifies itself so intimately with its object that it thereby becomes theory." Steven Cassedy discusses the formal nature of Bely's theory of symbolism and his attempts at a more purely literary theory, while indicating that the two were always intimately linked in his mind. In setting Bely in a general European context, Cassedy's second essay does something never before seriously attempted. His discussion of Bely's theory of language will serve as the starting point for any future assessment of Bely's contribution to such a theory.

Circumstances made it impossible for some of the new generation of first-rate Soviet scholars of Bely, such as A. V. Lavrov, N. G. Pustygina, and S. S. Grechishkin, to take a direct part in the symposium. One of this group, L. K. Dolgopolov, has recently gone so far as to assert that Bely is interesting above all as a "personality," not as the author of this or that work. This is testimony to Bely's power to fascinate, almost to hypnotize, not only his contemporaries but readers long after his death. And Dmitry Maksimov, the most distinguished Soviet specialist on Symbolism, gives us a glimpse of that incandescent presence in the memoir of Bely which he revised for inclusion in this volume.

As Maksimov observes, the study of Bely has just begun. We have not said the last word on any of the subjects covered in the essays in this volume. But I hope we have opened up new territory, have succeeded in capturing some of the excitement that attends this area of research, and have encouraged the adventurous to follow us to this fascinating new-found land.

A few final words of explanation and thanks are in order. The transliteration system throughout the volume is that used by the Oxford Slavonic Papers (citations of books or articles employing one of the several other systems must, of course, render them precisely). For easier reading, a few exceptions to strict transliteration have been made in the text: Gogol, for example (not Gogol'), and Daryalsky (not Dar'yal'sky).

Throughout the volume, I follow the sensible former Russian convention of capitalizing all words in the titles of periodicals and only the first word in names of books (e.g., *Russkie Vedomosti* but *Serebryanyi golub'*). The reader can thus tell at a glance whether the source is a journal or a critical study or a novel. The practice should never have been changed, and it's high time it was restored. Bely was addicted to ellipses in his writings; to avoid confusion with Bely's usage, ellipses in our citations are enclosed by brackets. Ellipses in the works of other writers indicate omissions.

Marshall Shulman, director of Columbia University's Harriman Institute for Advanced Study of the Soviet Union, lent enthusiastic support to the symposium and provided the funding that made it possible for us to meet in New York. The interest and encouragement shown by Jonathan Sanders, assistant director of the Institute, proved invaluable at every stage of the project. Bernadine Joselyn, program coordinator of the Institute (and now with the United States Department of State), and Carol Ueland cheerfully and efficiently attended to the multitude of details that accompany any international gathering, and helped everything run so smoothly during and after our week of meetings that I was able to be a participant rather than merely a stage manager. Stefani Hoffman prepared a translation of the Fleishman essay, to which Ruth Mathewson applied her formidable editorial skills. I owe a word of thanks to Joan Elliott and Richard J. Gale for their help in preparing and printing the texts on an often recalcitrant word processor. All of these people, along with other staff members of the Institute, helped make the preparation of the final manuscript as painless as such a task can be. Barbara H. Salazar of Cornell University Press wrestled considerably and expertly with the stylistic vagaries of the various contributions; any flaws that remain may be ascribed to our obstinacy. And my colleague Robert Maguire deserves special acknowledgment. He took time out from his busy schedule to give advice at many stages of this work, as he did throughout my years at Columbia. I shall miss him and the others who made that time memorable and productive.

I am grateful to Cambridge University Press for permitting John Elsworth to base his contribution on two chapters of his *Andrey Bely: A Critical Study of the Novels* (1983); to Harvard University Press for permitting Vladimir E. Alexandrov to revise a chapter of his *Andrei Bely: The Major Symbolist Fiction* (1985); and to the University of California Press for permitting Steven Cassedy to expand ideas first presented in his "Translator's Introduction" to *Selected Essays of Andrey Bely* (1985) in his two essays in this volume. These debts are more formally acknowledged on the opening pages of the essays in question.

JOHN E. MALMSTAD

Cambridge, Massachusetts

ANDREY BELY

1

Bely's Symphonies

ROGER KEYS

I

According to his memoirs, Bely began to write in the autumn of 1896, when he was sixteen years old. "I wrote a great deal," he tells us, "but I kept it to myself [. . .]. There was an endless epic poem in the manner of Tasso, and a fantastic tale featuring an American yogi who could kill somebody by merely looking at him. And lyric fragments, too, quite feeble, but with a hefty dose of 'home-grown' decadence (I hadn't done any reading yet)."[1] Like most very young writers, he turned to prose fiction with no fixed idea about the kind of thing that he wanted to write. Nor did he have any firm views on the way Russian literature was developing. Not unlike Aleksandr Blok at about the same period, Bely became aware of "the new literature" only after he had already begun to write it himself. Indeed, according to an autobiographical note written in 1933, Bely's creative interests did not begin with literature at all. Music was his first love, and it was through music that he came to poetry and prose. "I felt more of a composer than a poet," he wrote. "Music long overshadowed the possibility of a literary career for me, and I became a writer only by accident [. . .]. Had circumstances turned out differently I might have become a composer or a scholar."[2] Elsewhere he tells us that in the late 1890s he felt himself at "the meeting point of poetry, prose, philosophy, and music. I knew that each was defective without the other, but as to how to combine them all within myself, I had no idea. I hadn't sorted out whether I was a theoretician, critic, and propagandist of art, a poet, a prose writer, or a composer. But I could feel creative forces welling up within me, telling me that I could achieve

---

1. *Na rubezhe dvukh stoletii* (Moscow and Leningrad, 1930), p. 351.
2. "O sebe kak pisatele," *Den' poezii* (Leningrad, 1972), p. 269.

anything and that it was up to me to form myself. I saw my future as a keyboard, and it depended on me to play a symphony."[3]

Piano improvisations expressing his most cherished feelings and aspirations soon went hand in hand with the writing of poetry and lyric prose. Indeed, his first literary efforts actually arose, he tells us, as "attempts to illustrate those youthful musical compositions of mine."[4] It would perhaps be unfair to examine what survives from this preliterary period too closely were it not for the fact that Bely eventually published some of these pieces (the lyric fragments that he included in his first book of verse, *Gold in Azure* [*Zoloto v lazuri*, 1904]) and that, in any case, he quite rightly considered these early works to mark an important stage in his creative development.[5] Thus they can cast valuable light on the more mature works to follow. He was under the impression that much of his juvenilia had perished or otherwise gone astray,[6] but this has turned out not to be the case. A sizeable quantity survived in that part of his archive which he sold to the Lenin Library in Moscow,[7] and the most interesting finds have recently been published by Aleksandr Lavrov, including extracts from his early diaries,[8] yet more lyric fragments, an untitled märchen, a short story, and the so-called "Predsimfoniya" or "Presymphony."[9]

Bely had already been writing for five years when Valery Bryusov accepted his *Second Symphony* for publication by Scorpio in 1902. With one significant exception, it is possible to divide the prose work that Bely wrote before that symphony into two typologically related groups, both of them forms of unmediated lyricism in which no distance intervenes between the values of the implied author and those of the subject of discourse.[10] The first group consists for the most part of mood pieces, elegiac impressionist prose of the purest water, presented in the first person by a narratorial voice that bears no trace of irony. The influence of Turgenev's *Poems in Prose* is unmistakable. A few of these pieces have been published by Lavrov (e.g., nos. 8, 13, 14). In his introductory re-

3. *Nachalo veka* (Moscow and Leningrad, 1933), p. 17.

4. "O sebe kak pisatele," p. 270.

5. See the so-called "Lettre autobiographique à Ivanov-Razumnik" of March 1–3, 1927, published in *Cahiers du monde russe et soviétique*, 15, no. 1–2 (1974), pp. 54–56.

6. See the "Spisok propavshikh ili unichtozhennykh avtorom rukopisei," which he wrote in 1927 (Manuscript Division, Saltykov-Shchedrin Library, Leningrad [hereafter GPB], fond 60 [Bely], opis' 1, item 31).

7. Manuscript Division, Lenin Library, Moscow (hereafter GBL), fond 25 (Bely).

8. A. V. Lavrov, "Yunosheskie dnevnikovye zametki Andreya Belogo," *Pamyatniki kul'tury: Novye otkrytiya, ezhegodnik 1979* (Leningrad, 1980), pp. 116–39.

9. A. V. Lavrov, "Yunosheskaya khudozhestvennaya proza Andreya Belogo," *Pamyatniki kul'tury: Novye otkrytiya, ezhegodnik 1980* (Leningrad, 1981), pp. 107–50.

10. For a discussion of unmediated as opposed to mediated lyricism in fiction, see R. J. Keys, "Andrey Bely and the Development of Russian Fiction," in *Essays in Poetics*, 8, no. 1 (1983), pp. 35–39.

marks Lavrov makes the point that when Bely eventually selected some of these lyric fragments for publication in *Gold in Azure*, he preferred the more plot-oriented ones, those that told an eerie, prophetic, or fantastic story.[11] These form what I would call a second group, in which the individual lyric perceptions of the narrator are less in evidence. Indeed, some fragments are narrated in the third person and deal with invented characters and situations (e.g., "The Hair Worm" ["Volosatik"] and "The Quarrel" ["Ssora"]). But the fictional guise is so thin that we cannot help being aware of the author's lyric presence, offering us *his* daydreams, *his* nightmares, *his* allegorical interpretations of life's mysteries.[12] Also included in this second group are such fragments as "The Vision" ("Videnie") and "The Dream" ("Son"), in which the influence of Revelation and of Nietzsche's *Also sprach Zarathustra* is most strongly felt. "The Vision," for example, consists of a number of short sentences and groups of sentences, consecutively numbered as in the Bible. Anaphora, parataxis, and the repeated use of hieratic, archaic vocabulary evoke an apocalyptic vision that the first-person narrator has supposedly witnessed. At no point is the reader invited to question the narrator's prophetic authority. This vision is meant to be taken as factual prophecy and for that reason lacks any explicit fictional motivation.

This theurgic stance underlies much of Bely's early fiction, although the word "fiction" here is somewhat inappropriate, given the nature of his prophetic enterprise. One very early work, however, appears to fall at least partly outside the circle of unequivocal authority: "He Who Has Come" ("Prishedshii"), subtitled "Fragment of a Mystery Play That Was Never Written." This and one other scene ("The Jaws of Night" ["Past' nochi"]) were eventually rewritten and published in 1903 and 1906, respectively,[13] but Bely later wrote that he considered the printed versions inferior to his original drafts of 1898. The whole work was to be titled "The Antichrist," and as Lavrov has noted, it was the only venture of his preliterary period about which Bely was invariably serious when he referred to it in later years.[14] In a letter to Emile Metner of December 1912, he called it a "thing that has been pursuing me since adolescence,

11. Lavrov, "Yunosheskaya khudozhestvennaya proza," p. 112. Some twenty-six "lyric fragments," written between 1897 and 1900, survive in manuscript form (GBL, fond 25, folder 1, item 1), and of these Bely revised six for inclusion in *Zoloto v lazuri* (Moscow, 1904), pp. 177–96. Lavrov published six more in "Yunosheskaya khudozhestvennaya proza," pp. 121–25.

12. This is especially true of the fairy tale or *skazka* written in 1897, which according to Lavrov is the earliest of Bely's prose works to survive in complete form.

13. "Prishedshii: Otryvok iz nenapisannoi misterii," *Severnye tsvety*, no. 3 (Moscow, 1903), pp. 2–25; "Past' nochi: Otryvok iz zadumannoi misterii," *Zolotoe Runo*, no. 1 (1906), pp. 62–71. The latter has been translated by D. C. Gerould as "The Jaws of Night (Fragment of a Planned Mystery)," *Performing Arts Journal*, 3, no. 2 (1978), pp. 30–38.

14. Lavrov, "Yunosheskaya khudozhestvennaya proza," p. 110.

the main work of my life [*Hauptwerk*]. Its hour is approaching."[15] Yet he never returned to it, except to bemoan the noncompletion of a project that in 1927 he still considered to be "monumental" (*grandioznyi*). "I couldn't achieve it in the form I had planned," he said then; but the project and the experience that had given rise to it marked a significant shift in his spiritual development toward "apocalyptic longings and an expectation of the End."[16]

The mystery play was not a form of drama indigenous to the Russian tradition, and attempts to revive it on Western European models did not begin until the nineteenth century. One critic has pointed out that "various parodies of mystery plays received greater renown than did the mystery plays themselves,"[17] and this is scarcely surprising in view of what Mikhail Bakhtin, for example, regarded as modern art's intolerance of dogmatic utterance beyond that of the individual's private belief.[18] Religious faith may persist in the modern world, but it is no longer possible for mystically inclined artists to assume or demand that their audiences share their beliefs. Yet at the turn of the century Bely saw the mystery play precisely as a religiously oriented art form designed to unite actors and onlookers in a ritual celebration of humankind's kinship with the world beyond. "If the drama is turning into the 'mysterium,'" he wrote in 1904, "then the actor should become a priest and the onlooker a participant in the mysteries being celebrated."[19] His words may seem to imply that what he had in mind was yet another example of solemn, prophetic utterance, possessing, from our point of view, very little in the way of aesthetic as opposed to biographical or even psychopathological interest. And this would be a not inaccurate way of characterizing "The Jaws of Night." Yet, in the case of "He Who Has Come," things did not turn out that way. For one thing, the theme was poten-

15. Ibid., p. 149, n. 24.

16. "Lettre autobiographique," p. 54.

17. Zoya Yurieff, "'Prishedshii': A. Bely and A. Chekhov," in *Andrey Bely: A Critical Review*, ed. G. Janecek (Lexington, Ky., 1978), p. 46.

18. See Keys, "Bely and Russian Fiction," pp. 40–41. See M. M. Bakhtin, "Slovo v romane," written in 1934–35, partially published in 1972, but not published in full until 1975. The full text has been published in English as "Discourse in the Novel," in *The Dialogic Imagination*, ed. M. Holquist (Austin, Tex., 1981), pp. 259–422.

19. "Okno v budushchee (Olenina d'Al'geim)," *Arabeski* (Moscow, 1911), p. 141; first published in *Vesy*, no. 12 (1904), pp. 1–11. By 1906, Bely had become disillusioned with this "maximalist" conception of the role that the mystery might play in modern life. In his article "Na perevale, III: Iskusstvo i misteriya" (*Vesy*, no. 9 [1906], pp. 45–48; reprinted in *Arabeski*, pp. 318–21), he wrote that the origins of the mystery play had been religious and therefore beyond the sphere of art. Contemporary attempts to revive this religious dimension precisely through the realm of art were therefore, he felt, doomed to fail, although he could but applaud the spirit of the enterprise. The evolution of Bely's ideas on the mystery play in this and other articles is followed in George Kalbouss, "Andrey Bely and the Modernist Movement in Russian Drama," in *Andrey Bely: A Critical Review*, ed. Janecek, pp. 146–55. Maria Carlson discusses Bely's later use of the mystery in *The Silver Dove* in chap. 2 of this volume.

tially ambiguous as it involved the *questioning* of values, and was likely to defy a philosophically monolithic approach. In his memoirs, Bely defined the subject matter of the play as "the coming of Antichrist in the guise of Christ" ("prishestvie Antikhrista pod *maskoi* Khrista"),[20] and the theme of the mask develops important symbolic connotations as the plot develops. In a sense, doubt and irony are built into the play from the outset, for the reader has constantly to ask, along with one or two of the characters: What is the truth? What is the significance of certain phenomena that I observe? Who is the Antichrist foretold in the Bible, and who are his servants? Can I be certain that I am not deceived?[21] False messianism is the principal theme, and it is one that will recur in various forms in the best of Bely's work written before 1910, including the *Second Symphony*, the story "Adam," and his novel *The Silver Dove*.[22]

"He Who Has Come" opens with a long authorial stage direction that sets the scene and introduces us to two novice priests, Sergey and Mikhail, who are part of a larger company assembled in and around the Temple of Glory, awaiting the end of the world. The combination of solemn language and emblematic decor (a sunset, a comet visible in the darkening sky, steep cliffs plunging to the sea, etc.) seems to promise at best an abstract work peopled by schematic, allegorical characters mouthing cumbrous philosophical platitudes, but the opening dialogue between Mikhail, the skeptic, and Sergey, the true believer, belies such an assumption. For the first time Bely symbolizes or relativizes abstract universals by making them part of a character's individual outlook on life, which may or may not command the reader's acceptance. In Mikhail's words we see Bely's attempt to create a character who not only is capable of propounding a coherent philosophical point of view but also is psychologically convincing. (The fact that Mikhail's plausibility is inversely proportional to the "rightness" of his views in the context of the play in a way foreshadows the tragic irony of Bely's subsequent literary development.)

> Ah, how delightful it is to joke in pleasant complicity with others [. . .] all of whom are wearing masks on their faces! . . . Only sometimes, when everything is quiet, the mask slips off and a horror-stricken visage looks out into the velvety darkness [. . .]. We were in love . . . You [Sergey] still are in love—with a dream [. . .]. We still carry on the joke, all of us, [. . .] even

20. *Na rubezhe dvukh stoletii*, p. 401.

21. Compare Vladimir Solov'ev's *Kratkaya povest' ob Antikhriste* (St. Petersburg, 1900), which does not involve questioning of this kind. The contrast between Solov'ev's dogmatic, theological handling of the Antichrist theme and the skeptical, questing treatment it receives at the hands of a novelist has been analyzed by N. I. Prutskov in "Dostoevsky i Vladimir Solov'ev ('Velikii inkvizitor' i 'Antikhrist')," in his *Istoriko-sravnitel'nyi analiz proizvedenii khudozhestvennoi literatury* (Leningrad, 1974), pp. 124–62.

22. The theme is also to be found in his poetry of the period. Cf. *Zoloto v lazuri*, nos. 11, 12, 14, 67–69, in *Stikhotvoreniya i poemy* (Moscow and Leningrad, 1966).

when there is nothing left . . . Everything has blown away . . . Only the age-old thing that never changes is left [. . .]. We will die waiting. Our children will die waiting [. . .]. The crowd will venerate our beautiful dream, but all fairy stories come to an end [. . .]. The years will pass . . . The crowd will see nothing. Nothing new will happen. The shadows of the past will extinguish the future . . . The future, eclipsed, will sink without trace into the past [. . .]. Everything will fade, become covered with ashes and blow away as dust [. . .].

When I discovered that this was all just a joke, somebody's preposterous, eternal joke, I was filled with horror [. . .]. There is nothing. There will be nothing. Whatever is new has already been . . .[23]

Mikhail's view of the "eternal return" is infused with Schopenhauerian pessimism and has no share in the joyful affirmation of nontranscendence associated with Nietzsche's Zarathustra.

It transpires that Iliya, the "first teacher," is infected with the same philosophical nihilism, as one of the author's stage directions makes clear: "His frightened face stares out from beneath a mask into the velvety darkness."[24] This reprise of words uttered by Mikhail not long before anticipates Bely's use of recurrent verbal motifs in the "symphonies" and novels to expand the significance of a character's thought or action beyond its immediate context. As we shall see, this will become a key device in Bely's later attempts to transcend (some readers would say to subvert) the logic of realistic psychology and plot. But in this case, the meaning thus transferred is an uncontroversial one: Mikhail and Iliya both lack a firm inner faith in the inevitability of God's prophecies and so are potential victims of the Antichrist's deceits. Iliya's ideological counterpart is the teacher, Nikita, and their opposition is vividly symbolized in their interpretations of the reddish moon that suddenly appears on the horizon above the cliffs. For Nikita this is nothing less than the red eye of the beast whose appearance is foretold in Revelation. For Iliya the moon is merely one natural phenomenon among others, capable at best of reflecting his own inner state, nothing more.[25] Soon after, the novice Fedor arrives on the scene, claiming to have seen the Lamb wandering along the seashore. This news brings about a sudden change of heart in Iliya, who is convinced that the events predicted by St. John the Divine really are taking place. "Our fairy tale is a fairy tale no longer," he says. "The True One approaches."[26] And he departs to

23. "Prishedshii," pp. 3–4, 7–8.
24. Ibid., p. 13.
25. Ibid., pp. 16–17. Zoya Yurieff has written interestingly about the numerous echoes between "Prishedshii" and Kostya's play in Chekhov's *Seagull;* the "red eye" of the moon is one example. As she says, the "young Bely was not disturbed by accents of parody in Treplev's play and responded to it creatively in his early dramatic work. This response is an extremely rare example of a reaction to parody in a 'high key'" ("'Prishedshii': A. Bely and A. Chekhov," p. 49).
26. "Prishedshii," p. 21.

worship Him. Nikita goes on to condemn Iliya and his followers, however, and the stage directions make it clear that the "Prishedshii" is indeed the Antichrist. "His handsome face, convulsed and distorted, is like a terrible mask [. . .]. He who has come rises uncaringly to his feet, his features congealed and petrified like a mask."[27]

In "He Who Has Come" Bely goes beyond an attempt to portray a unitary, mystical vision of the kind observable in some of the lyric fragments. Instead, he gives us characters who are split in their spiritual allegiances, unable to distinguish with certainty between the true and the false messiah. Bely's deliberate choice of the dramatic form facilitates this inner division, of course, although what irony there is exists against a firm background of positive, extraliterary belief, embodied here in the figure of Nikita and expressed ex cathedra through the author's extremely prolix stage directions. The use of such a device to express an authoritative point of view external to the dialogue of the characters is a feature traditionally associated with narrative rather than drama, of course, and for this reason it is better to regard "He Who Has Come" as a work of fiction than as a play in the usual sense of the word. On the other hand, the work certainly has more in common with psychological drama as we have known it since the Renaissance than with the medieval mystery play that Bely was ostensibly intending to revive.

It may be worth asking why, if Bely thought so highly of the Antichrist project, he never managed to complete it. In his confessional novel *Notes of an Eccentric* (*Zapiski chudaka*, 1922), he gives as the reason the fact that he came to realize that he "had already entered the sphere of the mystery drama" himself: "I was already a participant in the events leading up to the catastrophe."[28] What could he have meant? We know from his original plan of the whole drama that the true prophets were to suffer death and resurrection,[29] and it might be assumed that the "mystery" would open out into real life at the point where history comes to an end and Christ's millennium begins. This outcome would certainly have rendered completion superfluous, given Bely's theory of the union of art and life in theurgy. But Bely referred specifically to "events leading up to the catastrophe" as the chief obstacle, not the final outcome of Apocalypse itself. *Notes of an Eccentric* is a doubtful source, of course, being a curious mixture of autobiography and fantasy, but the entry for April–May 1898 in Bely's "Intimate Biography" casts light on the question. It was about then that he had a prophetic vision in a Moscow church which gave him the original idea for his play. "I saw the two cupolas of the Temple of Glory, whither mankind would ascend. Then it began to

27. Ibid., p. 25.
28. *Zapiski chudaka* (Moscow and Berlin, 1922), vol. 1, p. 97.
29. "Yunosheskaya khudozhestvennaya proza," p. 110.

appear to me that Antichrist would enter the Temple, and in a flash I was struck by the thought that everything that is unclear and ominously vague in my soul/people's souls is a foreboding of the coming of Antichrist."[30] The idea that he himself might already be corrupted and that his whole theurgic undertaking might in this sense be a *d'yavol'skoe navozhdenie,* a suggestion or attack of the devil, may therefore have been present from the very beginning. It is no exaggeration to say that in the period between the 1905 Revolution and Bely's conversion to Rudolf Steiner's anthroposophy in 1912, this fear occasionally verged on the pathological. It was the chief psychological influence in the writing of *The Silver Dove* and *Petersburg.* "He Who Has Come" emerges as Bely's first attempt to articulate that dreadful possibility, although it was still severely distanced by its embodiment in the characters of Mikhail and Iliya. The central core of authorial certainty remains untouched.

II

Despite Bely's fascination with piano improvisations during the late 1890s, it is difficult to see how any of the works so far examined are connected with music, except in the general sense of being the lyric outpourings of an artistic personality. In that case, "musicality" is scarcely more than a loose metaphor linking two lines of creative development that, though parallel, are mutually distinct. However, Bely was much given to theorizing about his artistic activity and was always looking for ways to unify his creative interests at a higher level of abstraction. Kant and Schopenhauer seemed ready-made to help him. I have already pointed to Schopenhauerian echoes in "He Who Has Come," and Bely had read *The World as Will and Representation* a couple of years earlier, during the last few months of 1896. But it was not just the philosopher's metaphysical pessimism that drew him. He was equally impressed by Schopenhauer's irrationalist theory of aesthetic cognition, particularly as it related to music. "I had always loved music," he tells us in his memoirs, "but once I had mastered Schopenhauer's musical philosophy, I increased my attention to the art threefold. And music began to speak to me in a way it never had done before."[31]

It was Schopenhauer's contention that through music we gain access to the deepest forces underlying the universe: we are able to contemplate the noumenal Will itself. This metaphysical assertion lies at the basis of Schopenhauer's hierarchical classification of the arts, in which

30. Ibid., p. 110. The Russian—"vse neyasnoe i zlovesche smutnoe, chto zhivet v dushe"—is ambiguous here.
31. *Na rubezhe dvukh stoletii,* p. 353.

music is supreme. For music, unlike poetry, painting, sculpture, and architecture, is "quite independent of the phenomenal world. . . . [It is] a copy of the Will itself. . . . For this reason the effect of music is so very much more powerful and penetrating than is that of the other arts, for these others speak only of the shadow, but music of the essence."[32] Bely accepted this account of music's metaphysical grandeur wholeheartedly, as we can see from statements he made over the years. "Better than any other art, music is able to express the eternal," we read in a diary entry for July 1899. "And the eternal is closest to us and most accessible in music."[33] In a letter to Emile Metner of August 7, 1902, he actually referred to music as, "so to speak, the equivalent in this life of the next world" ("tak skazat', zhiznennyi ekvivalent potustoronnosti").[34]

But in at least one important area Bely disagreed with the philosopher, and that was with respect to art synthesis, particularly the way in which music and poetry may interact. According to Schopenhauer, music was the highest art form and had no need of support from any of the others. Program music or "painting in sounds" was particularly to be condemned, as was grand opera. Opera, he wrote, was "the creation, not of a pure artistic sense, but of the somewhat barbaric notion that aesthetic enjoyment can be heightened by amassing the means, by the simultaneity of totally distinct varieties of impression; and that the effect can be strengthened by an increase in the total mass." Instead of devoting itself to the music alone, "the mind is acted upon during such highly complex opera music, simultaneously through the eye by the most colorful spectacle, the most fantastic scenes, and the most animated impressions of light and color; and at the same time the plot of the work occupies it. The mind is diverted, distracted, stupefied by all this and is thus made unreceptive to the sacred, mysterious, intense language of tones." "When music joins too closely to words and seeks to mold itself to events," he wrote in another place, "it is attempting to speak a language which is not its own."[35] Schopenhauer's total rejection of the notion of the *Gesamtkunstwerk*, or synthetic art form, caused Richard Wagner a good deal of trouble in his time, and it was equally troublesome to Bely at the end of the century.

One of the problems was that although, as I have said, Schopenhauer's classification of the arts was based on metaphysical speculation about the capacity of individual art forms to reflect the cosmic Will, the philosopher was not averse to couching his arguments in immanent, non-

32. *The World as Will and Representation,* trans. E. F. J. Payne, 2 vols., vol. 1 (New York, 1966), bk. 3, no. 52, p. 257.
33. "Yunosheskie dnevnikovye zametki," p. 119.
34. GBL, fond 167, box 1, item 1.
35. Quoted in J. M. Stein, *Richard Wagner and the Synthesis of the Arts* (Detroit, 1960), p. 150.

metaphysical terms appropriate to the laws of aesthetic perception. In this respect he showed himself to be a follower of Lessing and Kant, and a rather unadventurous one at that. As we have seen, his objections to opera, for example, were based mainly on the empirical premise that the individual's aesthetic awareness should not be blunted through the mechanical accumulation of different kinds of sense impression. He agreed with the conclusions of Kant's first *Critique,* that our experience must take on a certain form in order to be considered experience of an intelligible world. In particular, Schopenhauer went on to postulate the a priori intuitions of space, time, and causality without which we cannot apprehend what is around us. This reasoning then led him to say that music is perceived "in and through time alone, with absolute exclusion of space, even without the influence of the knowledge of causality."[36] It is far from clear, however, how music can be regarded simultaneously as a temporal art in *form* and as an art that *transcends* time, space, and causality in *content* (that is, the noumenal Will).[37]

This contradiction is not overcome in any of Bely's writings on the subject, although his attention was drawn to it on more than one occasion.[38] Blok wrote to him in January 1903, for example, apropos of his article "The Forms of Art" ("Formy iskusstva"), published the previous year, which has a similar dual focus: music is seen now as a "real" art form empirically conceived, now as a mystical symbol pointing to something beyond itself.[39] Bely's reply shows that he grasped the problem perfectly: "I am combining musicality in the proper sense with its mystical, metaphorical connotation. If you were really to split hairs, then the result would be a total absurdity"; that is, something that was supposed to reveal a mystery beyond the bounds of time and space turns out to exist within time and space.[40] But Bely was not embarrassed by this objection. The truth was that he, no less than Schopenhauer before him, was not really concerned with music as an art *form* at this level at all. "I failed to

---

36. *World as Will,* bk. 3, no. 52, p. 266.

37. The two propositions appear to be based on entirely different premises, and Bely and others were tempted to argue in one sphere (that of formal aesthetics) a conclusion that could be theoretically sustained only in another (that of metaphysics).

38. E.g., by E. K. Metner in his letter of October 15, 1903 (GBL, fond 167, box 9, item 1), in which he objected to Bely's "theurgic" interpretation of music. Metner returned to the subject again in the article he published under the pseudonym Vol'fing, "Boris Bugaev protiv muzyki" (*Zolotoe Runo,* no. 5 [1907], pp. 56–62) and widened his attack to encompass the whole tradition of the "metaphysics of music," of music as irrational cognition, from Wilhelm Wackenroder, E. T. A. Hoffmann, and Ludwig Tieck through Schopenhauer to Wagner and Nietzsche and Bely himself.

39. Aleksandr Blok and Andrey Bely, *Perepiska,* ed. V. N. Orlov (Moscow, 1940), p. 3; "Formy iskusstva," *Mir Iskusstva,* no. 12 (1902), pp. 343–61, reprinted in *Simvolizm* (Moscow, 1910), pp. 147–74. Subsequent citations will refer to the translated version in Andrey Bely, *The Dramatic Symphony and The Forms of Art,* trans. R. J. Keys, A. M. Keys, and J. D. Elsworth (Edinburgh, 1986), pp. 159–82.

40. Blok and Bely, *Perepiska,* p. 8.

observe the proper perspective in my article," he wrote to Blok in the same letter. "I was making vague allusions to *what really matters* in the formal sphere which is alien to it."

Yet the fact remains that Bely *had* developed concrete ideas about the empirical synthesis and interaction of the arts, even if those theories were philosophically sustained in a way that closer examination revealed to be logically spurious.[41] And the validity of his attempts to translate those ideas into experimental literary forms was not something that could be prejudged. One thing, however, is certain. If all art, and literature in particular, was aspiring to the condition of music, it would not be because art was turning into life and life had as its final goal the reality beyond, which music could make more immanent ("muzyka, tak skazat', zhiznennyi ekvivalent potustoronnosti"). It would be because Bely and other contemporaries of a similar inclination were determined to conduct an open-ended experiment with the empirical materials that lay closest to hand, in their case the writer's stock in trade, in an attempt to discover what, if anything, a structure of sounds inseparable from sense could have in common with an art form made up of sounds most typically divorced from conceptual meaning altogether. Ostensibly their motivation might be different. In Bely's case it most decidedly was, since the impetus for his early work derived from a philosophical conception to which aesthetic experimentation was logically superfluous. But the results would be the same: literary structures that submit to our aesthetic judgment and not to any vague notion concerning their putative mystical or prophetic content.

Although so much of Bely's creative energy was spent in theorizing, it will come as no surprise to discover that he had no firm ideas about what he was actually doing when he wrote his first four prose symphonies. "Their structure arose by itself," he wrote in 1907, "and I had no clear idea about what a 'symphony' in literature should be."[42] He had definite ideas about the nature of symphonic music, however, although most of them appeared to derive from the metaphysical pole of his pseudo-Schopenhauerian analysis. "Program music is not the sublimest thing that the art has to offer," he wrote in 1899. "In terms of purity and directness of effect it is far inferior to nonprogrammatic music. This is why, when we listen to a symphony, we do not attempt to discover why it was written or what it is supposed to represent. For in a symphony we contemplate the sum total of all possible images in a given connection, all

41. A particularly glaring example of the way in which Bely conflates his two approaches to music occurs in *Forms of Art*, p. 175: "In all religions there exists a contrast between one world and another, better one. In the arts we have a similar contrast between spatial and temporal forms."

42. *Kubok metelei: Chetvertaya simfoniya* (Moscow, 1908), pp. 1–2; reprinted in *Chetyre simfonii* (Munich, 1971).

possible combinations of events, which come together to form a vast and fathomless symbol [. . .]. This is why symphonic music is infinitely higher and purer than operatic music."[43] The empirical reality was rather different, however. "I used to dream of program music," he admitted many years later. "The subjects of my first four books were drawn from musical leitmotifs [. . .]."[44] Symphonic music might occupy its noumenal realm unsullied by the arts beneath it, therefore, but other musical forms were open to interpenetration, and able themselves to influence the writing of literature. In particular, Bely was attracted by the orchestral suites and lieder of Edvard Grieg and by Wagner's *Ring der Nibelungen* during 1899.[45]

The first substantial prose piece of Bely's to be specifically associated with musical form was the work that he later referred to as his "Presymphony" ("Predsimfoniya"). He began work on it early in 1899 and had completed it by the autumn of that year. He apparently destroyed the final version of the work five or six years later, but an earlier version has survived and was published by Lavrov in 1981.[46] Bely later wrote that the symphonies "were born of 'cosmic' images within me. They had no plot. And this 'plotlessness' condensed into a program of little scenes."[47] This is certainly an accurate description of Bely's first essay in the genre, which is little more than a series of homiletic statements and exclamatory observations about man's fall from grace, his indifference to the Divine Will, and his determination to spurn the warnings of God's prophet, the unironized first-person narrator of the symphony itself. "Hearken unto me [. . .] and the One who is within me!" he entreats his fellows. "I speak, but they do not hear the symphony of eternity," he goes on to lament.[48] The fictional dimension of this "strange, wild, nebulous, cosmic epic in prose" (Bely's own words in 1927)[49] is as abstract and tenuous as it was in any of the lyric fragments, and indeed, as Lavrov has noted, the "Presymphony" is little more than a crystalline accretion of lyric images already familiar to us from the earlier works.[50]

The text is divided into some twenty-five sections, including a double "prelude" and a "postlude," with each section further segmented into numbered paragraphs of one sentence or more, varying in length from a single line to more than seventy. Each section is prefaced by indications of "reading tempi" ("andante," "adagio," "allegro furioso"), a somewhat

43. "Yunosheskie dnevnikovye zametki," pp. 134–35, n. 10.
44. "O sebe kak pisatele," p. 270.
45. "Rakkurs dnevnika," quoted in K. N. Bugaeva, "Andrey Bely: Letopis' zhizni i tvorchestva," GPB, fond 60, item 107, entries for February and April 1899.
46. "Yunosheskaya khudozhestvennaya proza," pp. 126–37.
47. "Lettre autobiographique," pp. 54–55.
48. "Yunosheskaya khudozhestvennaya proza," p. 133.
49. "Lettre autobiographique," p. 54.
50. "Yunosheskaya khudozhestvennaya proza," p. 113.

specious scheme that adds nothing to the meanings of the words on the page. The only other apparently musical device in the work is the repetition of certain key phrases as leitmotifs. ("And the Spirit of Eternity is over me. And I am affrighted in my beatitude" is one such motif that occurs fairly often in the first half of the work.) But the use of the device is entirely rudimentary and involves no transference of meaning beyond that of the one-dimensional, lyric context already established. If, as Lavrov contends, this is the most overtly musical of Bely's symphonies, a ne plus ultra by comparison with which subsequent examples of the genre involved a gradual retreat toward more purely literary structures,[51] then one might well wonder whether the prospects for interpenetration between music and literature were as extensive as Bely, in his more optimistic moments, appeared to believe. It is obviously time to look more closely at the possible connotations of the word "musicality" in literature.

III

The attempts of writers, critics, and musicians since the Romantic period to draw analogies between music and literature, and even to argue that the two arts may have certain techniques in common, have given rise to a complex set of connotations more than capable of bedeviling any rational analysis of the problem. We have already noticed that Bely typically speaks of music in a metaphorical sense as symbolizing otherworldly values, while continuing to imply that his words are also of nonmetaphorical relevance to music as an art. Terminological sleight of hand in the form of the word "musicality" then allows him to confer some of music's metaphysical grandeur on the "lower" art forms as well, and on literature in particular ("Poetry is the vent that lets the spirit of music into the spatial forms of art").[52] Occasionally he would alter the second term of his metaphor and define music as the expression of the artist's—any artist's—inner vision or mood, his "*nastroenie*,"[53] although since the Symbolist writer's vision was crucially linked to the world beyond, this was not as significant a surrender to impressionism as it might at first appear.

As for the idea that music and literature might be *literally* homogeneous, this is not an argument that Bely developed in great detail, at least not in his pre-anthroposophical days.[54] Both are acoustic arts, of

51. Ibid., p. 115.

52. *Forms of Art*, p. 173.

53. Ibid., pp. 180–81. Cf. also the foreword to the *Second Symphony* (*Chetyre simfonii*, p. 126; translated in *Dramatic Symphony*, p. 17).

54. See Rudolf Steiner's lecture "The Bearing of Spiritual Science on Art," given at Dornach on December 29, 1914, published as part of *Art in the Light of Mystery Wisdom*

course, involving the creation of sounds, and the French Symbolists, particularly Verlaine, had laid great stress on "verbal alchemy," poetry's "musical" resources of rhythm, rhyme, repetition, consonant and vowel harmony, and so on.[55] These were all, undeniably, subliminal, emotional effects of poetic language, and in this sense the close link between music and verbal art as a gamut of sounds was legitimate. But as Bryusov argued as early as 1894, these acoustic affinities were only one of the resources of Symbolism in literature, and not its essence. "Verse melody" was an auxiliary of sense, and nothing more. Some Symbolists, he agreed, had surrendered themselves entirely to acoustical play, and this was sometimes the only "meaning" their work possessed, but these were extreme cases that he had no desire to advocate.[56] The same point was made many years later by the musicologist Deryck Cooke, who wrote that in literature the sounds have been transformed into words, which "possess associations with objects, ideas and feelings—clear, rationally intelligible, but arbitrary associations; whereas in music, they have become elaborated into notes, i.e. sounds which have clear but not rationally intelligible associations." Nevertheless, Cooke continues, both arts "awaken in the hearer an emotional response; the difference is that a word awakens both an emotional response and a comprehension of its meaning, whereas a note, having no meaning, awakens only an emotional response."[57] In the period up to 1917 Bely never seriously argued that sound could be totally divorced from conventionally assigned lexical sense, although he did argue, after his conversion to anthroposophy, that the nature of sense, as embodied in the phonemes of Russian or any other language, had been misinterpreted since the scattering of tongues at Babel.[58] But this attempt to recover the original Logos and to assert the nonarbitrary nature of links between sound and sense belonged to a new phase in his creative development, which postdated his interest in

---

(1935; new translation, London, 1970). Here Steiner develops a genetic theory of artistic creation according to which every form of art is interpreted as an expression of the manifold spiritual processes at work within us. Interestingly, poetry occupies a higher position in Steiner's hierarchy than music, while eurythmy towers above all.

55. In her book *Word and Music in the Novels of Andrey Bely* (Cambridge, 1982), Ada Steinberg notices that Bely was dissatisfied with Verlaine's concept of musicality. "Neither Bely nor Mallarmé were satisfied with the mere musical effect of sound alone; they sought a closer analogy with music" (p. 34). This more direct analogy they pursued through the semantics of words and "principally, syntax, i.e., compositional elements organizing the 'music' of a poetic work after the pattern of the arrangement of notes in a musical score" (p. 26).

56. "Otvet," foreword to *Russkie simvolisty*, vypusk 2 (Moscow, 1894); reprinted in *Sobranie sochinenii v semi tomakh* (Moscow, 1973–75), vol. 6, p. 30.

57. Deryck Cooke, *The Language of Music* (Oxford, 1959), p. 26.

58. E.g., in *Glossolaliya, poema o zvuke*, written in the summer of 1917 but not published until five years later (Berlin, 1922).

the specific possibilities for forging a synthesis between music and literature.

Another area where Bely posited the homogeneity of the two arts was at the much more abstract level of the Kantian "transcendental forms," as adopted and modified by Schopenhauer.[59] At this level, music is viewed as a preeminently temporal art, as opposed to the truly spatial arts of architecture, sculpture, and painting. Literature occupies a pivotal position between these two poles, being both temporal and spatial, and therefore able to demonstrate the causal relationships between objects existing in space and time. The argument carries superficial conviction and is enlightening enough in some respects, but as a basis for defining any technical laws and sensible forms supposedly held in common by music and literature, it is much too unspecific. In particular, it is unclear how literature can be regarded as being literally spatial, since the simultaneous apprehension of words as acoustic carriers of separable meanings is not its mode of being. But the argument has metaphorical value in that the attentive reader of literature has constantly to add the significance of what he is reading at one moment to his memory of what has gone before. In that sense, the act of reading implies an interpretive spatialization of the words on the page, their removal from the temporal flow of the narration, or whatever. Furthermore, this way of regarding the matter allowed Bely to advance, albeit tentatively, a new theory of semantic structure in literature, one that was closely linked with the notion of recurrent leitmotif in Wagner and that in more recent years has achieved fame (some would say notoriety) as the theory of musical or spatial or poetic logic in literature.[60] The argument is of direct relevance to the interpretation of the symphonies and his later novels, although Bely never applied it himself, except in the foreword to *The Goblet of Blizzards* (*Kubok metelei*, 1908), the most spatial and for that reason, as we shall see, the least intelligible of his experimental works.

In the article "Forms of Art," the literal link between music and poetry as acoustic arts developing in time was identified as rhythm,[61] and in later years Bely would go on to develop an esoteric theory according to which poetry, like music, literally reenacts the fundamental rhythms of creation.[62] In that early article, however, he regarded words in poetry as expressing meaning rather less inaccessibly than that, and he appears to

59. See *Forms of Art*, passim.

60. One of the most influential formulations of this approach to the study of fiction was Joseph Frank's essay "Spatial Form in Modern Literature," first published in *Sewanee Review*, 53 (1945), pp. 221–40, 433–56, 643–53. Many years later Frank defended his ideas in "Spatial Form: An Answer to Critics," *Critical Inquiry*, 4 (1977), pp. 231–52.

61. *Forms of Art*, pp. 162–63.

62. Cf. J. D. Elsworth, "The Concept of Rhythm in Bely's Aesthetic Thought," in *Andrey Bely: Centenary Papers*, ed. B. Christa (Amsterdam, 1980), pp. 68–80.

define "rhythm" in a more metaphorical sense as it might be applied to a
succession of images, themes, and moods in a lyric poem. While using
Schopenhauer's terminology to emphasize the importance of causality
and "motivation" in literary (as opposed to musical) art, he went on to
criticize the demand that rational clarity should invariably accompany
such causal projections. "The internal coherence that connects a series
of poetic images," he wrote, "is frequently accompanied by an external
coherence, that is to say, by the expression of a conscious link existing
between these images viewed as a reflection of reality. It cannot be
inferred from this that conscious clarity is a necessary condition of poetic
creation." When he speaks of the "inner groundedness" (*vnutrennyaya
obosnovannost'*) of the images in a poem, Bely is, in one sense, implying no
more than that the lyric poet is himself the third term in any comparison
and that any apparent gaps in the poem's paraphrasable content are
explicable in terms of the poet's idiosyncratic vision. On the other hand,
when Bely emphasizes that the poet has every right to create those gaps
in the work's "rational" semantic structure, he is foreshadowing one of
the features that we associate chiefly with modernist poetry, namely, the
focus on an unelucidated image or series of images, each of which requires active interpretation by the reader, who thus needs to co-create
the poem's meaning, as it were, along with the writer. This kind of
poetry has been familiar in European literature since the time of Gérard
de Nerval's "Chimères," at least, and reached its apotheosis in the fan-
tastically impeded lyrics of Stéphane Mallarmé, but in the Russian context such a call for what the Formalist critics would refer to as "semantic
impedance" (*semanticheskoe zatrudnenie*) was a new phenomenon. There
was nothing particularly "impeded," however, about the lyric poetry that
Bely himself wrote before World War I; the difficulties associated with
his writing arise chiefly in relation to his prose works. The implications
of this spatial theory for fiction were particularly revolutionary, for it
was there that rationality as embodied in the laws of social and psychological causality was most firmly entrenched.

I shall say more about spatial form in connection with the analysis of
specific works by Bely, but for the moment it must be repeated that the
notion of the spatial element in both literature and music is still only an
analogy and must not be taken too literally. Counterpoint or polyphony
is a specialized branch of musical composition, for example, relating to
the "combination of simultaneous 'parts' or 'voices', each of significance
in itself and the whole resulting in a coherent texture" developing in
time,[63] and it is only in analysis that it yields a spatial impression. In this
sense, the idea of notes running "point against point" vertically down the
staves is a visual abstraction, no more. And so it is with verbal art.

63. P. A. Scholes, *The Concise Oxford Dictionary of Music*, 2d ed. (Oxford, 1964), p. 135.

Mallarmé's attempt to align "Un Coup de dés jamais n'abolira le hasard" with a musical score by printing different lines of sense in different type above each other across the page will always founder on the inability of the human brain to imitate and construe more than one verbal sound in any given instant of time. Bely hoped that when he moved to Munich in September 1906 to continue work on *The Goblet of Blizzards*, he would succeed where Mallarmé had admitted defeat. "But Munich was very far from being a creative city," he lamented many years later.[64]

The conclusion seems to be, therefore, that music and literature have their own autonomous modes of being and that interpenetration of the two art forms is for that reason problematic. As Schopenhauer implied, such syntheses as Wagnerian music-drama involve the juxtaposition of parallel effects rather than literal fusion of sensible forms. The argument by analogy may prove more fruitful, however, particularly in connection with such semantic features of spatial form as parallelism and contrast—all the possibilities for leitmotival theme and variation, in fact. The acoustic analogy will prove important, too, particularly in *Petersburg*, where sound symbolism, or what Bely later referred to as *zvukopis'*, is used widely as an adjunct to the leitmotif system.

IV

Between December 1899 and July 1902 Bely went on to produce four more symphonies. The first of these works, the so-called *Northern* or *Heroic Symphony*, took him a year to write and was completed during December 1900. The *Second* or *Dramatic Symphony* was composed in rapid bursts between March and July of the following year. The *Third Symphony, The Return*, was written between November 1901 and August 1902, partly overlapping with the first version of the "Fourth Symphony," which was completed in June and July of the latter year. They were not published in the exact order of composition, however. The *Second Symphony*, Bely's first venture into print, preceded the *Northern Symphony* by fifteen months or so. A few extracts from the "Fourth Symphony" appeared in a Moscow miscellany during 1903, but the rest of the work was never published in its original form. Bely made a number of frenzied efforts to rewrite it over the years that followed, and it was eventually published as *The Goblet of Blizzards* in April 1908, having been completed eleven months earlier. Meanwhile, *The Return* had appeared as a separate volume at the end of 1904.[65]

64. *Mezhdu dvukh revolyutsii* (Leningrad, 1934), p. 138.

65. *Severnaya simfoniya (1-aya, geroicheskaya)* (Moscow, 1904); *Simfoniya (2-aya, dramaticheskaya)* (Moscow, 1902); *Vozvrat. III['ya] simfoniya* (Moscow, 1905); *Kubok metelei. Chetvertaya simfoniya* (Moscow, 1908). All four symphonies have been reprinted in *Chetyre simfonii*

It was fitting that the *Second Symphony* should have been offered to the public before Bely's other early works, since it embodied better than any of them the themes that would engage his attention over the next few years and the literary strategies he would develop to express them. In this respect, it was quite different from the other symphonies, which are less complex in their way, less adventurous, less full of possibilities. Large claims have been made by critics over the years concerning the formal originality of the symphonies as a whole and their importance in the context of Russian literary history. Viktor Shklovsky, for example, was of the opinion that "without the symphonies modern Russian literature would probably have been impossible,"[66] and his words have been echoed by others. "Whatever we may think of Bely's symphonies as artistic achievements," writes Gleb Struve, "they must be viewed as significant experiments, foreshadowing important developments in modern prose fiction."[67] "These first works of Andrey Bely opened up a whole epoch in the development of the twentieth-century experimental novel," says Lena Szilard.[68] "Bely was the most audacious reformer of Russian prose," writes Ekaterina Starikova, "renouncing all its achievements and canons in the most demonstrative fashion in his search for new formal possibilities. . . . There are not even distant analogues to Bely's symphonies in the past history of Russian literature."[69] And so it goes on. In certain respects, these claims are difficult to justify, as I hope to show, for the works in question are not homogeneous achievements. The novelty of the *First* and *Third Symphonies* is largely superficial, for example, and certainly a lot less than many commentators have cared to admit, while *The Goblet of Blizzards* was, in its way, a monstrous aberration, a true ne plus ultra based on a fundamental misapprehension of the semantic possibilities of verbal art. The *Second Symphony* was a genuinely open-ended experiment, however, and one that broke through the barrier that so nearly ruins the rest of Bely's early prose work, that of unmediated, theurgic lyricism. And whenever critics attempt to substantiate their claims concerning Bely's early formal originality, it is invariably the *Second Symphony* to which they turn for convincing, concrete illustrations.

(Munich, 1971). "Otryvki iz 4-oi simfonii" appeared in *Al'manakh 'Grif'* (Moscow, 1903), pp. 52–61. Only the *Second Symphony* has so far appeared in English translation, in *The Dramatic Symphony and The Forms of Art*, trans. Keys, Keys, and Elsworth. Subsequent citations of *The Dramatic Symphony* will be to this edition.

66. Viktor Shklovsky, "Andrey Bely," *Russkii Sovremennik*, no. 2 (1924), p. 243.

67. G. P. Struve, "Andrej Belyj's Experiments with Novel Technique," in *Stil- und Formprobleme in der Literatur*, ed. P. Böckmann (Heidelberg, 1959), p. 467.

68. E. Silard (Szilard), "O strukture Vtoroi simfonii A. Belogo," *Studia Slavica Hungarica*, 13 (1967), p. 311.

69. E. Starikova, "Realizm i simvolizm," in *Razvitie realizma v russkoi literature*, vol. 3, ed. U. R. Fokht et al. (Moscow, 1974), p. 196.

Expressed in the broadest possible terms, Bely's perennial theme throughout the whole of his creative career was that of *dvoemirie,* the split between the world of matter and the world of the spirit, and how it might be overcome. This fundamental dualism underwent significant changes at various stages in his spiritual development. At the time when he wrote the symphonies he was concerned with the relationship between this world and the next, understood in the most literal way as the imminence of Apocalypse. At a later period he would focus attention more on the material world and the way it is transformed in human consciousness, before concluding with Rudolf Steiner that the phenomenal world is but a manifestation of the noumenal world in any case, at a lower grade of spiritualization. As we saw in regard to Bely's concept of the mystery play, this theme could be presented in two entirely different ways, either as the prophetic, mystical assertion of an unironized, usually first-person narrator (the lyric fragments, the early *skazka,* the cosmic "Presymphony") or as embodied in the epistemologically limited vision of an individual character or hero, open to doubt and disconfirmation (could he be mad or deluded by the forces of evil, like Iliya and Mikhail in "He Who Has Come"?). The four symphonies offer us further elaborations of this theme, although the precise angles of vision from which it is presented are different in each case.

The *Northern Symphony* appears to be the simplest of the four. A short introductory section or "prelude," spoken by an unnamed first-person narrator, is followed by the four parts of the symphony proper, recounted by the same narrator in a more anonymous fashion, with the first-person pronoun suppressed. It has a simple, unilinear story line, which is easily retold. Its unimpeded, vaguely poetic prose conceals considerable complexity of purpose, however.

The old king is dying (like most of the characters in this work, he is never named: Bely's depiction is as abstract and generalized as possible), and on his deathbed he enjoins his young son to "lead his people to the summits" and never to leave them. The new king takes up his father's words with alacrity and tells his people that he is determined to lead them into the light. (A very imprecise political program, this, but such is Bely's allegorical intention.) The young man's words fall on deaf ears, however. Eventually he loses heart and decides to seek solace and personal enlightenment by abandoning them and living in a lonely marble tower far away, with no one but his wife for company. Darkness, cold, sorrow, and old age appear to be the lot of all. After a time the royal couple have a daughter. They are visited by an old woman who turns out to be the personification of *Vechnost'* (Eternity), and she tells them that the princess is a chosen being who will eventually guide people in their search for the world beyond. (She is subsequently referred to as a "saint," in the Christian sense.) Thus ends Part I.

So far, the *Symphony's* meaning appears simple enough, even if the actual occasion of the plot was somewhat adventitious. Bely wrote later that the images of the work "hatched out" of melodies that he improvised on the piano.[70] He was inspired by Grieg (the *Symphony* is actually dedicated to the Norwegian composer) and particularly by his song "The Princess," written to words by Björnstjerne Björnson.[71] First the rhythm would come to him and then the melody, followed by visual images that he would later attempt to formulate in words. Only then did something resembling a plot emerge.[72] In the same place he refers to the *Northern Symphony* as a *skazochka,* a "little fairy story," and this characterization provides us with a key to its somewhat amorphous semantic structure. When we read a fairy tale, we subscribe to conventions of meaning that are very different from those prevailing in realistic fiction. Märchen are usually set in a distant historical or even mythical past, with the result that our expectations of social and psychological causality are severely weakened, if not abolished. In particular, characters may be in direct contact with supernatural powers, or may even be mythological or magical beings themselves. The "realistic" perspective that would allow the narrator to cast doubt on the veracity of his story or on the beliefs of his characters is missing in the *skazka.* The narrator is at one with his fictional world. There must be no ironic distance between him and the events he is recounting.

Bely was instinctively attracted to this kind of narratorial stance because it would allow him to construct a mythical, folkloric, or religious fiction without reference to verisimilitude. Furthermore, there might be ways of overcoming the perspectival limitations I have described. For, if carefully handled, the fairy tale structure could also be used as a means of preaching a syncretistic allegory whereby former systems of religious belief, including the overtly pagan, could be reconciled with Christianity through Christ's promise to save the world and all its peoples, both living and dead. As we have seen, the *Northern Symphony* begins innocently enough as a fairy tale about shadowy characters living in a vaguely medieval past. The tendency to graft allegorical meanings onto their actions is present from the start, however, and this will allow him to transform his märchen at the end into a theurgic prophecy about the imminent end of the world as relevant to events in the early twentieth century, as it is to the characters about whom he is ostensibly writing. In this connection, the opening prelude is particularly important. At first it appears to hark back to Bely's earlier work, and it is in fact a reworking

---

70. "Kak my pishem," in *Kak my pishem* (Leningrad, 1930), p. 17.

71. "Material k biografii (intimnyi), prednaznachennyi dlya izucheniya tol'ko posle smerti avtora," 1923, Central State Archive of Literature and Art (TsGALI), Moscow, fond 53 (Bely), opis' 2, item 3, entry for January–March 1900.

72. *Nachalo veka,* p. 120.

of an unpublished lyric fragment. That fragment, however, was written as late as October 1900.[73] In other words, Bely refashioned it and added it to the *Symphony* after he had completed the first three parts of the work. Mysterious, elegiac, and full of vague foreboding (whether for good or evil is as yet unclear), the prelude is obviously meant to set the mood for what is to follow. But more important, it asserts, in a manner not entirely untinged with irony, the reality in the modern world of some of those supposedly mythical creatures who will figure in the story to come. It allows the narrator, outside the structure of the *Symphony* proper, a single opportunity to bring himself and the present moment into a functional relationship with the plot that follows. "'Dreams, nothing but dreams,' whispered the windswept night."[74] But the narrator remains unconvinced. In his syncretic vision these things do exist, and the proof of that assertion is about to dawn. At this point the prelude breaks off, but not before the implied author, disguised as a lyric narrator, has managed to suggest to the reader the wider, more literal context in which he would like his symphony or fairy tale to be placed.

Part II begins in a slightly more concrete fashion. The medieval background becomes clearer, as we make the acquaintance of a young knight who, despite a tainted heredity (his father was a worshiper of the devil), "thirsts for dreams beyond the clouds."[75] The repetition of lyric leitmotifs from Part I is intended to show that he and the princess share a spiritual kinship and are both predestined to be saved in the world beyond. But in the meantime the negative side of the young knight's personality gains the upper hand, and in what the narrator portrays as a genuine struggle between the forces of good and evil, the knight eventually succumbs to temptation. The princess holds firm, however.

Part III presents us with a historically relativized, "realistic" narrative viewpoint ("In those years everything was held in the grip of Satanism," etc.),[76] although the spiritual generalities of the earlier sections (light versus darkness and so on) are by no means contradicted by this more specific detail. In the event, this realistic interlude is short-lived. The princess prays for the knight's immortal soul, and Eternity, cast in the role of guardian angel, intervenes on his behalf to defeat the forces of evil. The princess, now identified as a Christian saint, descends from her tower and continues Eternity's work throughout the land. In the end, both she and the knight are summoned by Death, to be reunited in the entirely mythical Land of the Blessed, which figures in Part IV. At this point both fairy tale and allegory give way to outright prophecy. God Himself appears, as does Christ, who announces to Adam and Eve, the

73. "Lyric Fragment in Prose," no. 23, GBL, fond 25, folder 1, item 1.
74. *Severnaya simfoniya*, p. 16; reprinted in *Chetyre simfonii*.
75. Ibid., pp. 52–53.
76. Ibid., p. 75.

creatures of ancient mythology and all the "white children" who inhabit this Pre-Raphaelite or Art Nouveau–style purgatory, that the world is about to end.[77] The daystar rises in the east and Apocalypse dawns. The moment anticipated in the prelude is nigh.

Enough has been said, I hope, to clarify the curious narrative strategy that lies behind this symphony. Bely's deeper purpose was, as ever, a theurgic one. He wished to present a vision of the other world which would be as valid for the reader of this fiction as for the characters and the narrator within it. The choice of a fairy tale structure overlaid with allegory was one way of avoiding direct perspectival clash between the reader's extraliterary beliefs (usually suspended during the reading of fiction) and the vision of the future presented at the end of the work. A disadvantage of this strategy was that the whole of Part IV might be interpreted as one writer's private, idiosyncratic view of Apocalypse, and little else. Bely accepted this limitation in the case of the *Northern Symphony*, while using the prelude to solicit the reader's sympathetic attention to a different view, beyond the perspective of the fiction itself.

As we have noted on several occasions, however, didacticism is usually the obverse of lyricism in Bely's early art, and all too often the prophetic stance that he adopts actually fractures the aesthetic integrity of his chosen genre, especially when the supernatural is asserted as a universal datum of experience in the contemporary world. The *Northern Symphony* generally avoids this dilemma, but *The Return* (the *Third Symphony*) is all but ruined by it. For all its apparent epic qualities, unmediated lyricism returns here with a vengeance.

Part I of *The Return* depicts a stylized mythological world outside time which bears scarcely any relation to specific earthly reality. (As Dmitrij Tschiževskij has noted, the scene might well be set on another planet.)[78] A nameless boy is playing on the seashore under the general protection of a mysterious but benign old man, who is apparently blessed with the ability to foretell the future. When a menacing sea serpent arrives in the vicinity, the boy becomes apprehensive, sensing that his carefree existence is about to come to an end. The old man asks the boy what he is afraid of. "The wind is whispering to me that I shall perish," he replies,

---

77. Gleb Struve, as long ago as 1959, claimed to see the "pictorial influence of the English Pre-Raphaelites and of Böcklin and the German Romantics" in Bely's early work, and went on to observe that the "question of the non-literary influences on Russian Symbolists still awaits its student" (op. cit., p. 464). As far as analyzing the influence of pictorial Impressionism and Art Nouveau is concerned, a valuable start has been made by Vera Kalina in her Ph.D. dissertation, "At the Crossroads of Modernism: Critical Studies in the Work of Elena Guro," Yale, 1978. Guro, although biographically associated with Russian Futurism during her short artistic career, was clearly influenced by Symbolist writing and especially by Bely's symphonies. For this reason many of Kalina's remarks about pictorial affinities in Guro's verse and prose are equally applicable to Bely.

78. D. Tschiževskij, introduction to *Chetyre simfonii*, pp. 19–20.

"[and] that the future cannot be changed [. . .]. I fear that this has already happened more than once in the past, and always with a sad ending." The old man tries to comfort him, while murmuring to himself: "No, there will be no saving him . . . Life will have to be repeated for him again [. . .]. Another of those needless recapitulations."[79] The boy's fear that he is about to be hurled into a new terrestrial incarnation is confirmed by the words of another threatening visitor, referred to variously by the narrator as a "ragamuffin," a "reprobate," a "murderer, capable of anything," and finally identified as the Tsar-Wind (*Tsar'-Veter*). After unsuccessfully engaging him in some kind of mental battle, the old man disappears, thereby allowing his adversary to tell the boy the "prophetic tale of Khandrikov," a story so frightening that the color immediately drains from the boy's cheeks. The old man now reappears to crown him with a wreath of red roses, symbolic of suffering, and to promise him that the time will come when all this will be resolved and the eagle will be sent to rescue him. The boy gradually drifts off to sleep.

Part II is set in turn-of-the-century Moscow and presents us with the "real" world of a young chemistry researcher named Evgeny Khandrikov. As the description of his everyday life develops, a whole battery of repeated motifs serves to connect contemporary events and characters with what has gone before. As he awakens from sleep, for example, he can still hear the sea roaring in his ears, but, the narrator tells us, "it wasn't like that at all. There was no sea behind the partition" in the apartment. There was nothing but the "sound of the samovar hissing."[80] When Khandrikov arrives at his laboratory later that morning, he suddenly feels two green eyes boring into him and catches a glimpse of blood-red lips and a "wolf's beard," all familiar to the reader as attributes of the Tsar-Wind in Part I. Now, however, these same descriptive features are applied to the chemistry lecturer, Tsenkh, who is ill disposed toward Khandrikov and is embroiled with the hero's future doctor and protector, the old psychiatrist Orlov (whose name is an obvious derivative of the Russian word for "eagle"—*orel*, pronounced *oryól*). In other words, Part II presents us with a psychological, apparently verisimilar, deciphering of what went before: it is possible that the whole of Part I is simply a translation of characters, events, and emotions of the real world to that of Khandrikov's dreams; that is, that everything there depicted is a function of his consciousness. Thus his metaphysical concerns and anxieties, in particular his fear that evil forces are trying to trap him in a vicious circle of pointless terrestrial reincarnations (an all too literal embodiment of Nietzsche's "eternal return"), are cast in a transparent allegorical form. Certain leitmotival repetitions in the plot work against this

79. *Vozvrat. III['ya] simfoniya*, p. 24–25. Reprinted in *Chetyre simfonii*.
80. Ibid., p. 45.

"realistic" relativization of the text, however, as when Tsenkh sends a telegram to his friend Vladislav Denisovich Drakonov at a village or estate named Serpent's Lair (*Zmeevoe logovishche*), inviting him to travel to Moscow and join him in his struggle against Khandrikov and Orlov.[81] The hero can know nothing of Tsenkh's specific action on this occasion, and for all that the narrator's treatment of the various phys- ical/metaphysical parallels is occasionally humorous (Drakonov's name is obviously derived from the word for "dragon," for example), the fact remains that by the end of Part II the anonymous narrator, not himself subjected to irony, has made it apparent that malign spirits *are* interven- ing in Khandrikov's life, independent of his hallucinatory fears.[82] The implied author thus attempts to enforce a belief in the existence of these forces as an item of dogma *outside* the limited perspective of his char- acter's consciousness, and the reader's dilemma is total.[83] Bely refuses to conform to the basic convention of a literary work that is inevitably bound up with its status as a fiction, significant, of course, but possessing no absolute epistemological validity beyond itself. There is a constant conflict in Bely's early work between the depiction of personal experi- ence (the lyrical mode) and the desire to universalize it, to confer upon it the distinction of general truth, beyond the individual instance. He takes a short cut, in other words, from the personal to the noumenal, which, although it may be acceptable in certain kinds of lyric or philosophical poetry, is not the stuff of which fiction is made.

V

Experimental works of literature often tend to be much less interest- ing than their creators' intentions. The theoretical possibilities that they are designed, consciously or otherwise, to test often exceed the author's ability to create an aesthetically satisfying whole. Bely was certainly aware of this danger. As early as 1902 he was writing to Emile Metner that the " 'symphonies' have no future as such; but as an intermediate stage in the formation of an assuredly important form, they have their

81. Ibid., pp. 80, 85.

82. Many of the work's leitmotival parallels have been tabulated in R. E. Peterson's article "Andrey Belyi's Third Symphony: Return or Demented Demise?" in *Russian Liter- ature and Criticism: Selected Papers from the Second World Congress for Soviet and East European Studies*, ed. E. Bristol (Berkeley, 1982), pp. 167–75.

83. Particular ambiguity attaches to the last chapter of the work, which deals with Khandrikov's fate after his death and where he appears to have returned to the mythical world of Part I, the "homeland of the spirit." Peterson suggests that this is "Khandrikov's last insane vision as he is drowning" (ibid., p. 170), although to relativize the scene by regarding it as the final flickering of the hero's consciousness still leaves unresolved the problem of perspectival breaches of the kind that I have described, to be found elsewhere in the *Symphony*.

significance."[84] Bely went on to explain that he was referring to the "beginning of the end of poetry proper." He returned to the thought in more secular vein nearly thirty years later. These works might be imperfect in themselves—he writes elsewhere of their naïveté and immaturity[85]—but as "laboratory experiments" they were valuable, in that their failure laid the foundation for future achievement.[86] He specifically excluded the *Second Symphony* from this stricture; he always regarded it as one of his finest creative works.

The *Second Symphony* belongs, like "He Who Has Come," to a different line in Bely's development, one that took him beyond the naive unmediated lyricism of theurgic writing toward the realm of modernist fiction proper, with its burden of doubt and irony and its inability to countenance a unitary source of cognitive authority. Although such works presupposed assertive lyricism as a terminus a quo, they were often composed alongside writing of a more purely theurgic kind; thus a simple chronological approach is an unreliable guide to Bely's creative development. He later wrote that his symphonic period extended from 1899 to 1902, and that the one symphony to be completed later than that—*The Goblet of Blizzards*—was the result more of spiritual inertia than of creative progress.[87] The *Second Symphony* provides the genuine link between Bely's early prose and his novelistic period; but before we examine that work in detail, it would be well to glance at *The Goblet of Blizzards*. Dead end though it turned out to be, it was the work in which Bely took the structural analogy between music and literature to its farthest limit and which, as he said later, revealed to him "once and for all the impossibility of creating a 'symphony' in words."[88]

The musical element in the *First* and *Third Symphonies* was rather superficial. Anton Kovač in particular has attempted to examine the first three published symphonies in terms of sonata form (exposition, development, recapitulation, and coda),[89] but this exercise reveals nothing of the works' significance that could not be discovered equally well by more traditional literary methods of analysis. As Raymond Furness has written, "to insist that a piece of writing has a fugal or sonata form says little more than that a theme is expanded textually from its point of focus . . . or that two contrasting themes are juxtaposed, which basically means very little." He goes on to note, however, that what is really important in the musical analogy is the technique of verbal leitmotif,

84. GBL, fond 167, box 1, item 1, letter of August 7, 1902.
85. He refers to them in *Masterstvo Gogolya* (Moscow and Leningrad, 1934), p. 297, as an "as yet childish rehash of Nietzsche's prose," for example.
86. *Kak my pishem*, p. 15.
87. *Mezhdu dvukh revolyutsii*, p. 296.
88. Ibid., p. 138.
89. A. Kovač, *Andrej Belyj: The "Symphonies" (1899–1908)* (Bern, 1976).

which the French Symbolists (like Bely and Thomas Mann some years later) regarded as deriving from Wagner's music-drama, and particularly *Der Ring des Nibelungen*. "This is the most consistent contribution of music to fiction," he continues, "a device most suitable to literature because it was originally a *literary* device taken over by music and by Wagner above all."[90]

I have already suggested that the use of verbal leitmotifs in fiction—that is to say, of words or phrases that recur at various points in the narration and may or may not be entirely explicable in terms of the logic of character psychology and situation at any given moment—is one extremely potent device by which the author may imply meanings beyond those made explicit in the immediate context.[91] As such, it is an important means of symbolization in fiction, by which I mean the totality of ways in which the implied author's meanings can be mediated to the reader. Some critics refer to this as *symbolism*, but as Furness implies, the use of symbolic leitmotif in this way is not confined to the Symbolist or modernist fiction of the late nineteenth and early twentieth centuries. Indeed, it is a device that occurs frequently in realistic fiction written much earlier in the century. Tolstoy's leitmotival use of the railway as a significant backdrop to developments in Anna Karenina's tragic life, for example, helps to signify—or symbolize—at a higher level, beyond that of everyday cause and effect, the implied author's suggestion that a superior power may be at work in human affairs, be it fate, divine predestination, or whatever. Wagner was particularly influential because his use of musical leitmotifs in opera both invited the search for verbal equivalents and drew the attention of writers and critics to the device in a more conscious fashion than anyone had done before. Later writers who worked at least partly under the influence of Wagner (Edouard Dujar-

---

90. R. S. Furness, *Wagner and Literature* (Manchester, 1982), pp. 16–17.

91. This device has been identified and analyzed by a number of critics, not all of whom use the same terminology. E. K. Brown, for example, refers to what he calls "expanding" as opposed to "fixed symbols" in his book *Rhythm in the Novel* (Toronto, 1950). This theory appears to parallel Viktor Shklovsky's distinction between actional (*syuzhetnye*) and unchanging (*prokhodyashchie*) images in the work of Zamyatin (see his *Pyat' chelovek znakomykh* [Tiflis, 1927], pp. 43–67). More recently Ursula Brumm has preferred the term "realistic symbol" (see "Symbolism and the Novel," *Partisan Review*, 25 [1958], pp. 329–42), while David Lodge has coined the phrase "metonymic metaphor" in *The Modes of Modern Fiction* (London, 1977). Meanwhile, some Soviet scholars have adopted the word "subtext" for a similar purpose. Cf. Tamara Sil'man's two articles: "'Podtekst—eto glubina teksta'," *Voprosy Literatury*, no. 1 (1969), pp. 89–102, and "Podtekst kak lingvisticheskoe yavlenie," *Filologicheskie Nauki*, no. 1 (1969), pp. 84–90. It seems to me that all of these critics are dealing with variations of what is essentially the same phenomenon, that of leitmotif as I attempt to define it here.

For an analysis of one of Bely's works making use of Lodge's terminological distinctions, see S. Fasting, "Andrej Belyj's *Simfonija, 2-aja dramatičeskaja*," *Scando-Slavica*, no. 25 (1979), pp. 37–55. E. Szilard prefers to adopt the Chekhovian notion of *podtekst* in her approach to the same work; see her "O strukture Vtoroi simfonii A. Belogo," p. 317.

din, Bely, Thomas Mann, Joyce, etc.) would underline the use of the device by paying far greater attention to actual verbal similarities, if not outright repetition, than earlier writers of fiction had done.

Of course, the motifs may be no more than mnemonic counters, a kind of verbal shorthand to speed the narration (*cartes de visite,* Debussy called them in music),[92] but their application can be much more complex than that. It is a protean device, able to adapt itself to any number of semantic strategies, some more successful from the aesthetic point of view than others. We noticed that the use of the mask motif in "He Who Has Come" is entirely realistic in that it acts as a verbal signal from the implied author to the reader that certain characters have certain psychological and ideological traits in common. This inference is not contradicted by subsequent developments in the empirical plot. In the *Northern Symphony* leitmotifs are used in a similar way to connect the princess and the knight, except that on this occasion they imply a relationship beyond that of normal causality, in that the two characters are preordained to a similar destiny. This strictly nonrealistic use of the device to imply the intervention of supernatural forces in human affairs is even more to the fore in the *Third Symphony,* where a whole system of recurrent motifs identifies characters in the real world of contemporary Moscow with their spiritual archetypes beyond the grave. I argued that certain uses of leitmotif in *The Return* are illegitimate, however, because the theurgic or symbolic implications that they embody contradict the reader's expectations of plot coherence raised elsewhere in the *Symphony* without showing them to be irrelevant.

The leitmotif system fails even more dismally in *The Goblet of Blizzards,* though for different reasons. One of the most characteristic uses of leitmotif in fiction is to permit the implied author to superadd to the meaning of his work without necessarily destroying its empirical foundation in plot and character development. This is where the *Third Symphony* came to grief. In a successfully realized work of art, symbolic meanings, such as those implied through the use of leitmotif, will overlie empirical ones, but they will not falsify or contradict them; the symbolic will thus be motivated by the empirical and will at the same time raise the empirical to a higher level of abstraction that comprehends it. Where this union of concrete instance and abstract implication fails to take place or is only partially accomplished—where, in other words, the empirical plane is falsified or distorted by an abundance of unmotivated symbolic implication—there we may suspect that the biographical author is gratuitously inserting abstractions into his text without embodying them in imaginative form. But at least in the *Third Symphony* there is a substratum of empirical reference to be falsified. The same does not appear to be

92. Quoted in Furness, *Wagner and Literature,* p. 7.

true of *The Goblet of Blizzards*, despite the valiant efforts of such critics as Sergey Askol'dov and Kovač to extract one.[93]

That Bely recognized the problem well enough we know from the preface he appended to the work. He began by admitting the lyric nature of his creative impulse. "I attempted to depict as accurately as possible," he writes, "certain experiences [*perezhivaniya*] which, so to speak, underlie everyday life and which are essentially inexpressible in imagery." But there was an even greater problem. His theme would have been difficult enough to express through the medium of lyric poetry, where there is at least one potentially reliable semantic focus, namely, the poet's own lyric persona. How much more difficult it would be to invent objective correlatives of these experiences in the form of characters and a plot! He expresses this difficulty in theoretical terms reminiscent of his earlier essay "Forms of Art." "How could I combine the inner [read: "lyric"] links between these verbally inexplicable, I would say mystical, experiences with the [external, i.e., causal] links between the images themselves?" In the end, he says, he decided to subordinate the symphony's plot elements to a mechanical elaboration of the lyric motifs and to treat the work more as a structural problem than as a communicative one. He expresses the rather pious hope that the "meaning of its symbols will become less opaque from an understanding of its structure," and that in order to penetrate the latter, the book should be reread time and time again.[94] Never would a writer be more in need of Joyce's "ideal reader suffering from an ideal insomnia"![95]

In *The Goblet of Blizzards* Bely produced a work that was as distant from genuine fiction as it was close to hermetic poetry. His almost exclusive concentration on developing ever more complex leitmotif clusters, to the detriment of what those leitmotifs meant in relation to a concretely identifiable set of characters or narrators, could but render the work incomprehensible,[96] if not literally unreadable (Blok certainly found it so).[97] There are no clear outlines, no concrete perspectives. Characters

93. See Kovač, *The "Symphonies,"* pp. 231–36, and S. A. Askol'dov, "Tvorchestvo Andreya Belogo," in *Literaturnaya Mysl'*, Al'manakh 1 (Petrograd, 1923), p. 86.

94. *Kubok metelei*, pp. 1, 3; reprinted in *Chetyre simfonii*.

95. J. Joyce, *Finnegans Wake* (London, 1939), p. 120.

96. See G. Janecek, "Literature as Music: Symphonic Form in Andrei Belyi's *Fourth Symphony*," *Canadian-American Slavic Studies*, 8 (1974), p. 511: "The reiteration and development of themes over both long and short spans of text are easily enough perceived, but the discovery that they fall into a large pattern is not so easily perceived. . . . Belyi's elaborate and extensive developments of his 'themes' have a tendency to wash away a firm recollection of the original theme, making the reiterations (which are rarely entirely literal anyway) seem like further developments. Only a reader with a photographic memory or the patience to do a lot of backtracking . . . is likely to discover the structural patterns of the work."

97. See Blok and Bely, *Perepiska*, p. 231, letter of April 24, 1908: "Even from the external (literary) point of view I completely reject this Symphony apart from two or three passages, if only for the reason that I can't understand half of it (but then neither does anybody)."

merge with the objects around them as well as with each other. The same words—verbs, nouns, and adjectives—are repeated as leitmotifs in relation to different people and things. For the average reader, the result is a curious interpenetration of all in everything. There is no recognizable grid of reference, no criterion of relevance. There are symbols everywhere, of course—but what do they symbolize? In this sense, the logic of Bely's structural calculations, developed algebraically in the preface for the benefit of would-be readers, is an irrelevance. All is relationship, and yet, in the final analysis, nothing succeeds in pointing beyond itself. This is "spatial form" taken to its ultimate—the destruction of all effective syntagmatic links in the development of the narrative.

As we saw earlier, Bely advanced the theoretical possibility of spatial form in literature as early as 1902, in the essay "Forms of Art," and there can be no doubt that he anticipated many of the theories concerning "poetic logic" and "reflexive reference" which have been advanced over the years to elucidate much Imagist and post-Imagist poetry written in the West, particularly that of Ezra Pound and T. S. Eliot.[98] The analogy with music on which the theory was originally based has been refuted with great eloquence by Graham Hough in *Image and Experience*. Hough's argument is so germane to what Bely was attempting in *The Goblet of Blizzards* and so relevant to the attempts of critics to interpret his later fiction, particularly *Petersburg*, in terms of spatial form that I shall quote it at length. Unlike the themes of a musical composition, Hough writes,

> themes in a poem are made of words, and words have meanings; our attention is never arrested at the verbal surface; it proceeds to what the words denote. They denote objects, persons and ideas; and it is very difficult altogether to dispel the notion that the objects, persons and ideas in a single poem should be in some intelligible relation to each other. . . .
>
> The collocation of images is not a method at all, but the negation of method. . . . A poem, internally considered, ought to make the same kind of sense as any other discourse. . . . The poem that abandons the syntax of narrative or argument and relies on the interplay of "themes" or the juxtaposition of images according to the mysterious laws of poetic logic is not, so far as it is doing anything positive at all, doing anything that poetry has not done before. Clustered and repeated images, contrasts or echoes among them, a half-heard music of this kind has always been part of poetic effect. . . . But in all poetry before our time this music has been background music. What we have heard with the alert and directed attention has been something different. It has been a story, or an argument, or a meditation, or the direct expression of feeling. . . . Modern poetry in the Imagist mode has performed the extraordinary manoeuvre of shifting its whole weight to this second level. It has shorn itself of paraphrasable sense, of all narrative or discursive line, and relies on the play of contrasted images alone. In

98. See n. 60.

doing so it has achieved a startling concentration and brilliance of the
individual image, and a whole new rhetoric of its own. . . .[99]

But he concludes that it is "an inadequate rhetoric, inadequate for anything but very short poems and very special effects."

Hough is writing specifically of poetry, of course, where reflexive
reference is, in a sense, more easily accommodated, since the main spatial coordinate of the imagery is the figure of the poet himself. But his
criticisms are particularly applicable to prose, which can scarcely be divorced from plot and character as constituting a narrated world outside
the circle of lyric reflexivity. Symbolic reference can only be an adjunct
to a fictional work's semantic system: it cannot exist by itself. To remain
within literature, even simple allegory depends on the existence of characters involved in actions at least partly independent of symbolic purpose. In the same way, leitmotif is just one of literature's symbolic resources: it cannot compose a work by itself. And those critics who look to
the labyrinthine leitmotif systems of *Petersburg* to provide an uncondi-
tional guarantee of the novel's thematic unity blind themselves to its
deeper meanings, which lie beyond resolution about a lyric center. It
may be possible to apply a similar procedure to *The Goblet of Blizzards* and
rescue it for coherence by interpreting the whole work as the ecstatic
vision of a mystically inclined lyric narrator, although I do not think that
very much is to be gained by doing so. In much of Bely's early work, as
we have seen, the musical analogy, metaphysically interpreted, took him
beyond art into the realm of didactic preaching. In the *Fourth Symphony*,
the musical analogy, literally interpreted, took him beyond meaning
altogether. Bely wondered in his preface whether the symphony on
offer was an "artistic work at all, or a document concerning the state of
consciousness of a contemporary soul, of interest perhaps to a future
psychiatrist," but to nobody else. He was content to let posterity
decide.[100]

                                    VI

Unlike most of Bely's early prose, with the notable exception of "He
Who Has Come," the *Second* or *Dramatic Symphony* was far from being a
fairy tale or theurgic allegory in any straightforward sense. Indeed, it
was the most obviously modern of his early works—I hesitate to call it
"realistic"—being set firmly among the characters and environs of the
Moscow of 1901, and Bely sometimes referred to it informally as his

99. Graham Hough, *Image and Experience* (London, 1960), pp. 23, 25–27.
100. *Kubok metelei*, pp. 1–2.

"Moscow Symphony." In his memoirs he was at great pains to depict the work as a freewheeling, questing affair, full of irony and scorn, and intended to cast doubt on some of the wilder forms of apocalyptic literalism current in his day.[101] In consequence, the symphony had a greater density of topical reference and was much richer and more varied in its lexical resources than anything he had written hitherto. The theme of the false prophet (*lzheprorok*) appears here once again, and it was his intention to depict characters who are led astray either by their own vanity or naïveté or, more ominously, by evil forces at work in creation. He saw it as a nondogmatic work, therefore, and in his willingness to create characters who were at odds with implied authorial values, he would indeed lay the foundations for future fictional achievements. But as he pointed out in his foreword, this negative "satirical" dimension was only part of the work's intended meaning. It had a "musical" component too (*muzykal'nyi smysl*), by which he meant at one level that the symphony would "express a series of moods, linked by a primary mood or harmony."[102] This was vague, since the moods depicted in the work, though lyrical in a broad sense, could be either positive or negative, mediated or unmediated, and could relate to either the characters or the narrator or both. Underpinning everything, however, was the work's "ideal" or "idealsymbolical" sense (*ideino-simvolicheskii smysl*), which, while it was everywhere implied, would destroy neither the satirical nor the musical (read: "lyrical") dimensions. This "third sense," as he revealed later in his memoirs, was nothing less than Bely's belief that "we were approaching the synthesis, or the third phase of culture."[103] A more skeptical work it might well be, therefore, but in its deepest layer of meaning it was hardly likely to be more secular. Bely still had faith in the theurgic answer to humanity's problems. How would he attempt to embody it in this most fictional of his symphonies?

As we have noticed, all of Bely's symphonies are disconcerting to the reader. To a large extent this is a result of their generic peculiarity, that "exceptional form" (*isklyuchitel'nost' formy*) to which Bely drew attention in his foreword to the *Second Symphony* and which was his reason, indeed, for writing those prefatory remarks. The reader has no very clear idea about how the work is to be read. Is it prose? If so, then what are we to make of its segmented structure, its exaggerated rhythm, its simplified syntax? Is it then poetry? But it looks like prose, has no obvious first-person narrator, and deals with imagined characters and events. It is a hybrid, in fact, a *mezhdoumok* composed of poetic and prosaic elements,

---

101. *Na rubezhe dvukh stoletii*, p. 13.

102. *Simfoniya (2-aya, dramaticheskaya)*, pp. 125–26, reprinted in *Chetyre simfonii; Dramatic Symphony*, p. 17.

103. *Nachalo veka*, p. 122.

and this ambiguity, like that of most overtly experimental forms of literature, immediately places us on our guard and makes us much more
attentive to the status of what we are reading as a literary artifact. It
sensitizes our aesthetic response, in other words. We are less likely to
take what we are reading at face value, as a naive analogue to our
extraliterary experience. At this point, what one might call the positive
critical dimension of Bely's symphonies, their tendency to sharpen the
reader's aesthetic discrimination, is likely to work against the author's
manifest intention to communicate universal, or in this case mystical,
truths in his fiction. Here the confusion between epic and lyric modes
will have negative consequences. The reader cannot help being struck by
the contrast between the sophisticated formal awareness that the structure of the symphonies betokens and the extraordinary crudity and
naïveté of some of Bely's semantic devices, those elements of unmediated dogmatic assertion that I have so often had reason to point to. To a
certain extent L. K. Dolgopolov is right to say that at the time Bely wrote
the symphonies, he had neither the experience nor the skill to avoid the
temptation of proclaiming ideas directly by way of authorial interventions or mouthpiece characters.[104] This strategy may indeed make it
easier, as Dolgopolov says, for the reader to grasp the abstract philosophical points at issue, but the price of such clarity is the impairment of
the symphonies as works of art.

   In the *First* and *Third Symphonies* we quickly come to terms with our
bewilderment because of the relatively firm framework of meaning provided by the development of plot and character. We are likely to remain
disconcerted throughout *The Goblet of Blizzards*—always assuming that
we continue to read the work at all—because neither plot nor character
nor recurrent imagery (Bely's assurances notwithstanding) serves to establish recognizable patterns of meaning. In the *Second Symphony* also,
Bely appears to go out of his way to disrupt the reader's conventional
expectations that plot and character will develop coherently, and it is this
aspect of the work that has led many critics to comment on its advanced
experimental character, in particular the way it anticipates similar structural displacements in later modernist fiction by Joyce, Evgeny
Zamyatin, Robert Musil, and many others. Askol'dov was one of the first
scholars to analyze this aspect of the *Second Symphony*. "The first thing
that strikes you," he wrote, "is the absence of a firm plot line. . . . The
first few pages are a fairly incoherent succession of different descriptions and images. . . . Ten or twenty plots succeed one another in a
confused way without beginning or end." Was it possible to unify this
apparent chaos of impressions and events? Askol'dov thought that it
was, and he did so by following the coordinates of the narrator's implied

   104. L. K. Dolgopolov, "Tvorcheskaya istoriya i istoriko-literaturnoe znachenie romana
A. Belogo 'Peterburg,'" in A. Bely, *Peterburg* (Moscow, 1981), p. 530.

angle of vision above and beyond the phenomenal world to a point where the confusion and purposelessness of earthly life were resolved in a higher, cosmic or spiritual purpose. It was Bely's great achievement, said Askol'dov, to embody the "symphonic" harmony that exists between the phenomenal and noumenal worlds.[105]

Askol'dov was one of that fairly numerous band of critics, as common in Bely's day as in our own, who were happy to appreciate the writer's works from a metaphysical position not far removed from his own. Their empirical observations about the structure and meaning of Bely's works are not necessarily invalidated by this approach, and in the case of the *Second Symphony* Askol'dov was right to point to Bely's attempt to unite its kaleidoscopic themes and variations at a higher level of abstraction. But the actual meaning of that symbolic concord, or rather the way it is arrived at, was more complex than the critic cared to admit. Is it really the case that the narrator's intimations of cosmic harmony in the world beyond are a sufficient resolution of the many this-worldly disharmonies that are the primary theme of the symphony? I have been using musical terminology up till now, since that is the metaphorical language in which these arguments are usually conducted, but it is not necessary to do so. What I have really been writing about is the way certain kinds of (by definition, nonmusical) meaning are produced in Bely's work, and since for the most part he succeeds in avoiding direct authorial comment in the *Second Symphony,* the key to its symbolic significance beyond the empirical plane is likely to be found in the author's handling of the work's leitmotif or image system.

It is essential, as we saw, to discriminate between different uses of the leitmotif device in Bely's works. The repetition of one series of lexical elements may imply a level of meaning that parallels that of another leitmotif network or, indeed, of the empirical plot. On the other hand, the semantic layers thus exposed may appear to contradict one another. In the case of the *Dramatic Symphony,* the first series of leitmotifs to be introduced—on the theme of metaphysical tedium or *skuka*—is emphatically negative and runs parallel to the "discontinuous" plot structure analyzed by Askol'dov and others.[106] The anonymous narrator looks around at the apparently pointless labors of so many nameless, isolated individuals in the Moscow streets and comments, in vaguely cadenced prose:

Vse byli bledny i nado vsemi navisal svod goluboi, sero-sinii, to seryi, to chernyi, polnyi muzykal'noi skuki, vechnoi skuki, s solntsem-glazom posredi.

105. S. A. Askol'dov, "Tvorchestvo Andreya Belogo," pp. 74–75.

106. Some critics have noted the way in which such "discontinuity" also affects the syntactic structure of individual sentences. See J. D. Elsworth, *Andrey Bely: A Critical Study of the Novels* (Cambridge, 1983), p. 57.

All were pale and over everyone hung the light-blue vault of the sky, now deep-blue, now grey, now black, full of musical tedium, eternal tedium, with the sun's eye in its midst.[107]

This and a number of related motifs are then repeated apropos of numerous characters and minor plot events throughout the symphony. The device, though preeminently lyric in its origin and its effect on the reader, is empirically recuperable. It embodies the implied author's negative philosophical concern with the theme of eternal return, the possibility despondently raised by Schopenhauer[108] and joyfully affirmed by Nietzsche[109] that there is no ultimate reality beyond that of the life force, that the only transcendent truth is that there is no transcendence and that humankind has nothing to hope for except an eternity of meaningless repetitions of the phenomenal world.[110] The chief consolation offered by Schopenhauer was that man could in some sense escape the pain of his subjection by retreating into the abstract contemplation of it, or by creating patterns of meaning within the charmed circle of art. This at least, he supposed, was better than nothing. Bely disagreed with the philosopher on this point, regarding his suggested remedies as passive, quietistic, even "Buddhist."[111] Art might redeem

---

107. *Simfoniya (2-aya, dramaticheskaya)*, p. 129; *Dramatic Symphony*, p. 19.

108. See *World as Will and Representation*, bk. 4, no. 54, p. 284.

109. In pt. 3 of *Also sprach Zarathustra* above all.

110. The earliest developed instance of this theme occurred, as we have seen, in Bely's depiction of the disciple Mikhail in "He Who Has Come." It will also be a major philosophical and psychological concern of *The Return*, where the hero's despair at the idea that there may be no meaning or purpose underlying the universe is very effectively conveyed, especially in pt. 2 of the work. In Khandrikov's case, awareness of the possibility of "eternal return" leads not to an affirmation of this-worldly values, as his eventual suicide demonstrates, but rather to a Platonic or even Christian faith in the existence of a paradise, a land of the blessed beyond the grave, to which all will eventually return. In this sense, as Oleg Maslenikov realized, for all the work's numerous Zarathustrian parallels, the Nietzschean spirit is absent from the *Third Symphony*, as, I hope to show, it is absent from the *Second* also. See O. A. Maslenikov, "Andrej Belyj's Third 'Symphony,'" *American Slavic and East European Review*, 7 (1948), p. 84.

111. See "Budushchee iskusstva," written in 1907 but first published in *Simvolizm*, pp. 449–53. Although Schopenhauer is not expressly mentioned in this article, it is obvious that Bely is engaging in a general polemic with many of his ideas. "Music dissolves the forms of adjacent [i.e., verbal] arts, as much as it nourishes them in other respects," he wrote. "The spurious infusion of the spirit of music is a sign of decadence; we are captivated by the form of this decline—and that is our infirmity; before it bursts, a soap bubble is suffused with all the colors of the rainbow [. . .]. If the art of the future were to structure its forms by imitating pure music, then that art would be Buddhist in character. Contemplation in art is a means whereby we become aware of the summons to create our own lives. In any art engulfed by music, contemplation would be an aim in itself: it would transform the subject of contemplation into a faceless witness of his own experiences; if the art of the future were to be swallowed up in music, then the development of the arts would be halted forever." Although the article was written six years after the *Second Symphony*, at a time when Bely's fascination with Schopenhauer's musical theories was already at an end, it is certain that many of the philosopher's basic ideas were anathema to him from the outset.

the world, but not in the metaphorical sense that Schopenhauer appeared to have in mind, and least of all, as Bely was coming to realize, through the unstrenuous reorchestration of a few lyric leitmotifs. Above all, art needed to focus on the experience of people who were struggling to make deeper sense of a world resolutely opposed to the possibility of transcendence. The notion of eternal return and various ways in which it might be philosophically and psychologically resisted are therefore tested in the plot and characterization of the *Second Symphony*, as Bely passes beyond the point of mere lyric assertion. And the chosen instrument of that testing is the work's principal hero, Sergey Musatov.

Musatov does not figure in the symphony until halfway through Part II, but from the moment of his appearance the work begins to acquire a much more traditional and coherent plot structure, as the narrator concentrates on revealing to us the nature of the hero's apocalyptic beliefs. He does so first by directly reporting a prophetic speech that Musatov makes at a gathering of mystics and other intellectuals in the capital. "The Third Kingdom is now dawning," says Musatov, "the Kingdom of the Spirit. [. . .] Now we shall have to suffer the terrible final battle. [. . .] The time of the four horsemen is dawning: the white, the red, the black and the pale rider of death. [. . .] This was the mysterious thought of Dostoevsky. This was the heart-rending cry of Nietzsche. [. . .] I hear the thundering of a horse's hooves: it is the first rider." And there would appear a man who "is to rule all nations with a rod of iron. [. . .] His mother is the woman clothed with the sun. And she has been given wings so that she might flee the Serpent and escape into the wilderness."[112] Although the narrator does not comment directly on Musatov's speech, it is ironized more or less overtly in the pages that follow, as motif after motif is systematically taken up in the plot and debunked. A little boy is seen playing with some other children in a Moscow courtyard, for example. The narrator describes the "austere and thoughtful" expression on his face and the way in which his eyes concentrate the deep blue of the sky. One hand is grasping a metal piston and he suddenly begins to belabor his little sisters with this "rod of iron." They begin to scream and throw fistfuls of sand at this "despot" of theirs. The boy meanwhile wipes the sand from his face with an inflexible gesture full of significance, looks up at the turquoise sky, and leans on the metal rod. Then he suddenly throws it to the ground, jumps down off the sandpile, and rushes out of the courtyard, whooping with joy.[113]

The mystical notions thus mocked are not necessarily to be regarded as completely devalued in the implied author's eyes, however. For, although numerous other "negative" satirical characters receive short shrift in this

112. *Simfoniya (2-aya, dramaticheskaya)*, pp. 211–13; *Dramatic Symphony*, pp. 74–75.
113. *Simfoniya (2-aya, dramaticheskaya)*, pp. 220–21; *Dramatic Symphony*, p. 81.

symphony, the narrator lavishes a great deal of attention on its hero and shows us more and more of the mental and emotional difficulties under which he is laboring. In particular, we become aware that he is both tortured and tempted by recurring images of the eternal return. Part III is almost completely given over to a description of Musatov's visit to the countryside, where he hopes to make sense of the different metaphysical beliefs at war within him. While there, he seems to hear a voice saying: "Everything returns . . . Everything returns . . . All is one . . . all is one . . . in every dimension . . . Travel to the west, and you will return to the east . . . The essence of all things is contained in the visible world."[114] And this refrain is then echoed in the sound of the trees around him. The narrator does not say so, but the real reason underlying Musatov's manic espousal of naive Apocalypse à la Vladimir Solov'ev may be the urgent need he feels to silence these siren voices inside him. At this point it is important to bear in mind part of the autobiographical significance that the symphony had for Bely. Some twenty years later, in his "Material for an Intimate Biography," he remembered that he had experienced the very things that Musatov was suffering, and in this respect the *Second Symphony* was a "random extract, almost a factual record of the real and immense symphony" that he lived through during the first few months of 1901.[115] Kovač has noted that many of Bely's most humorous satirical effects in the work were "achieved at the cost of considerable self-laceration," and this circumstance, he argues, "explains the *Symphony*'s marked degree of cynicism and gloom." In his opinion it is "doubtlessly the best portrait of the author's split personality," since it dramatizes "Bely's own uncertainty of the validity of his search for knowledge."[116] Self-doubt and the fear that he might himself be in thrall to malevolent spiritual forces oppressed Bely from a very early stage, as we saw in our examination of "He Who Has Come." These negative possibilities are given full and frightening expression in the *Second Symphony*.

Musatov struggles very hard against what he feels instinctively to be a potent and seductive force for evil within him, that of philosophical nihilism. For the most part the battle takes place below the level of consciousness and surfaces in the form of occasional leitmotifs related to the eternal return and, of course, in his fanatical desire to assert the imminence of events prophesied in Revelation. It is only when his eschatological dreams finally collapse (the people he had taken to be the "woman clothed with the sun" and her "man child, who is to rule all nations with a rod of iron" turn out to be an ordinary society lady and a little girl called Nina) that the kaleidoscopic view of reality prevalent before Musatov's appearance on the scene reasserts itself, now at least

114. Ibid., pp. 253–54; *Dramatic Symphony*, p. 101.
115. "Material k biografii (intimnyi)," entry for February 1901.
116. Kovač, *The "Symphonies,"* p. 162.

partially relativized as a function of the hero's emotional collapse. Musatov is not unnaturally overwrought and he gets very drunk. He then appears to be the victim of an extraordinary hallucination. I shall quote and summarize the scene at some length, as it is little known. "*They* pointed out the open door to him. He heeded *their* advice. Do not blame him, esteemed readers! It was *they* themselves who whispered to him: 'Here you will resolve your misunderstanding.'" He enters a room that we are told is just like any government office, with a smoky oil lamp hanging down from the ceiling, a table, a carafe of water, and a glass. Sitting on the floor is a corpulent man with a red nose and red hair, dressed in nothing but a white nightcap and underclothes. He is joined by another lean, untidy individual with beetling brows and a menacing gaze, also dressed in underclothes. He is called Petrusha or variations on the name and strikes up the following conversation with Musatov:

"People seldom call in here," [he said]. "I find that unforgivably thoughtless. [. . .] Well, sir? . . . What have you got to say?" [. . .] "What are the greatest truths in the universe?" [asked Musatov]. [. . .]

"Everything increases in refinement, as it grows more specialized. . . ."

"I already know that very well for myself," remarked the disappointed Musatov. [. . .]

"Is it possible?" [cried the other.] "Have you really got as far as *that*? [. . .] But surely you can't know yet that everything returns?" [. . .]

"But of course! I know that too," said Musatov, becoming irritated. "And that isn't what I came to find out, either . . . "

"In that case, there is nothing further I can teach you, most learned one!" squealed Peten'ka. [. . .] "But maybe I should just tell you the mystery of mysteries, to put your mind at rest: *there are no mysteries*. [. . .]"

"Could this really be the world of the fourth dimension revealing itself to me?" thought Musatov [. . .]. "Yes, yes, yes, yes, yes!" prompted the essence of things in the shape of Petrushka. "A million times yes! This is the so-called world of the fourth dimension! . . .The point is that it doesn't exist at all . . .[People have] gone on to invent this fantasy of the fourth dimension on the other side of their wall . . .And they began to beat against the wall in a desire to break through [. . .]. They should be careful, because the *Avenger* is alive! [. . .]"

"But *is* there anything behind the wall?" whispered Musatov, who had turned deathly pale.

"Just such a room with just such wallpaper as you'll see in any government office, with just such an eccentric as yourself hammering at the wall with his fists, thinking there is something on the other side [. . .]."

"Well and what *about* death?" Musatov was enquiring.

[. . .] "Death involves transferring the inhabitant of room no. 10,000 to room no. 10,001, assuming that all the proper documents are to hand," he said.[117]

117. *Simfoniya (2-aya, dramaticheskaya)*, pp. 305–10; *Dramatic Symphony*, pp. 136–39.

Musatov departs in terror. The narrator remains, and goes on to describe how the two occupants of the room actually grow horns before his eyes, thereby confirming to the reader their role as agents of the forces of darkness. The tone is somewhat jocular, as it is on other occasions when the narrator transcends the dimensions of realism in order to suggest that spiritual beings really do have access to the world here below. As if to back up his suggestion that such forces actually exist, the narrator switches to the Novodevichii Convent and shows us the figure of the recently deceased philosopher Vladimir Solov'ev, who has taken to appearing on the roofs and in the cemeteries of Moscow, often accompanied by one Bars Ivanovich, a friend of his from the other world. "I think, gentlemen, that you would have glimpsed two figures sitting on graves," says the narrator, although, of course, "perhaps I only thought I saw this," he adds a little later.[118] In other words, he does not insist on this interpretation, and this is where the *Second Symphony* differs from so many of Bely's theurgic works and anticipates *The Silver Dove*. The narrator does not attempt to impose total symbolic closure by way of an authoritarian mystical interpretation of events.[119]

On the other hand, the symphony is far from being devoid of dogmatic elements. A second network of positive leitmotifs runs through the work—apple blossoms, white lilacs, sunsets, the image of a nun dressed all in black tending the graves at the Novodevichii Convent, and so on— and it is these elements that such critics as Askol'dov have in mind when they write of the *Second Symphony* as expressing an ideal of cosmic harmony. These motifs are associated with a small group of relatively unironized characters, such as the elder Ioann and a "passive and knowing" individual called Petkovsky. They also eventually embrace a lady from Moscow's high society referred to throughout as *skazka* (literally, "fairy tale," and by extension a fantastic or alluring person or thing) and mistakenly identified by Musatov as the "woman clothed with the sun." What all these figures have in common, we come to realize, is their instinctive awareness that human love will eventually overcome the forces of evil and that the day prophesied by St. John the Divine will not, after all, be long in coming. Father Ioann implies as much to Musatov, who promptly retires to his brother's house in the country, presumably to ponder the elder's words and wait. It is interesting to discover that Bely had originally intended to end the symphony on a pessimistic note (the destruction of Musatov and of the whole human race, no less!), but

118. *Simfoniya (2-aya, dramaticheskaya)*, p. 313; *Dramatic Symphony*, p. 141.

119. Contrast *The Return*. That symphony, too, depicts a character ostensibly at the mercy of malevolent forces and tortured by the thought of cyclical repetition. But, *pace* Peterson (see n. 83 above), in Khandrikov's case the eternal return turns out to be no such thing. His soul returns finally to its spiritual homeland beyond the grave, there to remain beyond the call of future incarnations (*Vozvrat: III['ya] simfoniya*, pp. 123–24).

then thought better of it.[120] He replaced this ending with a scene set in the Novodevichii Convent the following spring and obviously intended in some sense to neutralize the effect of the "eternal return" motifs by integrating them ("and again, and again") with the positive images. The result was evidently meant to be a scene of some lyric power:

I opyat' byla yunaya vesna. Vnutri obiteli vysilsya rozovyi sobor s zolotymi i belymi glavami. Krugom nego vozvyshalis' mramornye pamyatniki i chasovenki.

Shumeli derev'ya nad odinokimi pokoinikami. [. . .]

I opyat', kak i god tomu nazad, u krasnogo domika tsvela molodaya yablonya belymi, dushistymi tsvetami.

Eto byli tsvety zabveniya boleznei i pechalei, eto byli tsvety novogo dnya [. . .]

I opyat', i opyat' khokhotala krasnaya zor'ka, posylaya veterok na yablon'ku . . .

I opyat' obsypala yablonya monashku belymi tsvetami zabveniya [. . .]

I opyat', i opyat' mezhdu mogil khodila molodaya krasavitsa v vesennem tualete . . .

Eto byla skazka . . .

I opyat', i opyat' oni glyadeli drug na druga [. . .].

Bez slov peredavali drug drugu, chto eshche ne vse poteryano, chto eshche mnogo svyatykh radostei ostalos' dlya lyudei . . .

Chto priblizhaetsya, chto idet, miloe, nevozmozhnoe, grustno-zadumuchivoe . . .

And once again youthful spring arrived. Within the cloister the pink cathedral with its gold and white cupolas rose into the sky. All around it were marble tombstones and little shrines.

The trees murmured over the lonely dead. [. . .]

And once again, as a year before, the young apple tree flowered, spreading its white, fragrant blossom near the little red cottage.

These were flowers of oblivion, the oblivion of suffering and sorrows, these were flowers of the new day [. . .]

And again, and again the red sunset laughed as it rippled the little apple-tree with a breeze . . .

And again the tree sprinkled the nun with flowers of oblivion [. . .].

And again, and again a beautiful young lady in spring attire wandered among the graves . . .

It was the fairy-tale.

And again, and again they looked at each other [. . .].

Wordlessly they told each other that all was not yet lost, that many sacred joys yet remained for people. . . .

That it was coming, that it was drawing closer, the cherished, the impossible, the pensively sad . . . [121]

120. See "Material k biografii (intimnyi)," entry for March 1901.

121. *Simfoniya (2-aya, dramaticheskaya),* pp. 324–25; *Dramatic Symphony,* pp. 149–50.

In a sense this structural resolution of the work's dissonant themes is rather spurious, little more than the implied author's attempt to impose a harmonious ending from above. We felt Musatov's travail from within and this was the symphony's greatest achievement, but we are told about the *skazka*'s inner serenity from without. (We learn even less about the inner world of the black nun, who is silent throughout the work.) Either Bely's positive theme about religious faith and the ability of human love to defeat the sense of purposelessness and evil, so well embodied elsewhere in the symphony, is not translated into character and action at all (the narrator's lyric monologue) or, where Bely does make the attempt, in the case of Father Ioann and the *skazka*, the results rarely rise above the level of flaccid sentimentality. Musatov encounters resistance from surrounding reality; the positive characters do not.

The critic Dmitry Tal'nikov argued in an article of 1914 that the Symbolists' lack of interest in everyday life was a result of their attempts to look through what they regarded as the lower forms of reality in order to glimpse the "noumena" beyond. However, if a Symbolist did not succeed in avoiding those empirical forms completely (literature could not help being a representational art in some senses, after all, said Tal'nikov), then he would depict the phenomena of existence by way of a series of superficial labels, schemas, and conventional signs. "It is not objects and the embodiment of ideas in objects that the Symbolist is aiming at, but the ideas themselves, naked and deprived of all 'lower' apparel. Looking through the empirical becomes looking past the empirical," and this, he went on to argue, was bound to have an adverse effect on the Symbolists' attempts to write fiction.[122] This is an exaggeration as far as the best examples of Symbolist prose are concerned, as we can see well enough from an analysis of the *Second Symphony*. The "negative" dimension of that work was a much greater imaginative achievement than the apparently "positive" side, although it was, of course, the lyrical, theurgic message associated with the *skazka* and Father Ioann that was more attractive to Bely as biographical author. Metner suggested as much in his early review of the work in 1903, and, Bely tells us in his memoirs, "I joyfully agreed with him."[123]

It was this positive construction that Bely attempted to embody in the years that lay immediately ahead, with what success we have already examined. In the summer of 1902 he worked on the first draft of his "Fourth Symphony," which, as he revealed in his "Material for an Intimate Biography," was "supposed to give a new, mystically correct transcription of the *Second Symphony*." He explained that his earlier conception of Apocalypse as an event in history, which was satirized in the

122. D. Tal'nikov, "Simvolizm ili realizm?" *Sovremennyi Mir*, no. 4 (1914), pp. 139, 144.
123. E. [Metner], "Simfonii Andreya Belogo," *Pridneprovskii Krai*, December 15 and 16, 1903; Bely, *Nachalo veka*, p. 81.

Dramatic Symphony but not completely disowned in that work, gradually gave way to a view that interpreted St. John's prophecies in terms of the individual's inward "symbolic ascent to Christ; the 'Apocalypse' is an 'Apocalypse' of the spirit: the way of initiation into the secret of Christ's Name." The message of the "Fourth Symphony" was to be that Christ's Second Coming was already taking place, "not in the thunder of apocalyptic historical events but in the quietness of people's hearts, whence Christ appears."[124]

It is impossible to reconstruct the plot of this symphony from the brief outline of it that Bely provided so many years later (very little of it survived in *The Goblet of Blizzards*, apparently), but it is clear from the few extracts that were published that we have to do with a work written at least partly in the old theurgic manner, filled with positive characters and purified of satire and irony. For some years Bely attempted to give direct, unmediated expression to what he later referred to as an "image of the radiant life,"[125] but this lyrical vision somehow eluded adequate embodiment in his fictional work. But when he finally allowed his artistic genius to follow its natural course, as he had done for a short while during the composition of the *Second Symphony*, he would produce a work as far removed from lyric or theurgic impressionism as it is possible to imagine. The result would be his fictional masterpiece, the novel *Petersburg*.

124. Entry for May 1902.
125. "Ibsen i Dostoevsky," *Vesy*, no. 12 (1905), p. 49; reprinted in *Arabeski*, p. 93.

2

The Silver Dove

MARIA CARLSON

Andrey Bely's first novel, *The Silver Dove* (*Serebryanyi golub'*), marks his transition from the experimental symphonies to a more traditional genre.[1] More ambitious than his previous efforts, *The Silver Dove* was the first volume of a projected trilogy in the broad manner of Dmitry Merezhkovsky's *Christ and Antichrist*, which Bely admired. Like Merezhkovsky, who "stood above history" while depicting it, Bely would show "the depths of the soul and the surface of history as two mirrors trained upon each other."[2] The theme of Bely's trilogy, to which he gave the sweeping title *East or West* (*Vostok ili Zapad*), was to be nothing less than the nature and destiny of Russia. The novels would describe the thesis and antithesis of "two Russias, between which lies an abyss," and would point the way toward synthesis and the renewal of disintegrating cultural values.[3] The emphasis of this first volume falls on the blindly destructive Russia of the East (the *narod* [the "common people" or the "people"], a spontaneous, undirected creativity), while the second volume, *Petersburg*, em-

---

1. Bely wrote *The Silver Dove* in installments, which appeared in *Vesy* in 1909 (nos. 3, 4, 6, 7, 10, 11, 12). In 1910 the Scorpio Press published the novel as a separate volume in an edition of 1,000 copies; "In Place of a Foreword" was added, but otherwise it was textually identical to the original. It was included in the Pashukanis edition of Bely's *Sobranie sochinenii* (vol. 7 [Moscow, 1917]). Only the first part (chaps. 1–4) had been printed when this edition was cut short, incomplete, by the events of 1917–18 and Pashukanis's death. In 1922 a second edition, with some minor textual changes (notably an abridged final paragraph) and without "In Place of a Foreword," was published by Epokha in Berlin in a printing of 3,000 copies. This edition has been reprinted twice, once by Wilhelm Fink Verlag (Munich, 1967) and again by Ardis Press (Ann Arbor, 1980). George Reavey's English translation was published in 1974 by Grove Press, New York. P. 154 of pt. 2 (1922 text) was omitted from the translation; it was published in the second number (1983) of *The Andrej Belyj Society Newsletter*, p. 12.
2. "Merezhkovsky: Trilogiya," *Arabeski* (Moscow, 1911), p. 420. The essay-review first appeared in *Zolotoe Runo*, no. 3 (1906), under the title "Mirovaya ekteniya (Po povodu 'Trilogii' Merezhkovskogo)."
3. *Mezhdu dvukh revolyutsii* (Leningrad, 1934), p. 46.

phasizes the cold, lifeless Russia of the West (the intelligentsia, a rational philosophy of cognition without the creative impulse to animate it). The third volume, tentatively titled "The Invisible City" ("Nevidimyi Grad") and presumably intended as a resolution of these antitheses, was never written.

Contemporary reviewers immediately saw *The Silver Dove* as a novel about the relation between the people and the intelligentsia. Most critics were unimpressed by this "long-familiar Slavophile construct, lately resurrected and slightly modified by some of our modernists."[4] Others saw it as "the first swallow of a new, mystical movement 'to the people,' of new attempts to bridge the abyss between the intelligentsia and the people based on the latter's religious quest."[5] More philosophically inclined critics recognized that the work was not just another populist novel, while some sympathetic reviewers close to Bely's circle were able to identify the novel as a mystical, specifically theosophical work.[6] Almost all were quick to criticize its ornamental, pseudo-Gogolian style, calling it pretentious, mannered, and in dubious taste. Recent criticism has been kinder to *The Silver Dove* but tends to emphasize its stylistic and narrative peculiarities and its significance in the history of modern narrative technique.[7]

The novel of a poet-critic-theorist who read widely in the philosophy of culture, the history of religion, and occultism, *The Silver Dove* is not a traditional representative of the genre; consequently, its deciphering by the critical reader requires special care in the selection of an approach. This essay recommends an eclectic means of explication that, while considering the sociohistorical attitude of a previous generation as well as the more formal criticism of the present day, turns ultimately to a cultural-philosophical approach as the most fruitful in untangling the com-

4. S. A. Adrianov, "Kriticheskie nabroski," *Vestnik Evropy*, no. 7 (1910), p. 383.

5. V. L. [V. L. L'vov-Rogachevsky], "Andrey Bely: *Serebryanyi golub'*," *Sovremennyi Mir*, no. 9 (1910), p. 169 (2d pagination).

6. N. A. Berdyaev, "Russkii soblazn: Po povodu *Serebryanogo golubya*," *Russkaya Mysl'*, no. 11 (1910), pp. 104–15; R. Ivanov-Razumnik, "Andrey Bely," in *Russkaya literatura XX veka*, ed. S. A. Vengerov, vol. 3, pt. 2 (Moscow, 1916), pp. 49ff.

7. For recent articles about *The Silver Dove*, see Thomas Beyer, "Belyj's *Serebrjanyj golub'*: Gogol' in Gugolevo," *Russian Language Journal*, 30, no. 107 (1976), pp. 79–88, and "Andrej Belyj's 'The Magic of Words' and *The Silver Dove*," *Slavic and East European Journal*, 22 (Winter 1978), pp. 464–72; John Elsworth, "*The Silver Dove*: An Analysis," *Russian Literature*, 4, no. 4 (1976), pp. 365–93, and his chapter on *The Silver Dove* in *Andrey Bely: A Critical Study of the Novels* (Cambridge, Eng., 1983), pp. 55–87; Johannes Holthusen, "Erzähler und Raum des Erzählers in Belyj's *Serebrjanyj golub'*," *Russian Literature*, 4, no. 4 (1976), pp. 325–44; Katalin Sëke, "Ornamental'nyi skaz ili ornamental'naya proza? (K problematike romana Andreya Belogo 'Serebryanyi golub'')," *Acta Universitatis Szegediensis: Dissertationes Slavicae*, 11 (1976), pp. 57–64. Mention should also be made of the "mythic" studies of Samuel Cioran ("The Pastoral Apocalypse," in his *The Apocalyptic Symbolism of Andrej Belyj* [The Hague, 1973]) and Ekaterina Kuleshova ("Potok soznaniya i mif v *Serebryanom golube* Andreya Belogo," in her *Polifoniya idei i simvolov* [Toronto, 1981]).

plexities of the novel. This emphasis on cultural values, philosophy, mysticism, and philology subordinates Bely the poet-critic to Bely the theorist. Such an approach, however, is suggested by the history of the novel's conception and its writing, which coincide with Bely's unrealized plan to write a book on the theory and philosophy of symbolism and his writing of "The Emblematics of Meaning" ("Emblematika smysla"), the central article of *Symbolism*.[8] *The Silver Dove* may be viewed as a programmatic work illustrating three fundamental concepts that Bely developed and refined between 1903 and 1909 and emphasized in the theoretical articles of *Symbolism* and *Arabesques* (*Arabeski*). They are *zhiznetvorchestvo* ("the creation of life"), theurgy, and *perezhivanie* (here understood as "mystical experience"). An examination of them, while by no means exhaustive, will serve to illuminate much of the structure and meaning of Bely's enigmatic first novel.

"Art Is the Creation of Life"[9] (*Zhiznetvorchestvo*)

"Art actually expresses living, experienced life. It affirms life as creativity, and not at all as perception," Bely wrote in 1908 in "Symbolism."[10] This notion was not uniquely Bely's. In his memoirs, Vladislav Khodasevich concisely describes the fundamental idea of the congruity of art and life that the second generation of Russian Symbolists had shared since the early years of the century:

> The Symbolists did not wish to separate the writer from the man, the literary biography from the personal. Symbolism did not wish to be only an aesthetic school, a literary trend. It constantly endeavored to become a vitally creative [*zhiznenno-tvorcheskyi*] method, and therein lay its most profound, and possibly unrealized, truth; its entire history, in essence, passed in the constant striving toward this truth. It was a series of attempts, at times truly heroic, to find the union of life and creativity, its own kind of philosopher's stone of art.[11]

8. In his "List of Manuscripts Lost or Destroyed by the Author," Bely notes: "The rough drafts of a series of chapters for the work 'The System of Symbolism' (incomplete); a reworked fragment of these materials is 'The Emblematics of Meaning'; another fragment is the article 'The Meaning of Art'; [. . .] the author kept looking for the chance to rework the material into a philosophical system; instead of the system, he had hurriedly to carve out of these materials two articles for the book *Symbolism* in 1909" (cited in A. V. Lavrov, "Materialy Andreya Belogo v Rukopisnom otdele Pushkinskogo Doma," *Ezhegodnik Rukopisnogo otdela Pushkinskogo Doma na 1979 god* [Leningrad, 1981], p. 36).

9. "Pesn' zhizni," in *Arabeski*, p. 43.

10. "Simvolizm," in *Lug zelenyi* (Moscow, 1910), p. 20.

11. V. F. Khodasevich, *Nekropol': Vospominaniya* (Brussels, 1939), p. 8.

Bely best defines the idea of *zhiznetvorchestvo* in his 1908 article "Art" ("Iskusstvo"): "The ability to live is uninterrupted creativity: it is a moment, stretched out into eternity: the conditions of external necessity tear apart the creative series and the moment. Eternity disintegrates into a waterfall of moments, the image of life disintegrates into thousands of images, the form of life into thousands of forms. These forms then are the forms of art, that is, the fragments of a single form; and this single form is the creatively lived life."[12] In other words, the colors, words, images, moods, and gestures that are the building blocks of the work of art are actually the exploded fragments of the author's own life in all its contexts (personal, historical, intellectual, and metaphysical). These fragments are then reassembled into an alternative but no less valid reality: a literary universe that in its turn becomes yet another fragment of the author's creatively lived life. The literary text becomes "an emanation of the all-embracing 'text of life.'"[13] Many of the "fragments" that make up the literary universe of *The Silver Dove* are traceable through the interconnections of Bely's articles, memoirs, and letters—documents of the creatively lived life of the Symbolist writer.

A brief overview of events in Bely's life between the completion of the *Fourth Symphony* and the writing of *The Silver Dove* also provides a clue to the sources of the novel's themes and images. Bely wrote the novel over the course of 1909, his year of spiritual crisis. The three years leading up to the writing of the novel had been marked for him by a growing sense of persecution and impending doom as deadlines, bitter polemics, and personal problems—above all the frustrated love affair with Aleksandr Blok's wife, which led to a break with both her and the poet—took their toll. Frustrated also in his theoretical work by what he perceived as the limitations of neo-Kantian philosophy, Bely sought refuge in the resumption of his theosophical studies. In September 1908 he began to attend the Moscow Theosophical Circle of Kleopatra Petrovna Khristoforova and to read the Theosophical writings of Helena Blavatsky, Annie Besant, and Edouard Schuré.[14]

---

12. "Iskusstvo," in *Arabeski*, pp. 215–16. *Zhiznetvorchestvo* was a theme that Bely regularly addressed in his lectures of 1908–9. On January 21, 1909, for example, in his lecture, "Ritm zhizni i sovremennost'" at the Polytechnical Society, Bely spoke of art as "the ability to live; in other words—uninterrupted creativity, the rhythm of life, the creation of life" (from a report on the lecture in *Russkie Vedomosti*, January 22, 1909).

13. A. V. Lavrov, "Mifotvorchestvo 'Argonavtov,'" in *Mif-fol'klor-literatura*, ed. V. G. Bazanov (Leningrad, 1978), p. 140. The article contains an explication of the theory of *zhiznetvorchestvo* and its corollary, mythopoesis.

14. In this discussion, I will differentiate between theosophy ("divine wisdom") as a general branch of speculative mysticism and Theosophy as a religious-philosophical movement initiated by Mme Blavatsky and Colonel H. P. Olcott in 1875.

Bely conveniently made a chronological list of his occult readings. By 1909 he had read a variety of Theosophical classics, including Mme Blavatsky's fundamental *The Secret Doctrine*

Bely projected his personal sense of persecution into his cultural milieu and saw his own suffering paralleled by the suffering of Russia, then in the grip of the social turbulence and political reaction that followed the suppression of the 1905 Revolution. "I found courage in the fact that my fate, the inhumanly vile years of 1906–1908, was a reflection of the illusions that had descended upon all of Russia: '*the evil eye, hating Russia*,'" he later wrote to Blok in 1911.[15] This dark, neurotic mood was reinforced by Vyacheslav Ivanov and the guru of the Theosophical literati, Anna Rudol'fovna Mintslova, during Bely's visit to Petersburg in January 1909. Both praised his recently published volume of verse, *Ashes* (*Pepel*), and claimed that in its gloomy poems he had unconsciously depicted the "evil illusion that had been spread in Russia by Russia's enemy," and "that '*enemies*' really do exist who are poisoning Russia with negative emanations; these enemies are Eastern occultists, acting on the subconscious of the Russian people, unleashing '*wild passions beneath the crescent of the waning moon*.'" Encouraging Bely to take a cosmic view of things, Ivanov and Mintslova told him that the "cultural forces of Russia" (i.e., the so-called God-seeking intelligentsia) were being attacked by "occult arrows shot from the world of darkness that was consciously demoralizing Russia."[16]

Bely's mood of persecution and doom reached a critical point when he returned to Moscow in January 1909. Exhausted and depressed, he broke down and caused a scene at the lecture given by Vyacheslav Ivanov on the mystical relationship between the people and the intelligentsia at a meeting of the Moscow Literary-Artistic Circle on January 27. Following this "scandal," Bely was removed by friends to the solitude of Bobrovka, the country home of the Rachinsky family. There, for five weeks in February and March, he rested, worked on his studies of poetic rhythm, read books on astrology and occultism, and charted his own horoscope. And he began to exorcise the events of the past three years by writing the first chapter of *The Silver Dove*. "A personal note reverberates in the novel," Bely wrote many years later, "a note that had tortured me throughout this whole period: a morbid sense of 'persecution,'

(1888) and *Voice of the Silence* (1889); Annie Besant's *The Ancient Wisdom* (1897) and *In the Outer Court;* Edouard Schuré's *Grands Initiés* (1889) and his translation of Rudolf Steiner's *Das Christentum als mystische Tatsache* (1902); and works by the leading Theosophists A. P. Sinnett and Charles Leadbeater. These works were available to him in French translation. Bely also read the French occultists (Eliphas Lévi, Stanislas de Guaita, Papus, and Saint-Yves d'Alveydre). (From Andrey Bely, "Kasaniya k teosofii," Manuscript Division, Lenin Library, Moscow [hereafter GBL], fond 25 [Bely], folder 3, item 2.)

15. Aleksandr Blok and Andrey Bely, *Perepiska* (Moscow, 1940), p. 263.

16. *Vospominaniya o Bloke* (1922–23) (Munich: Wilhelm Fink, 1969), pp. 623, 624. For a concise discussion of the "God-seeking" trend among the intelligentsia at the beginning of the twentieth century, see the entry "Bogoiskatel'stvo" in *The Modern Encyclopedia of Russian and Soviet History*, ed. Joseph L. Wieczynski, vol. 5 (1977), pp. 30–32.

a feeling of nets and a sense of impending destruction; it's all in the plot of *The Dove* [. . .] by externalizing my 'illness' in the plot, I freed myself from it."[17]

Bely claimed that he had "first heard the sounds of the theme of *The Dove*" in the summer of 1908.[18] He spent part of that summer, and the following one while actually at work on the novel, at Dedovo, the Tula estate of Aleksandra Grigor'evna Kovalenskaya, the grandmother of his childhood friend and fellow Symbolist Sergey Solov'ev. Dedovo and its environs contribute prominently to the atmosphere of the novel. "In the summers at Dedovo I read literary classics and collected material for the novel *The Silver Dove;* it became the place of my spiritual torment," Bely recalled in his memoirs.[19] The old estate house at Dedovo, its book-shelves stocked with Masonic volumes, the encyclopedists, and the works of the poets of old France, is reincarnated in the decaying Gugolevo manor, which exudes the aura of the French eighteenth century. The nearby village of Efremovo was the model for Likhov, while tiny Nadovrazhino became Tselebeevo; even the language of the novel's peasants is meant to be the Tula dialect.[20]

In the unpublished variant of "The Beginning of the Century" ("Nachalo veka"), Bely gives further information about the real-life sources of his characters. Solov'ev's pale and aristocratic grandmother "was a magnificent model for Katya's 'granny,'" the Baroness Todrabe-Graaben; her son "was a magnificent model for the senator." Petr Daryalsky's red peasant shirt, blacked boots, and ashen curls belonged to Sergey Solov'ev, then experiencing a passion for mystical populism (as was Bely himself), while the gentle Katya was inspired by Bely's new love, Asya Turgeneva. The sinister carpenter Kudeyarov was a mixture of the features of a carpenter from Nadovrazhino, the Theosophist M. A. Ertel' (with whom Bely was feuding in Khristoforova's Moscow Theosophical Circle in 1909), and Dmitry Merezhkovsky (with whom Bely had recently clashed over certain philosophical points). The figure of Matrena is a complex composite of several persons: "A woman from Tula province (large-bellied and pockmarked, with crossed eyes), Lyubov' Dmitrievna [Blok's wife] (eyes—ocean-sea-blue, sadness, prayers, sharp curiosity, daring), and Polya (a servant of Emile Metner's)."[21]

The relationship between Daryalsky, Kudeyarov, and Matrena not only hints at the strained relations that existed between Bely and the

17. *Mezhdu dvukh revolyutsii,* p. 354.
18. "Kak ya pishu [1929–30]," Central State Archive of Literature and Art [hereafter TsGALI], Moscow, fond 53 (Bely), opis' 1, item 76, p. 10.
19. *Mezhdu dvukh revolyutsii,* p. 10.
20. "Nachalo veka [Berlin, 1922–23]," TsGALI, fond 53, opis' 1, item 27, p. 82.
21. Ibid., pp. 81, 82.

Bloks in the years immediately preceding the writing of *The Silver Dove*
but also suggests the eccentric triangle formed by Bely, Valery Bryusov,
and Nina Petrovskaya in 1904. It is not too farfetched to suppose that on
one level *The Silver Dove* relives Bely's unsuccessful attempt to establish
the "*Eleusinian Mysteries* of our time" (with Nina Petrovskaya as high
priestess), an experiment that had ended with "the substitution of erot-
icism for the mystery."[22] Petrovskaya had run from Bely to the "great
magician," Bryusov, who in Bely's eyes had filled her with his "mediumistic spirit" and used her as a tool of the powers of darkness against
the prophet of light (a biographical scenario reflected in the plot of *The
Silver Dove*). Bely's novel could certainly be read as a polemical answer to
Bryusov's own depiction of this strange triangle in *The Fiery Angel* (*Ognennyi angel*).[23]

Immediately beyond the level of personal imagery in *The Silver Dove*
lies a suprapersonal, historical level that incorporates "fragments" from
the life of Russia in the hot revolutionary summer of 1905, when the
country, caught in the grip of widespread strikes, agrarian revolt, and
terrorist assassinations, must have seemed the victim of spells cast by
"dark forces." Bely transformed his own experiences and conversations
with peasants in 1905–6 into students ("shkubents," as the peasants in
the novel would have it) agitating among the peasants, sinister whispered conversations in taverns, and anonymous proclamations, half religious, half revolutionary. "Letting loose the red cock," a common expression for the arson that characterized revolutionary disturbances in
the countryside, becomes a realized metaphor in the novel as cockerels
appear on Matrena's tablecloth and on the Tselebeevo bell tower, and
finally materialize from the burning words of Kudeyarov's incantations
to chase Daryalsky into the forest.

While *The Silver Dove* is concretely set in Russia in the summer of 1905,
the mood it reflects is that of 1909, when the Russian intelligentsia was
attempting to assimilate the failure of the first revolution. The themes of
the novel are those that then obsessed the intelligentsia—the destiny of
Russia, God-seeking, mystical populism, sectarianism. On an intellectual
level, the novel explores the validity of various theories put forward by
the God-seekers of Bely's immediate circle.

Many in Symbolist circles had been caught up by mystical sectarianism
in particular, with its apocalypticism, soteriological emphasis, literaliza-
tion of the concept of transfiguration, and acceptance of the congruence

22. "Material k biografii (intimnyi) [1923]," TsGALI, fond 53, opis' 2, item 3, pp. 41
(verso), 44.

23. Bryusov's roman à clef was published over the course of 1907 and was thus fresh in
Bely's memory as he was writing *The Silver Dove*. For a detailed discussion of this interesting
history, see S. S. Grechishkin and A. V. Lavrov, "Biograficheskie istochniki romana
Bryusova *Ognennyi angel*," *Wiener slawistische Almanach*, no. 1 (1978), pp. 79–108; no. 2
(1978), pp. 73–96.

of religious and aesthetic activity. Dmitry Merezhkovsky and his wife, Zinaida Gippius, cultivated Old Believers and Flagellants (*Khlysty*), visiting them and inviting them to their Petersburg apartment; Konstantin Bal'mont imitated their spiritual verses (*dukhovnye stikhi*) in his poetry; the poet Aleksandr Dobrolyubov went off to the countryside to found his own sect; Sergey Gorodetsky and Aleksandr Blok visited the Flagellants. Bely, too, mingled with sectarians at the Merezhkovskys' and read the works of Aleksandr Prugavin and Pavel Mel'nikov-Pechersky about sectarianism.

The sectarians of *The Silver Dove* and their creed clearly represent Bely's polemic with Merezhkovsky's idea of the Third Hypostasis of God, that is, the synthesis of the religion of the Flesh (paganism) and the religion of the Spirit (Christianity).[24] Merezhkovsky was fascinated by the possibility that the blend of revolutionary apocalypticism, millennialism, and pagan and Christian traditions characteristic of Russian mystical sectarianism might indeed offer the possibility of the synthesis of flesh and spirit that he envisioned. When the novel first appeared, its readers jumped to the conclusion that the sectarians represented therein were Flagellants. In the "In Place of a Foreword" added to the 1910 edition of the novel, Bely made a point of addressing this question. He admitted that his Doves had "certain features in common" with the Flagellants, but he denied that they were meant to be identified with them: "The Doves I have portrayed do not exist as a sect; but they are, with all their mad inclinations, possible; in this sense my Doves are completely real."[25] The Doves are "completely real" in that they concretely embody the abstract ideas and expectations of the God-seeking intelligentsia of Merezhkovsky's persuasion, and by depicting the Doves as murderous, muddled fanatics Bely makes clear his own view of such notions.

The sectarians, the persecution complex, the summers at Dedovo, religious-philosophical polemics, Theosophy, the Revolution of 1905, mystical populism—all these are the constituents of Bely's kaleidoscopic literary vision, the creatively transformed "fragments" of his personal life and of the intellectual and spiritual life of Russia. By themselves, these fragments are only chaotic matter, unimbued with form and meaning. Before this matter can be utilized, it must be acted upon by an animating and organizing principle. This principle is theurgy.

24. Merezhkovsky elucidates this notion in the articles of *Ne mir, no mech* (Petersburg, 1908), specifically in the initial article, "Mech."

25. Bely's equivocating statement notwithstanding, he captures the spirit of Russian mystical sectarianism in *The Silver Dove* by drawing on the traditions of the Flagellants and the closely related Castrates (*Skoptsy*). Phrases and terms associated with these sects are used throughout the novel, directly and in puns. The influence of their wild and free spiritual verses is apparent in the novel's verbal texture (rhythm, assonance, repetition, and part-Biblical, part-folk style) and in the imagery (White Dove, Black Raven, Holy Spirit, Apocalypse, garden, plants, fire, crucifixion, ecstasy, etc.).

"The Creative Word Is the Word Made Incarnate"[26]
(Theurgy)

The idea of theurgy, standard in speculative mysticism, is rooted in the notion that the cosmos is created from sound. This sound is the spermatic Word, the creative principle that shapes, forms, and gives meaning to the fragments of chaos. As early as 1903, Bely had observed that the idea of theurgy was no longer to be found exclusively in the sphere of dogmatic religion, but had moved to a different medium that allowed its continued existence: "Art has become a surrogate for theurgy."[27] By "speaking" the creative, metaphysical Word, the artist becomes himself the creator of a new universe. After he has spoken the Word the artist cognizes the universe of his creation, that is, gives it concrete form by naming that which he has created:

> Every *word* is first and foremost a *sound* [. . .]. In sound a new world is created, within the boundaries of which I feel myself to be the creator of reality; then I begin to name the objects, that is, to recreate them a second time for myself. Striving to name everything that enters my field of vision, I am essentially defending myself against the hostile world that I do not understand [chaos] [. . .].[28]

In the light of such statements, Bely would say that *The Silver Dove* originated in a *theurgic act.* The entire novel becomes a complex outgrowth of a single set of "magic sounds" as "the creative word constructs the world."[29] The theurgic center lies at the approximate center of the novel. It is concealed in the horoscope prepared for Daryalsky by Schmidt, the theosophical adept who for many years has been his spiritual guide, "directing his fate, revealing to him the blazing path of secret knowledge" (II:14/239).[30] At first glance, this horoscope seems to consist of little more than vague threats of danger and arcane terminology. Actually, it contains in distilled, cryptic form the sounds that generate the universe of *The Silver Dove,* gives an indication of the novel's plot, and points to its larger occult meaning.

26. "Magiya slov," in *Simvolizm* (Moscow, 1910), p. 434.

27. "O teurgii," *Novyi Put'*, no. 9 (1903), pp. 102–3. Bely never republished this essay, but he did not abandon the idea of theurgy in his later writings. In 1905, for instance, he wrote in "Apokalipsis v russkoi poezii" that "creativity, carried to its conclusion, directly becomes religious creativity—theurgy" (*Lug zelenyi*, p. 230), and the idea is fundamental to the 1909 article "Magiya slov."

28. "Magiya slov," p. 430.

29. Ibid., p. 434.

30. All quotations from *The Silver Dove,* unless otherwise specified, are taken from the 1922 edition (see n. 1). A colon separates the part (in Roman numerals) from the page number. The number after the slash refers to the corresponding page in the Reavey translation of the novel. All translations are my own.

Daryalsky's horoscope is similar in many ways to the one Bely cast for himself at Bobrovka in February and March 1909, using the now obsolete method outlined in Paul Christian's *Histoire de la magie, du monde surnaturel, et de la fatalité* (Paris, 1870), a standard occult text with which Bely was familiar.[31] This method, supposedly based on the ancient, hermetic Book of the Tarot, uses twenty two Major Arcana, signifying "submission to the invariable laws of divine wisdom," to assign meaning to the astrological chart.[32] Each Arcanum consists of an occult meaning, a name, a number, and, most important, a letter supposedly preserved from the ancient and esoteric alphabet of the Egyptian Magi. When Bely wrote in the "Commentaries" to *Symbolism* that "the doctrine of the Logos already lies at the basis of astrology," he was referring to this occult alphabet.[33]

As Daryalsky enters Schmidt's hut, he sees the theosophist sitting before a large sheet of paper on which is drawn an astrological chart ("a circle with four intersecting triangles and a cross inside; within each angle lines were drawn outward, dividing the circumference into twelve parts, designated by roman numerals" [II:11/236]). These are the twelve houses that correspond to the signs of the zodiac with triplicities entered. Daryalsky is looking at a standard natal chart.[34] He particularly notices that in addition to being marked with the usual aspects, it has "inscriptions entered in red ink: '*The Sacrifice,*' '*The Scythe,*' '*three cups,*' '*The Blazing Light*'; on the side of the page more strange inscriptions were entered, such as X-10: The Sphinx (X) (99 wands); 9, Leo, Venus; 10, Virgo, Jupiter (Queen of Swords); 7, Mercury, 'The Mystery of the Septenary,' and so on" (II:11/237). These are the entries for the Fatidic Circle as governed by Mercury, for Daryalsky was "born in the year of Mercury [1880], on the day of Mercury [Wednesday]" (II:12/237). The Fatidic Circle reveals "the mysterious influence of the occult powers governing all lives."[35]

Schmidt explains to Daryalsky that when he was born, his moon was "in that part of the firmament that carries the name of 'The Dragon's Tail.' Your Sun, Venus, and Mercury are darkened by evil aspects; the Sun is darkened by its quartile with Mars; Saturn is in opposition to Mercury [the quartile and opposition are both malefic aspects] [. . .].

31. Bely's notes from this famous text and his horoscope charts are in the Manuscript Division of the Lenin Library in Moscow ("Vypiski iz knigi Christian *Histoire de la magie*," GBL, fond 25, folder 31, item 2). Some of these notes also appear in the "Kommentarii" to "Emblematika symsla" in *Simvolizm*, pp. 485–89.

32. Paul Christian, *The History and Practice of Magic*, trans. James Kirkup and Julian Shaw (Secaucus, N.J., 1972), p. 473.

33. "Kommentarii," in *Simvolizm*, p. 485.

34. A sketch of this chart as described in the novel is in Christian, *History and Practice of Magic*, p. 61.

35. Ibid., p. 473.

Saturn threatens you with destruction" (II:12/237). The motif of danger from Saturn is stressed a second time: "Jupiter in Cancer would foretell elevation, nobility, and priestly service for you, but Saturn has overturned everything; when Saturn enters the constellation Aquarius, misfortune threatens you; and just now Saturn is in Aquarius" (II:14/239). Aquarius, a "violent" sign, intensifies Saturn's natural malevolence.

On Schmidt's table is another sheet of paper with "sacred hieroglyphs." These consist of a drawing of a circle around which are set the heads of a man, a bull, a lion, and an eagle; inside is a magic star with numbers: "Written under this emblem in Schmidt's hand was 'Crown of the Magi—T = 400'; there were other figures, too; the sun, blinding two youths, with the subscript: 'Quitolath—Divine Truth: 100'; Typhon above two bound figures, under which Schmidt had written: 'This is the number *sixty, the number of mystery, fatality, predestination:* that is, *the fifteenth hermetic glyph,* "Xiron."* There were also the completely incomprehensible words 'Athoim, Dinain, Ur, Zain'" (II:13/238).

This lengthy and detailed casting contains two features that are of primary significance to the meaning of the novel. The first is a discussion of the configuration of the astrological chart, in which every element conspires to deflect Daryalsky from his mystic path and bring him to an early, violent death at the hands of the forces of Saturn. The role of this feature in the plot is obvious: Daryalsky is seduced away from the theosophical path by the Saturnian Kudeyarov and is eventually murdered by the Doves.

The second, more subtle feature is the placing of the Arcana in Daryalsky's chart. All the references to the Sphinx, the Blazing Light, Typhon, Quitolath, Ur, Xiron, and so on refer specifically to the Arcana that Schmidt has written into Daryalsky's horoscope. Ten Arcana are alluded to, by letter, name, or number; as we shall see, the basic sound complexes of *The Silver Dove* are built from their letter equivalents. These Arcana, extracted from the hero's own astrological chart, are the sounds of his fate and the source of the sounds that generate the universe of the novel.[36] *The Silver Dove* is highly orchestrated. Its verbal

36. For easy reference, here are the Arcana specifically mentioned in the text of *The Silver Dove* (Bely also copied them out into his notes on Christian):

Arcanum	Name/Letter	Number	Meaning
I	Athoim (A)	1	The Magus: Will
IV	Dinain (D)	4	The Cubic Stone: Realization
VI	Ur (U)	6	The Two Roads: The Ordeal
VII	Zain (Z)	7	Osiris: Victory
X	Ioithi (Jod)	10	The Sphinx: Fortune
XII	Luzain (L)	30	The Sacrifice: Violent Death
XIII	Mataloth (M)	40	The Scythe: Transformation
XV	Xiron (X)	60	Typhon: Fate
XIX	Quitolath (Q/K)	100	The Blazing Light: Earthly Happiness
XXI	Thoth (T)	400	The Crown of the Magi: Reward

complexity forces the reader to read slowly and with close attention to sound; its convoluted word order serves as an additional brake.[37] Gradually the reader begins to detect several acoustic-semantic complexes that are repeated over and over and that seem, therefore, thematically pertinent.

The primary acoustic complex is associated with the novel's unifying image: *golub'* (dove). It appears in the title, of course, and alludes to flight and bird imagery, as well as naming the religious sect. It generates a series of common words: *golubinyi* (dove, attr.), *golubchik, golubka* (little dove, dear fellow, darling), *golubyatnya* (dovecote); it spreads out into depths and blue spaces: *glub'* (the deep), *glubina* (depth, profundity, interior), *glubokii* (deep), *golubizna* (azure blue), *golubye prostranstva* (blue spaces). And its major letters are reassembled in *Gugolevo*. The letters *L* and *U* correspond with Arcana XII (The Sacrifice: Violent Death) and VI (The Two Roads: The Ordeal) from Daryalsky's horoscope.[38]

A second important acoustic complex is based on the word *dukh* (spirit). This complex leads to a spiritual series: *Svyatoi dukh* (Holy Spirit), *Dukhov den'* (Day of the Spirit, i.e., Whitmonday), *dukhovnyi* (spiritual), *dusha* (soul), *dushevnyi* (soul, attr.), and *vozdukh* (air). This complex also leads to a frequent semantic series, associated with smothering and suffocation, which serves as a verbal premonition of Daryalsky's murder: *dushnyi, dushno* (stifling), *dukhota* (stuffiness), *dushit'* (to smother). The first example occurs in the very first paragraph of the novel (*zhar dushil grud'*—"heat suffocated [or smothered] the breast"), foreshadowing the hero's end. The three relevant letters, *D, U,* and *KH (X)*, appear as Arcana IV (Realization), VI (The Ordeal), and XV (Typhon: Fate) in Daryalsky's horoscope.

A third complex, associated with evil forces, inverts the spiritual series *D-U-KH* to produce the arcanic *K/Q-U-D* (*demon est deus inversus*) which appears in *Kud*eyarov, in *kudel' pauka* (spider web), and in *kudesnik* (sorcerer). The vowel *U,* associated by Bely with the sound of primeval,

---

The remaining Arcana, not mentioned in *The Silver Dove*, are of little relevance to the novel's plot or characterization.

37. A few samples selected at random: "ot otradnykh i khladnykh dukha dykhanii" (I:105); "na tyazhkovesnuyu opirayas' trost'" (I:153); "kazhdodnevnyi na nego utrennii gnev" (I:162); "i besy iz ego vyshli dushi" (I:199). Bely has a predilection for inverted word order, which he often uses to emphasize a series of assonances. He also slows our reading of the text by recording peculiarities of speech (Chizhikov's inability to pronounce *r* or *l;* the use of peasant dialect; slang).

38. The letter *G,* unfortunately, does not appear in Daryalsky's chart; it is present, however, in the chart that Bely drew up for himself. Perhaps this indicates a literary fatidic connection between the two "symbolists." The letter *G* is Gomor, number 3, meaning Isis-Urania: Action. It expresses, "in the *divine world,* the supreme Power balanced by the eternally active Mind and by absolute Wisdom: in the *intellectual world,* the universal fecundity of the supreme Being: in the *physical world,* Nature in labour, the germination of the acts that are to spring from the Will" (Christian, *History and Practice of Magic,* p. 97).

undifferentiated chaos, appears also in the *pauk* (spider) that Kudeyarov becomes, in the *shu-shu-shu* of Kudeyarov's and Sukhorukov's whispers, and in the *tu-tu-tu* of the Doves coming to murder Daryalsky. The letter K/Q is Arcanum XIX (The Blazing Light: Earthly Happiness).

The arcanic M-A-T initiates the name *Mat*rena and *mat'* (mother, with its associations of Mother Russia and the *tellus mater,* the Damp Mother Earth of Russian folklore); *ma* ends the word *ved'ma* (witch), which Daryalsky uses to refer to Matrena. The Theosophists associated the syllable *ma* with the Great Goddess in all her manifestations, but especially with Maya, "meaning in truth the *'unreachable,'* in the sense of illusion and unreality; as being the source and cause of spells, the personification of ILLUSION."[39] The inverted sound complex T-M generates the darkness, spiritual and actual: *t'ma* (darkness), *temnyi* (dark), *mut'* (murk), *mutnyi* (muddy, murky). The combinations D-A and K/Q-A-T give the names of the other major characters, Daryalsky and Katya; T-D gives Todrabe-Graaben. The letter M is Arcanum XIII from Daryalsky's horoscope (The Scythe: Transformation), while A is Arcanum I (The Magus: Will) and T is Arcanum XXI, The Crown of the Magi: Reward.

Each Arcanum carries with it not only its particular "primordial" sound but also a triple meaning associated with the physical, intellectual, and spiritual worlds. Schmidt's mention of Arcanum XII points the reader toward "The Sacrifice: Violent Death," an indication of what lies at the end of Daryalsky's path. Arcanum XIII is "The Scythe," an image associated with Saturn-Cronos as Father Time, who will preside over Daryalsky's "Transformation." The threatening aspects of Saturn appear in both Bely's and Daryalsky's horoscopes. This planet is "the maleficus and abode of evil, the mysterious and sinister Senex (Old Man)";[40] it is destructive, all-devouring Time, the ruler of human destiny. Schmidt, in warning his young friend against Saturn, is warning him against Kudeyarov.

Arcanum XV expresses "predestination, mystery, fatality." Daryalsky feels pursued by some fateful mystery from the distant past: "Again you have looked into my soul, evil mystery! Again you look at me from the dark past . . . " (I:128/99). The symbol of Arcanum XV is Typhon, the Devil, the destructive force that holds man prisoner in matter. Typhon is the slayer of the god; he is associated with Kudeyarov and Sukhorukov, who engineer Daryalsky's death. Arcanum VI, The Two Roads: The Ordeal, symbolizes free choice and foreshadows the hero's impending passion. With Arcanum IV, The Cubic Stone: Realization, Arcana XV and VI generate the D-U-KH complex and associate spirituality with the

39. Mme Blavatsky, *The Secret Doctrine: The Synthesis of Science, Religion, and Philosophy* (1888; reprinted Pasadena, 1977), vol. 1, p. 396.

40. Carl Jung, *Mysterium Coniunctionis,* trans. J. F. C. Hull, 2d ed. (Princeton, 1970), p. 224.

hero's realization that his destiny lies in the experience of the mystery of death.

Arcanum XIX "illuminates those who know how to use it; it strikes down those who are ignorant of its power or who abuse it."[41] It initiates the acoustic complex (Q/K) associated with Kudeyarov and sorcery. Its reference to "The Blazing Light: Earthly Happiness" refers not to divine light but to the light of Lucifer, the Astral Light that Kudeyarov uses to spin the web that traps Daryalsky. Schmidt also mentions Arcana X (Fortune), I (Will), and VII (Victory), which imply that through an act of will Daryalsky can overcome the dark forces and emerge victorious. This positive conclusion is supported by one other feature: Daryalsky looks at Schmidt's paper and sees drawn there the Crown of the Magi. This is the final Arcanum and the synthesis, it is "the sign with which the Magus decorates himself when he has reached the highest degree of initiation and has thus acquired a power limited only by his own intelligence and wisdom."[42]

With the theurgic generation of the novel's sounding cosmos from the ancient occult alphabet of the Magi, Bely continues with "naming" (*naimenovanie*), which corresponds to cognizing that which has been created. The names of the characters are saturated with meaning; furthermore, the network of associations generated by the names in the novel is consistent with the visual imagery surrounding the characters and with the roles they play. The novel, born from sound, grows into names, names take on shapes, and shapes take on being.

Alternating between lyrical flight and crooked logic, the Gogolian narrator of *The Silver Dove* introduces the village of Tselebeevo and its inhabitants.[43] Tselebeevo, as its obviously toponymic name suggests, represents the hope of wholeness: *tsel'* (goal), *tselyi, tsel'nyi* (whole), *tselebnyi* (health-giving); the narrator calls it "holy, healing" (II:54/270). He proceeds to catalog the village inhabitants and to describe their distinctive features.

On the edge of Tselebeevo lives Dmitry Mironovich Kudeyarov, leader of the Dove sect. His first name, Dmitry, ties him to the realm of the Earth Mother, Demeter, and to the pagan mysteries. The syllable *kud* associates him with sorcery, evil spirits, and demons (through *kudesnik*) and with spiders, webs, and spinners (through *kudel'*). "In popular leg-

41. Christian, *History and Practice of Magic*, p. 109.

42. Ibid., p. 110.

43. Gogolian devices and allusions abound in *The Silver Dove* and are an integral part of its literary manner. V. M. Paperny has suggested that Bely's use of Gogolian style is not merely a literary device but a genuine attempt to grasp the rhythm of Gogol's "soul." "Closely linking Gogol's fate with the fate of Russia, A. Bely creates a mythopoetic structure at the center of which lies the fate of a new Gogol (Bely himself) and the new destiny of Russia" ("Andrey Bely i Gogol': Stat'ya I," *Uchenye zapiski Tartuskogo universiteta*, vypusk 604 [1982], p. 124).

ends," writes Aleksandr Afanas'ev, "the devil not infrequently appears in the form of a spider."[44] The syllable *yar*, defined by the dictionary of Vladimir Dal'—Bely's handbook to the Russian language—as "fiery," "hot," "evil," is Luciferian; from *yar* comes *yarkii*, "shining," "bright." This semantic aspect is associated with the spider image by the "tangled threads of light" that Kudeyarov weaves. The figure of the carpenter takes on one more semantic dimension; Dal' points out that in the Tartar language (which is, of course, "Eastern"), *yar* means "ravine, chasm, or abyss."

Kudeyarov lives with the browless, pockmarked, barefoot peasant woman Matrena Semenovna, the "virgin" (*bogoroditsa*) of the Doves. Her common peasant name reveals her connection to the Earth Mother; her patronymic means "obedient" in Hebrew, and she is submissive to Kudeyarov's will. Not personally attractive, Matrena is nevertheless irresistible, for she is the female principle in its fallen form, "the sensual, attractive, magnetic principle which fascinates and seduces, which throws the whole world into disorder, chaos, and sin."[45]

To the west of Tselebeevo lies Gugolevo, the country estate of the Todrabe-Graabens. Gugolevo, echoing the name of Gogol, whose presence is everywhere felt in *The Silver Dove*, preserves the nostalgic eighteenth-century world of *russkaya starina* (Russian antiquity). "The splendid manor house with its park, hothouses, roses, marble cupids overgrown with mold" (I:15/10), and inside, portraits from the court of Catherine II, porcelain shepherdesses, bookshelves bearing works of Pope, Diderot, and Racine, darkened gilt furniture, and the ancient, gray butler Evseich—all breathe the air of the "dear dead days," as Aleksandr Benois, Konstantin Somov, and Viktor Borisov-Musatov captured them in their paintings or as Bely described them in the poetic cycle "Then and Now" ("Prezhde i teper'") in *Gold in Azure*.

Living at Gugolevo is the Baroness Todrabe-Graaben, who is European and decaying like her estate, and her son, the eccentric Pavel Pavlovich, Senator Todrabe-Graaben, "an old man in the image and likeness of the West" (II:99/306). The Todrabe-Graaben name itself carries the taint of death and decay. *Tod* in German is "death"; *Rabe* is "raven," harbinger of death; *Grab* is "grave" or "tomb." The Baroness herself—a literary cousin of Pushkin's countess from "The Queen of Spades"—is an eighteenth-century relic, immutable, unchanging, death in life: "White as death [. . .] she reminded him of a phantom" (I:191/147). She is "old and dying Russia, proud and frozen in your greatness," now doing little more than observing "the rituals of antiq-

44. A. N. Afanas'ev, *Poeticheskie vozzreniya slavyan na prirodu* (Moscow, 1869), vol. 3, p. 135.

45. Blavatsky, *Secret Doctrine*, vol. 2, p. 104.

uity" (I:155/119). But she harbors no illusions about herself or Russia: "The Baroness had learned everything long ago; and she now dooms both herself and Russia to destruction and sacrifice in the fateful struggle; but she pretends to be deaf and dumb: as if she knows nothing of these new songs [of a new Russia]" (I:161/123–24).[46]

Living at Gugolevo with the Baroness is her granddaughter, Katya. Her full name, Katerina Vasil'evna, signifies in Greek "always pure" and "royal," revealing her "higher," mystical role in the novel. In fact she is a version of Vladimir Solov'ev's Divine Sophia, who is a gnostic-Christian amalgamation of the Wisdom of God, the World Soul, the Church, and the Bride of the Logos. This mystic concept of the Divine Feminine inspired the so-called second generation of Russian Symbolists, notably Bely and Blok, in their early works.

Katya is portrayed as a paradox—part child and part adult, very silly and very bright—and an ideal that cannot be achieved without first being abandoned: "There is only one Katya on earth [. . .] you will head West from Gugolevo—straight, always straight ahead; and you will return to Gugolevo from the East, from the Asian steppes: only then will you see Katya" (I:167/128). To the world Katya may be only a "little painted angel," but to the inner eye she is a spiritual ideal, visible only to the one who has journeyed west, into the sunset (death), and returned from the east (sunrise, rebirth).

Katya is the Sleeping Beauty of "The Green Meadow" ("Lug zelenyi");[47] she is Russia in potentiality, who slumbers, surrounded by the forest labyrinth (the oak grove that surrounds Gugolevo), and waits to be awakened. Like Gogol's Pani Katerina in "The Terrible Vengeance," whose soul is held captive by an evil sorcerer while she sleeps, Bely's Katya, the soul of Russia, is separated from her body, the Russian land and people, and held captive in the decaying world of the Todrabe-Graabens. She is to be awakened by the novel's hero, Petr Petrovich Daryalsky.

"Do you not find the name of my hero noteworthy?" asks the narrator (I:15/9). Indeed it is. The primary association is with the apostle Peter, the organizer of a new faith (Katya calls him "my apostle"). The name

---

46. The Todrabe-Graaben name associates the family with a Germanic esoteric tradition: philosophical alchemy. The Raven represents the first stage in the alchemical process of transformation, the state of *putrefactio* out of which the White Dove will arise. This stage must be achieved before the *rubedo* or dawn, the spiritual gold, can be attempted. It suggests the theme of cultural values in the broadest sense that runs through the novel: as the values of Western culture, which the Todrabe-Graabens represent, decay, they are to be transmuted into new cultural values by the "spirit imprisoned in matter," the mercurial Daryalsky; he is to achieve the *albedo*, the White Dove. Thus the Todrabe-Graabens represent a necessary first step, for alchemy teaches that there is no generation without corruption, no life without death.

47. See Bely's essay of that title in *Lug zelenyi*, pp. 3–18.

Peter literally means "rock," an image that additionally evokes the *lapis philosophorum,* which medieval alchemists identified with Christ. *Dar* implies "gift," "talent," and emphasizes Daryalsky's "chosen" status. In Persian *dar'yal* means "door, passage, or gate."[48] The image is potent, for in almost all esoteric doctrines the gate appears as the pathway to suffering and crucifixion: the "Path which leads up to the 'Strait Gate,' beyond which is the 'Narrow Way,' or the 'Path of Holiness,' the 'Way of the Cross.'"[49] Together the rock and the gate, the two parts of Petr Daryalsky's name, are symbols of Christ: "This *rock* and this *gate* are the Son of God," Blavatsky writes.[50] Daryalsky's spiritual destiny, the *imitatio dei,* is encoded in his name.

The name Petr also recalls Peter the Great, who at a critical point in Russian history set Russia on a westward-looking path that eventually led, Bely believed, to its present frozen immutability and to the polarization of the people and the intelligentsia. In 1905, as Russia approached another critical point in its history, another Peter, Petr Daryalsky, appeared for the purpose of resolving the crisis of "separations." As the one divided, so would the other unite. The circle would close.

East of Tselebeevo lies the town of Likhov. The narrator's description, while ironically Gogolian, recalls the broader category of provincial towns in Russian literature. In Likhov we recognize not only Gogol's Mirgorod but also Dostoevsky's Skotoprigonevsk and the muddy, dusty provincial towns of Mikhail Saltykov-Shchedrin, Nikolay Leskov, Aleksey Remizov, Fedor Sologub, Anton Chekhov, and the populist writers. As *Petersburg* would crystallize the urban myth, so *The Silver Dove* summarizes the myth of the *derevnya* (village, countryside) in Russian literature.[51]

Likhov evokes *likhoi* (evil) and *Likhoi* (a euphemism for the devil). Its residents live between "an abyss of dust and an abyss of mud," and the narrator says that the town "could not be saved" (I:97/74–75). The name, the dust, the pigs of Likhov all point to demonic (as well as Gogolian) connections. Likhov has a nest of Doves, headed by Fekla

48. L. D. Dolgopolov, "Simvolika lichnykh imen v proizvedeniyakh Andreya Belogo," in *Kul'turnoe nasledie drevnei Rusi: Istoki, Stanovlenie, Traditsii,* ed. V. G. Bazanov (Moscow, 1976), p. 351. Dolgopolov takes his information from the 1893 edition of the Brokgaus-Efron *Entsiklopedicheskyi slovar';* there is also a famous mountain pass in the Caucasus called the Dar'yal'skoe Ushchel'e. The etymology is not too obscure for Bely to have been familiar with it.

49. Annie Besant, *Esoteric Christianity, or the Lesser Mysteries* (1901; reprinted Wheaton, Ill., 1953), p. 119.

50. Mme Blavatsky, *Isis Unveiled* (1877; reprinted New York, 1975), vol. 2, p. 245.

51. For V. M. Paperny, this ability represents Bely's enormous (albeit unconscious) contribution to modern letters: "He created a poetics that made it possible to reprocess a *temporally existing tradition* into a structure purely spatial in character—into the semantic structure of a literary text" ("Andrey Bely i Gogol': Stat'ya II," *Uchenye zapiski Tartuskogo universiteta,* vypusk 620 [1983], p. 91).

*Mat*veevna Eropegina, wife of the wealthy miller, and her servant, Annushka *Golub*yatnya; dominated by the hypnotic Kudeyarov and the evil Sukhorukov, they poison Eropegina's husband.

By his own admission, the coppersmith Sukhorukov is "the smartest man in Likhov." His name (meaning "withered hand") is, like Kudeyarov's limp, a metaphor for his spiritual deformity. Sukhorukov is the real evil genius of the novel; he profanes and perverts the creative impulses of the Doves and uses them for his own selfish ends. He persecutes Daryalsky and eventually plots the young man's murder in return for the Eropegin money that Kudeyarov promises him. Claiming that "there's no sin: there's nothin'—no church, no judge in heaven" (II:189/374), the crudely sinister Sukhorukov is the nihilistic voice of the powers of darkness.

Such, then, is the literary universe created by the symbolist-theurgist. He first speaks the creative Word. The sounds of the cosmos, echoing through his novel's phonic structure, bring his universe into being. Finally, he organizes this universe by naming that which has been created. The name confers on an object the shape and form and action contained in the name in embryo, and grows into a character who then plays his predestined role in a drama that is not only personal but historical and spiritual as well. The actions of individual lives assume symbolic consequences on the macrocosmic level.

A Mystery Drama for the Modern Man
(*Perezhivanie*)

In "The Emblematics of Meaning," Bely wrote that "aesthetic and religious forms are united in the mystery [*misteriya*]."[52] The original function of the mystery was the symbolic reenactment of the passion, sacrifice, and rebirth of a divine figure for the purpose of enabling the participant in the mystery to experience spiritual identity with the deity, thereby promoting his psychic transformation and renewal. The pivotal point is the sacrifice, where, *in imitatio dei*, the participant symbolically gives up his lower earthly self in order to liberate his higher spiritual self. The energy hereby released recharges the noumenal force of the sacred.

Bely's interest in the mystery can be traced to the influence of Vyacheslav Ivanov's mystical Dionysianism, which is clearly present in Bely's novel. A specialist in the ancient Greek mystery cults and author of *The Hellenic Religion of the Suffering God* (*Ellinskaya religiya stradayushchego boga*, 1904), Ivanov saw in Dionysus and Christ the two historically important manifestations of the archetype of the dying and

---

52. "Emblematika smysla," in *Simvolizm*, p. 108.

resurrected god. This archetype gave rise to the mystery drama, which Ivanov regarded as the original source of art. The aesthetically expressed form of the revelation encountered in the mystery is the myth; its translation into culturally valid symbols and images is mythopoesis.

Bely had experimented with the medieval mystery play in his earlier prose works, as Roger Keys points out in his essay in this volume. In *The Silver Dove* Bely looks to the ancient roots of the mystery drama, grafting onto them his own brand of *zhiznetvorchestvo:* "Our individual life, when we attempt to define it from the point of view of aesthetics, is an extended mystery; in the end, all of man's history appears as such a mystery."[53] *The Silver Dove* finds modern dress for this ancient form, and presents the reader with a mystery drama for the psychic renewal of modern man.

As *mystes*, the hero of *The Silver Dove* reenacts the sacred tragedy. He passes through all the stages of the mystery drama, following the classic route mapped by succeeding generations of speculative mystics, as described by Blavatsky:

> Starting upon the long journey immaculate, descending more and more into sinful matter, and having connected himself with every atom in manifested Space—the *Pilgrim,* having struggled through and suffered in every form of life and being, is only at the bottom of the valley of matter, and half through his cycle, when he has identified himself with collective Humanity. This, *he has made in his own image.* In order to progress upwards and homewards, the "God" has now to ascend the weary uphill path of the Golgotha of Life. It is the martyrdom of self-conscious existence. Like Visvakarman, he has to sacrifice *himself to himself* in order to redeem all creatures, to resurrect from the many into the *One Life.* Then he ascends into heaven indeed; where, plunged into the incomprehensible absolute Being and Bliss of Parinirvana, he reigns unconditionally and whence he will re-descend again at the next "coming," which one portion of humanity expects in its dead-letter sense as the *second advent,* and the other as the last "Kalki Avatar."[54]

Daryalsky's path is as eclectic as Blavatsky's description: the symbols and imagery that flesh out his spiritual adventures are taken from the Eleusinian and Orphic mysteries, from gnosticism, Russian folklore, Theosophy, spiritualism, and, most important, esoteric Christianty.

The nature of Daryalsky's spiritual quest is made symbolically clear at the very beginning of *The Silver Dove.* Passing the village pond on his way to church on Trinity Sunday (Pentecost), his attention is suddenly caught by a hollow birch tree: "Daryalsky wanted to throw himself under

53. Ibid., p. 109.
54. Blavatsky, *Secret Doctrine,* vol. 1, p. 268.

it, and gaze, gaze into the depths, through the branches, through the shining spider web stretched tautly up there—there, where a greedy spider, having sucked his fill of flies, is sprawled out motionless in the air—and it seems as if he is in the sky" (I:17/11–12). Staring at the spider, Daryalsky senses that he is now being pursued by a mystery from the distant past: "It was as if a secret danger threatened him from up there, [. . .] as if some terrible mystery, immured for ages in the sky, secretly called him" (I:17/12).

The important image of the spider and the web comes from the occult tradition, which describes the radiant spider web of Maya, the eternal weaver of the illusory web of material existence. Daryalsky's vision of the spider becomes an allegory: his striving for spirituality is impeded by the illusions created in matter. The spider that weaves the illusory web that ensnares Daryalsky turns out to be Kudeyarov, who is "like a spider, weaving a radiant web out of himself" (II:107/312):

The spider weaves his web around the whole room; everywhere there is now a glimmer, a glitter, a twinkle of thousands of the finest, brightest threads—a crackling of threads: a golden, terrible thread; but all of those threads spun out of the carpenter came together again—either at his breast, or at his abdomen, while he, sitting in the corner, swiftly sorts them with his hands, as if a spider were sorting threads with its paws. [II:109/313–14]

This spider web grows to enormous proportions, and soon "Daryalsky looks—there is a spider web between his hands, it's stuck to his chest; he wants to disentangle himself, but he can't get rid of it [. . .] red, blue, gold, green threads draw into his white breast and out again"; "everything around him is in a spider web; in the sweet blue day the spider web settles on the grass and stretches out in the air" (II:128/329).

Vulgar mysticism (spiritualism, hypnotism, and black magic), which Bely regarded with contempt and not a little apprehension, probably serves as a further source of the imagery around the "spider" Kudeyarov. In the carpenter's hut "the air between objects is strangely tense, like some sort of tissue of spiritual force" (II:107/312); the luminous threads he produces parallel the various forms of ectoplasmic emanations described in spiritualist works.[55] Kudeyarov is the hypnotist who uses the astral light, "the source of all apparitions, all extraordinary visions and all the intuitive phenomena peculiar to madness or ecstasy,"

55. The famous medium Daniel Dunglas Home described ectoplasmic materialization as the production of a luminous cloud, while the celebrated Mme d'Esperance claimed that she could feel fine threads being drawn from her skin and had the impression of being covered with spider webs. The emanations would frequently be joined to the medium by faint, luminous threads. See Nandor Fodor, *Encyclopedia of Psychic Science* (1934; reprinted Secaucus, N.J., 1966), pp. 113–17.

to control the nervous systems of others.[56] Thus his threads of light envelop and influence the yielding Matrena, whom he "controls." Daryalsky eventually realizes that Matrena "was not herself, as such, but, so to speak, an extension of the carpenter [. . .] it was apparent that the carpenter inflated her soul with his own" (II:126/327). Only at the end of the novel will Daryalsky recall "the words of Paracelsus about how an experienced hypnotist can make use of human sexual powers for his own ends" (II:172–73/361).

In the beginning, however, none of this is clear to Daryalsky. In the church he has no idea of what is happening to him: "Had he been sleeping or not there in the church; had he had a vision or not?" (I:23/16). All he remembers is that the sight of Matrena has distracted him from the icon of the Queen of Heaven. "The pockmarked wench had asked for his soul" (I:21/15). This encounter affects his entire day. As he lingers at Father Vukol's after the liturgy, he remembers his past, the biography of a typical decadent: the rejection of Christianity, a flirtation with socialism, the promise of the "red dawns," and finally the mysticism of Jakob Böhme, Johannes Eckhart, and Emanuel Swedenborg. Only three days ago he had become engaged to Katya, "his new path and the inviolable pillar of true life" (I:59/45), and now the image of Matrena has entered his soul "like a stormcloud, a tempest, a tigress, a werewolf" (I:21/15).

That night Daryalsky leaves the Tselebeevo teahouse and in the darkness tries to make his way home to Gugolevo through the thick forest that surrounds the estate, praying meanwhile to Katya to "drive away the demon, keep the demon away" (I:127/99). His journey through the night forest, where he loses his way, marks his passage through the Gateway onto the mystic Path:

> Like a traveler surrounded by the darkness of tree trunks, bushes, forests, and forest bogs, which blow the icy sigh of fog in order to enter the breast of that traveler and then devour his blood as a fiery fever, so that later, staggering, he vainly seeks that forest path from which he had long been deflected—like such a traveler, Daryalsky had given his life, light, and nobility of soul to Katya, his betrothed, for she had become his life's path; and here this path is no longer a path [. . .] a day, a glance, an instant of the pockmarked wench's—and the light, and the path, and the nobility of his soul had turned into forest, night, swamp, and rotting bog. [I:129–30/101]

56. Eliphas Lévi, *The History of Magic*, trans. A. E. Waite (1860; reprinted New York, 1969), p. 40.

The forest labyrinth represents the originating point of the mystical journey.[57] The entrance into the forest is a common threshold symbol and usually signals a change of state. This is particularly clear in folktales (and the narrator frequently calls Daryalsky's adventure a "fairy tale" [*skazka*]), where the "thick, drowsy forest" (*dremuchyi les*) marks the point of transition between this world and the "other": "You look—and the whispering [*shepotnyi*] forest is already oozing drowsiness [*drema*] upon you; and there is no way out of that forest" (I:11/6). Daryalsky's mystery, waiting for him in the darkness, is hinted at by "the whispering of the trees" (I:129/100). In the forest labyrinth he feels "the terror of descent into chaos that calls us with the most powerful of calls, the most imperative of demands; it calls us—to lose our very selves."[58]

The forest is a traditional symbol of the Great Mother (together with the moon, the night, and the swamp); it represents the unconscious, with its attendant dangers and demons and possible death. It is no coincidence that as Daryalsky looks at the moon, he thinks he sees the "earth mother" Matrena. Only when dawn dissipates the powers of darkness does he stumble through the lion-guarded gates of Gugolevo, locking them behind him with the words "Away, be gone, avaunt demonic delusion!" (I:133/103).

Relieved to be back in the security of Gugolevo, Daryalsky feels that "the chaos that yesterday raged in his soul had just abated, and a victory had been achieved over the fateful feeling that had deflected him from his path—the demons had left his soul." But when General Chizhikov arrives to talk of the mystical and revolutionary sect of the Doves and to read their proclamation, Daryalsky suddenly senses that the demons "once again began swarming around him, assuming absurd but completely real images" (I:199/153). He runs away to the pond, where he has a waking dream in which "he understood that his soul was lost somewhere long ago, and that it is not in Gugolevo . . . " (I:207/159).

Katya goes outside to join him, and Daryalsky now realizes that he "loves Katya, but Katya is not that dawn" that he must seek (I:213/163). Poor Katya, looking at her betrothed, "in the twinkling of an eye experienced his stormy life; with her inner eye she foresaw his fall; but she foresaw also the punishment hanging over him: it seemed to her that his head was radiating an invisible, brain-burning flame; but she did not

57. In medieval literature, numerous Hermetic and Rosicrucian allegories begin with the pilgrim-initiate straying into the woods and becoming lost. Dante's mystical *Divine Comedy*, admired by the Russian Symbolists, opens with the poet wandering into the nocturnal forest.

58. Vyacheslav Ivanov, "Simvolika esteticheskikh nachal," in *Po zvezdam* (Petersburg, 1909), p. 31. The essay first appeared in *Vesy*, no. 5 (1905), under the title "O Niskhozhdenii."

know that this hellish flame was his tomorrow" (I:215/164). Daryalsky
receives his baptism by "hellfire" on the Day of the Holy Spirit (*Dukhov
den'*, Whitmonday). The couple returns to the manor house just in time
to see the Baroness explode at that "absurd creature," the "powerless
conductor of all kinds of astral filth" (I:204/156), as the narrator has
earlier described the student Chukholka, who has come to visit
Daryalsky. Now completely in the grip of "petty demons" released by
Chukholka's unfortunate astral forces, Daryalsky turns on the Baroness.
She slaps him, and he, offended, refuses to forgive the overwrought old
lady and leaves for Tselebeevo: "His vengeful enemy had executed him:
his fate was returning him to those places from which only yesterday he
had escaped" (I:224/171). He bids farewell to Gugolevo, now a lost
Eden, and turns "toward the East, toward darkness and debauchery"
(I:228/175).

The forces of darkness, who now hold Daryalsky prisoner, lead him to
the sectarians. Irrevocably cut off from his previous existence, feeling
that "there was no return; and living in a feverish dream had already
become sweet" (I:263/201), he waits for Abram, the messenger of the
Doves, at the ancient hollow oak. It is a noumenal moment, and
Daryalsky ritually marks it:

> Suddenly he wanted to tear off a fir branch, tie its ends together, and put it
> on his head in place of a hat, and so he did; and crowned with this green
> prickly wreath, with a diverging horn that stuck up over his forehead, with
> a green feather that stretched down his back, he climbed into the oak
> hollow; he could not remember if he waited for very long or not; and he did
> not know what he was waiting for. [I:264/201]

This brief drama is highly symbolic. Like other important moments in
which the sacred suddenly penetrates the profane world of the novel,
the scene is constructed of both pagan and Christian motifs. Sitting in
the tree, crowned with a fir branch, Daryalsky is the dead Osiris in the
trunk of the cedar tree; he is the horned Dionysus in the ark of wood,
ready to be sacrificed in his form as Dionysus Dendritis; he is the Christ
who, knowing that crucifixion lies ahead, puts on the crown of thorns as
a token of his passion. His blackened face, smeared with ashes, harks
back to ancient death rituals. The ancient oak, sacred to many deities,
foreshadows another sacred tree: the Tree of Death, the Cross.

When Daryalsky indicates to Abram his willingness to join the Doves,
he completes his descent into Hades, committing himself to the world of
material, illusory existence. The imagery is of hellfire. The shadows
from the fire Daryalsky has kindled dance "like some sort of winged
denizen of hell seeking to smother a man surrounded by a circle of fire"
(I:269/206). "I am yours," Daryalsky tells Abram. He moves into Kudeyarov's hut and becomes an assistant in his workshop.

Daryalsky visits his old friend, the adept Schmidt. At Schmidt's table, "he sat on the border of two worlds, distant from each other: the dear past and a new reality, sweetly terrifying, like a fairy tale" (II:9–10/236). Schmidt warns him against Kudeyarov, pointing out the threat from Saturn that is in his horoscope. But Daryalsky ignores the warning and returns to the Doves. In Blavatsky's terms, he is in the "valley of matter," he has "identified himself with collective Humanity," which he perceives as the common people. "He has stepped out of the circle of help—and for the time being his enemies are victorious over him, just as the enemy is victorious over and mocks our native land," says Schmidt (I:298/228).

In the novel's center, at the end of the fourth chapter, appropriately titled "Illusion" [*navozhdenie*], in the subchapter "Night," Schmidt explains Daryalsky's position to Katya, clearly stating the occult situation:

> Everything that is dark is now falling on Petr; but Petr can still be victorious; he must first defeat himself in himself, renounce the personal creation of life; he must revaluate his attitude to the world; and the phantoms that have for him assumed the flesh and blood of people will vanish; believe me, only great and powerful souls are put to such a trial; only giants break like Petr. [I:299/228]

This key passage is profoundly Theosophical. Daryalsky must learn that the world in which he is trapped is only "a bundle of the most varied illusions on the plane of deceptive perceptions" and that he himself is both creator and victim of these illusions.[59] The "collective Humanity" (the Doves, the common people) with which he associates himself "*he has made in his own image.*" Schmidt calls it "a terrible, oppressive hypnosis" (I:298/228). As long as he remains in the world of matter, Daryalsky remains the victim of the illusions created by the ubiquitous mediumism of the dark forces of matter, and "woe to him who does not disperse this sinister gleam by overcoming chaos. He will fall, crushed by a phantom," Bely had written in 1904.[60]

This is a variant of what would be refined in *Petersburg* as "cerebral play," the individual consciousness' creation and subsequent projection onto the astral plane of thought forms that then assume a palpable reality on the physical plane. Mme Blavatsky explains:

> As God creates, so man can create. Given a certain intensity of will, and the shapes created by the mind become subjective. Hallucinations, they are called, although to their creator they are as real as any visible object is to anyone else. Given a more intense and intelligent concentration of this will, and the form becomes concrete, visible, objective.[61]

59. Blavatsky, *Secret Doctrine*, vol. 2, p. 475.

60. "Svyashchennye tsveta," in *Arabeski*, p. 117. The essay first appeared in *Mir Iskusstva*, no. 5 (1904), as the third section of "Simvolizm, kak miroponimanie."

61. Blavatsky, *Isis Unveiled*, vol. 1, p. 62.

In the "Commentaries" to *Symbolism* Bely elaborates on the functioning of these thought forms:

> The entire astral atmosphere around us is saturated with "*artificial elementals*" [thought forms]; arranging themselves into a whole, these elementals form national, class, and other atmospheres, that is, a prism, individually refracting for us ideas and feelings common to all men, influencing in turn the *physical* atmosphere of life. They evoke and reinforce the everyday forms of life.[62]

From this point of view, Daryalsky's hopes for Russia (representing the idealistic but unrealistic hopes of the intelligentsia) have "generated" the Doves. His "strange truth" about the spirit of ancient Greece pulsing through the Russian people has, through his intensity of will, become "concrete, visible, objective." It has taken on the "everyday forms of life" among the sectarians. But Kudeyarov and the Doves are *not real;* they are, as Schmidt has pointed out, only "phantoms that have assumed the flesh and blood of people" (I:299/228), thought forms projected by an "impotent" and "sinful" intelligentsia into the class and national atmospheres.

As the summer passes, Daryalsky becomes more and more involved with the Doves and what he thinks is the "ineffable mystery" of Russia. He ignores the warnings of Father Vukol ("You shouldn't trifle with the Book of Revelation" [II:137/335]) and the Senator ("You're forcing yourself to dream dreams: Wake up" [II:102/308]). At last, on an evening in late summer, Daryalsky, Matrena, Kudeyarov, and his shaggy assistant succeed in producing the hoped-for revelation: a "radiant body," the "distant, sorrowful" eyes, the "wondrously youthful face" of the Dove Child materialize from their bodies. Dressed in the white garments of Revelation, the Dove Child presides over an apocalyptic scene reminiscent of the Last Judgment as described in sectarian scriptures:

> Below—a dark abyss and clouds floating there; on the clouds, stretching forth their arms to the Child, in snow-white garments, were the redeemed Doves, and there, in the distance, in the depths, in the darkness was a great red sphere enveloped in flames and belching smoke: that was the earth; the righteous were flying away from the earth.   [II:154/missing from Reavey]

The materialization is ephemeral; with the coming of dawn and cock-crow, "everything melts away, like someone's insubstantial dream, like a fleeting vision, and now there is no *child,* no red sphere enveloped in flames" (II:155/347). Daryalsky finds himself lying in the road with no memory of how he got there. Like the poor peasant in the folktale, he is

---

62. "Kommentarii," in *Simvolizm*, p. 498.

barely saved by the cockcrow that routs the powers of the night and wakes him just before he steps over the edge of a deep ravine.

Daryalsky at last begins to understand that his experience is not "ineffable mystery" but "horror, the noose, and the pit: not Russia but some sort of dark abyss from the East was forcing itself onto Russia" (II:147/342). The Dove has the head of a hawk; Matrena is a witch, a werewolf; Kudeyarov's light is astral, not divine. The Doves have no revelation.

Daryalsky is soon convinced that Kudeyarov means to destroy him. He leaves the carpenter's hut and goes to the village teahouse, there to think about the aberrations of the summer and his destiny. "He could not explain to himself his strange love and the wild rites [. . .] it seemed to him that something enormous and heavy had fallen on him, and was suffocating him" (II:178–79/366). The carpenter had offered him a cup of "new wine,"

> but once he had tasted of that cup, and he began to imagine heaven knows what; he didn't know, were they real, or dreams, these strange adventures that had happened to him; but after those rites he had risen with a dull ache in his head, and a feeling of nausea, and spiritual satiety,—and everything that had happened the evening before now seemed loathsome, shameful, and terrible; in the full light of day he fearfully shied away from bushes and empty corners; and it constantly seemed to him that someone was following hard on his heels; he sensed an invisibly oppressive hand on his chest; and he feared suffocation.   [II:179–80/367]

His disparate thoughts keep returning to a single focus, to an ominous image of oppressive death by suffocation in which *"the fourth"* plays a prominent part. In the little time that Daryalsky remains with the Doves, he is constantly in the shadow of "the fourth," feeling that "the fourth" has "firmly, so firmly, bound them all together into one fateful, shameful, and horrible mystery" (II:191/376). Daryalsky will encounter "the fourth" for the last time when he goes to Likhov to catch the train for Moscow. Anxious to get off the empty streets, "where he, *the fourth*, was waiting for him," Daryalsky allows Sukhorukov to direct him to the Eropegin house, where death awaits him.

Four is the number of the material world. This aspect of 4 is now "crushing" Daryalsky, suffocating him with the weight of material being. Four is the demonic number: the Devil is the fourth member of the Trinity. Like all symbols, however, 4 is also its own opposite, the transcendence of material reality. Blavatsky explains that "the circle of life circumscribes the four points of the cross, which represent in succession birth, life, death, and IMMORTALITY. Everything in this world is a trinity completed by the quaternity."[63]

63. Blavatsky, *Isis Unveiled*, vol. 1, p. 508.

Having reached the bottom of the "valley of matter," Daryalsky is now ready to begin his return to his spiritual home. He renounces the Doves, and as fire (the transmutative principle) breaks out in the village, he wanders into the countryside. A sense of the suffering soon to come overwhelms him. He understands that he has always been "doomed to pain and crucifixion which there was no way of avoiding, and he even tried to bless this crucifixion" (II:179/366).

Looking westward into the sunset, Daryalsky listens to the forest, now preparing to sleep through the autumn and winter; he goes out into the fields, now harvested and empty. And there, in the empty Russian fields, he hears the "Call of Eternity":

Petr's soul was bathed in tears: he followed the sunset over the empty field, he crushed the bitter-spicy grasses, gazed at the yellowish pearls that were departing with the sunset beyond the field; on his chest was the touch of unseen fingers, and on his lips—the kisses of tenderly trembling lips; and he walked on and on over the empty field; the evening sunset ran across the field in yellowish pearls; at times it began to seem to him that he was catching up with the evening sunset, but only the stubble stretched out beneath his feet, only he heard quietly wordless songs, and that same voice—familiar from time immemorial, forgotten long ago, sounding again: "Come to me—come, come." And he went on.

"I hear, I am returning—don't leave, wait for me . . . "   [II:206/387]

The Call of Eternity that also echoed in Bely's poems and symphonies belongs to the Gnostic traditions and symbolizes, according to Hans Jonas, "the form in which the transmundane makes its appearance within the world." The purpose of the Call is to awaken the individual from "the dream of this life," for occult tradition embraces the paradox that life in the world of matter is death, while physical death is in fact the "awakening," the "liberation" of man's divine spark from material being, the "tomb of the soul." "I am the call of awakening from sleep," goes one Gnostic text."[64] The Voice of Eternity, echoing across the abyss that separates spirit from matter, awakens Daryalsky from his "feverish dream" and calls him home to his rightful abode in the spiritual spaces.[65]

That night, as a pillar of fire stands over Tselebeevo, Daryalsky

64. Hans Jonas, *The Gnostic Religion*, 2d rev. ed. (Boston, 1963), pp. 74, 80. See also the 1903 poems "Vechnyi zov" and "Obraz vechnosti" in Bely's *Zoloto v lazuri*.

65. Bely wrote of the Call in "Feniks" (1906), using the same imagery that appears in *The Silver Dove*: The wise man "sees himself, thrown into the whirl of existence. He laughs at himself. He lovingly looks at himself. He calls out: 'Come to me.' And his distant call, like the dawn, penetrates the dream in which he dreams of himself. And the other him, shackled by the dream [of life], dreams of the dawn, and of someone's dear and familiar voice, tenderly soothing, calling, 'Come to me, come, struggling one; I will soothe you. Come, come . . . ' " (*Arabeski*, p. 155).

returns to Schmidt. Mentor and disciple talk. Schmidt explains the spiritual meaning of recent events in Daryalsky's life. As he leaves Schmidt's cottage to catch the train in Likhov, "Petr rendered his last thanks to the one who not only had been able to turn Petr's decision into action and give him the strength for the difficult struggle that still lay ahead, but also in one night to turn his shameful behavior and destruction itself into only an inevitable trial sent to him on the path of life" (II:210/390).

Daryalsky now begins the Way of the Cross as he journeys to Likhov with Sukhorukov. The text dwells on the "heavy cane with an ivory knob" (II:209/390) that he carries. This cane becomes his cross, the cosmic tree of death (traditional symbology portrays the Cross-Tree in various ways: rod, wand, branch, stick). In addition to its Christian symbolism, the rod also suggests the thyrsus of the Greater Dionysian Mysteries. It was "the wand borne by Initiates," explains Mrs. Besant, "and candidates were touched with it during the ceremony of Initiation. It has a mystic significance."[66] At the very end of the novel Sukhorukov will brag that he killed Daryalsky "with that stick of his" (II:246/419).

Imagery of passion and crucifixion appears throughout Bely's work, from the symphonies to the last novels. In a letter to Blok of early January 1903, Bely explained the significance of the cross: "the symbol of the fourth initiation of the Egyptian mysteries (so it seems) is the 'cross.' Here the powers of darkness are no longer mighty. The cross drives away the darkness."[67] Daryalsky's "crucifixion" will be his victory over the powers of darkness that now control him.

Arriving at the train station, Daryalsky is already in a different dimension:

> there was no day; but it seemed to him that there was no night either; there was merely a dark void; and even darkness did not exist: there was nothing at all in that place where just an hour before the petty bourgeois had bustled about and the trees had rustled [. . .] it seemed to him that he had arrived at the station premises from an azure world; and from there departed directly—to the city of shadows. [II:224/402]

The "city of shadows" is the world illusion, the "dream of this life." As his soul prepares to return to the azure world from which it came, the illusory forms of matter, time, and dimension disintegrate. Imagery of death abounds in this chapter: "everything was dim and as if draped in mourning" (II:225/402). Having missed his train and been advised by Sukhorukov to stay with the Eropegins, Daryalsky walks toward his ineluctable fate. He leaves the world of matter and enters the timeless, spaceless realm of the spirit: "It seemed to him that they had been walking for many long years, having passed future generations by many

66. Besant, *Esoteric Christianity*, pp. 51–52.
67. Blok and Bely, *Perepiska*, p. 10.

millions of years; it seemed to him that this path had no end, and couldn't have any, just as there could be no return either: infinity lay ahead; it, infinity, also lay behind; and even infinity did not exist" (II:227–28/404–5).

The final chapter of *The Silver Dove,* in which Daryalsky acts out the last, difficult act of the mystery drama, is appropriately called "Liberation" [*osvobozhdenie*], the term used for the mystic death in many mystery cults. The servant girl Annushka guides Daryalsky to his night's lodging. She is the psychopomp; with her black scarf, bloodless lips, and face pale as death, she is the guide of the dead who "opens the door into darkness": "Her outstretched hand seemed to indicate that he should unquestioningly descend into the place where he saw nothing but darkness" (II:236/411–12). This is the last trial. Trusting his guide, Daryalsky throws himself into the abyss. He is Mrs. Besant's "Mystic Christ": "Left still to suffer, crucified, to die to the life of form, to surrender all life that belongs to the lower world, surrounded by triumphant foes who mock him, the last horror of great darkness envelopes him."[68] He accepts his fate: "With his shout and his invitation for them *to carry out their intentions against him,* he himself, as it were, signed 'death' under the life he had lived" (II:243/416).

Petr Daryalsky's death comes at the hands of the spider that threatened him from the sky and wove the web of dark illusions in which he was trapped. Weaving in and out of the novel, the spider motif now appears for the last time as Daryalsky sits waiting for death in the dark room: "Petr saw how the door slowly opened and how a large dark spot, stamping on eight legs, pushed into the room" (II:243/416). The enormous "spider" seems at last to have Daryalsky entirely in its clutches:

> In the profound silence the heavy breathing of four stooped backs, grown together at the shoulders, could be heard above some object or other; there was then the distinct crunch of a crushed chest; then silence again . . .
> "Tu-tu-tu," legs started stamping in the darkness . . .   [II:244/417]

At the end of the novel, Daryalsky's initial vision of the threatening spider has been completely realized; that spider now sits on his crushed chest. The sound imagery reverberates with *T* and *U* (i.e., darkness and chaos: *Tashchi, tashchi!* . . . *"Tu-tu-tu"*—*topotali v temnote nogi,* repeated three times [II:244]).

The *dukh* sound complex, which has been repeatedly echoing in the final chapters of the novel as *dushit'* (to smother, to suffocate) and which is realized on the material plane in the suffocating death of Daryalsky, is transformed by that death into its analogues on the spiritual plane, *dusha*

68. Besant, *Esoteric Christianity,* p. 129.

(soul) and *dukh* (spirit). At the very moment the spider has him, he breaks the spell of the illusions perpetrated by the powers of darkness and enters into Eternity, whose call he had heard a second time only moments before his death. At the moment of death, "Petr lived billions of years in aether; he saw all the magnificence that is hidden from mortal eyes; and only afterward did he blissfully return" (II:244/417). In answering the Call of Eternity, he regains his memory of the "azure world."

When consciousness returns for an instant, Daryalsky recognizes in the Doves not enemies but his own dear sisters and brothers. The Doves, threatening and evil through the veil of illusion, are "kindly" and "without malice" once that veil has been lifted. In occult tradition the nature of evil is relative. Evil exists only as part of the binary opposition "good and evil," and binary oppositions belong to the realm of matter. Like Kudeyarov, Sukhorukov, and the Doves, evil is an illusion produced in matter. "The purification of the world," Bely had written to Blok, "[. . .] is reflected in art not as the union of good and evil, but, indeed, as the passage from external appearances to the center *through a system of evil.*"[69]

Petr Daryalsky's body is taken out and ritually buried in an orchard, another indication that his death is a spiritual event:

> They removed his clothing; they wrapped his body in something (bast matting, it seems); and they carried him out.
> A woman with loosened hair walked ahead with an image of a dove in her hands. . . .[70]

Like the gods in the ancient mysteries, Daryalsky undergoes a violent death, because the violent end of the god releases vital, creative forces. Like the sacrificed gods, who were wrapped in papyrus, leaves, or bark before being buried, Daryalsky's body is wrapped in bast. Like Dionysus, whose dismembered body was distributed among the celebrants to take

69. Blok and Bely, *Perepiska*, p. 16, letter of January 27, 1903. Daryalsky's forgiving attitude is further supported by the arcanic tradition: Arcanum XII, The Sacrifice: Violent Death, warns that "if the world makes an attempt upon your earthly life, do not die without accepting with resignation the will of God and without pardoning your enemies, for whoever does not forgive shall be condemned, beyond this life, to an eternal solitude" (Christian, *History and Practice of Magic*, p. 105). More important, perhaps, is Vyacheslav Ivanov's position that "the fear of the elemental becomes the fear of God [*timor Die (sic)*] in the religious consciousness of the Old Testament, and this already is a positive religious value; but the religious consciousness of the New Testament [i.e., a specifically Christian consciousness] removes all fear: love—that is the New Testament's equivalent to fear—love knows no fear" ("O russkoi idei," in *Po zvezdam*, p. 337).

70. *Serebryanyi golub'* (Moscow, 1910), p. 321. When Bely revised the novel for the 1922 edition, he abridged the final paragraph of the novel. He never explained why he had done so.

home for burial in their orchards and vineyards for its fructifying powers, Daryalsky, now the "fruit of the cross," is buried in a garden in anticipation of his future "germination." An old Daryalsky has died in order that a new, transformed Daryalsky, a bearer of new spiritual and cultural values, may be reborn as the god dies and is resurrected: "Except a corn of wheat fall into the ground and die, it abideth alone: but if it die, it bringeth forth much fruit" (John 12:24).

The original conclusion to *The Silver Dove* recalls that "the dawn is in sacrifice": "It was a fresh morning: the trees rustled; purple threads of feathery clouds, bright blood, passed across the sky in small bright streams."[71] Daryalsky's death has assumed the proportions of a cosmic event. He has found his dawn, and only the stream of bloody clouds, recalling the "small stream of blood trickling from the lip" of the dying man (II:245/418), reminds the reader of the price that was paid. *The Silver Dove* depicts dark illusions and death, but it also expresses hope of transformation and rebirth.

The Path of the Russian Intelligentsia

If the spiritual life of an individual can be plotted as a mystery drama, so then, by theosophical analogy, can the spiritual life of a nation. While the human soul acts out its role on the physical and spiritual planes, the national soul, being a projection of many individual souls through the prism of a physical and mental entity (a country, a nation), acts out its drama, theosophy would argue, on the intellectual plane. Petr Daryalsky's drama is that of the Russian intelligentsia, whose representative he is.

Contemporary critics had little trouble in recognizing *The Silver Dove* as a literary companion to *Landmarks (Vekhi)*, a collection of essays about the faults and weaknesses of the Russian intelligentsia published the same month as the first chapter of the novel (March 1909). *Landmarks* was a humanistic indictment of the intelligentsia's actions in the critical year of 1905 as a moral sin for which they must now atone. The book was a polemical bombshell. The liberal intelligentsia, offended by the public soul-searching and pious breast-beating of these legal Marxists turned God-seekers, attacked the collection with no less fervor than did the extreme left. Bely, however, enthusiastically defended it in the pages of *Libra*. In "The Truth about the Russian Intelligentsia," he called *Landmarks* "remarkable" and insisted it should become "the handbook of the

---

71. Ibid.

Russian intelligentsia."[72] The impact of *Landmarks'* main themes is apparent in *The Silver Dove*.

Bely's novel is less concerned with depicting the state of the relationship between the people and the intelligentsia as it was in revolutionary 1905 than with probing the intelligentsia's state of mind in 1909, when the events of 1905–6 could be viewed with some critical detachment. During those four years, the intelligentsia, Bely among them, were forced to rethink many of their original assumptions and come to terms with the fact that the link they had seen between themselves and the common people was essentially illusory. The idealized and romanticized populist stereotypes projected on the peasantry before 1905 did not coincide with the reality of peasant disturbances, violence, burning, and looting. The common people were not an innately noble and virtuous ally in the struggle against a corrupt and reactionary regime, but a chaotic and vicious dark force (*temnaya sila*). The hoped-for national catharsis never came; the identity that the intelligentsia had forged for themselves was shattered. The year 1905, Semen Frank wrote in *Landmarks*, had exposed "the impotence, ineffectualness, and bankruptcy of the Russian intelligentsia's traditional moral, cultural, and philosophical outlook."[73]

Instead of searching for political solutions, certain elements among the intelligentsia turned instead to introspective soul-searching, religion, even mysticism, and indulged in public self-flagellation. For Frank, the intelligentsia's impotence "is not a coincidence nor simply a misfortune: from the historical and moral standpoint, this is its *sin*."[74] As a sin, it demanded an act of atonement, a "religious action, invisible but powerful," suggested Sergey Bulgakov.[75] *The Silver Dove* documents this sense of guilt and the necessity of communal sacrifice and atonement. Bely, closely allied with the God-seeking intelligentsia, also advocates, in line with Bulgakov's plea for "religious action," a difficult (if not impossible) religious resolution.

The voices of *Landmarks* did not cry alone in the wilderness. On January 27, 1909, Vyacheslav Ivanov repeated for the Moscow Literary-Artistic Circle his lecture "On the Russian Idea" ("O russkoi idei"), in which he stressed the same oppositions that were to concern Bely in his planned trilogy: the individual and the community, culture and elemen-

72. "Pravda o russkoi intelligentsii: Po povodu sbornika 'Vekhi,'" *Vesy*, no. 5 (1909), p. 68.

73. *Landmarks: A Collection of Essays on the Russian Intelligentsia, 1909*, trans. Marian Schwartz (New York, 1977), p. 155. The other contributors were Nikolay Berdyaev, Sergey Bulgakov, Mikhail Gershenzon, Aleksandr Izgoev, Bogdan Kistyakovsky, and Petr Struve.

74. Ibid., p. 156.

75. Ibid., p. 62.

tal chaos, the intelligentsia and the people.[76] In their natural yearning to merge with the people, Ivanov suggests, the intelligentsia erred in not conceiving of that yearning in religious terms: "they did not realize that they do not need the people, but they need what the people need, too—a New Testament [i.e., Christian] synthesis of all the beginnings that determine life and all the energies that bring life into being; the intelligentsia did not know that the organic, primitive spiritual being of the people is the Old Testament, awaiting the exposure of its truth in a new religious consciousness." This is the intelligentsia's error, their "sin." Now they must hear within themselves the voice of humility that "ceaselessly sounds in the souls of our intelligentsia and ceaselessly calls them to a sacrificial act of self-abnegation and giving of self." On the one hand, Ivanov sees this sacrificial act as Dionysian self-destruction, an inherently Russian trait identified by Dostoevsky. On the other, he compares this sacrificial act to the sacrifice of Christ, which he describes in terms of the descent of the gnostic Logos: the intelligentsia must *descend* into the mass of the people in the same way that "the divine being sends down its light into dark matter, so that matter, too, can be imbued with light." People and intelligentsia will meet in "the light of the Christ."[77] Not only Ivanov's ideas but also his imagery left their mark on Bely's novel.

Vyacheslav Ivanov's religious-aesthetic blend of Dionysianism and esoteric Christianity everywhere permeates Daryalsky's mystical populism. Daryalsky has "composed with his life the strange truth" that "in the depths of his native people there pulses an age-old past, native to the people but not yet vitally experienced—that of ancient Greece" (I:174/133). He yearns for the paradise lost of ancient Greece, a paradise that is potentially preserved in the Russian people: "the sunny life of blissful Greece of years long past, with its wars, games, sparkling ideas, and always dangerous love, just like the life of the Russian common people, evoked on the surface of his soul pictures of a blissful Edenic life, of shady bushes, and breezy, honeyed meadows with games and round dances" (I:172/132). This age-old myth of Hellas must be fused with a modern myth of Christ. Daryalsky's "strange truth" is just such a blend of Dionysian and Christian mystery. But his theory is unproven. He is only "a man of the borderline,"[78] still searching and un-

76. This was the lecture at which Bely caused the "scandal" that eventually led to his breakdown, recuperation at Bobrovka and the writing of *The Silver Dove*. An account of the evening appeared in the Moscow newspaper *Russkie Vedomosti*, January 29, 1909. The text of Ivanov's suggestive (for *The Silver Dove*) lecture was first published in *Zolotoe Runo*, nos. 1, 2–3 (1909); it was included in his *Po zvezdam*, pp. 309–37.

77. Vyacheslav Ivanov, "O russkoi idei," in *Po zvezdam*, pp. 327, 329, 330, 332.

78. The image of the "borderline" (*rubezh*) is important for the second generation of Russian Symbolists. Bely called his contemporaries "the generation of the borderline," both literally ("children of the last and of this century") and figuratively; the borderline

sure of the future: his "whole decrepit heritage had already decayed within him; but the loathsomeness of decomposition had not yet been transmuted into good earth; and that is why the weak seeds of the future" cannot germinate in him (I:176/134). His adventures among the Doves are the test of the regenerative power of his truth, his opportunity to prove that he is, as he considers himself to be, "the future of the people" (I:176/135).

Bely started from a traditional mystical-populist assumption: "Our path lies in the unification of heaven and earth, religion and life, creativity and duty; in the light of this new unification, the individual personality approaches society in a new way, the intelligentsia approach the people."[79] His novel reflects the God-seekers' reluctance to surrender their mystical-religious concept of the common people as bearer of divine mysteries: "The Russian fields know the mysteries, just as the Russian forests know the mysteries," while the peasants' simple word becomes the word of God "received in silence" (II:95/303). In the characters of Daryalsky and Matrena, Bely portrays the attempted union of the people and the intelligentsia, the former contributing a "new theory" and the latter a vital sense of religious creativity. This *hieros gamos* was to produce a new religion of the Holy Spirit, a new heaven on earth; Russia's messianic mission would be fulfilled. This was the mood of 1905.

But the novel cannot mask the bitter disappointment that had taken hold of Bely and others by 1909, as the realization dawned that the intelligentsia were too weak and had nothing substantial to offer the people, while the boorish peasants concealed no divine truth, only darkness and death. Daryalsky cultivated the peasants, swore like them, dressed like them, worked with them, drank with them, but "all, all of this alienated people" from him (I:175/133). He joined the Doves, but "Petr did not have the strength on which the carpenter had counted" (II:191/376), and the radiant Dove Child, symbol of the new revelation, would never have physical being. The Doves scorned Daryalsky's weakness, they resented his condescension and suspected his motives. Unable to understand or trust him, they killed him. This was the mood of 1909.

Daryalsky's weakness is his sin. Alone he is unable to withstand the evil occult powers that threaten him and Russia, just as the common people, alone, are unable to withstand them: "The secret enemy did not sleep: he penetrated into the heart of the common people—and from there, from the poor heart of the people, he threatened Daryalsky" (I:177/135). The secret enemy can be overcome only if the common

---

runs as a leitmotif through the first volume of his memoirs, *Na rubezhe dvukh stoletii* (Moscow and Leningrad, 1930).

79. "Nastoyashchee i budushchee russkoi literatury," in *Lug zelenyi*, p. 61.

people and the intelligentsia join forces against it. But Daryalsky is impotent; his "truth" is not strong enough to lead anyone to a new revelation. Because of this weakness, the people have fallen prey, as Sergey Bulgakov wrote, to the "legion of demons [that] has entered into Russia's enormous body and is rocking it with convulsions, torturing it, and crippling it."[80]

Through Bely's particular mystical vision, the tragedy of 1905 becomes part of an enormous illusion perpetrated by "the evil eye, the eye that hated Russia" (I:177/135); "enemies have hidden in the darkness," according to Schmidt's diagnosis, "and no mere mortal knows who is really guilty of all the absurd things that are happening" (I:298/228). In 1905 Bely sensed that "the haze that veils our spiritual vision will fall on Russia, revealing all the horrors of wars and civil strife"; he waited for "external signs, hinting at what was happening internally."[81] The veiling haze "is not reality." It forms itself into phantoms, illusions that are

> an external symbol in the struggle of the universal soul with the horror of the world, a symbol of the struggle of our souls with the chimeras and hydras of chaos. The struggle against the horrible hydra is futile: new heads will keep growing back no matter how many dragon's heads we cut off, until we realize that the hydra itself is phantasmal; it is a Mask thrown over reality, behind which hides the Unseen One; until we realize that the Mask is phantasmal, it will grow, composing bloody worldwide historical pictures.[82]

As Daryalsky's spiritual goal is to understand that his involvement with the Doves is an involvement with world illusion, and that he then must conquer that illusion and liberate his soul from its net, so Russia's goal (led by a repentant intelligentsia) must be to conquer "the chimeras and hydras of chaos," to recognize their illusory, "phantasmal" character, and thus to liberate the land from the "horrors of wars and civil strife." Russia can achieve this goal in only one way: through "religious action."

In *Landmarks*, Sergey Bulgakov described the common people as the *cross* that the intelligentsia must bear. As atonement for the sin of impotence, the intelligentsia must carry this cross and sacrifice themselves, for in sacrifice is renewal of the human spirit and the values of human culture. "Russia cannot be renewed," he wrote, "without having first renewed (along with much else) its own intelligentsia."[83] Vyacheslav Ivanov also stressed decisive *Christian* action, sacrifice *in imitatio Christi*, as a way out of the labyrinth of Russian history.

80. Bulgakov in *Landmarks*, p. 62.
81. "Apokalipsis v russkoi poezii," in *Lug zelenyi*, p. 225.
82. Ibid., p. 227.
83. *Landmarks*, p. 26.

The Silver Dove documents this excruciating experience; man and nation walk the same path. Describing Daryalsky and hinting at his imminent sacrifice, ordained *in illo tempore,* Bely is in fact describing Russia:

> There was a sound of wild beauty in his verse, casting a spell on the darkness with an incomprehensible incantation in the rush of storms, battles, and ecstasies. And chaining together these storms, battles, and ecstasies, he forcefully broke their energy with Byzantinism and the odor of musk: but—oh, oh—the odor of blood rose smokily above the odor of musk.
>
> And for him this path was Russia's path—Russia, in which was beginning either a great transfiguration of the world or its annihilation.   [I:178/136]

Initially optimistic, the intelligentsia, like Daryalsky, turned to the people with what they thought was a new truth. The two forces were to join in a *coincidentia oppositorum* that would overcome the fragmentation of Russian reality and produce a new revelation, new cultural values, a new, whole Russia. But the intelligentsia did not "have the strength" to overcome the dark forces of reaction. For this failure they must now atone by sacrificing themselves for the renewal of Russia.

In *The Silver Dove,* Daryalsky takes the "religious action" advocated by Bulgakov. He sacrifices himself in the name of the people, for "one can only sacrifice *not in one's own name.*"[84] Bely's novel is an attempt to transmit a modern gnosis, a contemporary revelation of fundamental spiritual contents. Herein lies the essence of his mythopoesis and the purpose of his mystery drama for modern readers.

For Andrey Bely, who attempted to translate failure into positive action by summarizing and interpreting the events of 1905–6 and the following years through the prism of his own mystical vision, it was important that Russia understand the choice that now confronted it. Either it continued as before, locked in the dead rituals and dead values of its own past, unaware of its spiritual being and prey to mediumistic forces of illusion generated by "secret enemies," or, risking annihilation and the dangers that lurk in the darkness, it could step boldly onto the Path. Only by throwing itself into the transforming fire would Russia, like the Phoenix, achieve transfiguration and regeneration, new values and new life, "because only from the ashes of death can the sweet soul of paradise—the Firebird—arise" (II:96/303).

84. "Nastoyashchee i budushchee russkoi literatury," p. 71.

3

Petersburg

Robert A. Maguire and John E. Malmstad

Andrey Bely's enthusiasms tended to spill into several genres. Works written at more or less the same time often bear striking similarities. The year 1912 offers a particularly instructive case in point.

Bely had been shocked when Petr Struve, editor of the prestigious journal *Russian Thought (Russkaya Mysl')*, rejected the first chapters of his new novel in December 1911.[1] Nonetheless, he was determined to press on with it, buoyed by his Petersburg friends, one of whom, Vyacheslav Ivanov, suggested the title *Petersburg*. At the same time, he was deeply involved in the affairs of the Moscow publishing house Musaget, and particularly in its new journal, *Works and Days (Trudy i Dni)*, which he had helped found and edit. As article after article for that journal flowed from his pen in the winter months of 1912, work on the novel went into slow motion. In the hope finally of escaping the pressures and contentions of Moscow, he journeyed in March to western Europe with Asya Turgeneva, his wife in all but legal name. In May and June he took the novel up once more and managed to complete the fourth and fifth chapters. But single-mindedness again eluded him, for in April he and Asya had met Rudolf Steiner.

This meeting marked a turning point in Bely's life. He had been reading Steiner for several years, and now decided that he must study with him. That summer Bely dropped the novel completely as he traveled in Germany and Switzerland to hear Steiner speak. Steiner also gave him "meditative exercises," and expected to receive reports on them. After spending August in Munich and much of September in Basel attending a series of lectures given by Steiner and his associates,

---

1. See *Kak my pishem* (Leningrad, 1930), p. 19; the essay was reprinted in K. N. Bugaeva, *Vospominaniya o Belom*, ed. J. E. Malmstad (Berkeley, 1981), p. 318. This date, like others before 1917 referred to in this chapter, is given in the old style.

Bely settled for a few weeks at the resort of Vitznau, on the shore of the Vierwaldstätter See (Lake Lucerne). There he picked up his work on the sixth chapter of the novel and wrote two articles: "The Line, the Circle, the Spiral—of Symbolism" ("Liniya, krug, spiral'—simvolizma") and "Circular Movement" ("Krugovoe dvizhenie").[2] They appeared the same year in a double issue of *Works and Days*. We should not be surprised to find similarities between them and the novel.

Petersburg is Bely's best known work. It has been translated into many foreign languages and is coming to be reckoned one of the masterpieces of twentieth-century literature. As such, it has received more critical and scholarly attention than any other work by Bely. Aspects, sides, and angles have been examined, with approaches ranging from the Freudian to the Formalist.[3] The imagery has been studied in some detail, particular attention being given to the preponderance of the circle. But no scholar has yet examined the two articles of 1912 and the novel as interrelated parts of a single mental edifice. We propose to do so here.

We assume that the reader has some acquaintance with *Petersburg*. Such an assumption cannot be made about other works of Bely's, least of all the two articles of 1912. Even then they were known to only a small coterie of readers. Summary and paraphrase are therefore in order. The basic ideas will not be new to readers familiar with Bely's earlier work. He continues and develops the diagnosis of the crisis of modern life that he first undertook in 1904 in "Symbolism as a World View" ("Simvolizm, kak miroponimanie").[4] This diagnosis maintained certain

2. *Pochemu ya stal simvolistom* (Ann Arbor, 1982), p. 84. In August 1912 Bely had heard Steiner give lecture cycle 23 for initiates (*Von der Initiation; Von Ewigkeit und Augenblick; Vom Geisteslicht und Lebensdunkel*) and in September lectures on "The Gospel According to Mark" (see Bely's *Vospominaniya o Shteinere* [Paris, 1982], pp. 113–14). Both lecture cycles are reflected in Bely's two articles: "The Gospel According to Mark" is cited in "Circular Movement," while the opposition between *vechnost'* and *mgnovenie* (Bely's rendering of *Ewigkeit* and *Augenblick*) underlies "The Line, the Circle, the Spiral—of Symbolism."

3. Magnus Ljunggren, *The Dream of Rebirth: A Study of Andrej Belyj's Novel "Peterburg"* (Stockholm, 1982), a Freudian reading of the novel, contains a thorough bibliography of writing about *Petersburg*, as does J. D. Elsworth's *Andrey Bely: A Critical Study of the Novels* (Cambridge, Eng., 1983), in which readers will find a balanced and nicely nuanced general reading of the novel. Of works about *Petersburg* in Russian we must point to R. Ivanov-Razumnik's pioneering study *Vershiny: A. Blok, A. Bely* (Petersburg, 1923) and, more recently, E. Starikova's "Realizm i simvolizm," in *Razvitie realizma v russkoi literature*, vol. 3 (Moscow, 1974), and L. K. Dolgopolov's postface to the 1981 "Literaturnye pamyatniki" edition of the novel itself ("Tvorcheskaya istoriya i istoriko-literaturnoe znachenie romana A. Belogo 'Peterburg'"). In the West the early work of Johannes Holthusen must be credited ("Andrej Belyj und sein Roman 'Peterburg,'" in *Studien zur Ästhetik und Poetik des russischen Symbolismus* [Göttingen, 1957]), as well as Dagmar Burkhart's long article "Leitmotivik und Symbolik in Andrej Belyjs Roman *Peterburg*," *Welt der Slaven*, December 1964, pp. 277–323. The many more recent Western studies are detailed in the Ljunggren and Elsworth bibliographies.

4. First published in the journal *Mir Iskusstva*, no. 5 (1904), pp. 173–96. The first two sections were reprinted in *Arabeski* (Moscow, 1911) under the same title; sec. 3 appeared there as "Svyashchennye tsveta."

constants, despite the impact on Bely of thinkers as diverse as Vladimir Solov'ev, Schopenhauer, Nietzsche, Kant, the Neo-Kantians, the theosophists, and finally Rudolf Steiner. Among them were the problem of cognition, the definition of Truth as movement toward some goal, and the conviction that modern life was characterized by seeming dualities, even polarities. Bely assigned different terms to these polarities in his various essays, as in "The Crisis of Consciousness and Henrik Ibsen" ("Krizis soznaniya i Genrik Ibsen," 1910), which, as John Elsworth has pointed out, enumerates the contradictions "between consciousness and feeling; between contemplation and will; between the individual and society; between science and religion; and between morality and beauty."[5] The new terms of 1912 are "line" and "circle." In his early work, Bely often drew on his training in mathematics and the sciences for concepts and terminology. These two articles of 1912, however, appear to be the first instances where he created a new geometric model to embody, in more or less consistent if not systematic fashion, one key idea with which he had long been contending: "one must create life: creation before cognition."[6]

"The Line, the Circle, the Spiral—of Symbolism"

In "The Line, the Circle, the Spiral—of Symbolism" Bely posits two common ways of looking at the world: linear and circular.[7] Among his contemporaries, he says, linear thinking assumes two apparently different but ultimately identical forms. One, represented by the so-called decadents, emphasizes the unique value of the intensely experienced "moment" (*mig*). It is linear insofar as it sees human experience as merely a "succession" (*smena*) of such moments. This view claims to "stand above" time, but instead it "schematizes all past moments and orients them all on the present moment" (13); and as it examines that moment, time moves on. The other linear view, represented by the so-called evolutionists, sees human development as a "scheme of stages" (*skhema etapov*) guided by laws that operate in time. Neither view, however, takes account of the constant, relentless movement of time: "Time, a bridleless horse, races on and on and on" (13). (The personification of concepts is

5. *Andrey Bely: A Critical Study*, p. 10. "Krizis soznaniya i Genrik Ibsen" was first published in *Arabeski*.
6. "Otvet F. A. Stepunu na otkrytoe pis'mo v no. 4–5 'Trudov i Dnei,'" *Trudy i Dni*, no. 6 (November–December 1912), p. 16. See also the essays "Problema kul'tury" (1909) and "Smysl iskusstva" (1907), in *Simvolizm* (Moscow, 1910), pp. 8 and 210.
7. *Trudy i Dni*, no. 4–5 (July–October 1912), pp. 13–22. Hereafter this article will be referred to as "The Line," and page references will follow citations in the text.

typical of Bely.) The one view denies time, the other schematizes time and endows it with purpose.

Furthermore, neither view, Bely thinks, embraces the whole picture, for both are necessarily bound by experience (*perezhivanie:* Bely uses this word in various forms, all of which emphasize the epistemological *act* of cognition). The evolutionists deny that anything can be known beyond what is given to experience, and admit in effect that experience is limiting. The decadents choose not to look beyond immediate experience, believing that in such intensely lived moments they at least glimpse something of Truth. Bely grants that immediate experience would be Truth if it could embrace *all* moments, past and future; for if we could get back to the "prime source" (14), we would find that all moments would be but a single moment. However, experience is far too limited (and limiting) to make that even remotely possible. Thus both views divorce themselves from the absolute, or Truth. Finally, both views are ultimately circular: the philosophy of the moment because it is self-referential, moving endlessly around itself with no sense of any larger pattern; evolutionism because it posits endlessly repetitive patterns without, Bely thinks, any teleological impulse.

Circular thinking seems to be the opposite of linear. It denies the moment, as well as evolution, seeing both as subjectivism because both depend on experience. Instead, it claims to be timeless and objective, the "philosophy of an Eternity that cannot be experienced" (14). But, Bely insists, this cannot be. Circular thinking embraces not "eternity" but only a small part of the vast "circle." It can be expressed only conventionally, as dogma, that is, as motionless circular thinking; and dogmas, Bely argues, arise in time, and are grounded in particular ways of apprehending the world, that is, in experience. For Bely, then, linear and circular thinking ultimately amount to the same thing. Each fails to understand that the perceiving self is inevitably involved in its own perceptions: the proponents of the moment elevate that perceiving self above all else, while the proponents of dogma deny it altogether. Each view ignores the onward movement of time; each has become dogmatized, motionless.

Neither can capture eternity. Eternity exists, but its meaning lies "beyond the boundaries of all existing meaning" (15–16). All contemporary philosophies err, Bely asserts, in assuming that their very existence makes them meaningful, even when they proclaim the idea of nonmeaning. But there can be no meaningful philosophy of nonmeaning, no existing philosophy of nonexistence. Let us simply admit, he says, that philosophy is nonexistent. At most it can hope to be psychology, which is concerned with feelings and states of mind, particularly the general sense of meaninglessness and decay that afflicts us all.

Put another way, Bely accuses the decadents and evolutionists (proponents of the line) of showing no concern for the Ideal, and the dog-matists (Neo-Kantians, proponents of the circle)[8] of showing no concern for the Real. Both Ideal and Real must be accounted for. One way of accounting for them, in Bely's view, is to remember that everything is in constant movement. Neither line nor circle is in itself adequate to the reality of movement. But one geometrical image is: the spiral. Bely de-fines it as a "circular line" (that is, a line moving in a circle). For him it represents the true movement of time, inasmuch as it unites the moment (or the Real) with eternity (or the Ideal). The spiral has no straight lines and no closed circles, as we can see if we stand within it and allow ourselves to be carried along.

Are we, then, to be merely the passive victims of endless and pur-poseless movement? Is there no way we can touch Truth without turning it into lifeless dogma? Can we not give movement form without stopping it? To answer such questions, Bely introduces another geometric figure: the equilateral triangle. The apex, which touches Eternity, or Truth, always maintains the same angle, and for Bely represents the Ideal; the sides are constantly growing, and therefore represent the reality of time. Within it is the ever-moving spiral.

In another shift of terminology, Bely uses the word "Symbol" to rep-resent the perfect, ever-growing union of triangle and spiral, form and movement. Symbol "adjusts evolution to the immobility of dogma [. . .] throws the light of Eternity into evolution [. . .] makes dogma itself mobile" (19). Here "evolution" represents movement, "dogma" repre-sents form. Bely grants that these concepts are valid and necessary pro-vided they are given life and movement by the Symbol, and are not made absolutes. Through the Symbol, form, otherwise immobile, is given life; movement, otherwise formless, is given form. True Sym-bolism not only reconciles form and movement but is in constant move-ment itself: "it knows neither evolution nor return: it reincarnates itself" (21). In Bely's view, such symbolism has not yet been achieved. We must work to that end through theurgy: "man's only business is the act of deification: the action of creating oneself and others in God" (20). Until then, man himself will remain divided, with thought, *mysl'* (like dogma) and feeling, *chuvstvo* (like the moment), each proclaiming its primacy, and will, *volya*, helpless before both (21).

---

8. Bely includes both the Freiburg and Marburg schools in his condemnation of Neo-Kantian thought, and mentions Heinrich Rickert and Hermann Cohen, as well as lesser-known figures. Herbert Spencer, too, is named as the prime example of an evolutionist. Bely did not need to identify any decadent because his invocation of the cult of the "moment" would have instantly brought Konstantin Bal'mont and Valery Bryusov to the minds of his Russian readers.

"Circular Movement"

The "forty-two arabesques" gathered under the title "Circular Movement"[9] are lyrical musings and variations on the theme of "The Line." The subtitle evokes Gogol's *Arabesques*, where fiction and nonfiction coexist. Bely combines both genres, as it were, to produce something between the purely theoretical "Line" and the purely fictional *Petersburg*. We are back in that first world, for instance, when we read that "the line" is "half truth, half falsehood" but that "we think in contrasts. The thought of the line evokes in us the thought of the circle: in circular movement untruth is not all there is: here too truth and falsehood are intermingled. Truth is a spiral movement" (53). But in "Circular Movement" Bely also brings us much closer to the world of fiction, with a strong central narrative persona, a cast of characters (albeit "real" people), a definite setting (Basel), a system of concrete imagery, and a coherent narrative structure (each arabesque is a miniature chapter).

While working on this article, Bely was immersed in the writings of Friedrich Nietzsche.[10] Perhaps it is not surprising therefore that Nietzsche is its hero. Bely even gives Basel as the place of writing, although it was actually Vitznau. (Nietzsche had spent ten productive years—1869–79—at the University of Basel, and it was there that his mental illness had begun.)

In Russia at the turn of the century, Nietzsche became the hero of a myth whose outlines varied with the writers who took him up and used him for their own ends. What Bely himself called his "simply insane passion for Nietzsche" dates from that same time, when *Thus Spoke Zarathustra* became his "constant companion" (*nastol'naya kniga*).[11] Understandably, Nietzsche was a strong presence in Bely's fiction, verse, and theoretical writings for at least the next two decades, often explicitly, but often implicitly as well. The idea that philosophy is really psychol-

9. *Trudy i Dni*, no. 4–5 (July–October 1912), pp. 51–73. Page references will follow citations in the text. The image of the spiral (which first appeared in the *Third Symphony* [*Vozvrat*] [Moscow, 1905], pp. 82–83) culminates in *Krizis kul'tury* (*Na perevale* III) (Petersburg, 1920), with its two spiral diagrams (pp. 78–79). This work, signed "Basel-Dornach-Moscow, 1912–16–18," is in fact a greatly expanded and developed version of both "Circular Movement" and "The Line."

10. In the tenth chapter of the unpublished "Berlin redaction" of "Nachalo veka," Bely wrote of his time in Vitznau: "In those days *Zarathustra* spoke to me in a special way" (Manuscript Division, Saltykov-Shchedrin Library, Leningrad, Bely holding [no. 60], item 14, p. 172). Bely's long-standing interest in Nietzsche was another point of contact with Rudolf Steiner, who had written a book about him. As a result, Nietzsche's sister had invited Steiner to put the mortally ill writer's library in order and to share in the editing of his works, which Steiner declined to do.

11. *Na rubezhe dvukh stoletii* (Moscow and Leningrad, 1930), pp. 465, 466. In this memoir, Bely wrote: "The period from the autumn of 1899 to 1901 is for me principally colored by Nietzsche" (p. 466).

ogy, for example, is a basic notion of Nietzsche (see *Beyond Good and Evil*, 6 and 23), whether or not Bely was conscious of it when he wrote "The Line." In any event, like his fellow Russian Symbolists, Bely responded to Nietzsche creatively, less as a philosopher than as an "artist of genius" and a "personality" (*lichnost'*).[12] To Bely he "was never a theoretician [. . .] nor was he an aesthete [. . .] he was the creator of the most vital images, whose theoretical or aesthetic meaning would be revealed only when he was followed as creator and not just as thinker."[13] (This is obviously a variant of Bely's "creation before cognition.") By 1907, Bely was calling him "a symbolist, above all a symbolist in his creative work [. . .] the '*Superman*,' the '*Eternal Return*,' '*The Blessed Isles*,' '*Zarathustra's Cave*' are but religio-artistic symbols. And herein lies all of Nietzsche's power. But what rich material for allegories is offered by these symbols!"[14]

Nietzsche's notion of the "eternal return" fascinated Bely from the outset.[15] His understanding of it varied with the years. But it never represented the "joyful affirmation of nontranscendence" that Nietzsche had in mind;[16] Bely wrestled with that all his life. By 1912, when these two articles were written, Bely was using the idea of eternal return almost literally. We can of course say that this is "not Nietzsche." What concerns us here, however, is Bely's creative reading of him. (In many cases it could more accurately be called misreading.) For in "Circular Movement" Nietzsche became, as it were, the illustration of the truth of the diagnosis of modern culture that Bely made in "The Line."

In Bely's view, both Nietzsche and Zarathustra—the two are synonymous throughout "Circular Movement"—achieved greatness by ascending into the "mountains." Their tragedy was that once they had reached a certain height, they looked back, saw their shadow, took it for

12. John Foster, who read the present essay and made several valuable suggestions, has examined the wide range of responses to Nietzsche on the part of European writers in chap. 1 of his admirable *Heirs to Dionysus: A Nietzschean Current in Literary Modernism* (Princeton, 1981). Unfortunately, Bely largely falls outside his purview. M. L. Mirza-Avakyan deals with this enormous topic in the purely Russian context in a brief and therefore superficial article, "F. Nitsshe i russkii modernizm," *Vestnik Erevanskogo universiteta. Obshchestvennye nauki*, no. 3 (1972), pp. 92–103. A far more satisfactory account of Nietzsche's impact on one Russian writer is V. M. Paperny's "Blok i Nitsshe," in *Tipologiya russkoi literatury i problemy russko-estonskikh literaturnykh svyazei: Trudy po russkoi i slavyanskoi filologii: Literaturovedenie XXXI*, Uchenye zapiski Tartuskogo universiteta, no. 491 (1979). See also *Nietzche in Russia*, ed. B. G. Rosenthal (Princeton, 1987).

13. *Na rubezhe dvukh stoletii*, p. 466. In his important 1907 essay "Fridrikh Nitsshe," Bely wrote with contempt of those "ideologues and popularizers" who had turned the "living Nietzsche"—who must be experienced "within the self"—into abstract generalizations and a desiccated credo, i.e., into dogma (*Arabeski*, pp. 79–82).

14. "Smysl iskusstva," in *Simvolizm*, p. 226 (Bely's italics).

15. See, for example, the 1902 "Formy iskusstva," first published in *Mir Iskusstva*, no. 12 (1902), and reprinted in *Simvolizm*.

16. See the essay by Roger Keys in this volume, chap. 1.

reality, and descended instead of pushing on. Zarathustra was per-
suaded by the dwarf that everything repeats itself, that truth lies in the
eternal return (that is, in circular movement). This is the "untruth of
repeatedness" (*nepravda povtorennosti* [52]) and stands as an object lesson.
Every man has the capacity for greatness: "The sun is in our breast."
Sometimes we do "rush into the mountains," where we "sing"—song
being Bely's image for true freedom. Yet "while we are singing, we are
pursued by the black laughter of the band of Nibelungen: 'Where are
you going? Stop, turn back!'" If we heed them, "we see a slope that
frightens us and a treacherous shadow: it flies headfirst into the abyss"
(54). Yielding to "common sense," we think it is actually we, not the
shadow, who are falling, and we "return," only to plunge into an abyss
and smash ourselves to bits. In other terms, we return to bourgeois
comfort—our Basel—and to our "petty little interests." We may examine and revaluate what has happened to us on the mountain (the echo of
Nietzsche's "revaluation of all values" is, of course, deliberate, although
arbitrary, inasmuch as Nietzsche never used the word "revaluate" for
eternal recurrence, but reserved it for his criticisms of Western culture).
Even this, however, is a return that also opens an abyss. The time will
come when we are unexpectedly and forcibly reminded of what we have
forsaken and ought to regret. Secure in our familiar surroundings, we
will "suddenly" (a key word in *Petersburg*) experience a radical physical
displacement, when "the ground of [our] being [. . .] will be torn from
under [our] feet." We will try to explain even this in common-sense
terms, as "an ordinary nervous sensation" (55). But in fact we have been
vouchsafed a glimpse into the realm where our real "I" dwells.

So far, Bely has pursued his theme on three levels: the narrative
persona, Nietzsche/Zarathustra, and everyman. Only after his ideas
have been personified, as it were, does he then move to the kind of
general statements about the modern situation which make up all of
"The Line." He finds the same fatal attraction for return—that is, circularity—in every intellectual and cultural endeavor, especially philosophy, painting, the theater, and literature. He grants that the modern
enthusiasm for Nietzsche and for Ibsen (another culture hero) shows a
desire for the kind of ascent he urges; but he insists that we have not had
the courage to endure the enormous discomfort that such ascent entails,
and have opted for comfort instead. From Nietzsche we have accepted
"the lie of the return." He has been "the germ of our sickness," but he
can also become "the germ of our health" (68). That is to say, we need
not repeat his tragic error, but should move onward and upward.

Bely sees modern society perched on a precipice "between eternal
return and eternity" (analogous to the situation of Zarathustra and the
dwarf at the crossroads and before the gateway in the section titled "On

the Vision and the Riddle," in Part III).[17] Before we fall into the abyss, we must bestir ourselves and move "along the spiral," not in the circular motion described by Nietzsche. Here Bely makes one of the clearest statements in all his works of the need for constant movement: "our way is activity, limitless, tireless activity. Tiredness itself disappears when there is no time to get tired" (69–70). We must absorb the lesson of Zarathustra: "Zarathustra perished from *returning* in order that we, the witnesses of his death, might not return" (71), but push on and on, "higher and higher! This time—along the spiral" (68). Otherwise, we will find ourselves being pushed. Here Bely turns apocalyptic, in imagery that seems to prefigure the explosion imagery of *Petersburg*: "Atmospheric electricity will begin in the center of our study, we are turning the atmosphere of this study into the atmosphere of a thunderstorm; let's hope there won't be lightning. Lightning out of doors is not at all dangerous; there it is the play of violet-rose fires; but lightning indoors [literally, 'within four walls,' the image of a container that appears everywhere in *Petersburg* in a variety of forms—house, room, head, bomb, etc.] is a lightning that strikes us in the heart" (73).

Bely insists that the ascent can be made through what he calls "eternal books," embodying the "living, flowing word" (*zhivotekushchee slovo*) and thereby moving the reader along the "journey" toward the "unchanging center" that is our "motherland," the locus of "I, raised above myself" (57). The act of reading is an individual act. It therefore is appropriate to ascent, which is an individual, not a societal act. Through the reading of an "eternal book" we find the true self that is "outside the self" and become one with the universe: "You are now that very sun which has illuminated the page, and that sun which has been placed in you: from the occiput right down to the chest" (59). (We will later see how this process is supposed to work.) Bely writes that he had this same experience for the first time when reading *Zarathustra* in Basel. That is, the book was both revelation and revelatory of his self and its possibilities. This fact makes Bely once again intensely aware of his own "divergence from modern times" (73). For, he laments, such books are not really

---

17. John Foster has written that Nietzsche's reliance on imagery in *Zarathustra* is nowhere so striking as in this section: "Zarathustra's surrealistic account of the dwarf and gate . . . first shadows forth what Nietzsche saw as 'the fundamental conception' of his work, the doctrine of the eternal return. . . . The title of the episode captures the strategy he followed in writing it, for it does consist of a vision ending in a riddle, of vivid and disturbing concrete visual impressions that precede the idea which they render in an obscurely suggestive manner, and which in fact never receives a full discursive explanation in the rest of the book" (*Heirs to Dionysus*, p. 29). The section certainly captivated Bely, who quoted almost exclusively from it in "Circular Movement." Foster's statement that Nietzsche "in actual practice as well as in his claims . . . could be a daunting exemplar of how image could be mobilized to express idea" (ibid.) seems equally applicable to Bely's practice, both in his article and in *Petersburg*.

read.[18] If only people will "listen" (to him, clearly: this is Bely in his role of prophet), they too can ascend.

Bely's theoretical writings always aroused controversy among his fellow Symbolists. Most often they accused him of inconsistency from article to article. Fedor Stepun, for one, so charged in an open letter about "Circular Movement," which was printed in the same issue as the article itself. Bely's reply in *Works and Days*, no. 6, was a heated denial and an insistence that Stepun could not understand his "imagistic" means of expression. Here he put his finger on the quality that makes his critical writings difficult to grasp and opens them to attack. We may no longer believe that poetry is "thinking in images," as Aleksandr Potebnya had argued, but Bely's theoretical articles tend to be exactly that. It is their imagistic way of thinking that makes them fascinating in their own right, and important to a study of Bely's prose fiction. In "The Line," Bely used such imagistic thinking to pronounce judgment on the dreadful stasis of his time. In "Circular Movement," he exemplified the modern crisis in the tragedy of the man whom he regarded as having the greatest mind in Europe. In the novel *Petersburg*, he fully dramatized his vision.

The City

By the autumn of 1912, much of *Petersburg* was already written. Bely's conception of the physical image of the city had now taken form. This image was so basic that it remained untouched through several revisions. And it finds striking counterparts in "Circular Movement."

It is hardly surprising that a writer should begin a novel by establishing the place, as Bely does in *Petersburg*. What is surprising, however, is that he should begin an article in the same fashion, as if motivating

18. Bely singles out three such "eternal books" that always accompany him: the Gospels, Gogol, and *Zarathustra*. (He specifically states that Kant was no longer included [57].) Gogol is nowhere cited in "Circular Movement," although given Bely's reading of *Zarathustra* in the article, it is not hard to imagine that Bely envisions Gogol as another prophet who lost his way. The Gospel according to Mark, on which Bely had just heard Steiner lecture in Basel, is cited several times (69) to support the notion of ascent: "But when ye shall see the abomination of desolation . . . standing where it ought not . . . then let them . . . flee to the mountains. And let him that is on the housetop not go down into the house. . . . And let him that is in the field not turn back again for to take up his garment" (Mark 13:14–16). The words, of course, are those of Christ, although he is not mentioned by Bely (only "The Wisdom of God"), and he follows them with one of the most explicitly apocalyptic warnings in all the Gospels (Mark 13:17–37, often drawn on by Vladimir Solov'ev in his final apocalyptic phase), as Bely does in "Circular Movement" after the Gospel citations. Although it is left unstated, the "imitation of Christ" (in an anthroposophical spirit, to be sure: the physical transformation of man) is clearly Bely's ultimate model. One recalls, too, that Christ's famous "A prophet is not without honor, but in his own country, and among his own kin, and in his own house" is from this gospel (Mark 6:4).

everything that follows. Certain details of the description of Basel will be immediately familiar to readers of *Petersburg*:

> . . . hunchbacked *little hills* [. . .]. *Little houses* are sprawled on the *hills*. An *expanse* of tile roofs *glows* in the *sunset*. The *bright-flamed, bright-stoned* cathedral. The *purple air* has fallen on that *gray* tower.
>
> From everywhere *rage* the *leaves* of grapevines. A *rosy stream* of leaves has run along the wall. A *streaming* vine has fallen beneath the window. It has also fallen over the bronze *dragon* of the fountain, and over the signboard of the *tavern*. It has fallen over the slope as well. The strong-boned mountaineer has set to thinking: from the tiled *little house* to the tiled *little house*. Over there is an *idle little heap of worn faces* and *violet noses*.   [51]

The colors in this passage are pervasive in *Petersburg*: gray describes the inhabitants of the city, as well as Apollon Apollonovich; rose, purple, and violet are most often seen in the skies, clouds, and smoke. "Sunset" creates some of the most memorable effects: "flame-gold reflection" and "burning conflagration," with the "rust-red Palace" perhaps a counterpart to the "bright-stoned cathedral" of Basel at the same time of day. "Worn faces" and "noses" are seen in the passing parade on Nevsky Prospect (especially in chap. 6). The leaves in the Summer Garden "narrowed and curled in ever more restless spirals [. . .]. A vortex of leaves swirled, wound round and round."[19] "Expanses" are of course a typical feature of the Petersburg landscape, as Bely obsessively reminds us. "Dragons" are part of the important Oriental motif in the novel, notably in Nikolay's dream (chap. 5), where he understands that "the Ancient Dragon [the Turanian] was to feed on tainted blood" (166) and where he also recalls his own Bukhara dressing gown, "over whose smoky-sapphire fabric crawled sharp-beaked, golden, winged miniature dragons" (165). "Taverns" of various kinds are the scenes of significant encounters in the novel. We may also recall the mysterious "gleaming little house" where an old woman sits chewing her lips in Chapter 1. "Hills" are not a feature of the Petersburg landscape, but we are perhaps reminded of the apocalyptic vision of the city in Chapter 2, where, after the cataclysm that destroys the capital, "our native plains will everywhere come forth humped," and "Nizhny, Vladimir, and Uglich will find themselves on humps" (65).

---

19. *Petersburg,* translated, annotated, and introduced by R. A. Maguire and J. E. Malmstad (Bloomington, Ind., 1978; Hassocks, Sussex, 1979), p. 99. Hereafter all quotations from the novel will be taken from this translation of the 1922 Berlin edition of the novel and page references will be given in parentheses in the text. When we have occasion to refer to the first (1916) edition of the novel, quotations will be individually footnoted. For a discussion of the complex story of the writing and subsequent revisions of the novel, see our "A Note on Text and Translation," pp. xxiii–xxvii, and L. K. Dolgopolov's extensive "Tvorcheskaya istoriya i istoriko-literaturnoe znachenie romana A. Belogo" in the 1981 edition of the 1916 text (Moscow and Leningrad: Nauka).

Particularly noteworthy are the descriptions of the rivers on which Basel and Petersburg stand. In "Circular Movement" we find:

above the *green streams* of the Rhine, hunchbacked little hills. The *streams fly along rapidly* [. . .]. Here the Rhine is *stormily furious.* Capsizing in the streams, *the sun weaves rings* in them; a *golden sun ring rushes to the banks.* From one bank the Nibelungen are scooping up a *golden green stream*; they are trying to get the Rhine *Gold.* They are turning the *light* of the Rhine into *rot infected with germs.* [51–52]

In *Petersburg* we have the "expanse of the Neva," which "seethed"; "the greenish waters teem with germs"; "the soundlessly flying surfaces began glimmering green"; "the depths, the greenish-blue"; "the clear morning was ablaze with shimmering sparkles on the Neva, and transformed the whole expanse into an abyss of pure gold" (perhaps all that is left of the Rhine Gold of "Circular Movement").

How does such imagery allow us to conclude that two cities so different in physical appearance—as most tourists would certainly insist—are really so similar as to be virtually identical? Further parallels provide a clue. In the first arabesque, Bely calls Basel a "university town." This circumstance already endows it with a certain abstractness in his eyes. He reminds us that it is located in Switzerland, "the land of enlightenment." And with the word "enlightenment" Bely underscores the idea of abstractness. (Dostoevsky provides a ready literary precedent for Switzerland as an "unreal" place, a political but not a national entity.) Furthermore, in this university town "not a single soaring word cuts across your hearing; no sharp-winged verb arises. Here the word crawls. From one small heap to another [*kuchechka*; cf. the "heap of hovels" that make up "other Russian cities" besides Petersburg in the Prologue to the novel] a dullish word shuffles along in a somehow draggy way [*klyaklo*]" (51). The word is earthbound because it has been reduced to dogma here. Mindful of the argument in "The Line," we recognize that Basel, to Bely, represents the dead end to which life has been brought by ideological-minded theoreticians of every stripe.

Now, Petersburg has its university too; and two of the novel's major characters are its products: Apollon Apollonovich and his son Nikolay. Both are devotees of theories and dogmas. But the similarities extend beyond the two universities. Russia's earlier capitals, Kiev and Moscow, grew organically out of the demands of life, as trading centers, for instance. But Petersburg, which Dostoevsky called the "most intentional city in the world," is the product of one man's will. As such, it exemplifies Bely's conception of the appearance of dogma, as he sketches it in "The Line." The city arose in Peter's brain, at one "moment" in time (1703); it was then dynamic. But it took "form" in the edifices that gradually filled it, and finally became an artifact, a "dogma," whose sole function has been to impose its "will," through rules and regulations (themselves dogmas), on the life of Russia. In fact, and in the literary myth that has grown up around it, Petersburg became synonymous with bureaucracy, the triumph of static forms, alien not only to Russia (the eternal truth it claims to embody, if we apply Bely's paradigm) but to life itself. "Our life is Basel" (54), Bely writes in "Circular Movement." We might say that our life, even more, is Petersburg (and the novel *Petersburg*). In short, both cities function as emblems of the crisis of modern civilization. But ultimately the parallels work because Bely, in his novel, abstracts the image of Petersburg and delocalizes it, while persuading us of its "real" existence.

Bely posits these central questions from the outset. He begins the novel not with a traditional description of setting and character but with an invocation, in a formal "Prologue," of the city itself, or, as Pushkin called it, "Peter's creation." But the narrator who demands our attention in a series of "logical imperatives" adopts a mocking tone—"Your Excellencies, Your Worships, Your Honors, and Citizens." He then undertakes an exercise in cognition, richly comic yet deadly serious because it is unchallengeable from a logical point of view: a circular series of questions, answers, and definitions from which there is no escape. And he does so in language that is deliberately formulaic, that is, essentially dead. He begins with the question "What is this Russian Empire of ours?" By way of reply he quotes from official imperial proclamations. Gradually he narrows the focus to Petersburg itself, then to its main thoroughfare, Nevsky Prospect, and finally to the point or dot (*tochka*) that represents the city on a map of that empire and the world. Petersburg, in Bely's eyes, is the focal point of the crisis of modern life.

By the final paragraph of the Prologue, the city's existence has become tentative indeed. Yet the narrator hastens to assure us that it "not only appears to us, but actually does appear—on maps," and that from this "mathematical point, which has no dimension" (raising the age-old question of the city's "hallucinatory" quality), it "forcefully" proclaims its existence (2). Like any good dogmatist, it tirelessly does so in just those terms by which the narrator has defined its existence: the official "circular" (a nice irony in English as well as in Russian, in which *tsirkulyar* is a foreign word), that is, the rules and regulations expressed in bureaucratic language which issue in a "swarm" from this "invisible point" (*tochka*). The city can proclaim its existence only in words (as does Basel in "Circular Movement") and the words are devoid of the vital energy that originally gave birth to them and the city itself. The city has become a parody of creation, reproducing dead copies of itself that have no effect on anything, a point emphasized throughout the novel by the capital's inability to exercise control over a Russia that is being torn apart by revolution.

In the last arabesque of "Circular Movement," the narrator is back in Basel proper, where the cathedral dominates all. It has been reached by a circular movement, or a return. And we now see unmistakably that the cathedral stands for motionlessness (stone) and dogma (formal religion), which are the antitheses of life. In *Petersburg* there is no "return" in this sense. The city, which has been ever present throughout, disappears. However, returns do occur in other contexts. And as we shall see, they exemplify the same values as the cathedral in Basel.

The circle/dot imagery in the Prologue may well be related to the imagery of the final paragraph of the "Circle" section of "The Line." There Bely describes "dogma" as a circle "with a dot in the middle" (17). The dot (*tochka*) is that "moment" in time when dogma also had its inception (or "conception," as Bely says), although dogma tries to deny it, aware that the "moment" mocks its claims to "timelessness." This image has, of course, a different meaning and function in the novel. But in the Prologue, the city is defined in precisely those two geometric terms that will dominate all aspects of the novel to come: line (Nevsky Prospect, a "rectilineal prospect") and circle ("two small circles, one set inside the other, with a black dot in the center" on maps).[20]

Characters

Given Bely's view of line and circle, we should not be surprised that both—especially the line—figure prominently in the portrait of the first character we encounter in the novel: the archbureaucrat Senator Apollon Apollonovich Ableukhov. He quintessentially embodies what the city represents for Bely.

Apollon Apollonovich loves the straight line and every geometric figure associated with it: "After the line, the figure which soothed him more than all other symmetries was the square. At times, for hours on end, he would lapse into an unthinking contemplation of pyramids, triangles, parallelepipeds, cubes, and trapezoids" (11). He feels most comfortable in the cube of his carriage, and as he travels the "line" of Nevsky Prospect he dreams of the universe, even of infinity, as compartmentalized into neat squares and cubes. He strives always to remain within self-imposed confines—office, house, rooms, water closet, and

20. Elsworth argues a point similar to our own in this section without referring to the 1912 articles: "The city founded by autocratic decree is well suited to express the idea of a reality that owes its origin to human thought. The theme of the city's foundation parallels that of the senator's cerebral play in the first chapter" (*Andrey Bely: A Critical Study*, p. 97).

ultimately Petersburg itself. Their strict symmetries provide protection from the hostile "unformed" vastness of the Russia that lies beyond.

It is as if in Apollon Apollonovich the "philosophy of evolution" has indeed "burst into the philosophy of dogmatism," as Bely put it in "The Line." There he had argued that just as modern thought has ended in dogmatism, so too modern art must "burst" into "the finality [*za-konchennost'*] of classicism" (15). Although Apollon is no artist, his very name, reduplicated in the patronymic, alludes to the god associated with art, and, for Nietzsche, with form. This modern Apollo has surrounded himself with neoclassical objets d'art, including a painting by David; he lives in one of those neoclassical columned mansions that line the banks of the Neva; and he would like to "freeze" Russia, that is, render it static and immobile. In "The Line" Bely associates this "ideal of stasis" not with ancient Greece but with ancient Egypt: "If classicism would be truly immutable, the pyramid, not the Venus de Milo, should, of course, serve as its emblem. The pyramid, after all, is a stereometric figure" (15). He thinks that cultural history has now come full circle: "The Egyptian is awakening in the contemporary artist." At several points in the novel Apollon Apollonovich is likened to an Egyptian. At the ball in Chapter 4, for instance, he sits "imperious, ramrod-straight [. . .]. His little legs with their sinewy calves rested perpendicularly on the rug, so that the lower and upper parts formed ninety-degree right angles. Apollon Apollonovich looked like an Egyptian depicted on a rug" (123). The pyramid is one of the geometric shapes that most soothe him and at times inspire his dreams of absolute order (cf. "The Line": "There is no inspiration in the pyramid, but of course people are inspired in the proximity of the pyramid" [15]).[21] Bely also argues in "The Line" that modern art has become "stone images" (*kamennye baby*). Throughout the early parts of the novel, the Senator is associated with stone (one of the first physical descriptions mentions his "stony senatorial eyes"), unyielding hardness, and routine. And we recall that the image also appears in the final

21. The travel sketch (*ocherk*) "Egipet," written in 1911 and based on Bely's experiences in Egypt the year before, certainly informs the image of the pyramid both in "The Line" and in the novel (think only of Nikolay's visit to the pyramid-Sphinx complex at Gizeh in the Epilogue, which, Bely admitted, was based on his impressions). Later, in his memoirs, Bely described climbing the Great Pyramid at Gizeh. He then experienced what he was told is called the "pyramid illness" (*piramidnaya bolezn'*): a feeling of being "turned inside out" (*naiznanku*). The climb, he continued, was a turning point in his life, for the "result of the pyramid illness was a change in the organs of perception [. . . my] changed attitude to life informed *Petersburg*, which I began soon after" ("Vospominaniya, tom III, chast' II, 1910–1912," *Literaturnoe nasledstvo*, nos. 27–28 [1937], pp. 433–34). In the travel sketch and the later memoirs Bely emphasized the "deadness" and the "desert" of ancient Egypt, which seemed, however, more alive to him than the reality of modern colonial Egypt. The Egypt of 1910, he felt, was the lifeless forerunner of the future of Western civilization. Also, retrospectively in *Krizis zhizni* (*Na perevale* [1923], pp. 16–17), he wrote that when he was in Egypt he recalled the attempts that Vasily Rozanov (who is not named) had made to connect ancient Egypt with Dostoevsky's Petersburg novels.

description of Basel in "Circular Movement": "frozen on the wall was a knight clad in armor, motionless, in the act of attacking a dragon. The knight was of stone; and the dragon was also of stone" (73). In effect this is a mirror image of the unicorn goring a knight which appears on the coat of arms of the Ableukhov family. And at several points the Senator is described as a "little knight."

In none of the other major characters do we find such close parallels to "The Line" as we do in Apollon Apollonovich. Thus we see how central he is to the idea of the impasse of modern thought that informs *Petersburg* from beginning to end. (From what we know of the process of the novel's composition, it seems to have begun in Bely's mind with the figure of the Senator.) He stands apart from the other characters—excepting the narrator—in another respect as well. Only he is endowed (in chap. 1) with all the attributes of what Bely calls "cerebral play" (*mozgovaya igra*).[22] In "The Line," Bely argues that every "moment" must assume static form and crystallize into "dogma." So it is with the Senator's thoughts: "And one fugitive thought was the thought that the stranger really existed. The thought fled back into the senatorial brain. The circle closed" (21). But that dogma-circle contains the "moment" that ultimately engendered it and will annihilate it in turn, because time does not stand still. The "stranger," Dudkin, who is spotted by the Senator on Nevsky Prospect and then haunts his thoughts, embodies all those forces that will bring Apollon down and destroy him. And at an earlier "moment" a son, Nikolay, was engendered; he will become the unwitting agent of the Senator's downfall. Similarly, Lippanchenko, who is dedicated to the destruction of the Senator's "order," creates a conspiracy that will destroy *him* through the agent *he* has created, Dudkin. Those who would control are the most controlled; circles inevitably close, only to be shattered in turn.

The emphasis on Apollon Apollonovich's mental capacities in Chapter 1 recalls another aspect of "The Line." At the beginning of that article, Bely states that a divorce of thought from feeling and emotion has reduced the "organism of experience" to "bone covered with skin" (14). (At several points Apollon Apollonovich is described in this way or as a skeleton.) He rephrases this idea in the final section of the article when he speaks of the "triangle" of "head-heart-hand—thought, feeling, will" that resides in all of us, but has lost its unity in modern man, thus producing a rotten corpse, not a living being. It is not difficult to see how Bely has realized this notion in the fiction. From the beginning, the narrator contrasts the "unprepossessing little figure" of the Senator with

22. For a discussion of the relation of *mozgovaya igra* to Bely's theory of symbolism and the relation of both to the problem of cognition in *Petersburg*, see Vladimir Alexandrov's article "Unicorn Impaling a Knight: The Transcendent and Man in Andrei Belyi's *Petersburg*," *Canadian-American Slavic Studies*, 16, no. 1 (Spring 1982), pp. 9–18.

the "explosion of mental forces" that pour forth from his cranium. We never really see him *act*. Instead we "see" his thoughts, hear his words, and are told about his endless dictation of directives, all of which have no effect on the world that is crumbling around him. The first real *physical* action he performs, apart from his daily gymnastics, comes after his fall from power, when he bustles about dusting his books. Here we think of Bely's image, in "The Line," for the end product of dogma: "Evolutionism is the dust of edifices that have collapsed [i.e., all the previous dogmas that inform it]. The philosophy of the moment is an edifice made out of dust" (20). For all Apollon's talk of the progress of reason and "humanism," concepts fixed in his mind in the names of Auguste Comte and Giordano Bruno, the result for him is a life marked by a loss of feeling, emotional vitality, and will. He can no more manage his personal life (his wife has run away with another man, his son has become estranged) than he can control the state. In a final restatement of this theme in the article, Bely writes: "The philosophy of dogmatism is thought torn out of the brain" (22). He goes on to draw a terrifying picture of the fate of such dogmatic thought, disconnected from the "heart" of feeling and the "hand" of will: "congealed, it hangs in immobility [. . .] this is an old, long-buried time of old, the time of gray China, which is now ready [. . .] to devour us" (22). Again the novel offers striking parallels. Apollon Apollonovich is everywhere associated with the color gray; his son, in a nightmare about his genealogy, sees Saturn devouring his own children and himself becomes a "mandarin of the Middle Kingdom" (chap. 5, "The Last Judgment"). Once again the circle has closed; there is no escape. In "The Line" Bely insists that the only hope is to be found in the utter transformation of the "corpse of our thought," which lies rotting in a "yellow desert" (an image perhaps suggested by Nietzsche's "desert of our exhausted culture" in *The Birth of Tragedy*). In *Petersburg* he is far less specific and far less optimistic.

If Apollon Apollonovich betokens such disembodied thought, the other components of the dismembered triangle in modern man can be seen in Nikolay Apollonovich and Dudkin. In Nikolay there is no connection between instincts and thought (his Neo-Kantian studies, which have engendered philosophical nihilism). He represents "heart-feeling" (*serdtse-chuvstvo*). Of all the major characters, he is the one who is most ruled by his emotions and passions. For instance, his infatuation with Sofia Petrovna, when frustrated, erupts in murderous rage against his father. And throughout the novel he is associated with blood and the color red, which for Bely signifies violence, disintegration, and death, the present condition of the "heart" of modern man. (In the color scheme established in "The Line," "purple blood" will flow in the veins of unified and harmonious man.)

Dudkin represents, as it were, "hand-will" (*ruka-volya*). Though a committed terrorist, and therefore supposedly the very embodiment of revolutionary action and will, he can no longer make meaningful connections between what he does and what he thinks, and has become the pawn of others. Bely describes his first appearance as follows: "Rhythmically swinging in his hand [*ruka*] was a not exactly small and yet not very large bundle [the bomb, his creation and the "agent" of his will as terrorist] [. . .he] slipped [. . .]. He then grasped the railing with one hand; the other hand (with the bundle) described a zigzag" (12). In "The Line," the zigzag describes what Bely calls the "ideal of a kinematic conception of art," and represents the opposite of the static ideal of dogma and classicism. It does not, however, betoken true movement or creativity.[23] Rather, it is "the zigzag of a nervous tick: a neurasthenic moment" (15), and thus could well describe not only Dudkin's gesture but his lack of true creativity.[24] Perhaps, too, the yellow Semite or Mongol face on the wallpaper in Dudkin's room which torments him for his paralysis and "imprisonment" by Lippanchenko is a reflection of the yellow dust in "The Line:" "Our will [. . .] torn loose from the head and the heart; and in the mechanics of life it is like a lion amidst the sands; its golden sunlight has verily become a yellow desert" (22).

We must take care not to overdraw the parallels between the triangular scheme of "The Line" and the characters of the novel. They are, after all, characters, not allegorical figures. Bely is dramatizing the extremes of the division of the modern self as exteriorized selves, as a conflict, projected into reality, between different selves or parts of a missing totality. His techniques of characterization all support this idea. For example, each character is endowed with one or two striking physical traits that are highlighted again and again: Sofia Petrovna has luxuriant tresses and an incipient mustache, Lippanchenko has a low narrow forehead, Apollon Apollonovich is possessed of large greenish ears (in fact, all the details of his physiognomy are associated with his head).

23. Before the confrontation between father and son, which results in Nikolay's winding of the bomb, a mirror cracks in chap. 5: "a jagged needle-thin line cut through it like a flash of lightning [. . .] and it froze there for all time in a zigzag" (156). The "bad omen" betokens only the shattering of the facade of the familial relationship. It is a kind of explosion, the result of accumulated forces, and might be likened to the lightning bolt that shatters the complacency of the enclosed study in "Circular Movement" (73); but it is merely destructive, not "real" movement or "real" creativity.

24. There is one other character in the novel who can be said to represent "hand": Sergey Sergeevich Likhutin. This association first appears when he learns of Nikolay's "base" conduct toward Sofia Petrovna, his wife, and tries for the first time—and unsuccessfully—to assert his will, by forbidding her to attend the ball: "In agitation he began to pace the tiny little room, his fingers clenched in a fist, raising his fist each time he made a sharp turn [. . .]. The blow of a fist smashed the dressing table in two" (pp. 88, 92). His failure of will here leads to his comically frustrated suicide when word and deed are so disconnected that he crashes not into death but onto the floor. In the 1916 version (p. 195), Likhutin actually cries out "word and deed" (*slovo i delo*), a formulaic appeal to the tsar's justice that is comically out of place in the context.

Here Bely borrows a trick—the so-called marking device—from Tolstoy and other nineteenth-century realists and exaggerates it. Each person, in the crisis phase of modern life, is dominated by one part or aspect to the point of hideous caricature. (This is a view that Nietzsche also puts forth in *Zarathustra*.)[25] Thought, feeling, and will have become destructive parodies of themselves. And man, lacking organic wholeness, is but a sum of warring parts.

Dogma, as Bely defines it in "The Line," finds yet another correspondence in the constructs created by the characters in the novel (houses, rooms, and the like). For them, the world of objects is a correlative of their inner worlds. Thus Apollon Apollonovich seeks refuge as much by fleeing into his own cranium as by fleeing into the rooms of his house and into the city itself. Yet the skull box is not completely enclosed: it has openings, or eye sockets. Likewise, the rooms, the houses, and the Senator's boxlike carriage have windows and doors. Petersburg itself was built as an opening onto Europe, or a "window," to use the term made famous by Pushkin's *Bronze Horseman*. All these openings belong to the generic and often repeated image of the "slit" (*prorez'*) or "breach" (*bresh'*). Whatever form they take—and "eye" seems by far the most common—all allow not only movement out but also movement in, and therefore make nonsense of any hope the characters may have of inhabiting hermetically enclosed interiors. Thus, as a "window," Petersburg may have been designed to look out on Europe, but Europe also looks in on Petersburg. The same situation holds for all the characters in relation to the world around them. For instance, the Senator's eyes look out the window of his carriage, but madly widening eyes peer back through the

25. Gogol, of course, had pictured inhabitants of Petersburg in this way, i.e., as parts, not wholes. More relevant to Bely's even greater tendency to hyperbolize is Zarathustra's description, in "On Redemption," of the "cripples" around him: "for there are human beings who lack everything, except one thing of which they have too much—human beings who are nothing but a big eye or a big mouth or a big belly or anything at all that is big. Inverse cripples I call them. . . . [I] looked again, and said at last, 'An ear! An ear as big as a man!' I looked still more closely—and indeed, underneath the ear something was moving, something pitifully small and wretched and slender. And, no doubt of it, the tremendous ear was attached to a small, thin stalk—but this stalk was a human being! If one used a magnifying glass one could even recognize a tiny envious face; also, that a bloated little soul was dangling from the stalk." (Compare the description of Nikolay in chap. 7, in "The Conversation Had a Continuation": "A quintillion—oh, oh, oh!—dangles from a frail little stick [. . .]. Nikolay Apollonovich lived as a human numeral one, that is, as an emaciated little stick [. . .]. And all the hideous monstrosity of a quintillion [. . .] had fallen right on this little stick. An indecent something had taken a nothing into itself; and this had been swelling from time eternal" [226].) "The people, however, told me that this great ear was not only a human being, but a great one, a genius. [So too, in the novel, another "ear"— that is, Apollon Apollonovich—has the same reputation.] But . . . I maintained my belief that it was an *inverse cripple who had too little of everything and too much of one thing* . . . [our italics; the standard Russian translation of *Zarathustra* by Yu. M. Antonovsky (St. Petersburg, 1911) gives *kaleka naiznanku* for 'inverse cripple']. Verily, my friends, I walk among men as among the fragments and limbs of men" (*The Portable Nietzsche*, ed. and trans. Walter Kaufmann [Harmondsworth: Penguin, 1981], p. 250).

window and into his eyes, with enormous consequences for all (chap. 1, "And Catching Sight, They Dilated, Lit Up, and Flashed . . ."). Bely uses the same imagery in the same way in "The Line." An "eye" (*oko*) is that "moment" (*mig*) which "winks" (in a nice pun: the expression *migayushchee oko*, "winking eye," contains the word *mig*) at dogma and mocks its claims to timelessness and self-referential sufficiency. "The *'eye'* gazing at the contemporary philosophy of dogmatism is the weakest point of the philosophy of dogmatism," he asserts, *"that very place where the circumference is not closed"* (18). In imagery similar to the novel's, he compares this "place" to a head whose sinciput has not grown shut.

The major characters also attempt to make sense of their world by conceiving of it as polar opposites: here/there, manmade/natural, now/then, west/east, Christ/Satan, the first term in each pair representing the "positive" values of order, system, and good, and the second the "negative" values of instability, chaos, and evil. These pairings, too, are shown to be illusory and false, dogmatic schematizations of a far more complex reality.

One particularly striking instance in the novel occurs during the dinner-table conversation between Nikolay and his father, immediately preceding the Senator's dream. Here they argue over who is more "scientific," Kant or Comte. They become thoroughly confused because of the similarity (in Russian) of the pronunciation of these two names (*Kant/Kont*). Their inane conversation makes Bely's point that the positivist and Kantian philosophies are in essence the same, as Nikolay will recognize in his dream. Both lead to the total negation of values. Bely makes this same point on every level of the novel. Reaction, in the person of Apollon Apollonovich, opposes revolution in Lippanchenko, the representative of the mysterious terrorist "Party." But these seemingly polar opposites prove to be but different sides of repression and stasis: in Bely's favorite image of the period, one is but the other "turned inside out" (*naiznanku*). The grossly fat Lippanchenko, compared to a rhinoceros, and the elegant Senator, associated with a unicorn, could not seem more different, but they share a repertory of identical gestures (just as both beasts have one horn for goring) and submit the egos and wills of their "sons" to preordained laws and schemes that provoke murderous if ultimately futile reactions. Bely, in a novel full of mirrors and reflecting surfaces, even hints at the inside-out principle in their names, Apollon and Lippanchenko, in which the consonants *p* and *l* are doubled and reversed. There is a subtler identity, too. In "Circular Movement" Bely writes that "creation" does not lie in "protection" (*okhrana*): "The protective branch of art is the museum: in the museum that which is being created is covered with dust and devoured by mice" (70). The Senator's house, we recall, is a kind of museum that the servants cannot keep free of dust or mice. But the essential point is linguistic, and English cannot render the pun that Bely realizes in the novel. For "the protective branch" (*okhrannoe otdelenie*) is also the Russian term for the secret police, the Okhrana, of which the double agent Lippanchenko is an employee. Once again we see not an opposition but an essential identity.

Even the most significant antithesis in the novel, East and West, is not really that, all appearances to the contrary. To be sure, the details associated with Mongolism in the novel are specifically Eastern (the color yellow, the Japanese, the Oriental face on the wall of Dudkin's room, among others), but by 1912 the concept was no longer strictly Eastern as far as Bely was concerned. It now subsumed all that was noncreative—that is, stagnation and repression—and was a part as much of West as of East.[26] Opposites are merely apparent. Revolution and reaction are but different sides of the same coin. Both have brought the characters, and Russia itself, full circle to the same dead end: Lippanchenko is childless, like Dudkin and the Likhutins; Nikolay remains a bachelor; Apollon and his Institution are merely a meaningless "paper mill." The appropriate model of reality is not either/or but both/and. We have already seen that Bely in effect so argues in his two articles, where line and circle are but one and the same.

Critics have noted the many allusions to earlier Russian literature in the novel. Clearly Bely employs such allusions as a kind of shorthand technique of characterization. They also reinforce his idea of circularity: there is no escape from the past, from meaningless repetition, even in the realm of literary history. As Bely says in "Circular Movement," "the same circle has been described by literature" (63). At the same time, the allusions reflect his belief that modern man lacks true identity: in Petersburg he has reached stasis, and can merely repeat himself by allusion to the literary types that characterize the myth of the city in the works of Pushkin, Gogol, Dostoevsky, Tolstoy, and others. Finally, by choosing bits and pieces from different literary characters for each portrait and exaggerating each detail, Bely points up the lack of wholeness of these new Petersburg types.

26. In the 1923 "Vospominaniya o Bloke," Bely wrote: "Vladimir Solov'ev saw a menace to Russia in the Mongol East; [his] '*Panmongolism*' is a symbol of the darkness, the barbarism [*aziatchina*] that overwhelms our consciousness from within; but the darkness is also in the West [. . .] there, no less than here, '*Tartar eyes*' also menace Russia" (*Epopeya*, no. 4, p. 260). And further: "The dominant note of the *Tartar*, the *Mongol* in my *Petersburg*, is a deception whereby a spiritual and creative revolution is replaced by its antithesis, which is not revolution, but the implanting into humanity of a new impulse of benighted reaction, numeration, mechanization; social revolution (the '*Red Domino*') turns into the revolt of reaction when there is no spiritual shift of consciousness. And the result is the stasis of the numbered Prospect in social consciousness for time immemorial; and the unleashing of '*wild passions*' in individual consciousness" (p. 265). See also pp. 262–65 of this memoir, where Bely further specifies "Mongol" details in the novel. More generally, Bely saw Mongolism as a manifestation of baneful occult powers in the world, an aspect of the "universal provocation" that held Russia in its grip (see his letter to Ivanov-Razumnik of December 1913, cited in the Nauka edition of *Peterburg*, p. 516).

Dreams

At moments of greatest stress all the characters glimpse the futility of attempting to make meaningful distinctions. Likhutin prepares to kill himself when he fails to order time into meaningful units; he feels that he has been imprisoned "ever since the creation of the world," and is left merely with the "zero" of a noose. Sofia Petrovna, during her wild carriage ride home from the ball, experiences "only a void" that swallows up piece after piece of her life while a "metallic steed" pounds at her back.

But these are minor revelations, appropriate to the relatively minor position of these two characters, in comparison with the dreams of the Senator and his son and the understanding achieved by Dudkin.

As befits a man whose mental constructs have earlier been shown as encompassing his own house, Bely describes Apollon Apollonovich's dream world—his "second space"—as beginning with a walk down a long corridor that opens out from his own head. This is an analogue of his daily "journey" down his "first" or "material" space: the corridor leading from his bedroom to the "room that was comparable to no other," the water closet. The dream journey in Chapter 3 is preceded by an awareness of both spaces:

> one, material (the walls of the rooms, of the carriage), the other, not exactly spiritual (it was also material) [. . .] over Ableukhov's head, Ableukhov's eyes saw bright patches and dots of light, and iridescent dancing spots with spinning centers. They obscured the boundaries of the spaces. Thus one space swarmed in the other space; you know, the kind that seems to be made of Christmas tree tinsel, of little stars and of little sparks [. . .]. Apollon Apollonovich flew out through the circular breach, into darkness, above his own head (which looked like the planet *earth*), and—he flew apart into sparks. [93, 95]

Let us compare the description, in "Circular Movement," of the way Bely thinks we move into the universe through the reading of an "eternal book." Here the images of pulsation, expansion, and contour also figure, as they do, of course, elsewhere in *Petersburg*:

> you will sense a pulsating beating all around you a yard away; and this is what will outline your real contour for you now; this contour will play above you in gold and blue sparks; in gold and blue sparks it will start playing— above you; you will move into the earth, under the earth—through the earth; the sparks of the firmament, pulsating, will lie on your breast, and your eagle-like, soaring head will proudly survey your *heaven* and *earth*. Thus in the beginning were created the heavens with their earths, for in actuality thought created the heavens and their earths. [59]

Interestingly enough, Bely uses the same kind of imagery in an un-published memoir fragment to depict what happened to him during his anthroposophical "meditations" of 1912 ("the experience of the awaken-ing etheric body").[27] But the Senator is no occultist; this "cerebralist" tries to maintain conscious control of his life even in his meditations before falling asleep. "Apollon Apollonovich, while falling asleep, would remember all the inapprehensibilities of the past [. . .]. He would re-member everything he had seen the day before so as not to remember it again" (93). On this occasion, however, the "timeless void" he enters has prepared a nasty surprise, which his "code of rules had not foreseen"; it is analogous to, and perhaps caused by, the unexpected encounter with the stranger on Nevsky Prospect. When he goes to investigate an odd sound, he comes face to face with his son as an ominous Mongol, and hears a voice announcing the absence of all law, upon which he is whirl-ed outside himself ("something scandalous had taken place" [95]), only to return to "consciousness" after a "double dream."

The dream is one of those moments when time past and future is revealed, when a character glimpses an essential truth about his situation because his consciousness loses control and ceases to "experience experi-ence." (As Bely wrote in "The Line," "the Eternal cannot be experi-enced" [14].) The image of the corridor and the sound of the hooves recall the long excursus on cerebral play in Chapter 1 (e.g., "And when the door to the small hollow-echoing corridor slammed shut, it was only a hammering in the temples" [21]). They look ahead to the ball in Chap-ter 4, when the Senator, now awake, sees himself as he does in the dream, reflected in a mirror as a little knight whose "luminous phe-nomenon" is shattered (symbolic of his loss of authority and power be-cause of the actions of his son). There he also encounters Nikolay Apol-lonovich as the red domino, at which point "something scandalous"

27. In the unpublished Berlin redaction of "Nachalo veka" (pp. 173–75), in the Sal-tykov-Shchedrin Library, Bely describes how the "flashes of fire—stars" in his eyes "were experienced in a completely real way" during his meditations in July–August 1912. He felt that his body was "electrified," that his thoughts "pulsated outside his body," and he saw his "I" as the body of a "world giant" stretched through space. He likewise drew on these meditative experiences in the description of Apollon Apollonovich's feeling of an abyss in his dream ("With the opening up of the sinciput, something could run along the corridor *until it plunged into the abyss*" [93]). In a published fragment from the same memoirs he wrote: "An '*abyss*' opened wide under your feet, yes, yes: the Symbolists had talked loftily of the *abyss*; now I felt this *abyss* in all its staggering realism" ("Iz vospominanii," in the journal *Beseda*, no. 2 [July–August 1923], pp. 123–24). All this reflects Steiner's teaching that the "two worlds" (the physical and the spiritual) touch in the dream state and we then experience one opening into the other as an abyss. The city of Petersburg is frequently described as just such a place in the novel, a "point" (*tochka*) where the physical and spiritual planes touch, and which seems, therefore, to hang over an abyss. The parallels between Bely's anthroposophical experience on the one hand and the article and *Petersburg* on the other, while interesting, are not essential to an understanding of the latter. In the novel Bely creates an internally consistent world in which we can believe, even though it may not resemble the world in which we live our day-to-day lives.

(*skandal*: the word is used both here and in the dream) literally takes place and awakens "in his consciousness the memory of some incident in the past" (112). The "clatter of small pounding hooves," of course, also prefigures the appearance of the Bronze Horseman, who haunts all the characters; and its transformation into the "clicking of the tongue of some worthless Mongol," who is Nikolay Apollonovich, hints at what will later be made clear: Peter the Great is as much a manifestation of "Mongolism" as is anything else in the novel. This Mongolism, which affects "fathers" as well as "sons," is lodged deep *within* the characters, and finds physical expression on this occasion in the Senator's own son, Nikolay. Even in his dream Apollon Apollonovich strives mightily to hold this unpleasant truth at bay ("Apollon Apollonovich did not want to understand this" [94]) through his usual appeal to ordered routine, here the Code of Laws. And when "space" announces that there are "neither paragraphs nor regulations!" then "*suddenly*" his consciousness whirls through a "breach" in his head into the void. For his "dogma" has been shattered, and he too will "fly apart into sparks." (The "roar" that occurs when his consciousness is pulled outside will reappear when the bomb explodes and creates a "breach" in his house.) But there is no escape. The "linear" journey becomes a "circle" as consciousness "turns back," takes "form of some kind [. . .] filled with stinking abomination," which is the "little old yellow man" (95). The sewer-like tub containing the Senator's consciousness suggests, of course, the water closet where he likes to spend so much of his time. But it also graphically represents that "nuance of putrefaction," that "rotting corpse of our thought" (22) about which Bely wrote in "The Line," as well as the circular trap of modern thought depicted in "Circular Movement": consciousness that fills itself with its own waste, its own dead thought, until eventually it must explode. The dream does reveal a terrible truth: the circular entrapment of the Senator in his own dogma. It does not, however, reveal any way out of the impasse.

Bely apparently completed the dream of Apollon Apollonovich before he wrote "The Line" and "Circular Movement," and merely retouched it in the light of his own meditative experiences. Nikolay's dream, however, was written after these two articles. It is more closely tied to them than is Apollon's dream. The same is true of the "sensations" that Nikolay experiences in the final chapter, when he drifts into sleep while the bomb ticks to its explosive climax. The circularity explored in both articles obviously underlies the very conception of motion and time in Nikolay's dream and is spelled out far more explicitly than in the Senator's dream ("The circle of time had come full turn" [167]). In "The Line," the condition of modern thought is described as "the time of gray China, now ready [. . .] to devour us" (22); this image is realized in Apollon Apollonovich's appearance in the dream as the emperor of

China and as Saturn. And Nikolay's vision of his past incarnations recalls the condition that Bely, in "The Line," insists cannot be experienced by experience, the condition where all moments of the past (and future) are seen in the present moment.

The shattering revelation of the dream is elaborately prepared. Nikolay has just received a letter informing him that the "bundle" he took from Dudkin is a bomb that will enable him to fulfill his promise to kill his father. As he rereads the letter on the street and realizes its full implications, he "felt a stabbing pain [. . .] in the place where his heart was located, a spark flared. With frenzied speed it turned into a swollen crimson sphere. The sphere expanded, expanded, expanded, and the sphere burst" (128). At that moment a "mangy little fellow," the secret police agent Morkovin, who will torment him in the cheap restaurant, materializes beside him. Nikolay's reaction recalls what his father experienced on the Nevsky when he encountered the stranger ("His heart pounded and expanded, while in his breast arose the sensation of a crimson sphere about to burst into pieces" [14]). In both cases these sudden shocks prepare the eruption of the unconscious in the dream visions to come. Morkovin's mental torture of Nikolay, followed by the appearance of Peter the Great, both as a mysterious Dutchman and as the Bronze Horseman, a "bronze hulk [. . .] glowing phosphorescent [. . .] he who dooms us all—irrevocably" (148; *bez vozvrata*—a parallel with Apollon Apollonovich's dream), further shatters the shell of commonsensicality that Nikolay has constructed. Now, as he awaits the meeting with his father in the early morning after the ball, a "primordial terror, long forgotten," returns: his delirious childhood vision of an "elastic blob," a "spherical fat fellow," Pepp Peppovich Pepp, which "kept on expanding, expanding, and expanding and threatened to come crashing down upon him" (158). The parallels with "Circular Movement" are obvious. There the "modernist philosopher" is described as having a "rubber head," which allows him to bounce back when he hits the bottom of the abyss, describe "a circle in the air," and then "run down the street of the university town" (56) to announce his discovery (Nikolay is, of course, a student). And it is not difficult to see in the "rubber head" an early version of the passages in which Nikolay imagines himself to be a Pepp Peppovich Pepp, a fat, spherical creature made of rubber (e.g., p. 158).

The dreaded confrontation with his father follows. It unleashes a murderous impulse just at the point where they have almost achieved reconciliation. Nikolay then winds the bomb and "tumble[s] headlong into that abyss which he had wanted to escape" (163). He imagines the explosion, and seems to return from that "abyss" long enough to think rationally about disposing of the primed mechanism. But he feels "nauseated, as if he had swallowed the bomb like a pill," and has a "bloating sensation" in his stomach. And as he sits in his study ("everything seemed peaceful"), his head sinks onto the bomb, and a "Nikolay Apollonovich number two," an "unconscious" Nikolay Apollonovich, emerges. (Bely excised this detail from the revised version, perhaps feeling that it established too obvious a parallel with the "second space" notion that precedes Apollon's dream.)[28] He enters that "very strange state" in which it seems that beyond the door lies "the measureless immensity of the cosmos," into which one can only "plunge headfirst" (164). The dream—"The Last Judgment"—begins.

In the open door to the corridor appears an "age-old head," a "hallowed Turanian," Nikolay's Oriental ancestor ("Heredity told"). They engage in conversation about Kant, who, we are told, was also a Turanian. The Kantian "Mongol cause" that Nikolay outlines to his visitor— "Value as a metaphysical nothing!," "the destruction of the Aryan world by means of a system of values"—recalls Bely's critique of contemporary philosophy as nihilism in "The Line": "it maintains that it is an *existing* philosophy of *nonexistence with its meaning existing in nonexistence*" (16). The Turanian, however, chastises Nikolay for not understanding the "task," and advances another dogma. Nikolay has spoken of "value" when he should have spoken of "numeration," "the destruction of Europe" when he should have understood "its immutability." This is the "Mongol cause," arrived at as "logically," in a series of "paragraphs," as Nikolay has arrived at his conclusion. The circle of dogma—stasis—is closed. At this point Nikolay realizes that the "wrinkled countenance" and "ear" before him are those of his father, Saturn, whose mission he has misunderstood and against whom he has dared to "raise his hand." And he is cast into the void and witnesses his former reincarnations. The "circle of time" has come full turn, and now, like his father in his dream, Nikolay returns to his body, which is simultaneously the container of the "zero" chronology of the Ableukhovs, the bomb, and Pepp Peppovich Pepp. And with his realization that "he himself was a bomb," Nikolay "burst with a boom" and awakens: "The ravings had passed, so that morning could remain morning, day could remain day, evening could remain evening" (168). But he has wound the bomb and in twenty hours it will burst, as all dogma must burst—but into what? That its explosion may be futile, that it may explode into yet another dogma, as Bely had written in "The Line," we shall see in Dudkin.

28. In the 1916 version the passage reads: "In the second place: in the second place (we observe for our part), Nikolay Apollonovich Ableukhov was an unconscious man (not Nikolay Apollonovich number one, but Nikolay Apollonovich number two); from time to time, as he passed from the outer door to the inner door of the entryway, a certain strange, very strange, extraordinarily strange state came over him (as it did over Apollon Apollonovich) . . ." (p. 234 of the Nauka text). The 1922 text has: "And in the second place: from time to time, while passing from the outer door to the inner door of the entryway, a certain strange, very strange state came over him [. . .] (p. 164).

Besides the circle pattern, "Circular Movement" provides other interesting parallels with Nikolay's dream. His conversation with the Turanian looks very much like a reworking of a passage in which Bely describes an enormous disembodied head that resembles the face of a clock
and begins to chime as follows:

> One! Deep midnight, scholasticism! . .
> Two! Windelband's new history of philosophy—Volume One . . .
> Three! . . Kantkantkant! . .
> Four! Fichte and schschsch . . .
> (Where Schelling was to come the clock was broken and exclaimed,
>   inappropriately: the philosophy of Vladimir Solov'ev!)
> Five! Hegel and Cohen! . .
> Six! The devil take it—
> Rickert! . .
> Seven! The sacred septenary for two weeks: Simmel, Husserl,
>   Christiansen and Natorp.
> (What followed was indistinct and languid.)
> Sig—gw—art!
> (What followed was not at all distinct; on the contrary, it was completely
>   distinct, with heavy wheezing):
> Ca—ssi-rrrer!!!
> Eight! Kant!
> Nine! Kant!
> Ten! Kant!
> Eleven! (with a loud cracking) The philosophy of Lask! . .
> Twelve! . . The revival of scholasticism . . .
> (And once again the chiming began:)
> One! The deep midnight of scholasticism! etc.
>
> [67–68]

With its enumerative, even syllogistic structure, this passage (surely a
parody of sec. 3 of "The Other Dancing Song" in *Zarathustra*, pt. 3) could
easily be transferred into the fictional world of *Petersburg*. In turn, it
illustrates a sarcastic formulation of circular reasoning that Bely advances some ten pages earlier in the same article: "consciousness is the
form of the form of consciousness" (italics omitted). This formulation
does not find its way into the novel; but other aspects of the passage in
which it is situated do:

> [. . .] its name is contemporary philosophy, where over-refined reason—
> Kantian reason, in which almost nothing of Kant has remained—*hurls itself
> into the abyss*, taking with it the *modernist philosopher*; the modernist *falls
> headfirst*; along with him goes *The Critique of Pure Reason*, which he continues
> to read upside down and right to left: instead of *Reason* he reads some
> Eastern nonsense, provided it is not some Eastern incantation, for he reads:
> *Nosaer*. [56; italics ours]

Reason/Nosear (Razuma/Amuzar) is structured as a palindrome; the second element is lexically meaningless, both in Russian and in English. As Bely says, however, it does suggest an "Eastern incantation." In this way, he economically makes the point that modern philosophy is a combination of Kant and Eastern thinking, that there is no difference between the rational and irrational. As Nikolay discovers in his dream, all is "the Mongol cause."

Bely's personification in "Circular Movement" of the state of contemporary philosophy (by which he always means Neo-Kantianism) shows further similarities with both of the great "reasoners" of his novel. Let us cite the larger part of the relevant section of that article:

> The movement of philosophical modernism is a circular movement; here consciousness *impregnates itself*: it is *hermaphroditic*; the Neo-Kantian, as a collective entity, is *hermaphroditic*; this hermaphrodite, having had a taste of Nietzsche, has toppled over as an *enormous spherical head*, having converted the whole vainglorious little body of the system into the cube of a sphere [. . .] a head with a forelock . . . without any organism attached. The Neo-Kantian, who as a collective entity is composed of people who, taken individually, are clever and eminently reasonable, is just such a monster: a *combination of a boy and an old man—neither a child nor an adult, but a nasty little boy who has been castrated* before the onset of puberty and is then surprised that he does not grow a beard. [. . .] His brain, *excessively swollen, shatters his cranium from within*, in order to rotate all its convolutions bonelessly [. . .]. The poor little head with *a sinciput that has not grown together*. [56–57; italics ours]

Again, swelling imagery is prominent here, only now it is associated not with bouncing, as in the earlier passages, but with something that looks very much like the operation of what in *Petersburg* would be called "cerebral play." As we are reminded here, too, the head and the cranium form part of the cube/sphere image system of *Petersburg*, including the detail, common to both article and novel, of the sinciput that has not grown together. The references to hermaphroditism and castration reinforce Bely's theme of the sterility of modern philosophy, particularly of the Neo-Kantian variety, but also parallel the larger theme of sterility, in a variety of senses, that we find in *Petersburg*. More specifically, we may recall that Nikolay is scrawny, hairless, and unsuccessful with women, and that he seems to be suspended, emotionally and physically, somewhere between childhood and adulthood; "boy" and "old man" remind us that Nikolay and his father are but versions of each other, and as such, interchangeable. Finally, we note the tendency to treat ideas in terms of bodily parts—of which more later. Some of these same images are also used to describe Lippanchenko and the eunuch-like Senator. The Neo-Kantian of the article is "extraordinarily learned and brainy," but he is "a perfect idiot" (*sovershenneishii idiot*: this is the same expression used to describe Likhutin after he has shaved his mustache just before his aborted suicide).

These dreams are involuntary journeys on the part of Apollon and Nikolay, representing moments when their ordered world "suddenly" takes a jolt and opens up into other dimensions. Again they find a compelling parallel in "Circular Movement." There Bely warns us of the dangers of attempting to take refuge from experience in familiar surroundings. "You" will be sitting in "your" comfortable house, which is very much like the Ableukhovs' in certain details of furniture:

> The day will come: the *study* will remain the same; the same sounds of the *grand piano*; the same small *clock* and the same *"methodology."* But the ground of your being—*suddenly*, without any transition—will be torn from under your feet: you will see that you and your armchair are directly suspended in an empty horror, out of which the malicious moon stupidly has slithered right under your feet. With anguish you will raise your eyes to the *non-existent*, formal heavens (having confused the position of the horizon-line); instead of *non-existent* heavens you will see a *speeding* stone globe of indescribable dimensions—speeding directly at you, or no, remaining motionless, but pulling you toward it with dreadful rapidity. [55; italics mostly ours; cf. *Petersburg*, chap. 5, p. 165; chap. 3, pp. 92–96]

Obviously, such displacements are profoundly disturbing for the Senator and Nikolay. Father and son have achieved momentary glimpses of truths greater than the worlds that they have constructed for themselves; but they are thoroughly frightened, and unable to push on toward the possibilities revealed. Instead, they return to where they were: Apollon to being "a little old yellow man" with his "yellow heels" resting on a rug (95); Nikolay to his bewildered, almost sleepwalking existence. They do not act, but instead are acted upon. Apollon is forced to retire and face the "sewer" of his household. Nikolay is to remain caught in the grip of the scheme engendered by his "promise," there to experience the "oppressive confluence of circumstances," the "pyramid of events," and the "horror" of the "quintillion," with himself as a "human numeral one," an "emaciated little stick" followed by thirty zeros (the line/circle imagery again). The pyramid image figures in "The Line" as an emblem of immutability: "Eternity *exists*, although its meaning lies . . . beyond the bounds of all existing meanings: in this sense, the meaning of the pyramid is *nonexistence*" (15–16). "Quintillion" recalls the "decallion" image in that same article—an unimaginably large figure (and Bely's neologism) which, when coupled with zero, represents the source of all being. If that source could be reached, then "the decallion of [individual] moments would be equal to one single moment, the sum to the component items. In only one case can the component item be equal to the sum: if the component is a zero. The equality of the decallion to one decallionic component should be imagined as the equality of zero to a decallion of zeros" (14).

Neither reason nor familiar surroundings provide father and son with any real consolation or understanding. Yet they refuse to face what they have seen, and even, in Chapter 8, try to return to "normal." This process of denial and return is described in "Circular Movement" as well. But it is a "dangerous pastorale" for the "you" of "Circular Movement" as well as for Apollon and Nikolay. "Suddenly" is sure to intrude and shatter all illusions of security, whether it is the "suddenly" of radical physical displacement or the "suddenly" of the explosion of the bomb that has been ticking away throughout.

The only character in *Petersburg* who seems potentially capable of breaking out of the circle of existence is Dudkin. He is the most complex and problematical of all Bely's characters; and it is he who raises the whole question of Nietzsche, the central figure of "Circular Movement."

Dudkin

Dudkin is well aware of the presence of Nietzsche in modern life. As he says to Nikolay Apollonovich during their first long encounter in the novel, in Chapter 2: "I was a Nietzschean. We are all Nietzscheans, and you are a Nietzschean, although you wouldn't admit it. For us Nietzscheans, the masses, who (as you would say) are stirred by social instincts, become an apparatus of implementation, where all people (and even those like you) are a keyboard, on which play the flying fingers of a pianist [. . .] surmounting all difficulties" (57). This appears to be a vulgarized version—the admixture of Dostoevsky's underground man is significant—of the "superman" idea, which was accessible to any reasonably intelligent reader of the popular press at the time. Dudkin's conscious understanding of Zarathustra does not go beyond this; at least, it is never articulated. But he is a Zarathustrian figure through and through, despite some associations with the imagery and ideas of *The Birth of Tragedy*.[29] It is

29. See especially the section titled "Dionysus" in chap. 6. H. J. Gerigk, in "Belyjs *Petersburg* und Nietzsches *Geburt der Tragödie*" (*Nietzsche Studien: Internationales Jahrbuch für die Nietzsche-Forschung*, 9 [Berlin, 1980]), and Virginia Bennett, in "Echoes of Friedrich Nietzsche's *The Birth of Tragedy* in Andrej Belyj's *Petersburg*" (*Germano-Slavica*, 3, no. 4 [Fall 1980]), discuss specific instances of this particular work in the novel. Their readings of the novel are seriously skewed by their reliance on this work, as are Carol Anschuetz's speculations about Nietzschean connections ("Bely's *Petersburg* and the End of the Russian Novel," in *The Russian Novel from Pushkin to Pasternak*, ed. John Garrard [New Haven, 1983]). Never again did Nietzsche rely so heavily on polarities; and by the time *Petersburg* was being written, Bely found this kind of thinking antithetical to his own, as is clear from his treatment of line and circle. He makes no reference to *The Birth of Tragedy* in the articles of 1912, where his attention falls almost exclusively on *Zarathustra* and, to a lesser extent, *Ecce Homo*.

he who enacts what Bely sees as the tragedy of Nietzsche—and of modern man.

Dudkin's whole way of life presents striking parallels with the later life of Nietzsche, who, let us remember, is synonymous with Zarathustra in Bely's mind. To quote a passage from Stefan Zweig's biography of Nietzsche:

> And up again into the small, narrow, modest, coldly furnished *chambre garnie*, where innumerable notes, pages, writings, and proofs are piled up on the table, but no flower, no decoration, scarcely a book and rarely a letter. Back in a corner, a heavy and graceless wooden trunk, his only possession, with the two shirts and the other worn suit. Otherwise only books and manuscripts, and on a tray innumerable bottles and jars and potions: against the migraines, which often render him all but senseless for hours, . . . and above all the dreadful sedatives against his insomnia. . . . A frightful arsenal of poisons and drugs, yet the only helpers in the empty silence of this strange room in which he never rests except in brief and artificially conquered sleep.[30]

Let us remember Dudkin's isolation, self-medication, insomnia, and poverty. Let us also remember that he lives in a shabby, virtually unfurnished rented room on the top floor, which can be reached only by a dark, fetid, and seemingly endless flight of stairs. This room is often referred to as the "habitation" (*obitalishche*). Of course this term is ironic; but it also signals that the room may have an importance disproportionate to its physical appearance. Indeed, that proves to be the case. The "habitation" functions in the novel as the equivalent of Zarathustra's mountain: it is the place to which Dudkin "ascends" from the "abyss" of the city, the place where he has his major visions and comes to understand (or to think he understands) the meaning of his life and the course of action he must follow.[31]

Much of the specific imagery associated with Dudkin is familiar to readers of *Zarathustra*: solitude, the wanderer, heaviness, iciness.[32] Particularly prominent is the image of the shadow. Again, let us recall

---

30. Quoted by Walter Kaufmann in his preface to *Thus Spoke Zarathustra*, in *Portable Nietzsche*, p. 104.

31. We might recall that both Apollon Apollonovich and Nikolay experience their dream visions while on the upper floor of their mansion. Even Likhutin climbs onto a chair before his suicide attempt. Characteristically, Dudkin, who sees more than any other character, lives in the "highest place" of the novel.

32. It is Apollon Apollonovich who is most often associated with ice. In Bely's verse ice is often a symbol for loneliness, as it is in *Zarathustra*. With Apollon Apollonovich, however, ice is above all an image of stasis and nonmovement, as seen, for instance, in his desire to "freeze" Russia. This reminds us that we have to do with multivalent imagery and with a symbolist novel, not an allegory. Still, both the Senator and Dudkin are fundamentally loners and try to use force to deal with the world, as Dolgopolov remarks ("Tvorcheskaya istoriya," p. 600).

"Circular Movement," where Bely seems to draw upon the "Shadow" chapter in *Zarathustra,* Part IV. For Bely, the shadow represents a constant temptation to return, a temptation to which Zarathustra (and Nietzsche) yielded.[33] In other words, Bely sees the shadow as a problem in identity and mission, and in *Petersburg* he employs it in the same way, notably in his treatment of Dudkin. The narrator neatly sums it up when he says: "So let our stranger [Dudkin] be a real stranger! And let the two shadows of my stranger be real shadows!" (36).

Dudkin is described as *being* a shadow—"bluish," or "idle"—and as *casting* a shadow. As Nikolay observes: "Now I understand where you cast your shadow from—the shadow of the Elusive One" (59). The place Nikolay has in mind is the habitation. Again we are back in the landscape of *Zarathustra*: mountain (habitation), shadow, abyss (city). And it is in the habitation, in Chapter 6, that all the shadow's implications for Dudkin are explored.

Dudkin is making yet another of his returns to the habitation, this time after visiting Lippanchenko. He is followed up the stairs by Shishnarfne, whom he has seen earlier that day at Lippanchenko's, and before that in some place he cannot for the moment recall. Now, Dudkin has always been a linear thinker, in Bely's sense, a believer in meaningful distinctions between there and here, then and now. There/then is the place/time where he has once been but no longer is and never again will be. It represents menace, insecurity, danger, but is, he thinks, safely behind him. Specifically, then/there represents Helsingfors, where the symptoms of his illness began. It also represents Teheran (which is Shishnarfne's home town), as well as something called the "shadow state," where he has committed some dreadful, unspecified act. "Here" represents Petersburg, the habitation, and relative security. Yet Dudkin is already half aware that his distinctions are flawed. For one thing, the illness contracted in Helsingfors is still very much with him. Then, too, Teheran, an "Oriental" city (specifically Persian, as of course is Zarathustra), is perhaps suggestively present in the mysterious yellow face that appears on one of the four yellow walls of the habitation. And Shishnarfne makes certain, in this scene, that Dudkin understands the falseness of the here/there, now/then distinction—and with it the falseness of linearity. "Our capital city, adorned with monuments," says Shishnarfne, referring to Petersburg. Dudkin objects: "You say 'our capital city,' but it's not yours. *Your* capital city, I believe, is Teheran. For you, an Oriental. . . ." But Shishnarfne is having none of it: "Why no, I've been to Paris and London. As I was saying [. . .] it's not customary to

33. In both "The Line" (p. 20) and "Circular Movement" (p. 72), Bely also introduces the figure of Ahriman to emblemize the fatal attraction to a return to the ordinary and the comfortable. In anthroposophy, Ahriman represents the force devoted to the maintenance of the status quo, which prevents human spiritual evolution.

mention the fact that *our* capital city belongs to the land of the spirits [. . .]" (205). In other words, "there" and "here" are the same geographically.[34] They are interchangeable, just as for Nietzsche—again as Bely reads him—there is no essential difference between Persia and Europe, East and West. The identity depends on circularity, not on linearity. To emphasize the point, Shishnarfne picks up a circular image that is invoked in the prologue of the novel, that of the dot:

> Petersburg is the fourth dimension which is not indicated on maps, which is indicated merely by a dot. And this dot is the place where the plane of being is tangential to the surface of the sphere and the immense astral cosmos. A dot which in the twinkling of an eye can produce for us an inhabitant of the fourth dimension, from whom not even a wall can protect us.   [207]

Now, to Dudkin, Shishnarfne represents "there" and Dudkin "here." But that distinction too is soon eradicated. For one thing, Shishnarfne has returned from Dudkin's past—in Helsingfors and at Lippanchenko's—and is actually in the same room with him. In other words, by returning to the habitation Dudkin does not escape what is "out there" but brings it back with him, ensuring that it too will "return." For another thing, the attentive reader will have noticed that Shishnarfne is simply a reversal (a return, as it were) of the word Enfranshish, that puzzling and incomprehensible sound that Dudkin has been hearing in the habitation. In the course of this scene, he comes to understand that Shishnarfne and Enfranshish are the same, and that both are "here" in the most immediate sense possible—within him. Let us recall how this happens. Gradually, Shishnarfne becomes more and more insubstantial:

> A man of all three dimensions had entered the room. He had leaned against the window and had become a contour (or, two-dimensional), had become a thin layer of soot of the sort you knock out of a lamp. Now this black soot had suddenly smoldered away into an ash that gleamed in the moonlight, and the ash was flying away. And there was no contour.   [207]

All that is left is a "voice" that moves "very perceptibly away from the window in the direction of" Dudkin, and finally enters him, "becomes" his own voice. The two are one. And this joining takes place in a fourth dimension too, like the joining of the cities of Teheran and Petersburg—

34. In a letter to Aleksandr Blok, dated November 26, 1911—while work on *Petersburg* was still in its earliest phases— Bely clearly regards Helsingfors and Finland as "Eastern," as manifestations of "Mongolism": "*the yellow fascination*—yield to it and—an automobile, Tartars, Japanese guests, and then— Finland, or '*something*' present in Finland, and then— Helsingfors, Azef, revolution—always the same gamut" (Aleksandr Blok and Andrey Bely, *Perepiska* [Moscow, 1940], p. 280). Interestingly enough, all these motifs are prominent in *Petersburg*.

a dimension that Dudkin entered when he committed that mysterious "act" and has, all unwittingly, inhabited until now. In that dimension, "everything [. . .] flows in reverse order. Ivanov becomes some sort of Japanese: Vonavi" (208). Similarly, Shishnarfne ("there") becomes Enfranshish ("here"), and both are within him: "And he understood: 'Shishnarfne—Shish-nar-fne. . . .' From his vocal apparatus came the reply: 'You summoned me. . . . Here I am. . . .' *Enfranshish* had come for his soul" (208).

This passage bears a startling resemblance to one in *Zarathustra*. There the shadow says:

> I am a wanderer who has already walked a great deal at your [Zarathustra's] heels—always on my way, but without any goal, also without any home . . . I have already sat on every surface; like weary dust, I have gone to sleep on mirrors and windowpanes: everything takes away from me, nothing gives, I become thin—I am almost like a shadow.

In *Zarathustra*, shadow and source are never quite identified— "even when I hid from you I was still your best shadow: wherever you sat, I sat too."[35] But in *Petersburg* the two become one.

As we have said, Shishnarfne is a Persian, as of course is Zarathustra. In effect, this encounter can be seen as a fictional gloss on Bely's statement, in "Circular Movement," that "To Nietzsche [Dudkin] came adherents of Zoroaster from Persia" (52). What Shishnarfne does is to convert Dudkin from linear to circular thinking, just as the dwarf converts Zarathustra. Dudkin becomes convinced of the truth of circularity, at least as it concerns his own past experiences and encounters. Among them is the "act" he has committed in Helsingfors. Its nature is never specified. We are told only that

> his preaching of barbarism had come to an unexpected end (right there in Helsingfors). Alexander Ivanovich had seen himself (while in a somnolent state) being whirled through what might most simply be called interplanetary space, for the purpose of performing *a certain vile act* [our italics]. That had been in a dream, but a hideous dream which had decided him to stop preaching. Alexander Ivanych did not remember whether he had committed *the act* or not [. . .]. [204]

The 1916 version is no more specific: "being whirled [. . .] for the commission of a certain act which was ordinary *there*, but nonetheless vile from our point of view."[36] In an early manuscript of the novel, Bely does say that Dudkin had been "whirled" to a witches' sabbat "for the commis-

35. *Zarathustra*, pt. 4, "The Shadow," in *Portable Nietzsche*, p. 385.
36. P. 293 of the 1981 Nauka text.

sion of a satanic act (kissing the Goat's behind and stamping on the Cross)."[37] "There," in other words, is demonic; and Dudkin has been possessed by evil powers ever since. But Bely deleted this explanation, obviously wishing to leave matters unclear. Still, the expression "vile act" should alert the careful reader. It is the term that Nikolay Apollonovich uses for the "sin" of his conception. Thus the theme of parricide seems to be transferred to Dudkin. If this is the case, then who is his father? So far we have assumed that his putative victim is Apollon Apollonovich, who is a "father" to him in the sense in which any authority figure would be. Much closer is Lippanchenko, his ideological and spiritual father. Bely does not elucidate. But as this crucial encounter with Shishnarfne draws to an end, the "act" is again mentioned, this time by the "voice" that is now within Dudkin. The voice tells him that he has been registered in the "fourth dimension" ever since he committed "the act," and will be granted the right to live there when he signs his internal passport, as it were, if he performs "an extravagant little action" (*postupochek*). Again we are not told what the action is (and the 1916 version is no clearer). Hindsight suggests that it refers to Dudkin's impending murder of Lippanchenko; and the fact that it occurs in a passage that simply rephrases the earlier one, with its reference to "vile act," lends some support to this supposition. But Bely deliberately keeps the matter vague, leaving it to Dudkin—and the reader—to discover what he must do, guided by the inexorable logic of circle and line.

In any event, by the end of this scene Dudkin realizes that he has entered into a pact whose terms are binding. He further realizes that he must bear the responsibility for his own situation: "he had committed it. He had joined himself to them" (208). Until now he has tried to see the pact as something imposed on him by evil forces that have kept him in thrall. But Shishnarfne will not allow it: "with water you swallow germs, and I'm no germ" (206). Enfranshish (Shishnarfne) is not some substance that is unwittingly consumed, like tainted water; the consumption is deliberate. Nor does Shishnarfne allow Dudkin to bring in illness as an explanation of what has happened.[38] In other words, Dudkin can no longer dismiss the pact as being over and done with, as having happened "there" and "then," in Helsingfors; there is no undoing it, any more than Nikolay can undo his promise or the march of events by throwing the bomb into the river, as Dudkin urges. Once he accepts responsibility for the act, Dudkin sees that he has imprisoned himself in a circular process. In fact, he sees that his entire life has been circular—an endless

37. Quoted by Dolgopolov in ibid., p. 630.

38. The 1916 version is slightly more specific here: "all this [the "connection between his theory and Satanism"] had been rejected by him as an illness; and now, when he was again ill, all of that was being disgustedly returned to him with interest by the black contour" (ibid., p. 296).

going out and coming back, or a series of eternal returns. In this sense, he is following the pattern of Nietzsche and Zarathustra, as Bely interprets it in "Circular Movement."

Unlike Nietzsche and Zarathustra, however, Dudkin understands that such a pattern is ultimately sterile and futile, an enslavement of his body and mind. He wishes desperately to liberate his "imprisoned will" (Nietzsche's term), to break out of the circle of eternal return, to move ahead "without return"—*bez vozvrata*, a phrase that becomes virtually a leitmotif in the novel.[39] And he thinks he knows how he can. In a final epiphany—experienced from the very top of the house, the garret above his room, an analogue, as it were, of the very summit of Zarathustra's mountain—he decides what he must do. He must commit another act, an act of the will, and thereby liberate himself from this circular prison. The act cannot be directed against Enfranshish/Shishnarfne, for they are within him and the result would be suicide. But there is an external counterpart to these forces—Lippanchenko. Dudkin calls him the "image" of his imprisonment, the one who has "enslaved his will." It was Lippanchenko, apparently, who drew Dudkin into terrorism and who has made him responsible for entrapping Nikolay in a new terrorist plot, directed against Apollon Apollonovich. Dudkin feels intense guilt for his role in these matters, as suggested in the song about Pontius Pilate that he hears from the garret ("I see, oh Lord, my iniquity" [209]). This awareness of guilt and moral necessity helps prepare him to acknowledge his own responsibility in the enslavement and the entrapment of Nikolay:

> He had given Nikolay Apollonovich up to Lippanchenko out of fear [. . .]. Without believing, he had believed, and in this lay his betrayal [. . .]. Lippanchenko had enslaved his will. The enslavement of his will had occurred because he kept wanting to dispel the horrible suspicion, and he kept driving away suspicion by keeping company with Lippanchenko [. . .]. Thus they had become tied one to the other. [211–12]

To kill Lippanchenko, then, is to kill the jailer, open the doors of the prison, and escape "without return."[40]

In terms of the line/circle imagery of the book—and of the two companion pieces we have been discussing—Dudkin looks to the line to solve

---

39. In our translation of the novel, we consistently rendered this phrase as "irrevocably." Had we then been aware of the implications of Bely's two articles, we would have remained literal.

40. In "Circular Movement" (53) Bely notes Zarathustra's loss of vision when he descends the mountain, and connects it with the sea, which he calls "flowing picturesqueness" (or "figurativeness": the Russian is *obraznost'*). Hereby he suggests the corruption of the "passionate" clarity of vision into "strange images." We recall that it is Lippanchenko, the double agent and provocateur, who alone of all the characters lives by the sea, and that it is he whom Dudkin connects with the "strangeness" of the hallucinations he suffers, especially the Mongol-Semite face that stares from the wallpaper of his room.

the problem of the circle. The act of will, as he conceives it, is linear. In effect, he is right back where he started. For the way out will be yet another terrorist act—the murder of Lippanchenko. The cycle simply begins again. The futility of his final act finds expression in the weapon he chooses. We recall that he first attempts to buy a knife, but is refused by a suspicious shopkeeper. He then purchases a pair of scissors. Like the knife, scissors are a correlative of "something steely" that enters his soul when—from his own mountaintop, the garret above his room—he resolves to commit the act. Their blades, like that of the knife, are straight, and thus appropriate agents of the rectilinear act of the will. Like the knife, they have the function of cutting through a circle—most immediately, the bloated sphere of Lippanchenko's body, and ultimately the circle of enslavement. The knife, however, is *all* straight lines. Scissors have *circular* handles (a detail not specified in the book), and thus are the perfect emblem of an act that proves futile. They catch up the basic line/circle imagery of this book—and of the two companion pieces—and remind us, once again, that for Bely, the contrast between line and circle is only apparent. The line invokes the circle; both are false ways of conceiving the world.

Dudkin is found straddling the corpse of Lippanchenko, one arm outflung, in a grotesque parody of the Bronze Horseman. His act of will has ended in madness: the straight line has become the circle, for madness too is a circular condition. As Bely writes in "Circular Movement": "The prisoner becomes a madman" (54). This is a quote from *Zarathustra*; and it is instructive, for our purposes, to look at the larger context in Nietzsche. "Will—that is the name of the liberator and joy-bringer; thus I taught you, my friends. But now learn this too: the will itself is still a prisoner . . . Willing liberates; what means does the will devise for himself to get rid of his melancholy and to mock his dungeon? Alas, every prisoner becomes a fool [or "madman"]; and the imprisoned will redeems himself foolishly."[41] Surely Dudkin exemplifies this foolish attempt at redemption. He ends up a madman. This is not the creative madness of which Nietzsche speaks in *Zarathustra*—the madness experienced on mountaintops, a clairvoyant and liberating madness. (Let us note that the murder does *not*

41. *Zarathustra*, pt. 2, "On Redemption," in *Portable Nietzsche*, p. 251. The German word that Kaufmann translates as "fool" is *Narr* ("Ach, ein Narr wird jeder Gefangene! Närrisch erlöst sich auch der gefangene Wille"). It can also mean "madman." The Russian version of "Alas, every prisoner becomes a *fool*" is "Akh, *bezumtsem* stanovitsya kazhdyi plennik" (*Tak govoril Zaratustra* [St. Petersburg, 1911; reprinted New York: Chalidze, 1981], p. 121). *Bezumets* also carries both meanings, "fool" and "madman." In "Circular Movement," Bely renders this sentence as "*bezumtsem* stanovitsya *uznik*." The use of *uznik* (not *plennik*, as in Antonovsky's 1911 version) suggests that Bely translated directly from the German. *Uznik* also appears in *Petersburg* just before Dudkin realizes that it is Lippanchenko who has enslaved his will: he "seemed to himself merely a captive *prisoner*" (211), "*poimanny uznik*" in the Russian.

take place in the habitation, but at Lippanchenko's, he emblematically being another version of the dwarf who tempts Dudkin/Zarathustra down from the mountain.) Rather, it is a garden-variety madness. Dudkin has not escaped the circle, but has merely reenacted it.

What does all this say about Peter the Great as he is presented in the novel? As we recall, the Horseman crashes into Dudkin's habitation after he has resolved to kill Lippanchenko ("'I know what I shall do.' Everything would come to an end [. . .] his mission took shape" [212]). This in itself represents a triumph of circularity: past and present meet, and, as the narrator says, "the destinies of Evgeny [in Pushkin's *Bronze Horseman*] were repeated" (213). Even more strikingly, the Horseman, who has always been an awesome, menacing figure, now turns benevolent and calls Dudkin "my son." He proceeds to infuse Dudkin with his very being: "Now he turned white hot, and flowed over Alexander Ivanovich, who was kneeling before him [. . .]. He poured into his veins in metals" (214). One could interpret the appearance of the Horseman at this point as a reminder of the futility of trying to change history, which Dudkin, a revolutionary and therefore a linear thinker, presumes to do. History is also circular; even Dudkin, we are told, has existed before, as Evgeny. What, then, does Dudkin inherit from Peter? We are never specifically told. But our awareness of the line/circle theme suggests the following: Peter's creation, Petersburg, results from an act of the will. By creating it he seemingly broke out of the age-old circularity of Russian life. Now he apparently passes on this power to Dudkin, giving him a way out of the fateful circle of his life, a way that is "without return" (*bez vozvrata*). This motif is associated with Peter as well as with Shishnarfne/Enfranshish throughout the book. East and West, once again, are not polarities: the Persian Shishnarfne and the Westernizing tsar meet, both impelling Dudkin to the same ultimately futile act.

This entire scene is played out against the backdrop of the universe—really, *in* the universe: the walls of the habitation have fallen away and "the black room opened up—into ineffabilities" (213). This opening up seems to confer on the encounter the validity of universal law, as if Dudkin is to be exempted from the iron law of return by performing an act of the will, as Peter once did. But there is that awkward final scene, with Dudkin totally mad, mimicking the Horseman.[42] What sort of legacy has Dudkin received?

Here we can suggest two possibilities. One is that Peter all unknowingly is as much deceived as Dudkin. This interpretation would make him a pitiable figure, tragically unable to escape the trap of circularity

42. The 1916 version leaves no doubt of Dudkin's total madness; the final sentence of chap. 7, cut from the 1922 version as obviously unnecessary, is "Vidimo, on rekhnulsya" (p. 386 of Nauka ed.), i.e., "Evidently he had gone mad."

himself, doomed to travel in the same fateful circle, as his frequent incursions into the "present" of the book suggest, not to speak of his enduring, unchanging presence as the statue on the Senate Square. The other is that Peter is aware that his legacy as a creator and builder has fossilized into dogma, as represented by both the bureaucrats and the terrorists, who, as Bely sees it, are really dedicated to the same end, all outward dissimilarities to the contrary. He must again destroy in order to create new life, as he destroyed the old Russia in order to make way for the new. The destroyer/builder idea finds a neat parallel in *Zarathustra*: "Whoever must be a creator always annihilates."[43] In this reading, the Horseman would use Dudkin to destroy terrorism, in the person of Lippanchenko, as Lippanchenko has used Nikolay—through Dudkin—to destroy bureaucratism, in the person of Apollon Apollonovich. The way would then presumably be open for a new creation. But Peter disappears along with Dudkin, at the end of Chapter 7. His disappearance suggests that he is as much a victim of the forces of destruction as are his heirs, that he, the ultimate "father" of the novel, shares the fate of the other fathers, Apollon Apollonovich and Lippanchenko. If he can easily be associated with Apocalypse (he does, after all, appear in the novel as the Bronze *Horseman*, suggesting the four riders of John's Revelation), his revelation to his "son" is both false and futile.

If Peter *is* aware of what has become of his creation, he may also be aware that he cannot undo what has happened: he too is imprisoned in circularity. In other words, he may be moved by revenge, and feel impelled to destroy "without return." The revenge motif does not occur in Bely's reading of Zarathustra in "Circular Movement." But it is found in Nietzsche, in the passage from which Bely quotes the phrase "every prisoner becomes a madman." Zarathustra goes on to say: "the imprisoned will redeems himself foolishly." His explication of this idea is highly suggestive for the figure of Peter in Bely's novel, and for Dudkin as well, particularly in the final, mad scene:

> the will itself is still a prisoner. Willing liberates; but what is it that puts even the liberator himself, in fetters? "It was"—that is the name of the will's gnashing of teeth and most secret melancholy. Powerless against what has been done, he is an angry spectator of all that is past. The will cannot will backwards . . . the imprisoned will redeems himself foolishly. That time does not run backwards, that is his wrath; "that which was" is the name of the stone he cannot move. And so he moves stones out of wrath and displeasure, and he wreaks revenge on whatever does not feel wrath and displeasure as he does. Thus the will, the liberator, took to hurting; and on all who can suffer he wreaks revenge for his inability to go backwards. This,

43. *Portable Nietzsche*, p. 171.

indeed this alone, is what *revenge* is: the will's ill will against time and its "it was."[44]

Read this way, Peter's revenge is directed against his inability to go backward, to the liberating, creative moment when he broke out of the circularity of the old Russian way of life, and through a creative act of the will established a new Russia, in Petersburg. This Russia, this Petersburg, has fossilized into the dogmas of bureaucracy and terrorism and can only be destroyed, not revived. We might recall Zarathustra's words about the "law of time that it must devour its children,"[45] and Bely's similar use of the myth of Saturn in the novel.

As Peter's heir, Dudkin finally enacts the impulse to destroy that seems to have drawn him into terrorism in the first place. At this point, however, he directs this impulse not at a civilization, political system, or bureaucracy, but at one particular man—his "father," Lippanchenko, who certainly "does not feel wrath and displeasure," as Dudkin does. Perhaps Dudkin acts out of revenge for all that has happened to him, notably the imprisonment of his will. Whatever the reason, his "action" is futile, a point Bely graphically makes by ending this chapter—and Dudkin's presence in the novel—with the cockroach that crawls over his face as he straddles the corpse of Lippanchenko.

Endings

The circle or sphere is ever present on all levels, and is intrinsic to the workings of the novel as a whole. For instance, the characters return to the same place again and again, often involuntarily; they "run in circles," and their running seems inevitably to bring them to the Senate Square, where the Bronze Horseman stands, even when the routes they follow do not correspond to the geography of the real city.[46] "Cerebral play" is circular or spherical too. It is often likened to an explosion that bursts forth from the skull and expands, but never entirely detaches itself from its point of origin, and in fact returns there, albeit in different form. Explosion is of course the ultimate purpose of the bomb. But before it explodes, the bomb generates the action of the second half of the novel, just as Nikolay's conception by his parents has generated the conflict and the promise that have brought the bomb and thus the novel's plot into being. A full circle has been described. Shadows become people, but people can become shadows in this hallucinatory world where the mind

44. Ibid., pp. 251–52.
45. Ibid., p. 252.
46. See the section "Printsipy i priemy izobrazheniya goroda" in Dolgopolov's postface to the 1981 Nauka edition, especially pp. 609–15.

creates realities that not only assume independent existence but exist beyond the control of the mind that produced them and in turn exert a reciprocal influence on their creators. (This is also a paradigm of Bely's view of artistic creation.) Father and son commit an act of mental terrorism against each other, and find that these acts turn back on them: Nikolay thinks his father a scoundrel and wishes him dead, the plot arises and Nikolay becomes *its* agent; the Senator thinks his own flesh and blood a scoundrel, and is destroyed by Nikolay, if not physically, then as a bureaucrat. And so it goes, circle after circle, on every level of the book.

As we have seen, the circle appears as early as the Prologue, where Petersburg is described as consisting, on maps, of "two small *circles* [*kruzhki*], one set inside the other, with a black *dot* [*tochka*] in the center" (2). In retrospect, these images become symbols that convey the nature and destiny of the city that is the theme of the novel that follows. And we also realize that the image of the city established in the Prologue describes the novel's structure of double circularity: the outer circle of Prologue/Epilogue enclosing the "center," like dots within dots on a map.

The circle/sphere symbol underlies the insistent repetitions in the novel as well. They become especially noticeable toward the end, when entire paragraphs from earlier sections are repeated verbatim. No doubt, too, circularity motivates the rising theme of childhood, which involves all the major characters, even the loathsome Lippanchenko. For example, shortly before he is killed Lippanchenko sings a song that takes him and his mistress, Zoya Zakharovna (whom he addresses ironically as *matushka*, "little mother"), back to their youthful years of first love. At this moment she calls him a "big baby, just incorrigible" (*neispravimyi rebenok* [260]), and we recall that earlier she has told Dudkin that Lippanchenko plays with toy soldiers and with dolls. She refers to him throughout by the endearing diminutive Kolechka, and announces that "he's just a child" ("on—*rebenok, rebenok*"). As Dudkin stares at him he sees, to his astonishment, "the lip of a nursing infant [*molokosos*] of a year and a half" and "the head of a premature child" (*nedonosok* [191]).

These are only suggestions of the theme more fully developed in the final chapter that has puzzled so many critics. We now catch the tone of those nineteenth-century novels devoted to family happiness, and are aware of yet another closing of the circle of Russian literature in *Petersburg*, which has begun with a deliberate evocation of the European eighteenth-century novel, and has thereby hinted at the infancy of the genre itself. The emphasis of Chapter 8 is on the ideal of bourgeois serenity and comfort, which is to be attained, as analogous passages of "Circular Movement" suggest, by a return to the old ways of the family. Everything points to a new beginning. Anna Petrovna has returned home; husband and wife recall their honeymoon in Venice (another city on canals, like Petersburg). The family settles back into a semblance of harmony and peace as father and son experience reconciliation ("they retraced their steps" [282]). But another return has been made too, as the bomb returns to the bedroom of Apollon Apollonovich, reminding us that it is the result of the "cerebral play" (itself a circular process) of both bureaucrats (Apollon) and terrorists (Lippanchenko). At length it explodes, bringing this chapter, and the novel proper, to an end. Petersburg disappears; the Ableukhovs are destroyed as a family; only individuals are left, who wither and die.

The Epilogue's emphasis is on fragmentation. The components look like "returns" from the rest of the novel. For instance: "Nikolay Apollonovich, in a blue gandurah and a bright red Arabian chéchia [Eastern motif], *squats motionless on his haunches* [as he does in chap. 8, p. 270]. An extraordinarily long *tassel* dangles from the chéchia [cf. the tassel on Apollon's dressing gown]. His *silhouette* [common in the novel] is distinctly etched [. . .] the sounds of a *tom-tom* [a virtual homonym of *tam*, 'there,' a word that appears frequently in the earlier parts]: they strike the ears with a *hollow, oppressive quality* [the sound of the exploding bomb]. Everywhere are the white *cubes* of *hovels* [. . .]. [Cubes describe the houses on the Nevsky (10) and are generally a pervasive geometric figure; *hovels, domishki*, recall the statement in the Prologue that 'other Russian cities are a wooden heap of hovels' (2).] The Berber is *olive-skinned* [. . .] [recalling the yellow 'Eastern' face on the wall of Dudkin's room]. In the distance is the *pink* of an *almond tree* [pink is a feature of the city landscape; almond tree, *mindal'*, echoes the name of Anna Petrovna's Italian lover, Mindalini (translated Almondini in our version to preserve the wordplay)]. That *jagged* mountaintop is bright violet-amber [jagged perhaps suggests the zigzag motif found earlier; it is repeated a few lines later in the Epilogue as 'the *jagged* gray forest distance'] [. . .] the *glittering wedges of moonlight* and the *little squares of parquet floor*. Nikolay Apollonovich [. . .] kept stepping out of *shadow*—into the *lacework of light cast by the lamp. He kept stepping out of this bright lacework—into shadow* [the Ableukhov house]" (291–93).

Several of the images just specified, as well as others that come later in the Epilogue, are drawn from the image system that is found also in "Circular Movement": the starkness of the settings; the moutaintop, with "jagged" suggesting difficult access; the dismissal of Kant; the "Eastern" references generally (Zarathustra being a Persian); the survey of the ruins of culture; the solitary seeker of the truth (in this case not Dudkin but the equally helpless Nikolay). The motif of childhood is strongly articulated in the Epilogue as well, in Apollon's reversion to childhood and in Nikolay's trip to Nazareth, the childhood home of Jesus. These are of course returns. Traditionally, childhood is an emblem of growth, energy, vitality. But it is hard to detect those qualities here: Apollon is sinking into senility, and Nikolay's "return" to Nazareth, as to Egypt, feels like an excursion through a museum. The Ableukhov family has come to a sterile end, like a cycle of time and history. The last sentence of the novel is uttered with the impersonal finality of a news item: "His parents had died" (*Roditeli ego umerli*). We are left with the fact of death.

Given the views outlined in "The Line" and "Circular Movement," *Petersburg* could perhaps conclude in no other way. The city need not be destroyed physically (nor are its analogues, the Senator's house, which is only damaged, and his head). But its time in history is clearly over. And here the career of Apollon Apollonovich is emblematic of the fate of the city. As he loses his "post," his "function," he ceases to exist in any way that is meaningful to him and can only relive his past in his memoirs. As he sits paralyzed in his wheelchair, lifeless and immobile, he is surrounded by nature. So too, we might argue, does Petersburg sit surrounded and isolated by Russia as a whole. That it will "explode" Bely insists in the Epilogue: "There will be an explosion: everything will be swept away" (292). But whether it will explode into yet another "dogma" or be reborn and transfigured, free of the cycles of reincarnation and recurrence, he does not say.

In "The Line," Bely uses the spiral as the image of creative movement. But there are no spirals in *Petersburg*. In the Epilogue, even lines have pretty much disappeared; the circle dominates, and with it the sense of futility and sterility that Bely associates with the circle throughout his writings of this period. Are we left, then, with no way out?

To be sure, we are told in the Epilogue that Nikolay has abandoned Kant and is reading a new philosopher, Skovoroda. Bely may be hinting at the beginning of some internal transformation, but if so he gives only the vaguest of hints; we are not shown the result.[47] Certainly Dudkin's madness, as we have argued in the previous section, is neither "liberating" nor even remotely "creative," as others have stated.[48] His will has

47. John Elsworth has written that "the epilogue intimates a replacement of the 'eternal recurrence' of the novel's eight chapters by a return of a different kind, a retrieval of the innocence of man's childhood and the commencement of a new culture" (*Andrey Bely: A Critical Study*, p. 111). Nikolay's actions may indeed evince a *desire* for rebirth, and he seems to be at a somewhat higher point on the spiral than where he began, but the next phase of the spiral movement is nowhere shown in the novel. As Elsworth admits, rebirth "can be no more than intimation."

48. Dagmar Burkhart argues ("Leitmotivik und Symbolik," p. 310) that Dudkin's final madness indicates his accession to a higher truth. Carol Anschuetz makes essentially the same point, seeing Dudkin as a "creative artist" in his murder of Lippanchenko, and argues further that the "fate of Dudkin recalls that of Nietzsche" ("Bely's *Petersburg*," p. 134). But Bely's view of Nietzsche's tragic fate is clear in "Circular Movement": "In *Ecce Homo* he is all contorted, he is—an idiot"; "*Eternal return* overpowered Nietzsche" (pp. 64, 68).

not been "unharnessed yet from his own folly," as Nietzsche puts it in *Zarathustra*.[49] He is a tool in the hands of Peter; we should not forget that his resolve wavers repeatedly before the murder: he implores the "phosphorescent intervals between the branches, which were forming the body" (259) to release him from his mission. But an arm (Peter's) sternly directs him to his victim and he commits the murder. Dudkin remains a prisoner, a man under compulsion who redeems his will foolishly. We should recall the conclusion of "On Redemption," that so shall the will remain "until the creative will says to it, 'But thus I willed it.' Until the creative will says to it, 'But thus I will it; thus shall I will it'."[50] That *creative* will does not speak to Dudkin or anyone else in the novel.

Before we conclude, however, that Bely's vision of Petersburg and Russia is utterly without hope, we must look at one more circle in the book: the bomb. The shape of its container, a sardine tin, actually combines line and circle to make four walls, as it were, that are placed within the four walls of the Ableukhov house. And we know from "Circular Movement"—and indeed from the novel itself—that Bely regards such walls as symbolic of the stasis and dogma of modern life that must be blown apart. (We think too of the cranium—the "skull box"—as a container to be broken by the "bomb" of cerebral play.) The bomb, then, betokens necessary and inevitable apocalypse. In *Petersburg*, its explosive force is purely destructive. Dudkin, who manufactures the bomb and delivers it to the Ableukhov house, acts as an agent of destruction, but all unwittingly, for he believes that he is merely delivering the "little bundle" for safekeeping. In one instance he does consciously become a destroyer, when he murders Lippanchenko (who at the moment of his death becomes a kind of bomb, as gases explode from him and a "volcano" opens up in his stomach). But the act ends in the annihilation of the self, that is, in madness. Likewise, the explosion of the bomb in the sardine tin removes the Ableukhov house and Petersburg (if not literally destroying them), and makes impossible any reconstitution of the Ableukhov family. However, the evidence of "Circular Movement" and other works—Bely expects his readers to have his entire oeuvre always in mind—shows that Bely believed that destructiveness should go hand in hand with liberation and creativity.

In the 1910 essay titled "The Crisis of Consciousness and Henrik Ibsen" Bely observes: "To place dynamite under history itself in the name of absolute values, which consciousness has not yet revealed—this is the terrible conclusion to be drawn from the lyrics of Nietzsche and the drama of Ibsen. To explode, along with one's age, in order to strive toward genuine reality—that is the only way of not perishing." Nietzsche

49. *Zarathustra*, pt. 2, "On Redemption," in *Portable Nietzsche*, p. 253.
50. Ibid.

and Ibsen were for him the "two greatest revolutionaries of our time," but could "only see the way out"; they did not show us how to bridge the "catastrophe that awaits us."[51] A year later, in *The Tragedy of Art* (*Tragediya tvorchestva*), Bely makes a similar point about Nietzsche: he is "the greatest artist in Europe" who "throws his bomb at us—*Zarathustra.*"[52] Presumably Bely sees his own *Petersburg* as a bomb in this sense. However, it is a bomb that does not merely destroy, but—like the works of Ibsen and Nietzsche—clears the way for new creativity, a rebirth.

That Bely believed in the possibility of rebirth can be seen from the novel he intended to write as a sequel to *Petersburg*: "The Invisible City" ("Nevidimyi Grad").[53] Was Nikolay to be reborn in this sequel? Was he or a new hero to go beyond mere cognition to cognition animated with the creative principle hinted at in *Petersburg*—the "White Domino," whom several of the characters glimpse but fail to recognize?[54] In other terms, was someone to recognize the teleological principle that can turn meaningless cycles and repetitions into the whorls of the spiral moving toward ultimate illumination, making what seems like an ending into a new beginning? We shall never know, because the novel was never written. As it was, Bely's next novel, *Kotik Letaev,* is set entirely in the mind of a child and is the first chapter, as it were, of the grandiose epic (*epopeya*)

51. *Arabeski*, p. 174. Ibsen also figures in "Circular Movement," though much less than Nietzsche. Bely calls both of them "mountain dwellers," and adds that "everyone is aware of the clear vision [or "clairvoyance"—*yasnovidenie*] of mountain dwellers" (61). As early as December 1905, in the essay "Ibsen i Dostoevsky" (where Nietzsche is also present), Bely had written of the need to leave behind the fetid air and hysteria of Dostoevsky's vile taverns, where "mystics fraternize with policemen," and "ascend": "mountain clarity demands ascent" (*Arabeski*, p. 94). The parallels with Dudkin in the novel are obvious. All this suggests that the ideas that resulted in *Petersburg* were long in gestation.

52. *Tragediya tvorchestva: Dostoevsky i Tolstoy* (Moscow, 1911), p. 13. The image of the bomb, the favorite weapon of Russian revolutionary terrorists, and the 1910 reference to "dynamite" were very likely prompted by a sentence in the first part of the "Why I Am a Destiny" section of Nietzsche's *Ecce Homo*: "I am no man, I am dynamite" (*Basic Writings of Nietzsche*, ed. Walter Kaufmann [New York: Modern Library, 1968], p. 782). In an essay titled "Iskusstvo," written in the autumn of 1908, Bely had stated: "My art is a bomb that I throw; the life that lies outside me is a bomb thrown at me" (*Arabeski*, p. 216). It is doubtful, however, that this image was drawn from *Ecce Homo*: that work had been published in 1908, but only in an expensive limited edition of 1,250 copies; it did not appear in the generally accessible collected works until 1910. *Ecce Homo* is mentioned in "Circular Movement," as well as in the later *Krizis kul'tury.*

53. On June 10 (23), 1912, Bely wrote to Blok: "I have totally exhausted myself working on the novel [*Petersburg*], and I have promised myself to refrain from depicting the *negative sides of life* for a long time to come. In the third part of my series '*East and West*' I will depict wholesome and ennobling elements of 'Life and the Spirit.' I am sick and tired of having to rummage around in vileness." By December 28, 1912 (January 10, 1913), the title had come to him: "When the second part is finished [. . .] I would like to start on the third, '*The Invisible City*' [. . .]" (Blok and Bely, *Perepiska,* pp. 301, 309).

54. The White Domino has been identified by some readers as the "etheric Christ" of anthroposophy, by others as anthroposophy's Archangel Michael (he is called Misha). His presence suggests that a means of uniting human beings may exist in a world where the forces of evil are in ascendancy and where "universal provocation" abounds.

called "I," the "panorama of human consciousness" itself which he planned but never completed. The "Symbol," Bely argued in "The Line," was to be the means for this transfiguration. And the novel may be Bely's "sermon" (*propoved'*) on the necessity for such transfiguration, for as he remarked in "Circular Movement," the "sermon is creation" (69).

Bely may well, in fact, have meant the "sermon"—his novel—to be the vehicle of such creation. Perhaps that seems improbable at first. To the outer eye, *Petersburg* looks highly conventional. It has a prologue and an epilogue; eight chapters of more or less equal length, each with an epigraph, the fourth functioning as a pivot; a fairly consistent unity of time and space; and a simple plot (the terrorist conspiracy). This structure can be likened to a solid edifice. But pulling against it is an element of sheer sound, suggested, for instance, in the "ooo" that echoes throughout. Movement is created, we might say, from the pull of these two opposites. Put another way, we see a double emphasis. On the one hand, there is presentation, the actual narrative, which is linear; yet in the numerous references to earlier Russian literature it is circular as well, a kind of summation or "return" of an entire period of culture. On the other hand, there is "creation," as expressed in what Bely calls, in "Circular Movement," a "living, flowing word" (57), which differs from sheer sound in that it is structured, and from sheer structure in that it moves.

None of the characters in the novel is capable of such "living speech." Apollon Apollonovich is all words in his government capacity, where "every verbal exchange had to have a goal, plain and straight as a line" (122). Yet in encounters with his son or the servants he becomes almost inarticulate. His puns are most telling. Of course, they are laughably moronic. More important, they mix animate and inanimate, thereby suggesting that he has no real sense (*smysl*) of language whenever he cannot make his bureaucratic abstractions. And for years on end he has been repeating the same puns, over and over. This is not so much an indication of his attachment to routine as it is yet another manifestation of his essential lack of creativity (despite his name, Apollo) and of the automatization of his life and thought. For him, language has become idiotically self-referential, like everything else. It refers to nothing live and is fatally separated from the life that produced it. So is the speech of all the characters, but this characteristic is taken to an extreme in the Senator. By the end all speech, for him, has come down to one "point," the Egyptian name Dauphsekhrut (with all that Egypt implies for Bely), about whom his son is writing. Once more we are reminded that Bely saw the degeneration of language as yet another manifestation of the "mouldering head" of modern culture.

Let us remember, however, that for Bely the book is not coextensive with the experiences of its characters. If it is a "true" book, like the Gospels, Gogol, and *Zarathustra*, which are singled out in "Circular Movement"—and presumably *Petersburg* too—it is an embodiment of universal truth. Bely means this literally, as is clear from an elaborate argument in "Circular Movement." Thought, he says, precedes all: "in the beginning were created the heavens with their earths, for thought actually did create the heavens and their earths" (59). And the true "you" is "out there" too, in the "spaces," as an "enormous and shining giant," "you yourself" who are "outside yourself," while also embodied in the bones and tissues of your organism:

> Your ordinary thought is now the firm-boned skeleton of this solar thought; the sun's thought has now thrown your ordinary feeling over thought's head: this feeling is the feeling of space, for space is the muscles of solar creation; your will is now thrown over the head of thoughts, and beyond the muscles of feelings, for that will is time; times are nerves of a radiant being, and it itself is the blood of the universe: spark-begetting lights.
> You are now that very sun which illuminated the page, and that sun which has been placed in you: from the occiput to the chest. [59]

The book, Bely insists, bears the same relationship to universal thought as does the body. He even resorts to anatomical imagery to make his point:

> The soul of time is the unity of a center aware of itself. This center is our "I." The soul of lines [on a page] is the unity of a thought building itself (for man's thought builds itself—it does not hang in the air ready-made). The line is the first corporeality [*telesnost'*] in thought; a nerve filament that surrounds the electrical current of a mighty cerebral blow. In blows is the pulsation of the lines; and the line ought to strike on *an object*, not strike the air. The body of the line is connective tissue which twines around the nerves (the bones are built from connective tissue: the nervous system has to be set on something; a nervous system without bone amounts to picking around in oneself [*samokovyryanie*]). The aggregate of pages is muscles; and the title page is the skin. [58]

Just as the body does not incorporate only the thought of the individual possessor of the body, so the book is not merely the creation of the author. Rather, it is "the final investiture in flesh of all-joyous and *living* creation, the three-dimensional projection of a four-dimensional being: the book itself is always the body of the Angel. The luminous and immense Archangel who has been crucified for our sake into the bony chaos of matter: that is the book" (58). Like the body, the true book is not merely physical: "the visible world itself is only the beating heart of some electric being flying from universe to universe" (57). One difference, however—and here we are interpreting Bely—is that it is very difficult to transcend the body. Two instances of failure can be seen in *Petersburg*, in Apollon and Nikolay, and two in *Zarathustra* (as Bely reads it), in Nietzsche and his hero. Another difference is that the body perishes but the true book does not.

Yet the true book does not really live until it is set in motion by the act of reading. And Bely describes this process in his favorite line/circle/spiral imagery.

> The run-on line that forms the surface of the page is the uniting of circular movement to linear movement; in moving from line to line the eye describes a circle. The uniting of one page to another combines circular and linear movement and forms a spiral. The truth of the book is spiral; the truth of the book is the eternal changing of unchanging positions. That truth does not lie either in evolution or in the unchanging nature of repetitions. That truth lies in the reincarnation *of that which has been posited* once and for all. But that which has been posited once and for all is Eternity.
>
> If only the *line* of evolution predominated in the world, then there would be no books: while you are writing a book, everything in you has changed. If a circle described once and for all predominated in the world, then all the books would have been created before the creation of the world, and there would be nothing to write; everything that had been written would have the appearance of a single plane: the circle is a plane. But the book is possible in the spiral: in it are the endless reincarnations of the book that has been written once and for all—the book of Destinies. [58]

Through the act of reading, then, we become one with the universe that is embodied in and through the book. And Bely suggests strongly—at least in this article—that books are the only way in which this movement into the universe can be accomplished. "People do not read books," he says, and therefore never experience what books can do.

The point, with reference to *Petersburg,* is not that the characters do not read books—all of them do—or even that they do not read "true" books. Dudkin has perhaps dipped into Nietzsche; Nikolay is steeped in Kant; Apollon has certainly read important writers. The point, rather, is that the characters are too limited and in most cases too frightened to read as Bely thinks they should. The process of making and reading the book is reserved to the transaction between reader and writer—between us and Bely (and his various narratorial hypostases). Reader and writer survive the novel; the narrator distances himself—and us—from the characters in various ways, making it impossible for us (and him) to identify ourselves fully with any one of them, and thus with their fates. In reading, then, we create the spiral that pulls us out of ourselves, detaches us from the fate of Nikolay, Apollon, Dudkin, Petersburg, and Russia. Bely does not say what happens once we have completed the book and return to our normal modes of existence. We may take the book up again. But is that not one of those fateful "returns" against which we are warned, again and again? Bely leaves us in doubt on this question; but he leaves us in no doubt at all that we as readers—and he as narrator—have moved beyond the book yet have been able to do so only in and through the book, which, like the Symbol-Word, has both cognitive and creative possibilities.[55]

For the book offers the possibility of movement without end along the spiral. And any interpretation of this particular book, *Petersburg*, should not be limited to or by the articles of 1912 that we have been examining. They provide no keys to its mysteries. If we attempt to find a philosopher's stone in Bely (or worse, outside him altogether, say in anthroposophy), we fail: readings of Bely must honor his addiction to plurality and his concern with dynamism, the notion of continuous creation, which occupied a central position in all his writings after 1910 as he combated what he considered the chronic tendency of human thought to render static that which it purports to explain. Nothing irritated him more (especially in his later years, as his wife's memoirs show)[56] than people who regarded him as some kind of prophet with answers to life's mysteries. He intended that his readers (and listeners) should fend for themselves among a proliferation of meanings. Any reading must take account of the full range of contrasting, even contradictory elements in *Petersburg*. Otherwise we neglect the discontinuities and fail to honor the possibility even of incoherence in the text. This is not to say that any and all readings of Bely's works are equal, but that the authority of different readings cannot be tested by references to one idea or single line of thought in his mind. As he wrote in "Circular Movement," "we think in contrasts" (53). The "truth" of *Petersburg* is given in no postulate, but takes form from a complex of contradictions and half-truths that are in ceaseless movement.

55. In such earlier articles as "Magiya slov" (1909) and "Emblematika smysla" (1909), Bely had argued that the Symbol-Word created as it named. It brought something into being, yet was in touch with an Ideal as well. It was thus both objective and subjective: "The word creates a new third world—a world of·sound symbols, by means of which the mysteries of the world posited outside me are illuminated, just as are the mysteries within me" ("Magiya slov," in *Simvolizm*, p. 430).
56. See K. N. Bugaeva, *Vospominaniya o Belom*.

4

Kotik Letaev, The Baptized Chinaman, and Notes of an Eccentric

Vladimir E. Alexandrov

Shortly after completing *Petersburg,* Bely began to write a cycle of autobiographical novels that he intended to unify under the title "My Life" and that he projected might fill ten volumes. *Kotik Letaev* (written 1915–16, published 1917–18), *The Baptized Chinaman* (*Kreshchenyi kitaets,* written 1920–21, published 1927), and *Notes of an Eccentric* (*Zapiski chudaka,* written 1918–21, published 1922) are the works that grew out of this plan.[1]

The common genesis of the three works explains numerous thematic and formal interconnections among them. But they also represent the culmination of several major trends in Bely's fiction that begin in his earliest belletristic efforts—the experimental symphonies. At the same time, they signal Bely's turning toward overt autobiographical and memoiristic writing, which became one of his main preoccupations during the last dozen years of his life.

All three works are difficult to characterize generically. The most important difference between them and Bely's works from the symphonies to *Petersburg,* as well as the majority of long prose narratives that one normally thinks of as novels, is their subject matter. As one concludes from the close parallels among Bely's published memoirs of his childhood, *Kotik Letaev,* and *The Baptized Chinaman,* the latter two works

This revised version of chap. 4 of my *Andrei Bely: The Major Symbolist Fiction* (Harvard University Press, 1985) is published here with the permission of the publishers. Copyright © 1985 by the President and Fellows of Harvard College.

1. K. Bugaeva, A. Petrovsky [and D. Pines], "Literaturnoe nasledstvo Andreya Belogo," in *Literaturnoe nasledstvo,* no. 27–28 (Moscow, 1937), pp. 604–6. For an illuminating discussion of the three works and the connections among them, see John D. Elsworth, *Andrey Bely: A Critical Study of the Novels* (Cambridge, Eng., 1983), chaps. 5–7.

are actually very thinly veiled accounts of periods of the author's infancy and boyhood. Similarly, Bely's comments in *Notes of an Eccentric* also place that work firmly in the realm of autobiography. It should be stressed, however, that a significant autobiographical bent can be discerned in all of Bely's earlier works of belles-lettres as well. Indeed, there is an intensification in his commitment to the experienced minutiae of his life from the symphonies to *The Silver Dove* to *Petersburg*. However, this should not be understood simply as yet another instance of the perhaps inevitable phenomenon of an author incorporating personal experiences into his fictions. Chance ultimately rules over such inclusions. In Bely's case, by contrast, autobiography can be seen as an outgrowth of the symbolistic epistemology that is the foundation of his art.

Bely's view of symbolic art as based in a special type of perception appears in his first published essay, "The Forms of Art" ("Formy iskusstva," 1902). In "Criticism and Symbolism" ("Krititsizm i simvolizm," 1904) and the important later essay "The Magic of Words" ("Magiya slov," 1909), he makes the perceiving individual's "inner experiences"—his ideas and feelings—one of two components in a symbol, the other being that aspect of the outside world upon which the perceiver casts his gaze.[2] In other essays, including "The Apocalypse in Russian Poetry" ("Apokalipsis v russkoi poezii," 1905), "The Emblematics of Meaning" ("Emblematika smysla," 1909), and "The Crisis of Consciousness and Henrik Ibsen" ("Krizis soznaniya i Genrikh Ibsen," 1910), Bely progresses to a view of human inner experiences as being rooted in or stemming from a transcendent realm.[3] Thus, in the theory of symbolism that Bely had formulated by the end of the first decade of this century, the individual cognitive act that constitutes a symbolic perception or that underlies the creation of a literary symbol is expressive of a cosmic truth as well as of the individual's inner state. As a result, a gravitation toward first-person narrative would seem to be inevitable, as would a preoccupation with autobiography. And by virtue of their relation to the transcendent, the personal, inner experiences of an individual acquire a validity and truth value that "mere" fiction lacks.

Bely's immersion in Rudolf Steiner's anthroposophy starting in 1912 could only reinforce his belief in the validity of his own theory of symbolism. He found in Steiner's numerous lectures and writings a vast image-laden cosmology that was essentially congruent with the abstractly formulated world view he had developed in his essays. The goal of anthroposophy is for the adept to become aware of his place in a com-

2. The three essays were reprinted in *Simvolizm* (Moscow, 1910).
3. "The Emblematics of Meaning" was first printed in *Simvolizm*. "The Apocalypse in Russian Poetry" was included in *Lug zelenyi* (Moscow, 1910). "The Crisis of Consciousness and Henrik Ibsen" first appeared in *Arabeski* (Moscow, 1911). For a different reading of Bely's theory of symbolism, see Steven Cassedy's essay, chap. 8 in this volume.

plex physical-spiritual cosmos that is undergoing an elaborate teleological evolution, and in which Christ is the central regenerative force. The initiate achieves this goal through special meditative praxis, which again puts personal occult experiences at the center of both the individual's life and the art he may create.[4]

Of the three works, *Kotik Letaev* has fared best with readers from the time of its first publication to the present day. Indeed, *Kotik Letaev* is invariably mentioned together with *The Silver Dove* and *Petersburg* as one of Bely's greatest achievements in belletristic prose. The reasons for this judgment are complex. Suffice it to say that the dazzling formal and stylistic effects of *Kotik Letaev* are largely absent from *The Baptized Chinaman*, whereas *Notes of an Eccentric* suffers from chaotic organization and what seem to be self-indulgent *longueurs* on Bely's part. This evaluation of Bely's legacy is reflected in the pages that follow, most of which deal with *Kotik Letaev*. My primary focus throughout is the core of Bely's art—the metaphysical beliefs that determine the themes, style, and form of his works.

Kotik Letaev

1

In accordance with Bely's own practice, *Kotik Letaev* is usually labeled a "novel," and for convenience I will refer to it by the same term.[5] However, Bely's references to the work after he completed it suggest that he did not think of it as fictional.

In his memoir *On the Border of Two Centuries*, Bely says that in not a single one of his books had he given as straightforward "a copy" of something he had actually experienced as in *Kotik Letaev*: "it was not *Andrey Bely* who wrote it, but Boris Nikolaevich Bugaev who naturalistically drew what he remembered all his life."[6] A most unusual feature of the work is its forays back in time to the moment of Bely's birth

4. Strictly speaking, the transcendent realm of Bely's theoretical essays cannot be equated with the spiritual realm of anthroposophy. According to anthroposophy, the spiritual world is immanent rather than transcendent. However, because anthroposophical occult experiences, such as those that Bely depicts in his works, resemble what an impartial observer might call contacts with a transcendent realm, it seems simplest to equate the two. It is also worth stressing that Steiner's use of the word "occult" has no pejorative connotations.

5. Bely also called the work a "Symphonic tale" (*Simfonicheskaya povest'*); see K. Bugaeva and A. Petrovsky, op. cit., pp. 604–5. Page references to the following edition of the novel will be given in the text: *Kotik Letaev* (Petersburg, 1922; reprinted Munich, 1964). The second page reference in each pair of references indicates the English translation by Gerald Janecek (Ann Arbor, 1971), which I have silently corrected in many places.

6. *Na rubezhe dvukh stoletii* (Moscow and Leningrad, 1930), p. 165. Bely makes the same claim in a preface to the novel that was first published in *Novyi Zhurnal*, no. 101 (1970), pp. 69–70.

and to his prenatal existence; associated with them are depictions of the spiritual cosmos. Here *Kotik Letaev* obviously and markedly differs from any number of autobiographical novels of childhood, such as Tolstoy's *Childhood, Boyhood, Youth* (1852–1857) and Sergey Aksakov's *Years of Childhood of Bagrov-Grandson* (1858). As one might expect, Bely could not acknowledge his occult beliefs publicly in the Soviet Union in 1930. Thus, in *On the Border of Two Centuries* he attempts (unsuccessfully) to give a purely physiological motivation for the occult imagery that fills the work. Nevertheless, his testimony provides evidence to support a view of *Kotik Letaev* as bridging reality and fiction.

In *Notes of an Eccentric,* a frankly memoiristic work published in Berlin in 1922—a less repressive place and time— Bely states openly that he came to know the prenatal experiences he described in *Kotik Letaev* by means of anthroposophical meditations.[7] Later, in a letter of 1927 that was obviously not intended for publication, Bely speaks of the "anthroposophical academic task" that is embodied in *Kotik Letaev*: "through an expansion of memory truly to see something of what had not been seen" in infancy. And in *Why I Became a Symbolist,* an important memoir he wrote for his "desk drawer" in 1928, Bely continued to claim that he described his spiritual development "most exactly" in *Kotik Letaev.*[8]

Bely actually wrote the novel while helping to build the Goetheanum, the combined theater and temple that Steiner designed and anthroposophical initiates took part in constructing in Dornach, Switzerland. Given his total immersion in the "occult science" at this time in his life (1914–16), and given the central importance in anthroposophy of the "Akashic record"—a cosmic transcript of all human experience that can be read with great accuracy by the initiate who has undergone the requisite training—there is every reason to assume that Bely meant all his depictions of his seemingly fanciful spiritual experiences to be taken as literally true. In fact, the inviolate authority of the Akashic record for the anthroposophist lends weight to the accuracy of the clairvoyant's recovered past experiences that simple memory lacks. From this point of view, therefore, the sole features of *Kotik Letaev* that can be called fictional are the characters' names (most have been changed) and a reference to "sisters" (assuming he is not making a figurative reference to his cousins), while Bely was in fact an only child.[9] Clearly, however, the high degree of artistic organization the work evinces—its widespread use of leitmotifs, metrical passages, structural echoes, alliteration, and the

---

7. *Zapiski chudaka,* 2 vols. (Moscow and Berlin, 1922; reprinted Lausanne, 1973), I, 46.

8. Bely's letter to Ivanov-Razumnik was published by Georges Nivat in *Cahiers du monde russe et soviétique,* 15, no. 1–2 (1974), pp. 74–75. *Pochemu ya stal simvolistom* (Ann Arbor, 1982), p. 9.

9. For a key to the actual identities of characters that Bely hid behind fictional names, see Dmitrij Tschiżewskij's "Erläuterungen" in the reprint of the novel cited in n. 5 (pp. xiv–xvi).

like—should serve as a reminder of the fact that *Kotik Letaev* records the occult experiences of a *writer*. Steiner's anthroposophical writings and mystery dramas differ greatly in style from Bely's works.

Inevitably, given the subject matter, *Kotik Letaev*'s focus is the formation and development of the eponymous protagonist's personality. External events are relatively few as a result, and Kotik's story consists largely of his gradual withdrawal from and loss of unmediated contact with the spiritual realm out of which he descended when he was born. This general process clearly derives from Steiner's view that "the human soul and entire being are, during the first years of earthly life, in much closer connection with the spiritual worlds of the higher hierarchies than they are later."[10] Concurrent with this process is the gradual crystallization of Kotik's sense of self as differentiating from the external world of matter.

Bely had earlier intended the work that became *Kotik Letaev* to be the final volume of a trilogy that began with *The Silver Dove* and continued with *Petersburg*. Stylistically and formally *Kotik Letaev* is of a piece with those works, although there are interesting new developments in the devices Bely employs, especially with regard to narrative point of view. The importance of leitmotifs, rhythmicized passages, and alliteration is even greater in *Kotik Letaev* than in *Petersburg*. As in earlier works, both the form of the narrative and the protagonist's life progress along spirals, with cyclical repetitions of Kotik's experiences looping around a teleological progression toward ultimate illumination.[11] And more than in previous works, but less than in those that would follow, Bely coins numerous neologisms in *Kotik Letaev* to render his unique world view.[12]

As for the content, the single most important stimulus for the total immersion in autobiography that resulted in *Kotik Letaev* (and in Bely's plan to write the autobiographical epic of which *Kotik Letaev* was supposed to be the beginning) was Bely's involvement in anthroposophy. The goal of this teaching is to transcend the limitations of the self and to achieve enlightenment. The matter of how the individual ascends to this state inevitably becomes all-important to him. Thus, although Viktor Shklovsky was correct in signaling Bely's growing involvement with autobiography beginning with *Kotik Letaev*, he erred in suggesting that anthroposophy and autobiography are at odds in Bely's work.[13] If anything, the anthroposophical belief that one's past can be retrieved from the cosmic Akashic record should motivate autobiography. Moreover,

10. Rudolf Steiner, *The Spiritual Guidance of Man* [trans. of *Die Geistige Führung des Menschen und der Menschheit*, 1911] (Spring Valley, N.Y., 1950), p. 6.

11. For more on the spiral, see Gerald Janecek, "The Spiral as Image and Structural Principle in Andrej Belyj's *Kotik Letaev*," *Russian Literature*, 4 (1976), pp. 357–64.

12. For a good discussion of the novel's style, see Georges Nivat, "Le Palimpseste de l'enfance," in *Kotik Letaiev* (Lausanne, 1973), pp. 282–88.

13. See his "Andrey Bely," *Russkii Sovremennik*, no. 2 (1924), pp. 231–45.

given the general harmony between Bely's theory of Symbolism and anthroposophy,[14] it is not surprising that the anthroposophical world view underlying *Kotik Letaev* should be in fundamental agreement with the metaphysical schema found in the earlier novels, especially that of *Petersburg*.

To be sure, there are several shifts in emphasis. With the disappearance of the Solov'evian theme of pan-Mongolism and the attendant mood of febrile apocalyptic dread, the atmosphere in *Kotik Letaev* is somewhat lighter than that of *Petersburg*. However, the change is not wholly to the generally calm and roseate atmosphere of Steiner's descriptive writings (his "mystery dramas" are another matter). Kotik, like his predecessors in Bely's other works, is very much under the *coercive* sway of a spiritual realm; in fact, he is immersed in it more deeply than any other character in Bely's canon. In part, such absorption follows inevitably from Steiner's belief that the human soul sojourns in an otherworldly realm before birth and remains attached to it in early childhood. But Kotik also expects to suffer a Christlike passion in the future. This belief may be due as much to the simple fact that Bely did not have a happy childhood as to the important role that Christ has for the intitiate in anthroposophy. It was typical of Bely to give cosmic significance to his own and his characters' troubled spiritual states.

The most striking innovation in *Kotik Letaev* (though an inevitable feature of childhood autobiographies) is its double first-person perspective. As the narrator makes clear in the Foreword, he is thirty-five years old at the time he is telling his story. He has achieved a state of clairvoyant "self-consciousness," which "has burst open my brain and hurtled into childhood." The result is that he and his infant self can now "converse" and "understand" each other (9/3). This image of the adult confronting himself as a child comes directly from Steiner's explanation that the adept who has achieved occult insight "beholds his new-born self as another being standing before him."[15] The achievement of "self-consciousness" is the pivotal event in the narrator-author's life because it makes possible the work he is writing.

The adult narrator also draws a parallel between the special form of cognition that his self-consciousness denotes and the beginning awareness of a child: "Self-consciousness, like an infant within me, opened its eyes wide." Thus Bely is implying that his procedure in the rest of the work will be to present his own development from the point of view of the "occult science" of anthroposophy, which retroactively

---

14. See my study *Andrei Bely: The Major Symbolist Fiction* (Cambridge, Mass., 1985), chap. 3.

15. Rudolf Steiner, *An Outline of Occult Science* [*Die Geheimwissenschaft im Umriss*, 1909], trans. Maud Monges and Henry B. Monges, rev. Lisa D. Monges (Spring Valley, N.Y., 1972), pp. 338–39.

illuminates for him the physical and spiritual sides of his infancy. Implied also is that the child's spiritual development will be given in the terms of an anthroposophical conception of an adept's ascent to ultimate illumination. (This indeed proves to be the case in the body of the novel, and represents an interesting variant on Ernst Heinrich Haeckel's seminal idea that "ontogeny recapitulates phylogeny"—that the development of an individual reflects the evolution of the species. Haeckel's notion reappears in various forms in *Kotik Letaev*, and is a fundamental characteristic of Steiner's world view and conception of man in general. Indeed, Steiner is known to have admired Haeckel's ideas.) The effect of Bely's tactic, therefore, is that the same phenomenon—namely, Kotik Letaev himself—is examined from two obviously interrelated but still widely divergent points of view: that of the infant's confused and uncomprehending perception of the world in which he exists (presumably preserved in the adult Kotik's normal memory) and that of the infant's spiritual experiences as retrieved, ordered, and illuminated retroactively by the adult's occult clear vision. This was, presumably, the ultimate significance of Bely's remark about the "anthroposophical academic task" that motivated his writing of the work. The fact that the second point of view is occult rather than simply adult is Bely's greatest innovation in the genre of childhood autobiography. One must assume, however, that some overlap between these two viewpoints is inevitable because the adult's clairvoyance should also be able to resurrect the totality of the child's experiences, including the confusion.

The narrative shifts often and easily between the two poles. Rapid shifts in point of view and narrative voice appeared in earlier works of Bely's as well, and contributed much to their nervous narrative texture, as well as to their elliptical suggestiveness. But *Kotik Letaev* contains the first instance of perspectives that both derive from and are directed at the same multidimensional persona, which exists on both spiritual and material planes, rather than at some phenomenon external to it.

The ultimate result of this practice, however, is comparable to that in the earlier works. In *Petersburg*, for instance, the shifts from the Senator's rigid and unimaginative cogitations to an indented passage about the Flying Dutchman conjuring land out of fog, then back to the Senator, sketch several different but interrelated planes of reality that define the complex material and spiritual world posited by the novel. In *Kotik Letaev*, the shifts in point of view sketch the different planes of being—both eternal and time-bound—on which Kotik himself exists. As a result, he emerges as a composite of physical and spiritual dimensions—indeed, as the entity that bridges them. Like the city in *Petersburg*, Kotik is both embedded in and a symbol of the entire cosmos.

In addition to defining in the Foreword the parameters that he will use in the work—in contrast to *Petersburg*, where the Prologue serves as a foil for the remainder of the text—the narrator adumbrates the major themes that will constitute the work itself: (1) the "triangular" relationship among the protagonist, the realm of the spirit, and the world of matter; (2) the path one must follow to achieve "self-consciousness"; (3) the role that an exalted being will play in Kotik's destiny; and (4) the relation of language to reality.

Intimately connected with the first theme—the nature of the connection between the individual and the transcendent—is the entire question of perception and cognition, as it also was in *Petersburg*. And it is to this topic, or rather to this complex of ontological and epistemological interrelationships, that I would like to turn first.

2

In the Foreword, the narrator depicts a rugged mountain landscape that one is inevitably tempted to relate to the Swiss Alps which Bely enjoyed climbing while in Dornach.[16] The fact that the Foreword ends with an indication of the Swiss locales and the year in which Bely (as opposed to Kotik Letaev) wrote it reinforces the autobiographism of the text as a whole. More important, however, the narrator clearly wants the dramatic scenery to be understood as a record of his turbulent past existence as well as a prefiguration of his future. He presents himself as being at a summit in his life, which one must conclude is the consequence of the "self-consciousness" that he has achieved.

But the jagged mountain scenery is not merely a metaphor, emblem, or objective correlative for the narrator's spiritual development. Rather, it appears also to be the actual physical deposit of the narrator's spiritual growth: "At your feet is all that once grew out of you painfully and that was you;/that kept falling away from you like dead stone and kept solidifying as cliffs" (12/5). In this instance, the narrator has described what appears to be the same reification of thought into matter that Bely dramatized as occurring in the first chapter of *Petersburg*. It will be recalled that both Dudkin and the Senator's house were shown to be products of the Senator's "cerebral play," which in turn was a "mask" for occult forces that intruded into the narrator-author's mind as well as that of the characters.[17]

Extrinsic support for the view that the cognitive creative process established in *Petersburg* also operates in *Kotik Letaev* is provided by Bely's

16. K. N. Bugaeva makes this connection openly in her memoir *Vospominaniya o Belom*, ed. John E. Malmstad (Berkeley, 1981), p. 52. See also Bely's memoir *Vospominaniya o Shteinere*, ed. Frédéric Kozlik (Paris, 1982), pp. 220, 234.

17. See Andrey Bely, *Petersburg*, trans., annot., and introd. Robert A. Maguire and John E. Malmstad (Bloomington, Ind., 1978; Hassocks, Sussex, 1979), pp. 20–22, 35–36.

revealing essay "On the Meaning of Cognition" (1916).[18] Because it is written entirely from an anthroposophical perspective, its argument is difficult to follow in places. Nevertheless, it clearly constitutes a theoretical disquisition about the same process of spiritual development that is dramatized on the pages of *Kotik Letaev*. The essay's relevance for the novel is further indicated by its year of composition and, most important, by the fact that it contains numerous specific formulations of key concepts that are nearly identical to those found in the novel. It is also worth noting that Bely underscored the significance of the essay long after he wrote it by referring to it as part of his lifelong attempt to produce a complete theory of symbolism. As he put it in his memoir *Between Two Revolutions*, "On the Meaning of Cognition" contains "traces" of the "skeleton" of the entire theory, which, although remaining unfinished, was clear in his mind.[19] This avowal provides additional evidence for the general continuity of Bely's thought before and after he fell under Steiner's influence. Moreover, it inadvertently reveals Bely's continuing loyalty to anthroposophy at a time when he took pains to hide it from public view in the Soviet Union.

The essay's particular utility is that it suggests a framework for understanding *Kotik Letaev* and shows the novel to be based in a much more orthodox conception of anthroposophy than was the case with *Petersburg*.[20] In the light of the essay, the narrator's task in *Kotik Letaev* is confirmed as the depiction of the achievement of "self-consciousness"— a direct knowledge of the higher worlds, which is the ultimate raison d'être of anthroposophy.

The idea of thought descending from the realm of spirit through man to create matter recurs in the essay a number of times. Speaking of the act of cognition, Bely affirms that "the world thoughts [*mirovye mysli*] are deposited [*slagayutsya*] in us by the world of thought, and through us incarnate the universe./We create a world in the world." In characterizing this created world, Bely echoes the Alpine imagery from the Foreword of *Kotik Letaev* when he says that "the world of concepts, objects, forms and images *crystallizes* within cognitive acts" (39; italics mine).

Numerous parallels can be found between Kotik's experiences with the worlds of matter and spirit and those of the narrator and characters of *Petersburg*. Moreover, because the novel is primarily concerned with the process of the individual's spiritual development, it is possible to

18. *O smysle poznaniya* (Petersburg, 1922; reprinted Chicago, 1965). Page references to the essay will be given in the text.

19. *Mezhdu dvukh revolyutsii* (Leningrad, 1934), p. 211.

20. Gerald Janecek provides another anthroposophical reading of *Kotik Letaev,* based directly on Steiner's own writings rather than on Bely's refraction of them, which is analogous to mine: "Anthroposophy in *Kotik Letaev,*" *Orbis Litterarum,* 29 (1974), pp. 245–67.

discern several stages in Kotik's relation to the material world on the one hand and to the spiritual cosmos on the other.

First of all, the narrator establishes the primacy of the otherworldly realm in the appearance of thought and the creation of the material world (as was also the case in *Petersburg*): "The world and thought are only the spumes: of menacing cosmic images; blood pulses with their flight; thoughts are lit by their fires; and these images are—myths" (19/11). Similarly, in "On the Meaning of Cognition," Bely speaks of matter and concepts as the "spumes" that "cool" out of the boiling of undifferentiated reality during the initial stage of cognition (44).

As in *Petersburg*, the thoughts that derive from an otherworldly realm are shown to have an intrusive and ultimately deterministic relation to the individual. In the early stage of his existence Kotik appears as a mere physical receptacle for thoughts: "an arising childly thought reminds one of a comet; now it falls into the body; and—its tail bloodies." This image recalls comparable ones for the transcendent's relation to the earth in the first two symphonies.[21] Significantly, the descent of thought into the body occurs immediately after Kotik's physical birth; in the preceding paragraph the narrator had described the moment when Kotik's head had emerged into the world while his feet were still in the womb (20/11–12).

An integral part of the narrator's description of the first, tentative, and ultimately ephemeral formation of Kotik's sense of self is the reification of intruding cosmic thoughts into the matter that defines Kotik's world. After experiencing the sensation of being a point that swells to a sphere, then bursts and re-forms a number of times, the narrator describes in an indented paragraph how "gloom (like a snakeskin from a little snake) began to crawl from me; sensations separated from skin: they disappeared under my skin: out fell lands born of blackness." The last phrase recalls the tortured mountain landscape of the Foreword.

The impression that the Alpine range truly was the by-product of the protagonist's spiritual development is supported by his explanation that his skin became "a corridor" for him. Immediately he extends this notion by asserting that "rooms are parts of the body; they have been cast off by me; and—they hang over me." Indeed, the narrator describes

21. See Andrey Bely, *Sobranie epicheskikh poem. Kniga pervaya: I. Severnaya simfoniya (1-aya, geroicheskaya). II. Simfoniya (2-aya, dramaticheskaya)*, vol. 4 (Moscow, 1917); both were reprinted in one volume: *Chetyre simfonii* (Munich, 1971). An English translation of the *Second Symphony* has been published: *The Dramatic Symphony and The Forms of Art*, trans. R. J. Keys, A. M. Keys, and J. D. Elsworth (Edinburgh, 1986). A "bloody meteor" that is associated with human evil appears in the *First Symphony* (p. 52) and a "heavy, interplanetary sphere" (p. 195) that is linked to the apocalypse appears in the *Second*. In the essay "Symbolism as a World View" ("Simvolizm kak miroponimanie," 1903), Bely speaks of a falling meteor as an "intrusion of Eternity" that acts as a reminder of the paltriness of man's state (*Arabeski*, p. 228).

throwing strange buildings out of his body, including a "temple of thought" which he solidifies as a skull. A time will come, he explains, when he will be able to remove his skull and walk through it as through a temple (26–27/16–17). The creation of the temple of course recalls the creation of Apollon Apollonovich's house by his "cerebral play" in *Petersburg*, as well as the actual physical appearance of the Goetheanum: the two intersecting spherical cupolas that formed the roof of the original building (which no longer stands) had a cranial shape. And Bely's description in *Notes of an Eccentric* of a night watch in the Goetheanum recalls the skull imagery in *Kotik Letaev*.[22]

Another direct association between thought and its condensation into matter appears in a scene where Kotik redefines both himself and the space around him after a moment of fright (52/35–36). At the end of this passage, as well as later in the work, when the narrative spirals back to Kotik's first moments (111/81; 186/139), the narrator establishes a connection between the transcendent and the ability to generate physical reality (including himself!) by saying that he "pulsed with time . . . with the corridor, the dining room, the living room." As subsequent passages in the novel make clear, a pulsation or rhythm is the way in which Kotik perceives an ordering principle or energy to be flowing into him and communicating with him from the spiritual universe out of which he descended into his fleshly being. The "pulses" are thus analogous to the "occult forces" that the narrator-author of *Petersburg* said are hidden by the "mask" of "cerebral play"—the thoughts that occur spontaneously in characters.[23] The presence of metrical passages in *Kotik Letaev* inevitably reinforces for the reader the effect of the narrator's words about the occult meaning of rhythm. But for reasons to be discussed below, the rhythm in the novel's narrative should be taken at most as an inducement for the reader to search his own existence for comparable experiences, rather than as a bridge thrown between reality and fiction, which was the way "cerebral play" was meant to function in *Petersburg*.

In *Petersburg* the scene of Dudkin's confrontation with Shishnarfne was modeled on the anthroposophical conception of "thought beings" and "sound beings" whom the adept could come to know, and who in turn can enter the human world through the adept.[24] This process constitutes an anthroposophical variant of the reification of thought discussed above (and helps explain why Bely found Steiner's ideas congenial). The same schema operates in *Kotik Letaev*, albeit without the

22. *Zapiski chudaka*, I, 93. Photographs of the first Goetheanum appear between pp. 36 and 37 of Bely's *Vospominaniya o Shteinere*.

23. See Bely's essay "Zhezl Aarona (O slove v poezii)" in *Skify*, 1 (1917), for a discussion of the connection between rhythm and meaning on the example of Fedor Tyutchev's poetry (pp. 201–3).

24. See Alexandrov, *Andrei Bely: The Major Symbolist Fiction*, pp. 118–19.

atmosphere of hallucinatory terror that colors many of the occult experiences characters have in *Petersburg*. For example, sound is presented as a means of contact between the individual and the transcendent in passages about Kotik's doll, Ruprecht, which is like "the life of sound in me [. . .]. I experienced it not in myself, but in a being of the realm of sound into which I was raised" (204/153). The narrator then explains that he was not given a clear view of the "realm of sound," but did manage to glimpse a "sound apartment with all the domestic belongings of rooms of sound." There is no indication here that this otherworldly version of the apartment is the source of the rooms Kotik deposited in a material version outside himself. Nevertheless, the "sound apartment" bears a relation to the Letaev apartment similar to that between a Platonic Idea and its material embodiment.

Kotik's spontaneous ability to have such experiences is lost after he turns four (94/68). Indeed, he finds this age to have been the turning point of his entire life: "the age of four had cut my life into two parts" (128/94). Here Bely is again following Steiner, who taught that the child's spiritual composition undergoes a radical change after the third year.[25] And a number of passages in the novel detail his growing estrangement from the spirit world (e.g., 76/54, 96/69, 150–51/112).

3

In addition to helping to illuminate the continuity between the creative-cognitive processes in *Petersburg* and *Kotik Letaev*, "On the Meaning of Cognition" serves to demonstrate the later novel's dependence on anthroposophy. Specifically, the essay reveals the extent to which *Kotik Letaev* is structured in accordance with Steiner's tripartite conception of the individual's ascent to "self-consciousness."

According to Steiner, a special form of meditation, which leads to a new sort of "sense-free thinking," is the path by which the initiate could come to a knowledge of the "higher worlds" and of his place in them. Steiner outlined the nature of this path in *The Philosophy of Freedom* (1894), his first major work, and returned to it repeatedly in later writings and lectures.

Numerous passages in *Kotik Letaev* appear to be transcripts of occult meditative experiences that Bely actually had. Perhaps the most striking is one describing a continuum between the adult narrator and his infant self:

> I close my eyes: I catch up to the spirits
> with my thoughts; there appear: —

25. See Steiner, *Spiritual Guidance of Man*, pp. 14–15.

—quiverings, sparkles
beneath my eyelids; I sense: the quiverings of the child's body; in the
quiverings a head—sprouts; arms and chest sprout for me like grass.
[267/202]

Here we seem to be presented with the narrator's cognitive entry into a
"higher realm" in which he perceives—or "remembers"—himself as a
child. The flashes of light that the adult sees are evidence of an occult
experience, as *Notes of an Eccentric* and some of Bely's anthroposophical
poetry confirm: both contain references to comparable displays.[26] Indeed, as I shall suggest, the whole experience resembles a transition
from the first to the second stage in Steiner's tripartite cognitive schema.

Other instances in which the novel's adult narrator appears to be
describing what might be termed meditative "curves" that lead from
some initial symbol or image he is contemplating to an occult insight
include his contemplation of a human skull and his invitation to the
reader to "imagine" one (33, 37/22, 24), his contemplation of clouds
(181–82/136), and his sensation that the hemispheres of his brain are
melting and preparing to take flight (271/205).

In anthroposophy, the first cognitive step the beginning adept can
reach by meditating on symbols is called "imagination." As Steiner puts
it in *An Outline of Occult Science,* the individual who achieves this stage
perceives "spiritual facts and beings to which the senses have no access."
The dominant characteristic of the higher world at this stage is that "a
continual transformation of one thing into another" takes the place of
earthly phenomena: "Birth and death are ideas that lose their significance in the imaginative world," and "in it there exist everywhere constant motion and transformation, nowhere are there points of rest."[27]

In "On the Meaning of Cognition," Bely speaks of "imagination" as
typified by a chaos of ideas, sensations, fantastic images, dreams, and the
like, in which "neither the world nor thought exists," and in which the
"crust" of familiar concepts is removed from the world and the world
melts "like ice" (46–47). This description bears a very close resemblance
to several passages in the Foreword to *Kotik Letaev,* where the narrator
says that "self-consciousness [. . .] has broken the ice of words, concepts
and meanings" (13/6). There are also passages, primarily in the earlier
chapters of the novel, in which the narrator describes the *instability* of the
infant's world in a way that suggests that Kotik is perceiving "imagina-
tively": "swarm, swarm—all was swarming," "metamorphoses envelop
one" (92/66).

One can also find throughout the text recurring instances of imagery

26. See the poems listed in n. 41 below; see also n. 27 to chap. 3 of this volume.
27. Steiner, *Outline of Occult Science,* pp. 271–72, 303–4.

that is ordered in accordance with the characteristics of anthroposophical "imagination." Recalling his father's mathematical notes and his
mumbling over them "Just so!" (*Tak-s* in Russian), Kotik says:

> These are—*little x's, y's, z's* [*iksiki,igreki, zetiki*] . . . *little dachshunds* [*taksiki*]; I
> encountered dachshunds on the boulevard.
>   I thought:—
>   —the "*x*"'s sprout in a shoot from the little lecture notebooks:
> in a greening, murmuring leaflet—from the swelling bud; they woodify as
> twigs; and they stick out afterwards . . . as a young man kept on: at the
> University, for Papa. [178/133; a similar passage appears on 97/70]

Comparable metamorphoses occur in relation to Kotik's memory of a
Greek vase (181/135), of his father's friends appearing as aquatic creatures (195/146), and about the flow of days (254/192).

It is worth stressing that Steiner's tripartite cognitive process is meant
to provide a mature adept with a way of gaining insight into the ultimate
spiritual truths of existence. This naturally raises the question of what
relation the above-mentioned instances of "imagination" have to the
double narrative viewpoint out of which the novel arises. It is a legitimate goal in anthroposophy for an adept to examine his past (including
his past lives) through meditation. But what about three-year-old Kotik,
who is simply too young to do very much consciously? Are we to assume
that the infant was *spontaneously* experiencing "imagination"? Or is this
the adult narrator's meditative experience coloring his presentation of
his childhood experience—the Heisenberg uncertainty principle of
means distorting the results, as it were? Since Steiner does not provide
for meditation by children of Kotik's age, we must conclude that Bely
has embroidered on orthodox anthroposophy by presenting Kotik's
childhood experiences in anthroposophical terms (a practice that recalls
his distortion of anthroposophy in *Petersburg*[28] and his conflation of
Nietzsche with Vladimir Solov'ev both in early essays and in works of
belles-lettres).

It is still possible, however, to understand Bely's ascription of meditative experiences to his infant self in a way that does not go against the
grain of the anthroposophical world view contained in the novel. Given
the importance of Haeckel's principle for both anthroposophy and *Kotik
Letaev* (where it is evoked often), one could see it as fitting that Kotik
would experience the stages of man's cognitive ascent to enlightenment
as he develops physically. In this way, the child recapitulates the highest
spiritual stages that Steiner taught initiates could achieve. And Bely
could be said to have preserved the spirit of anthroposophy, if not the
letter.

28. See Alexandrov, *Andrei Bely: The Major Symbolist Fiction*, pp. 117, 119.

The second stage of anthroposophical cognition is "inspiration," which provides the initiate with "points of rest" absent from the metamorphoses of "imagination": "one learns to know the inner qualities of *beings* who transform themselves [. . .] and discerns a great number of relationships between one being and another." It is most interesting for understanding *Kotik Letaev* specifically that Steiner goes on to explain that "observation in the world of inspiration may only be compared with *reading*: and the beings in the world of inspiration act upon the observer like the letters of an alphabet, which he must learn to know and the interrelationships of which must unfold themselves to him like a supersensible script." Thus, according to Steiner, without cognition through inspiration "the imaginative world would remain like writing at which we stare but which we cannot read."[29]

In "On the Meaning of Cognition" Bely's description of "inspiration" also involves the initiate's gradual awareness of the higher beings in the realm of "sense-free thought," but by discerning *rhythms* that link him with the higher world:

> We grasp the life of ideas in two ways: by means of the hierarchical life of rhythm within and outside us; what is music within us, is voices of hierarchies outside us; the worlds of angels and archangels—are thoughts; and the life of hierarchies in our thought and the life of our thought in the formations of the world—are a unity.   [47]

In the novel, this stage is embodied in passages describing Kotik's attachment to his doll, Ruprecht, and the "sound apartment," both of which I mentioned above in connection with "sound beings." It is also clearly present in Kotik's perception of candle flames dancing in a candelabrum: in the resulting "gleaming rhythms the land of rhythm would begin to beat"; "the pulse of the rhythm of gleamings is—my own," Kotik continues, "beating in the land of the dances of rhythm." Bely strains language nearly to the limits of intelligibility in such passages in order to communicate what was obviously not a verbal experience during his infancy—a practice with far-reaching implications to be discussed below. However, it is possible to understand the "pulse of the rhythm of the gleamings" as being a link between Kotik and the otherworldly "land of rhythm"—which evokes Bely's formulations in "On the Meaning of Cognition," and, in turn, anthroposophical teaching about "inspiration." The effect of a common pulse beating in Kotik and the otherworldly realm is the formation of "a passageway into another world," through which "beings of another life will freely pass into our apartment" (thus giving Kotik the "insight" into "higher beings" that "inspiration" is supposed to provide). The one being that does appear before Kotik is associ-

29. Steiner, *Outline of Occult Science*, pp. 304–7.

ated for him with the Russian vowel sound *yu* (close to the English "you"). It seems to Kotik as if the being is "trying to make sound out of the air, or to sculpt it" (183–84/137–38).

In *Kotik Letaev* Bely also refers to his occult investigation of the connection between his childhood and the "higher worlds" of spirit by the same metaphor of "reading" that Steiner uses when he speaks of "inspiration." The novel's narrator says that "the transfiguration by memory of what happened previously is in fact reading: of the universe that is not ours—that stands behind what happened previously [. . .] memory—is a reading of the rhythms of the sphere [. . .] of the realm where—/—I lived before birth!" (187/140–41). Because the subchapter in which this passage appears ("Impressions") contains a description of flowing light pulses out of which forms arise (as I mentioned, an experience Bely also describes in both *Notes of an Eccentric* and a series of poems that are obvious records of his meditations), there is every reason to connect the narrator's references to "reading" with Steiner's description of "inspiration."

The transition from imagination to inspiration can be summarized as the change from fluidity to fixity, and this is an experience Kotik has often. As the narrator puts it at the beginning of Chapter 2: "I began to live in the state of being, *in what has become* (as I had earlier lived in *becoming*)" (62/43). The widespread opposition of "swarm" (*roy*) and "form" (*stroy*) in the novel is a reflection of the same transition: for example, "My first moments are—swarms; and 'swarm, swarm—everything swarms' is my first philosophy; I was swarming in swarms [. . .] the circle and the sphere are my first forms: conswarmings in a swarm" (64/45). Among others, the experiences to which this transition is applied include Kotik's reaching age four, when he begins to live "on land" rather than "in oceans," or as he also puts it, when the "angel of the epoch" appears out of the flow of human time (128/95).

The third and highest stage in anthroposophical cognition, intuition, involves understanding the "inner nature" of the "beings of the higher world" that the adept has come to know during the second stage, inspiration. To know a higher being "means to have become completely one with it," and this final stage of cognition is what "makes possible an adequate research into repeated lives and into karma."[30] More specifically, the highest insight of which the clairvoyant is capable in anthroposophy is the recognition of his own unity with Christ. Bely speaks of this overtly in his description of intuition in "On the Meaning of Cognition": "Finally in *inspiration,* in the union of our thought with the universe, in [sic] the wings of this thought as in an angel, 'I' fly over the chasm separating me from the boiling of the universe; 'I' *unite with the*

30. Ibid., pp. 309–11.

world in the unity of the divine [italics mine]: this union is in fact *intuition*" (47). This is the aspect of the three-step cognitive process that is perhaps the most obvious in *Kotik Letaev,* and it finds its clearest expression in Kotik's overt and elaborate identification with Christ in the last pages of the novel. For this reason, further discussion of imagery scattered throughout the text that is related to intuition can be left until the next section of this study, which will be concerned with the role of an exalted being in Kotik's life, and the relation this being has to the major theme of the trauma that his parents' discord caused him—a preoccupation in all of Bely's autobiographical writings.

Assuming that the three cognitive stages Steiner describes do appear in the novel, it is still necessary to explain why they should appear throughout the text, seemingly at random. A simple explanation can be found in Steiner's view that the stages in question "need not be thought of as successive experiences . . . the student . . . may have reached only a certain degree of perfection in a preceding stage when he begins exercises that correspond to a subsequent stage."[31] The combination of this view of the results of meditative praxis with Bely's spiralic narrative form—in which he returns to earlier events at the same time that Kotik grows older—results in the appearance of intuitive moments at the beginning of the text while imaginative ones can be found near its end. The general, large-scale tendency in the novel, however, is from imagination to intuition, despite repeated local countercurrents.

4

In "On the Meaning of Cognition," Bely states that achieving the highest state of intuition yields the realization that "'I' am not 'I,' but Divinity within me." In keeping with this insight, which recalls a similar formulation in Paul's Epistle to the Galatians (2:20), Bely draws an overt parallel between the story of Christ on Golgotha and the anthroposophical conception of cognition. As a result, the individual who achieves the highest cognitive state relives, in a way, the "Golgotha mystery," which is the central event in cosmic evolution, according to anthroposophy.[32] The essay concludes with the statement: "Not 'I'—but Christ in me [. . .]. We—are born in God. In Christ—we die. And—we arise in the Holy Spirit" (51). The last sentence in the Epilogue of *Kotik Letaev* is nearly identical: "In Christ we die in order to be resurrected in the Spirit" (292/222). It is clear, as a result, that Bely is making in the novel the

---

31. Ibid., p. 344.
32. See Steiner, *The Fifth Gospel* (1913; London, 1968), p. 151. The syncretic nature of anthroposophy, which draws from Eastern and Western religious teachings, accounts for both the similarities and differences to be found between Bely's ideas and the tenets of Eastern Orthodoxy.

same identification between Christ and intuition that he had made in the essay.

In addition to concluding a series of images in the Epilogue that portray Kotik as a cross-bearing Christ approaching Golgotha, the narrator's final words are the culmination of a series of references throughout the text to an exalted being that accompanies all the phases of Kotik's spiritual development. Because this being is an omnipotent, benevolent guiding spirit, it represents a major change from the atmosphere of *Petersburg,* in which the dominant forces were evil, and the "white domino"—modeled on the anthroposophic "Etheric Christ"—appeared as distinctly alienated.

Starting as early as the Foreword of *Kotik Letaev,* Bely speaks of *"that very one (but who—you don't know): and—with that very same glance* (what kind—you don't know) he will look, having cut through the cloaks of nature; and—reverberating in the soul: with the immemorially familiar, most cherished, never to be forgotten . . ." (11–12/5). The narrator's relation to this higher entity is comparable to what is implied elsewhere in the novel by the notion "memory of memory" (to be discussed below), and resembles the Gnostic conception of the earthbound soul's stirring in response to a call from its spiritual homeland. This latter possibility is implied by Kotik's description of the descent of his "I" (as distinct from the divine "I") into a physical body during the actual moment of incarnation. He recalls the sensation of being "terribly compressed" after having been "diffused throughout the cosmos." "But the decision has been made," he continues, "the hour of life has struck; and letting me out of parental arms, Someone ancient stands there behind 'I'" (50/34).

This exalted being resembles an entity that appears in many mythic quest patterns and that is called the "greater guardian of the threshold" in anthroposophy. During his spiritual exercises the initiate who has achieved inspiration encounters this being as "an ever present exhorter to further effort [and] . . . the ideal toward which he strives." Eventually the adept recognizes that this guardian is Christ, and thereby gains insight into the ultimate mystery of existence.[33]

The exalted being in the novel is implicitly identified with Christ in the scene of Kotik in the skull temple (36–37/24). It is also evoked repeatedly in the text in a more elliptical form (30/19, 35/22–23, 48/33, 80/57, 105/76, 209/157) until it becomes associated with the central trauma of Kotik's (and Bely's) life—his being torn between parents with antipodal characters. In trying to please one, young Bely always automatically disappointed the other. The result was that he was made to feel guilty even though he was not really at fault, and thus eventually came to identify with the ultimate guiltless victim, Christ. Near the end of the

33. Steiner, *Outline of Occult Science,* p. 345.

novel, after describing his sensation that he was at the intersection of the father's and mother's lifelines (which inevitably evokes the image of the cross), Kotik states: "But it stood in my soul:/—'You are—not Papa's, not—Mama's . . .'/—'You are—mine!' . . ./'He' will come for me" (217/163). The idea that Kotik crucified belongs more properly to a divine being than to the physical world is in keeping with anthroposophical teaching about the central role of the "Christ impulse" in human and cosmic evolution.

Thus we again return to Christ, but via Kotik's experiential role as a Christ figure, instead of through the practice of a special form of cognition. The extent to which this identification became rooted in Bely's imagination is revealed by his continuing to express it even in his official memoirs about his childhood, which are otherwise characterized by his attempts to adapt his past life to the requirements of the Soviet regime.[34]

But the exalted being is not only Christ. Shortly before the novel ends, the heretofore unspecified and tantalizingly familiar "he" is also identified as Vladimir Solov'ev. "It seemed," the narrator writes upon recalling his childhood impressions of adults' conversations about the philosopher, "I saw Vladimir Solov'ev: and he is—*that very one* (but who—you don't know)" (262/198).

Solov'ev had occupied a sacrosanct place in Bely's imagination since the beginning of the century. Thus it is not surprising that Bely would elevate the image of this beloved personage to a supernatural realm (as he had already done in the *Second Symphony*). The implicit identification of Solov'ev with Christ should probably be understood as Bely's way of suggesting that the philosopher had achieved the highest level of anthroposophical cognition (intuition) in which his individual "I" becomes dissolved in Christ. The incorporation of Solov'ev into an anthroposophical schema is yet another instance of Bely's habitual syncretism (and at the same time a reflection of Steiner's known admiration for Solov'ev).[35] The little girl Sonia Dadarchenko, whom Kotik likes, and whose first name is a diminutive of Sophia—and thereby an evocation of Solov'ev's Divine Wisdom (Hagia Sophia)—also becomes linked to the exalted being in the novel by the mere mention of her "violet eyes" that "speechlessly pass into" Kotik (228/171).

Before we continue with Kotik's identification with Christ, it is worth mentioning that an important effect of Solov'ev's appearance in Kotik's life is that it induces in him "the sensation of self-thinking thoughts, rushing about in wing-horned flocks" (260/197). Reference to thoughts

34. See *Na rubezhe dvukh stoletii*, p. 181.
35. Christ, Solov'ev, and Steiner were linked later by Bely as well. In his *Vospominaniya o Shteinere*, p. 335, after describing the enormous effect that Steiner's lecture series *The Fifth Gospel* had on him in 1913, Bely remembers that his thoughts turned back to the beginning of the century and visits to Solov'ev's grave.

thinking themselves first appeared in *The Silver Dove* when Daryalsky felt the intrusion of demonic otherworldy forces into his life. In *Petersburg* "cerebral play" and "self-thinking thoughts" grew in importance, and became the names for the transcendent's moving into human consciousness and constituting the world.[36] Now, in *Kotik Letaev*, Bely seems to refine the meaning of this central idea of his own world view in accordance with anthroposophy. Following Solov'ev's identification with Christ in the novel, the appearance of these thoughts in Kotik becomes associated with the attainment of the highest, intuitive stage of cognition. This inference is supported by the association of "self-thinking thoughts" with the image of "wing-horns" (*krylorogi*). Bely's striking neologism reappears throughout the text, and culminates in an extended passage at the end of the novel when Kotik's head seems to dissolve and the two halves of his brain sprout wings and soar (268–71/203–5). As implied in the idea of flight, wings when related to the mind suggest the achievement of transcendence—which is the state Kotik is indeed experiencing at the end of the novel. Bely also employs this image in "On the Meaning of Cognition" (47) and in poems describing his meditative experiences;[37] it also appears in Steiner's writings.

As I mentioned, the most overt identification of Kotik with Christ occurs in the Epilogue. Bely has his alter ego anticipate "the torments of my cross," "dragging a wooden and shoulder-breaking cross," and "hanging" from "nails." These emotional-charged passages undoubtedly represent the peak of Bely's lifelong quest for the true tie between the transcendent and the human. As Christ, Kotik will become the living perfect mediator between heaven and earth.

5

With the possible exception of *Petersburg*, all of Bely's earlier works are centrally concerned with processes that might be defined as quests for a metaphysical absolute. The fact that the Princess and the Knight in the *First Symphony*, Musatov in the *Second*, Khandrikov in the *Third*, Svetlova and Adam Petrovich in the *Fourth*, and Daryalsky in *The Silver Dove* are not masters of their own lives does not detract from the impression that they are enacting an extended search for a principle that will bring them into harmony with the transcendent. An argument could be made that in *Petersburg* Dudkin and Nikolay Apollonovich are involved in a similar pursuit, the first through his mystically colored revolutionary activity, the second through his philosophical and then mystical investigations. But the world of *Petersburg* is so charged with cosmic forces, and every-

---

36. See Alexandrov, *Andrei Bely: The Major Symbolist Fiction*, pp. 116–17.
37. See, for example, "Dukh" (1914), in Andrey Bely, *Stikhotvoreniya i poemy*, Biblioteka poeta, Bol'shaya seriya (Moscow and Leningrad, 1966), pp. 372–73.

one in the city is so thoroughly overwhelmed by them (whether they realize it or not), that a quest in the sense of a physical or spiritual journey to the source of power and ultimate enlightenment is neither necessary nor even possible. Everyone in the city has already arrived, or, perhaps better to say, the transcendent hovering throughout the city has already drawn all of the inhabitants into itself.[38] In *Kotik Letaev*, by contrast, Bely returns to a more familiar quest pattern, but one that has become entirely internalized.[39]

The narrator's use of a Steinerian cognitive methodology results in a form of contact between man and the realm of spirit that differs in an important respect from what we find in Bely's earlier works. The narrator's memory, which has been illuminated by clairvoyance ("spiritual *sight*") through the achievement of self-consciousness, is made to operate like a perceptive glance. The "target" of the narrator's memory, however, is not the external world around him, but his own childhood as recorded in an otherworldly realm. The analogy between visual perception and apprehension of the past through memory is underscored by the fact that Bely uses visual images to communicate the meaning that memory produces. Thus *Kotik Letaev* contains two processes by which the protagonist experiences contacts with the spiritual realm, depending on whether we have the infant's experiences or the adult's apprehension of those experiences.

The first occurs spontaneously as a given of the infant's existence and has as a consequence the constituting of the world around him. The second is encapsulated in the formula "memory of memory," which is the clairvoyant adult's way of referring to the memory of having had memories of a spiritual life while an infant—memories that were subsequently lost with age. It is these memories from infancy that the birth of self-consciousness in the adult can recapture, and it is this attempt to recapture the past that is comparable to a quest. But the ontological status of these memories, which are thought processes of course, is not simply that of purely mental images: "The memory of memory is such: it is—a rhythm in which thingness is absent; dances, mimicry, gestures— are the dissolution of the shells of memory and a free passage into another world [. . .] these dances are—flights into the never-having been, and nonetheless real; beings of other lives have now intruded into the events of my life" (188/141). The meaning of this passage (and

38. See Alexandrov, *Andrei Bely: The Major Symbolist Fiction*, pp. 110–22.

39. See Anna Lisa Crone, "Gnostic Elements in Bely's *Kotik Letaev*," *Russian Language Journal*, 36 (1982), pp. 88–105, for a Gnostic reading of Kotik's quest. Although this study illuminates a number of images in the novel, it does not take sufficient account of the substantial differences between anthroposophy and gnosticism (even though, as Crone realizes, Steiner borrowed from the latter). Thus, although spiritual transcendence is central to both teachings, anthroposophy is not a dualistic system, and its concept of evil is very different from that of gnosticism.

others like it: 22/13, 112/82, 122/90) is that through clairvoyance the adult narrator can enter into conscious contact with the land of rhythm, which the infant Kotik entered spontaneously as a function of his young age (a fact the adult also learned through clairvoyance). It will be recalled that in "On the Meaning of Cognition" Bely described inspiration, the second meditative stage, in similar terms. Like Kotik, the adult can have his world "enriched" with beings from this spiritual realm. Thus a form of memory, understood as meditation, emerges as a means of tapping into an otherworldly dimension in which the narrator's past—the infant's immanent experience, which in turn is based in a cosmic past—exists eternal and unchanged.

This is, in effect, Bely's personal version of the important anthroposophical belief that there is in the spirit world a permanent recording of all that ever occurred called the "Akashic record." Steiner claimed to have derived his cosmogony from reading this record and taught that properly prepared adepts could do the same.[40] In fact, as I suggested above, following Steiner's likening of inspiration to reading, Bely also refers to the act of reading when he speaks of his occult experiences in *Kotik Letaev*.[41]

The function of language in apprehending reality was from the start a fundamental concern in both Bely's theory and his art. Thus the metaphor of reading the indelible cosmic record represents a radical shift from the claims Bely made about the reality of his own fictions in *Petersburg*. If the reader was asked at the end of Chapter 1 to accept the contention that the fictional characters embodied in the language of *Petersburg* were as real as the reader's own world,[42] in *Kotik Letaev* language is repeatedly shown to be inadequate to the task of expressing the narrator's clairvoyant images.

Conditional constructions that have a direct bearing on this question appear often in *Kotik Letaev*. "Thus would I thicken with words the unutterability of the advent of my infant life," the narrator remarks on the first page, following an indented paragraph in which he attempts to describe his first vague sensations of existence. In this and similar instances, the verbal embodiment of experience is clearly something that *follows* the experience, rather than actually being the mode of existence of that experience, as was implicitly the case in *Petersburg*.

---

40. See, for example, Steiner's *Outline of Occult Science,* p. 105, and *Fifth Gospel,* pp. 30, 41.

41. Evidence for my assumption that Bely himself read the Akashic record can be found in poems from his collection *Zvezda.* They suggest that his meditations resulted in visions of a spiritual reality like the one Steiner described. See John E. Malmstad's variorum edition of Bely's complete poetry: *Stikhotvoreniya/Gedichte,* vol. I, pt. 2 (Munich, 1984), poems nos. 345, "Samosoznanie" (1914); 346–50, "Karma" (1917); 369, "Dukh" (1914); 371, "Vospominanie" (1914); 387, "Inspiratsiya" (1914).

42. See Alexandrov, *Andrei Bely: The Major Symbolist Fiction,* pp. 109–14.

This might seem to be another consequence of the fact that *Kotik Letaev* is a childhood autobiography—of the notion that children do not think in words (which have a reality for them independent of things). But the narrator also makes it clear that his approximate renderings are not due simply to the adult's personal inability to recapture the infant's preverbal state. He acknowledges the existence of supreme experiences that remain ultimately incommunicable, such as what he felt as a child, and, later, "on the rib of the pyramid of Cheops" (78/55). Thus even though the narrator recognizes in later life what he felt as a child, he still cannot communicate it. This recalls the narrator's essentially Romantic paean to the unutterable Russian word in *The Silver Dove*, and thus suggests Bely's return to a view of language such as he held before *Petersburg*.

The implicit gap between language and reality is also addressed explicitly by the narrator of *Kotik Letaev*. A number of passages deal with the young child's literal understanding of metaphors, such as those about a certain Ezheshekhinsky, who "flew off through a pipe" and "is walking through fire and copper pipes" (65/45). Both phrases are familiar Russian idioms for having had a rough time of it in life. But the child imagines Ezheshekhinsky literally wandering through pipes, and this image triggers his memory of his own movement through pipes before birth, as he puts it—a recollection that in turn echoes the formation of the corridor and Letaev apartment out of him at the beginning of the novel.

This process of Kotik's fitting something from his own prenatal experience to a metaphor also occurs when he hears that "someone fell into a swoon" (75/53). He imagines the person falling through the floor, which becomes an image for his spontaneous ability to move beyond the limits of consciousness at an early age: "for me the threshold of consciousness is movable, penetrable, openable like the floorboards of the parquet." The experiences he had when he was capable of crossing the threshold easily, however, "are not applicable to anything," and are therefore forgotten after infancy. Nevertheless, they revive later as a memory of his having had a memory of some lost experience (76/54), which he will recapture through meditation.

The process that the narrator dramatizes by understanding metaphors literally is fully explicated in the important subchapter "Self-consciousness." He states that "an unknown word is made intelligible in the recollection of its gesture; the gesture is—within me; and for words I select gestures; the world is formed out of gestures for me" (115/84). This is basically a description of an aspect of anthroposophy known as "eurythmy." It has to do with the belief that sounds are linked to particular physical gestures of the body, which are also reflected in the movement of the tongue that produces the sounds—with all being an accurate expression of cosmological verities. (Bely wrote a treatise on this subject titled *Glossolaliya* [1922].) The primeval, cosmic meaning with which Kotik infuses the words he hears by supplying images of physical movement from within himself is what the adult then presumably tries to recover through clairvoyant memory from the Akashic record. Although the point of contact with the otherworldly realm is within the self, according to anthroposophy, the fitting of eurythmic gestures to words leads not to solipsism but to an expression of cosmic truths. As Bely put it in a memoir, "The subconscious is filled with gestures that depict the life of the spirit world [. . .]. A gesture is the root of the verbal tree."[43] The assemblage of cosmically significant gestures is thus a true expression of the nature of the world, while words without their underlying eurythmic significance are not. The gestures of which the narrator speaks most likely derive from the same inspirational world of rhythm that generated the cognitive-creative impulses that through Kotik deposited his world around him. This is why the narrator can say "impressions of words—are recollections for me" (117/86). The gestures words evoke recall the ultimate transcendent reality of which he is trying to become aware again through clairvoyance.

6

Kotik Letaev is the culmination of a major line in Bely's fiction that begins with the *First Symphony* and that is marked by an ever-deepening immersion of the individual in the realm of spirit. The last novels Bely wrote, beginning with *The Baptized Chinaman*, are characterized by a sudden decrease in this metaphysical preoccupation. However, it is worth noting the ironic fact that this reorientation is also prefigured in *Kotik Letaev*—in the heart, as it were, of Bely's most otherworldly novel, and at a time when he was committed to anthroposophy.

Entire pages in *Kotik Letaev* consist of seemingly straightforward recollections of childhood experiences. They appear especially frequently in and after Chapter 3, at the opening of which the narrator announces that he is now four years old—the age that marks the turning point in his spiritual evolution. No unusual perceptions or especially metrical or orchestrated passages appear for several paragraphs or pages at a time. These pages recall Bely's three volumes of memoirs more than any of his earlier belletristic works. Were it not for the context, one would have

---

43. *Zapiski chudaka*, I, 154. See Bely's essay "Zhezl Aarona (O slove v poezii)" for similar formulations and other illustrations of how Bely supplied gestures for words (especially pp. 186–89) which recall the earlier essay "The Magic of Words." For another discussion of these metaphors—which, however, places undue emphasis on the novel's metalinguistic dimension—see Carol Anschuetz, "Recollection as Metaphor in *Kotik Letaev*," *Russian Literature*, 4 (1976), pp. 345–55.

hardly any suggestion on the basis of these passages alone that the work at hand is not a "realistic" one. Only an occasional leitmotif or other brief digression appears every once in a while, recalling the esoteric cosmogony that had been established earlier and was to be developed later in the novel.

There would of course be nothing remarkable about straightforward recollections in a childhood autobiography that was written from a non-occult point of view. But although the adult narrator in *Kotik Letaev* has explained how he lost his spontaneous contact with the otherworldly when he turned four, that adult narrator has presumably achieved clairvoyant insight. One would expect, therefore, that his insight should inform even passages dealing with the child's life after the age of four. Otherwise one is left with an impression that is antithetical to an anthroposophical world view—that a terrestrial existence ever could be free of cosmic significance.

Thus one cannot avoid the impression that the pages in question are lapses in a vision of existence that at other times caused Bely to write in a uniquely nonrealistic manner. This impression of inconsistency is augmented by the fact that after interludes of simple prose, Bely returns to the unique style of his visionary passages. Nothing quite like this had appeared in Bely's earlier works.

Several hypotheses come to mind when one attempts to account for this segmentation of the text into different "fields." The first is that Bely tries to make language work in a way it cannot. In the subchapter "The Formation of Consciousness," for example, he begins by saying that in the distant past " 'I' did not exist"—that there was an "enormous gap" in the body where consciousness was to be. But at the same time he speaks of the "seethings of delirium" that "were appearing to me"; and he adds that "warmth seethed up for me; and I was tormented" (17–18/10). In these passages Bely wants nothing less than to describe an absence of self-awareness from the point of view of the as yet unborn and unformed infant. But this is clearly an overly ambitious project, given the way in which language functions, and leads to the striking paradox of referring to oneself even when that self does not exist. Thus an already difficult series of passages is complicated further. There is, in short, an inevitable irreconcilability between the ideas Bely wants to express and the means available to express them. Perhaps, therefore, Bely felt compelled to lapse into simpler prose dealing with mundane reality to provide relief through contrast, both for himself and for his readers.

Behind these opposing tendencies in Bely's prose, which grow out of the opposition between a conception of the self as integrated in the cosmos and one of the self as separate from it, lies the double point of view that operates throughout the work—that of the experiencing infant on the one hand and of the recollecting adult on the other. Bely attempts to capture the elusive experiences of the child in highly allusive language that often skirts the edge of intelligibility. As a consequence the narrator often has to add a simple explanation from the adult's linguistic resources to the child's impressions. For example: "the live-flowing lightscript of lightning bolts is—words; and the pulsation is—meanings" (116/85). The narrator's explanation that the child's visual impressions are "words" and "meanings" is in effect a brief lapse from the way he normally tries to use language to render the child's experiences. The point of these departures is of course to clarify what might otherwise be unintelligible, to provide a point of definite contact with the reader.

The appearance of small-scale "realistic" narrative passages in the context of cosmic visions suggests that clarity, even if it betrays unmediated accuracy of representation, was important for Bely (and clarity—indeed, the scientific reproducibility of occult experiences—is a hallmark of anthroposophy, or "occult science," as it is also known). This is ultimately something like an admission of incomplete success in carrying out an artistic project that Bely had defined as his "anthroposophical academic task." The description of the father's name day (188/141), for example, sits like a block of material whose occult significance is not illuminated in a context where the constant emphasis is on the spiritual significance of things and events (assuming, of course, that there is no deeply encoded occult significance below the surface of the memoiristic passages).

The Baptized Chinaman

1

Bely returned to his vast autobiographical epic "My Life" in 1920, and published the first chapter of the continuation the following year with a title that suggested what his long-range intentions were: *The Crime of Nikolay Letaev. (The Epic—Volume One). The Baptized Chinaman. Chapter One.* He shortened the title to *The Baptized Chinaman: A Novel* in 1927, when he published a revised version of the chapter in book form.[44]

Bely's boyhood is the subject of the new work, which thus constitutes an obvious sequel to *Kotik Letaev*. The visionary, anthroposophical imagery that dominates the earlier work, however, has been moved into the background of the later one. The bulk of *The Baptized Chinaman* consists

---

44. For a description of the writing and publication history of the work, see *Literaturnoe nasledstvo*, no. 27–28, p. 605. The Introduction by D. Tschiževskij and A. Hönig in *Kreshchenyi kitaets* (Munich, 1969) provides additional information. All page references to this reprint of the work, which has yet to appear in English translation, will be given in the text. Elsworth, *Andrey Bely: A Critical Study*, pp. 138–39, provides a lucid discussion of the relation between this novel and Bely's other works.

of the child's realistic impressions of his life, and there are few passages in it dealing with the ties between the protagonist and the otherworldly realm. This is what may have led Bely actually to quote his descriptions of his father as he appears in *The Baptized Chinaman* in *On the Border of Two Centuries,* his official memoir of the period portrayed in the novel.[45]

At the same time, a dual point of view continues to operate throughout the work, although it differs from what we find in *Kotik Letaev.* As one might expect, since there are few visionary passages, the two dominant points of view are the conventional ones of childhood autobiography—the earthbound child and the earthbound adult. The child occasionally also has visions of something like an ancestral past, but it is not clear whether such visions are due to the adult's ability to read the Akashic record or are simply the child's memories of moments of spontaneous clairvoyance experienced during infancy. Presumably, since the work is the putative continuation of *Kotik Letaev,* the former is the case. In any event, the perceptions that are clearly those of the adult are found in digressions and occasional asides that ironize at the child's expense.

Apart from the relatively rare occult passages in the work, what evidence is there that Bely is still operating within a world view that is a continuation of the one in *Kotik Letaev?* The answer lies, I believe, in the significant role played by alliteration and metricization of the prose in *The Baptized Chinaman.* The narrator of *Kotik Letaev* made clear that rhythms connect the spiritual and human worlds (as Bely had done also in "On the Meaning of Cognition"). Numerous scenes depict a variety of repetitive pulses as the most fundamental means by which both information and literally creative energy were transmitted from the cosmos to Kotik, and through him into his world. Sounds in anthroposophy fulfill a similar function; and it is likely that the numerous neologisms in the novel were meant to do so as well. Thus passages filled with sound repetitions and a recognizable meter in *The Baptized Chinaman*—many pages of which are written in regular amphibrachs—appear to be implicit expressions of an occult world view even when no overt occult imagery appears. It should be stressed, however, that when the reader is presented with only such abstract and relatively mute phenomena as meter and alliteration, it becomes very difficult indeed to speak of the specific nature of man's links to the transcendent.

As he did in *Kotik Letaev,* Bely places the central event of his young life at the heart of *The Baptized Chinaman*—namely, the trauma of being torn between his parents, which leads him to identify with Christ. In *The Baptized Chinaman,* however, Bely's emphasis is on the suffering he had to endure rather than on the achievement of ultimate wisdom. As a

45. *Na rubezhe dvukh stoletii,* pp. 19–20.

result, one is forced to conclude that either *The Baptized Chinaman* covers a period in Bely's life during which he had been removed somehow from the path of enlightenment that was the focus of *Kotik Letaev* or that Bely's tone became more pessimistic under the influence of the ghastly hardships he had to endure in Soviet Russia in 1920.[46] My guess is that the latter case is more likely, because after the narrator of *Kotik Letaev* turned four—an event that supposedly decreased his spontaneous contacts with the spirit world—visionary passages continued to appear (as they would in *Notes of an Eccentric*) as a consequence of the adult's retroactive illumination of his childhood by means of clairvoyance.

Bely often communicates his pain and sense of guilt with great power, as when he laments: "I committed a crime against mother by having appeared before her; and later: I initiated discord between her and papa; self-consciousness—is criminal" (171). It is this childhood experience that of course explains the original title of the work, *The Crime of Nikolay Letaev.*[47]

2

The changed emphasis in the final title of the work is more difficult to understand, as is the function of the Asian imagery in the novel as a whole. On numerous occasions the narrator describes his father—who is obviously Bely's own father—as having "Scythian" features (7, 35, 94, 154), or as recalling a Chinese who has fathomed the wisdom of the *I Ching* (21), or as Zoroaster (141). Near the end of the novel, after relating the charming story of his father's dream of Christ, in which Christ agrees with the father's sui generis philosophical system, Kotik concludes, "Papa is probably a baptized Chinaman!" Although this makes clear that the change in titles indicates an apparent shift in focus from

46. Paramount among the descriptions of Bely's hardships before his departure for Berlin in 1921 is his letter to his first wife, Asya Turgeneva, dated November 11, 1921, and published in *Vozdushnye puti*, no. 5 (1967), pp. 296–309. For a description of his tormented state in Berlin, see Marina Tsvetaeva's brilliant short memoir "Plennyi dukh (Moya vstrecha s Andreem Belym)" (1934), reprinted in *Izbrannaya proza v dvukh tomakh* (New York, 1979), vol. 2. A translation is available in Marina Tsvetaeva, *A Captive Spirit: Selected Prose*, trans. J. Marin King (Ann Arbor, 1980).

47. It is somewhat surprising that in *Na rubezhe dvukh stoletii* (p. 331) Bely would suggest that the "crime" in question was his going to a library instead of to school for a period during his early adolescence—another major incident in his life, and one he had planned to depict in *The Crime of Nikolay Letaev*. (This traumatic period is discussed in John Elsworth, *Andrey Bely* [Letchworth, 1972], pp. 10–12.) *The Baptized Chinaman* offers ample evidence that Bely thought of himself (albeit ironically) as a criminal during his early childhood because no matter what he did, one parent was always displeased (e.g., p. 89). Perhaps the incident with the library from a later time in his life should be understood as a further manifestation of the original childhood trauma. It is also possible that in his memoir Bely was trying to deemphasize his self-identification with Christ in order not to antagonize the Soviet censorship.

the narrator to his father, or to the narrator's relation to his father, the meaning of this shift remains unclear.

Given the importance of the apocalyptic meaning of Asia in *Petersburg*, it is tempting to hypothesize that the references to Asia in *The Baptized Chinaman* have a comparable significance, despite the fact that they were totally absent from *Kotik Letaev*. Thus the narrator's father as a baptized Chinaman may be an echo of Apollon Apollonovich Ableukhov, whose ancestor was a baptized Mongol.

It is likely, however, that the frequent references to Scythians specifically are a reflection of a Russian cultural and political movement known as Scythianism and associated with the social and literary critic Ivanov-Razumnik. D. S. Mirsky characterizes it succinctly as a "sort of mystical revolutionary messianism, laying great stress on the revolutionary mission of Russia and on the fundamental difference of Socialist Russia from the bourgeois West."[48] The Scythians saw the Bolshevik Revolution as a manifestation of the new world and order to come. (Aleksandr Blok's poem "The Scythians" [1918] is a well-known expression of this ideology.) Bely was a close friend of Ivanov-Razumnik for a long time, is known to have found his ideas congenial,[49] and first published *Kotik Letaev* in his miscellany *The Scythians*. Be that as it may, it is clear that the significance of Asia has changed for Bely since *Petersburg* because the apocalypse as such is no longer his central concern in *The Baptized Chinaman*.[50]

Indeed, the occult significance of things Scythian in the novel could be characterized as more broadly occult and diffuse than anything as specific as the end of world history. In general, Bely adapts Scythian imagery to his own needs and presents it in a form that recalls the narrator's prenatal cosmic existence in *Kotik Letaev*. But since the achievement of self-consciousness is not an overt theme of *The Baptized Chinaman*, and since the narrator lost spontaneous contact with the spirit world at the age of four, the fact that he continues to have occasional occult experiences in *The Baptized Chinaman* could be understood as either inconsistencies on Bely's part or as natural but rare events that constitute exceptions to the rule.

Unlike the situation one finds in *Kotik Letaev*, the narrator's occult visions in *The Baptized Chinaman* arise primarily during moments of emo-

48. D. S. Mirsky, *A History of Russian Literature*, ed. and abr. Francis J. Whitfield (New York, 1966), p. 461. See also Stefani Hoffman, "Scythian Theory and Literature, 1917–1924," in *Art, Society, Revolution: Russia, 1917–1921*, ed. Nils Åke Nilsson (Stockholm, 1979).

49. See Roger Keys's study "The Bely–Ivanov-Razumnik Correspondence," in *Andrey Bely: A Critical Review*, ed. G. Janecek (Lexington, Ky., 1978), pp. 193–204.

50. Samuel Cioran, *The Apocalyptic Symbolism of Andrej Belyj* (The Hague, 1973), mistakenly equates Solov'ev's Pan-Mongolism with Scythianism and thus concludes that *The Baptized Chinaman* is an apocalyptic work (p. 36).

tional turmoil. A hysterical outburst from the narrator's mother leads to an especially painful scene with the father, which in turn prompts a complex sequence of images revolving around a Scythian slaying a Persian. This violent image is awakened somehow in the narrator's imagination by his father's practice of smashing a rusty nail into a metal washbasin in order to "tame" his wife, who, as a result of the hideous noise, invariably collapses in tears (153). The horror of the scene apparently causes the narrator to swoon, and he has a vision of his father in the guise of an enraged Scythian on horseback. The narrator then begins to identify with this vision himself: "the galloping [of the Scythian] became bound together through a compaction of the dust; compacted dust—is my body [. . .] the hooves pound; in my little breast—there's a growing lump, a bloody lump: my Scythian!" (156). In this passage the rhythm (of a gallop) is made to take on material substance that is the narrator himself ("compacted dust—is my body"). This image recalls the fundamental pattern of the relationship between the spiritual and material worlds of *Petersburg* and *Kotik Letaev*, where the spiritual created the material. Moreover, the narrator's reference to a "growing lump" in his heart echoes the expanding crimson sphere in Apollon Apollonovich's chest, although, again, here the image is not apocalyptic. The importance of the rhythm as the primary link between man and the otherworldly realm is underscored by the fact that in the Russian original this passage is composed entirely of amphibrachs.

This passage may also constitute evidence for an occult dimension in the novel because it is concerned with reincarnation. According to Steiner, intuition, the highest cognitive state, "makes possible an adequate research into repeated earth lives and into human karma."[51] Thus the narrator's vision of himself as a Persian and of his father as a Scythian (and all the other avatars in which the father appears throughout the text) may be taken as evidence of the continuing relevance of the tripartite anthroposophical cognitive schema for the narrator, although its form is more muted here than in *Kotik Letaev*. At the same time, the fact that a swooning child had this vision spontaneously goes against Steiner's explanation that man can attain enlightenment "only through soul-spirit exercises"—a departure from anthroposophical orthodoxy that characterized *Kotik Letaev* as well.

Bely does not use amphibrachs exclusively in visionary passages, however. The image of the Persian (an exemplar of old effete culture?) and the Scythian (a healthy, barbaric destruction of the past?) continues to develop until the narrator identifies himself with the Persian, whose head is being pierced by a spear thrown by the Scythian. This and related images are interrupted by the sudden appearance of the nar-

51. Steiner, *Outline of Occult Science*, p. 311.

rator's parents, who have obviously come to his room because he has been having a nightmare (162). Even though this passage represents a return to reality, it, too, is composed of amphibrachs. It differs from the visionary passages only in its lack of striking alliterations. The general significance of the widespread amphibrachic rhythm in the novel is thus probably as evidence of man's dependence on a spiritual cosmos.

Although the specific occult significance of Scythians and Persians is unclear, the image of the narrator as a Persian being slain by a Scythian does suggest a connection with Christ's torment. This possibility is confirmed later in the novel when Bely presents an esoteric, anthroposophical version of the Old Testament in which the narrator's father appears as Abraham and the narrator himself as Isaac. The latter is of course a well-known biblical type for Christ. Inevitably, the narrator identifies himself openly with Christ and says, "I wanted to crucify myself" (227).

The significance of Christ in *The Baptized Chinaman* continues to be anthroposophical, as in *Kotik Letaev*. In an important passage the narrator speaks of Christ in distinctly Steinerian terms as the central regenerative force in the cosmos. The page in question is of particular interest because it contains one of the most striking typographical arrangements in Bely's entire canon. The narrator's text, as he speaks of Christ as a "sun Disk," suddenly splits into two separate columns of print, each containing a different sentence. In one the "Christ Being"'s body enters "like a Sword into the world's/Nothingness!"; in the other it enters "like a Sword into the world's/Everything!" The text then merges into a funnel shape that narrows toward the bottom of the page as the narrator speaks of the occult, archangelic names of the anthroposophical Christ's attributes (217). The entire typographical design thus describes the movement toward an ultimate unity in Christ of everything in the cosmos—a view that typifies anthroposophical teaching as a whole.

So few passages of *The Baptized Chinaman* deal openly with the occult that one has little to go on in attempting to understand the precise nature of man's relation to the spiritual world in the work. But in addition to the passage quoted above about the seeming compaction of the narrator's body out of rhythm, occasional hints suggest that Bely has not abandoned the world view that dominated his earlier works.

For example, as he puts it in the novel, "I know: that chute which you can't overcome in a hundred thousand years: is the spinal column; I crawled from the worm to the gorilla, to . . . to . . . the expansion of the sphere: my head, on which I try to seat myself; and fall again: into the antedeluvian past" (168). This sounds like a conflation of Haeckel's principle with an image for the mind expanding to the point of contact with the spirit realm—both of which figured prominently in *Kotik Letaev*.

Another particularly intriguing instance is the child narrator's description of how a nanny of his came into being; it bears a resemblance to the process by which Dudkin arose before Apollon Apollonovich and Shishnarfne appeared before Dudkin in *Petersburg:* "She simply appeared (very many things in life *simply* appear: fleas, crumbs, motes of dust!) [. . .] and so someone breathed Henrietta Martynovna onto a mirror for me" (42). In part, this passage is concerned with capturing the ebb and flow of the child's unstable memories of the woman. But there is also a complex connection between perception and creation: the woman appears in a mirror in which, presumably, the child had earlier seen only himself. It will be recalled that Shishnarfne had returned to an otherworldly realm through Dudkin's throat after becoming a two-dimensional figure on a windowpane. Now, however, a human being appears on a mirrored glass surface as a reified exhalation from what may be a spiritual dimension as well. It is interesting to note, moreover, that Bely uses the same tactic to suggest the ultimately mysterious origins of the nanny as he did for the occult events in the *First Symphony*.[52] He does not specify the subjects of the verbs that indicate how she arose, and simply says "[they] breathed [*nadyshali*]" Henrietta Martynovna, "*someone* exhaled," "[they] breathed again [*dokhnuli eshche*]."

The narrator's existence continues to be cyclical in this novel, as it was in *Kotik Letaev*. There are numerous references to reincarnations in which characters enact what appear to be familiar events from past lives. Thus, in addition to having been a Persian, the narrator was a Hebrew in Sinai, and draws a parallel between his fear of transgression against both parents and the constraints of the Mosaic Commandments (214). Similarly, the struggles between the parents are represented as reenactments of those between Xanthippe and Socrates, and the father appears as one who has lived in ancient Rome and in Palestine at the time of Christ (215). The difference between the implied cyclical shape of time in this work and the spiralic time in those preceding it is that the teleological component that converts cycles into whorls of a spiral is muted in *The Baptized Chinaman* by the weakening of the narrator's identification with the transcendence that Christ represented for him earlier.

Notes of an Eccentric

Although very digressive, *Notes of an Eccentric* centers on the year 1916, and, more specifically, on Bely's journey from Dornach in Switzerland through France, England, and Scandinavia to Russia in response to a draft notice.[53] The work is thus focused on a period in the author's life

52. See the *First Symphony:* "something flew in" (p. 21), "someone sad swam up" (p. 24), "Someone waved to them" (p. 113), etc.

53. All page and volume references to *Zapiski chudaka* will be given in the text. All translations are my own.

some thirty years after we last saw him as a child in *The Baptized Chinaman*.

In many formal and thematic respects, however, this memoir is a direct continuation of the earlier autobiographical novels, especially of the more occult *Kotik Letaev*. The return to a frank concern with anthroposophical issues and experiences in *Notes of an Eccentric* in comparison with *The Baptized Chinaman* may be due to Bely's having published the *Notes* in Berlin rather than the Soviet Union.

I suggested above that a melding of fiction and reality seems to be an inevitable outgrowth of Bely's theory of symbolism, and was a fact in his two autobiographical novels. The confusion of life and art is central to the *Notes* as well.

On the one hand, Bely goes to some pains in the work's prefatory remarks to distinguish beween himself and the protagonist in the text, whom he names Leonid Icy (Leonid Ledyanoy). On the other hand, in several places in the body of the text, the narrator makes remarks that blur this difference; for example, "there is not a single line in the 'Notes' that I did not experience exactly in the way I depicted the experiences" (II, 235).

This seeming discrepancy can be resolved if one understands the distinction Bely drew between himself and Leonid Icy as the difference between two separate aspects of his own persona—the public author and the private man. Indeed, Bely refers to Leonid Icy as the "corpse" of a writer who has died (I, 15) and whom he now rejects (II, 157). Thus, rather than conclude that *Notes of an Eccentric* is something like a novel, one should see it as a recollection of a period in Bely's life that he rejects as no longer relevant from the point of view of the new state of being he has entered.

Bely expressly connects the spiritual transformation that allows him to shed his former self with his abandonment of the novelistic form, despite the fact that formally the *Notes* are of a piece with all of his earlier belletristic works. Bely refers to the pseudonymous Leonid Icy as a being that has transformed itself from "a shadow into me myself"; the result is that Bely feels his position in the world has been usurped by his public writer's persona (I, 73). A similar formulation appears in the subchapter "The Writer and the Man" (I, 62–63), where Bely states that his attempt to tell about an event of prime importance for himself in novelistic form is an attempt with "unfit means." This is what leads him to conclude that "each novel is a game of hide and seek with the reader; and the meaning of the architectonics of the phrase is to avert the reader's eye from the sacred point: the birth of myth." This is, in effect, an expression of romantic irony, which recalls Bely's narrative digression in *The Silver Dove* about the unutterable wisdom contained in the "Russian word."[54]

54. See Andrey Bely, *The Silver Dove*, trans. George Reavey (New York, 1974), p. 303.

Bely's reason for writing *Notes*, therefore—to which he refers as a "diary" (I, 63)—is to "tear off my writer's mask, and to tell about myself as a human being" (I, 63–64). This change was not easy to accomplish, he explains, and it was only when a guiding "star" appeared in his life that he was able to overcome Leonid Icy.

Given Bely's description of the star bringing him to an "infant" lying in a "manger"—an infant that is he himself—it seems clear that Bely is referring to his spiritual rebirth through anthroposophy. It is interesting to note that Bely's description of his old alter ego's demise recalls the process by which Shishnarfne disappeared in *Petersburg:* Leonid Icy was transformed from "a three-dimensional state into a two-dimensional one, as befits a decent flat shadow that has not forgotten its place" (I, 75). This image evokes the entire complex of connections among mental creation of reality, anthroposophical "thought" and "sound beings," and "reality" and "shadows" in *Petersburg* that I have discussed elsewhere.[55] The ultimate meaning of these associations is that Leonid Icy can be understood to have been an emanation of Andrey Bely's mind that was created by occult forces acting through him.

Although the *Notes* suggest that Bely overcame his old alter ego, it remains unclear when he did so—before or during the writing of the text. Bely's Afterword suggests it was the latter. From the vantage point offered by the completed work, he refers to it as having been written by an "eccentric" who had endured a "terrible illness" during the years 1913–16. The truthfulness of his depiction of his spiritual illness leads to his profoundly ambivalent attitude toward the book: "I love the 'Notes' like the truth of my illness from which I am now free" (II, 236).

Many pages of the *Notes* have an atmosphere of hysteria, confusion, and seeming paranoia. Bely describes repeatedly and at length his conviction that he was followed during his long journey to Russia by agents of a malevolent occult organization masquerading as British spies. This dominant theme of the work is augmented by its highly fragmentary and often confusing narrative form—numerous rapid leaps from one topic to another, highly elliptical comments, and choppy typographical arrangements. What, one may ask, was the "terrible illness" that gave rise to such a text?

On the level of "normal" human experiences, Bely's sense of disorientation was due to his separation from his wife, Asya Turgeneva (whom he calls Nelly in the *Notes*), who stayed in Dornach when Bely returned to Russia in 1916. In his view, their meeting (they met before they became anthroposophists) was instrumental in his overcoming the spiritual stagnation that he describes as the "underground" into which Leonid Icy had put him (I, 79). During the years he spent apart from her his sense

---

55. See Alexandrov, *Andrei Bely: The Major Symbolist Fiction*, pp. 109–14.

of loss was aggravated by her sporadic communications, from which he inferred that she was becoming increasingly alienated from him. His agony reached a peak in 1921 after he arrived in Berlin, where he eventually saw her in the company of another man.

The *Notes* also deal at length with a very severe problem of a spiritual order. As Bely formulates it in his Afterword, the "leitmotif" of the work is a "morbid psychological confusion" that caused him to ascribe to himself the great spiritual achievement of intuition when he was actually still quite "mortal" and entirely "undistinguished" (II, 235). He realized too late that although his true spiritual achievements lay in the future, he was transferring them into "this life": "at times I ascribe to myself perfections that belong to The Man [i.e., the individual united in Christ]; that is the profanation of The Chalice" (I, 81). It is most ironic that this self-chastisement should echo what might be termed the sin of hubris, which Bely dramatizes in the *Second Symphony* through Sergey Musatov and in *The Silver Dove* through Petr Daryalsky. Both characters conceive of themselves as harbingers of apocalyptic changes in man's spiritual state, and both are explicitly condemned for this. Bely's portrayal of characters' errors in the two earlier works thus emerges as a prefiguration of the erroneous path he himself followed during the period described in *Notes*.

The consequence that Bely claims for this grave error—a cognitive one in the context of the anthroposophical tripartite schema I discussed in relation to *Kotik Letaev* and *The Baptized Chinaman*—is that he lost insight into the "higher realms" of spiritual reality. To illustrate this loss he quotes a conversation he apparently had with Nelly in Berlin shortly before he published the *Notes:* "Now we have descended from the mountains and are crossing the plains; we, Percevals, to whom a vision of Mont Salvat was revealed: for a moment. We must wander for years in order to find *that Temple* again" (I, 159; a similar passage appears on I, 80). The "Temple" is probably the Goetheanum; and the implication is that Bely will attempt to rediscover the anthroposophical path to illumination that he has lost.

Perhaps the most revealing evidence of Bely's plight is his inability to read the "occult script" of events taking place around him. It will be recalled that Steiner likened the second, inspirational stage in his cognitive schema to reading, and that Bely made extensive use of this metaphor in *Kotik Letaev.* As in the earlier work, however, Bely continues to apply Steiner's ideas to experiences outside actual meditative visions: "the events of the journey" from Dornach to Russia, for example, are "not even a sign, but perhaps part of a sign: the circle of the letter '*yu*' [written in Russian as *I* and *O* joined at the middle by a short horizontal bar]" (I, 156). Bely explains that even under the best of circumstances, it is difficult to combine correctly individual letters into words, and his conclusion is that he has lost this ability altogether: all the "perceptions changed in me; [it] was ending: the *code* was not being read; I saw empty fantasies of someone's fate, which was cutting [me] off from Nelly" (II, 199).

Bely's recognition that he has been misreading his relation to the cosmos, and has been ascribing to himself the enlightenment he will achieve only after "two or three incarnations" (or, as he also puts it, his error in confusing his individual self with the divine supraindividual self), allows a malevolent emanation of the spirit world to attack him (I, 81). This, then, is the origin of the occult British "sir" who follows Bely on his long journey home. Thus the "paranoia" that colors many pages of the *Notes* should be seen not as simple madness but as a response to authentically occult events, at least from Bely's viewpoint.

Despite the author's frequently despairing tone and his remarks about achieving enlightenment only in the future, *Notes of an Eccentric* does contain brighter passages dealing with what appear to be ongoing occult experiences. One can, for example, find elements of the tripartite cognitive schema in which Bely's identification with Christ takes the form of references to the "cross" that he "now carries for [his] Motherland" (II, 117). The suffering Bely stresses here of course needs to be understood in terms of intuition, as in *Kotik Letaev*.

Perhaps the most widespread evidence for Bely's continuing involvement with meditation is found in the many highly unusual typographic arrangements of text in the latter two-thirds of the *Notes*. I have suggested elsewhere that the specially indented passages in *Petersburg* may be understood as a graphic representation of the intrusive relationship the transcendent has to the novel's narrator-author and his characters.[56] Similar typographically offset passages can be found in *Kotik Letaev* and *The Baptized Chinaman*. Passages of *Notes of an Eccentric* are frequently offset both when Bely is recalling occult experiences from his past (e.g., I, 124–25, 133, 140–41; II, 86, 220) and when he seems to be recording meditative experiences contemporary with his writing of the text of *Notes,* as when he digresses from describing his journey to discuss the history of ornamental design, and his invitation to the reader to accompany him. What follows resembles an anthroposophical meditation on metamorphosing designs that yields an indented passage containing a reference to a "wing-arm [*kryloruk*] flying around" (II, 105). As Bely makes clear elsewhere in *Notes,* as well as in *Kotik Letaev,* winged things of various kinds constantly inhabit his meditative visions. Thus the indented passage in question takes on the appearance of a sudden shift in perspective due to the initiate's—Bely's in this case—cognitive penetration into a higher realm.

56. Ibid., pp. 123–26.

It should be noted, however, that unusual typographic arrangements are not always overtly linked to occult experiences, a variation one does not find in Bely's earlier works. (An anthroposophical world view cannot be said to allow an entirely nonoccult reading of human experiences.) For example, Bely seems to be stressing primarily the illusory nature of the world in wartime Britain—which, as he puts it, seems to have been produced on a duplicating machine—by arranging the text on a page in the shape of an hourglass, and by placing a period at the narrowest point (II, 50).[57] Similarly, he arranges texts to resemble both a ship's wake and the waves through which the ship moves (II, 63–64).

There is a playful dimension to such typographically marked passages that counters the frequently anguished and hysterical content of much of *Notes of an Eccentric.* But because the text offers little if any evidence of self-parody in such passages, it would probably not be possible to reconcile Bely's laments about having strayed from the true occult path with the passages describing his seemingly late meditative experiences in any other way than by acknowledging that there were gleams of light in his despair. The widespread amphibrachic passages in the *Notes,* as in *The Baptized Chinaman,* are also ultimately evidence for Bely's continuing faith in a connection between the transcendent and the human.

In the final analysis, the dominant feature of the three works that grew out of Bely's plan to write a vast autobiographical epic is a preoccupation with the problem of how the individual—and, more specifically, the practicing anthroposophist—achieves spiritual regeneration. In this respect, *Kotik Letaev, The Baptized Chinaman,* and *Notes of an Eccentric* represent a continuation of a theme present in all of Bely's earlier works. It is all the more striking, therefore, that in Bely's next novels, *Moscow* and *Masks*—the last two that he wrote—the problem of spiritual regeneration disappears from the surface. Neither the narrators nor the characters speak openly about or experience contacts with a transcendent realm, as all had done in earlier works. Indeed, only familiarity with anthroposophy allows one to discern the theme of spiritual regeneration underlying the common plot connecting *Moscow* and *Masks.* At first glance, this fact may seem to indicate a major change in Bely's attitude toward the nature of the link between the human and the transcendent. However, the numerous writings Bely produced for his "desk drawer" during the late 1920s (some of which have been published in the West) make it clear that he remained a passionate admirer of Steiner's teachings and practitioner

---

57. This passage recalls the introduction of *Petersburg,* in which the narrator describes the city as an illusory point on a map, but a point that establishes its existence by emitting streams of printed documents—a view that can also be connected with what Shishnarfne says about Petersburg later in the novel. When the hourglass passage in *Notes of an Eccentric* is viewed from this vantage point, it takes on occult significance.

of anthroposophy while he worked on his last novels. The reason for the change in his art beginning with *Moscow* must therefore be sought somewhere other than in a change of heart. And the most likely answer seems to be that in order to be published Bely had to try to hide from view what was unacceptable to the Soviet politico-literary establishment.

5

Moscow and *Masks*

JOHN ELSWORTH

1

Bely's Moscow cycle, like all his preceding novels, was envisaged as a single work in many volumes but was never completed. The two parts of the first volume, *The Moscow Eccentric* (*Moskovskii chudak*) and *Moscow in Jeopardy* (*Moskva pod udarom*), were published together in 1926, and these two parts are customarily known as the novel *Moscow* (*Moskva*). It was declared then that the entire work would consist of two volumes, but when the second volume eventually appeared under the title *Masks* (*Maski*), in 1932, the projected volumes had risen to four.[1] However, Bely died in January 1934 without redeeming his promise, and the cycle as we have it consists simply of *Moscow* and *Masks*.

Critics have almost universally rejected these novels. Contemporary reviewers expressed a modicum of qualified approval, particularly for *Moscow,* and Leonid Timofeev went so far as to assert that its clarity of characterization, the tension of its action, and its descriptive power made it Bely's best work to date.[2] Konstantin Loks found only an alternation between a few effective passages and others that produced no impression at all.[3] Some Soviet critics dwelt at length on questions of ideological correctness, finding that Bely must have learned his Marxism from such disgraced tutors as Aleksandr Bogdanov (pseudonym of Aleksandr Ma-

---

This essay is based on chaps. 8 and 9 of my *Andrey Bely: A Critical Study of the Novels,* published by Cambridge University Press (1983).

1. *Moskva pod udarom* (Moscow, 1926), "vmesto predisloviya," signed "September, 1925. Kuchino"; *Maski* (Moscow, 1932; reprinted Munich, 1969), p. 5. Further page references will be given in the text; those to *Moskva pod udarom* will be preceded by the roman numeral II. Translations are mine.

2. L. Timofeev, "O 'Maskakh' A. Belogo," *Oktyabr',* no. 6 (1933), p. 213.

3. K. Loks, "O spornom i besspornom," *Krasnaya Nov',* no. 11 (1926), p. 239.

linovsky), long since unmasked as idealistic and bourgeois, or declaring that the moral victory of his hero, Professor Korobkin, was actually impossible in a capitalist society.[4] With the years these views have hardened into outright rejection, though *Moscow* and *Masks* are not often mentioned in Soviet criticism at all. Mikhail Kuznetsov concludes that *Masks* "is the terrible but logical end of a sick talent, unable to overcome the blind alleys of a false philosophy."[5] Even Boris Pasternak found the novels impossible to read, and wrote that he rejected "this tormented prose."[6]

Soviet and émigré critics have differed somewhat in the grounds for their rejection, but hardly in their final judgments. Vladislav Khodasevich found the plot and characterization of *Moscow* utterly beyond credibility, and took Bely particularly to task for his claim in the preface to be depicting the helplessness of science, which is essentially free, in a capitalist society; the novel, he declared, contained nothing of either science or capitalism.[7] Bely's language has also been condemned; Khodasevich, again, found the language of *Moscow* debased and vulgarized in comparison with that of *The Baptized Chinaman*.[8] Gleb Struve has described the novels as "almost unbearable," "because of the utter absurdity of their plots in combination with excessive lexical tricks."[9] Only isolated voices have expressed differing opinions. Vyacheslav Zavalishin writes: "No other work of post-revolutionary Russian literature can compare with [*Moscow*] in intellectual depth, intuitive premonition of Russia's future, understanding of Russian psychology, or vastness of conception." Yet even he has to conclude that *Masks* is "a much weaker effort."[10] As for Bely's style, almost the only commentator with kind words to say of his continued linguistic experimentation was Evgeny Zamyatin.[11] Otherwise the insistent ternary rhythm and the abundant neologisms that characterize these works have been seen only as a source of irritation.

Quite apart from the aesthetic question of the novels' readability, commentators in the West were handicapped by the sparseness of available information about Bely's life and thought during this last decade of his

4. A. Bolotnikov, "Neudavshiisya maskarad," *Literaturnyi Kritik*, no. 2 (1933), pp. 84–86; A. Tarasenkov, "Tema voiny v romane A. Belogo 'Moskva,'" *LOKAF* (*Znamya*), no. 10 (1932), p. 176.

5. M. Kuznetsov, *Sovetskii roman* (Moscow, 1963), p. 111.

6. Jacqueline de Proyart, *Pasternak* (Paris, 1964), p. 239.

7. V. F. Khodasevich, "Ableukhovy—Letaevy—Korobkiny," in his *Literaturnye stat'i i vospominaniya* (New York, 1954), p. 191 (first published in the Paris journal *Sovremennye Zapiski*, no. 31 [1927]).

8. V. F. Khodasevich, "Andrey Bely: *Kreshchenyi kitaets*," *Sovremennye Zapiski*, no. 32 (1927), p. 455.

9. G. Struve, "Andrey Bely redivivus," in *Andrey Bely: A Critical Review*, ed. G. Janecek (Lexington, Ky., 1978), p. 41.

10. V. Zavalishin, *Early Soviet Writers* (New York, 1958), p. 36.

11. E. Zamyatin, "Andrey Bely," in his *Litsa* (New York, 1955), p. 80.

life. As it was impossible to reconstruct reliably the intellectual context in which he was working, his works were subject to misinterpretation. This problem was inevitably exacerbated by the political division between Soviet and émigré cultures, and the inescapable elements of accommodation to the Soviet regime (*prisposoblenchestvo*) in Bely's work made the task of his distant critics doubly hazardous.

A particularly contentious issue, and one on which the interpretation of the novels was bound to depend, was the question of Bely's relations with Rudolf Steiner and the anthroposophical movement. It was common knowledge in émigré circles—and duly documented in the many memoirs of the period that have appeared over the years—that during Bely's two years in Berlin he had suffered profoundly from the final collapse of his marriage to Asya Turgeneva and from his inability to reestablish a close relationship with Steiner. He was grieved by the impossibility of returning to the anthroposophical colony in Switzerland, and Steiner's cool response made him feel rejected. He had imagined that the Western brethren would wish to hear of his intense spiritual experiences during the extreme privation of the Civil War period, but he encountered so little sympathy that he reacted by quarreling publicly with Steiner and the Anthroposophical Society.[12] What the émigré community did not know was that shortly before Bely left Berlin for Moscow in 1923, he had been reconciled with Steiner, and that although his attitude toward the Anthroposophical Society as an institution did change irreversibly, his attachment to Steiner himself had been largely restored.[13] In the absence of this information, and in the presence of clear textual evidence of an obeisance to Marxism, it was not difficult to reach the conclusion that Bely had abandoned everything he once held dear and sold himself to the Communist regime. Konstantin Mochul'sky first established this view of Bely's last novels in his monograph of 1955.[14] Fedor Stepun, who had always held the view that Bely was devoid of intellectual consistency, saw no problem in interpreting his Moscow novels as a complete ideological volte-face. He was so convinced of Bely's apostasy that he interpreted the rape of Lizasha in *Moscow in Jeopardy* as a deliberate blasphemy on the Symbolists' cult of Sophia, although nothing in the text suggests that Lizasha and Sophia have anything in common at all.[15]

Until some twenty years ago, then, Soviet critics either passed over

12. See, for example, V. F. Khodasevich, "Andrey Bely," in his *Nekropol'* (Brussels, 1939), pp. 61–99, and Marina Tsvetaeva, "Plennyi dukh," in her *Izbrannaya proza v dvukh tomakh* (New York, 1979), II, 80–121.

13. Georges Nivat, "Lettre de A. Belyj à Ivanov-Razumnik," *Cahiers du monde russe et soviétique*, 15, no. 1–2 (1974), p. 80 (letter of March 1–3, 1927).

14. K. V. Mochul'sky, *Andrey Bely* (Paris, 1955), pp. 264–65.

15. F. Stepun, *Mystische Weltschau* (Munich, 1964), pp. 349–51.

these novels in silence or condemned them as neither Marxist nor readable, while critics in the West agreed by and large that they were not
readable but found them Marxist in their ideology. Since that time,
however, the emergence of new information has made it possible to put
the record straight. One of the most important documents in this respect
is the memoirs of Bely's widow, Klavdiya Nikolaevna Bugaeva, published in full with extensive notes and commentary only in 1981, but
known to scholars from archival sources and partial publications for a
number of years previously.[16] Only a small part of Bely's copious correspondence with Ivanov-Razumnik, the only confidant to whom he wrote
regularly and in detail in this period, has been published, but the bulk of
it has been selectively available to scholars in archives.[17] Two substantial
memoirs written by Bely with no prospect of publication at that time, his
Recollections of Steiner and *Why I Became a Symbolist*, have also been published in the last few years.[18] In addition it has been possible to gain
access to the oral tradition sustained by people who knew Bely in those
years but wrote little or nothing down. In comparison with most earlier
periods of Bely's life, this last decade is still sparsely documented, and it
remains possible that future publications will necessitate a revision of
any views expressed now; but it seems unlikely that any radical misinterpretation of his work is still possible.

Only very recently has any attempt been made to reexamine the established critical opinion about these novels. The task that it seems necessary to address now is to take a fresh look at every aspect of these
rebarbative texts and attempt to interpret the aesthetic system on which
they are based. For, clearly, if they are not simply the impenetrable
gibberish that most critics have held them to be, then they are making
demands on their readers that have yet to be properly identified.

2

The element of plot was one of the essential features Bely sought to
reintroduce into his work once he had abandoned the multivolume auto-

16. K. N. Bugaeva, *Vospominaniya o Belom*, ed. John E. Malmstad (Berkeley, 1981). The
typescript of these memoirs is held in the Manuscript Divisions of Leningrad's Saltykov-
Shchedrin Library and Moscow's Lenin Library. Separate chapters were published in *Novyi
Zhurnal*, nos. 102, 103, 108 (New York, 1971–72), and in *Cahiers du monde russe et soviétique*,
15, no. 1–2 (1974).

17. See n. 13; see also R. Keys, "The Bely—Ivanov-Razumnik Correspondence," in
Andrey Bely: A Critical Review, ed. Janecek, pp. 193–204. The letters are held in the Central
Archive of Literature and Art (TsGALI), Moscow.

18. *Vospominaniya o Shteinere* (Paris, 1982) and *Pochemu ya stal simvolistom i pochemu ya ne
perestal im byt' vo vsekh fazakh moego ideinogo i khudozhestvennogo razvitiya* (Ann Arbor, 1982).

biography of which *Kotik Letaev, The Baptized Chinaman,* and *Notes of an Eccentric* were all to be part and had returned, at first unwillingly, to the novel form. As was noted at the time, the strong element of adventure found in the plot of *Moscow* particularly was a feature of Soviet literature in the period of the New Economic Policy (1921–28).[19] The specific difficulty Bely faced in constructing an adventure plot was that his basic concern, as ever, was with inner experience, with the human spiritual response to the world, rather than physical action upon the world. His hero is thus inevitably passive, and the action is that of others upon him. Nevertheless, the source of the action is a mathematical discovery that the hero, Professor Korobkin, has made, news of which has filtered through to German military spies, who have realized its great military potential and seek to acquire the details. A parallel invites itself with the image of the bomb in *Petersburg,* which expressed the power both of the apocalyptic transformation of self and world and of their annihilation. The essential difference is that the ambiguity of the bomb image is missing here. The novel is indeed concerned with the transformation of the self, but the destructive power of the discovery is an entirely separate issue, and the professor's activity, such as it is, consists in the deliberate and ultimately self-sacrificial prevention of its use.

The central strand of the plot of the first volume is concerned with how the initial information falls into the hands of Mandro, the German spy and villain extraordinary, with his attempts to elicit the details, and with the professor's gradually increasing awareness of the threat, including the practical implications of his discovery, which he had not originally perceived. This scenario culminates in what is undoubtedly the most gruesome scene in Bely's prose, as Mandro, gaining access in disguise to the professor's apartment, ties him to a chair and burns his eye out with a candle in a final, and still unsuccessful, attempt to wrest the secret from him.

The action of the novel is set on the eve of World War I; the outbreak of war orchestrates the melodramatic ending. The social environment is a mixture of the professorial circles of Bely's childhood, known from his childhood novels and later memoirs, and a highly satirized version of the social and intellectual milieu of the Symbolist period. Into this scene is set a domestic conflict not unlike others in Bely's novels. Professor Korobkin has a wife, who has been conducting a longstanding affair with his colleague Professor Zadopyatov; a son, Mitya, whose theft and sale of his books has put the Germans on the track of the discovery; and a sallow and sickly daughter, Nadya, of whom he is very fond. The domestic conflict is integrated into the adventure plot only at the point of the son's thefts. For the rest it forms a separate theme, which, however, runs in parallel with the theme of the professor's increasing insight. On the spiritual level he comes to realize that his lifelong view of the self-sufficiency of reason is inadequate; the collapse of his intellectual system is paralleled by the collapse of the sham that is his family. By the end of the novel he is entirely alone.

Mandro, whose social facade is that of an international businessman, has as family only his teenage daughter, Lizasha, whose friendship with Mitya Korobkin is the social contact point for the fathers. A process of dislocation takes place here, too, as increasingly lurid rumors fly about concerning Mandro's perversions and villainies; Lizasha becomes imperfectly and belatedly aware of these rumors, but the realization of her father's true nature comes about only through an incestuous rape. The theme of transformed awareness, central to Korobkin, is reflected in other characters: it is in evidence in a muted form in Lizasha before the rape; it is found in Mitya Korobkin after the discovery of his theft and his truancy from school; and it appears in Zadopyatov and Korobkin's wife after Zadopyatov's wife has discovered their liaison and collapsed with a stroke. It is also latent in Korobkin's friend Kierko, who emerges more fully in *Masks,* but is seen in the first novel giving solace and political instruction to Lizasha after the rape.

Thus the thematic parallels between the various elements of the novel's action are clear enough to see. A unified plot structure, however, is not to be found. In motivational terms the central strand of the mathematical discovery does not need Korobkin's family except at the one point of Mitya's theft. Its revelation and Mitya's apparent moral regeneration when he is forgiven for his misdemeanors have no further consequences, since the character makes no further appearance. The change of heart in Zadopyatov and Korobkin's wife does not affect the action. Most particularly, the crimes of Mandro, including the rape of Lizasha, are not needed for the central plot at all.

Loose ends are to be expected in a novel that was envisaged as the first of several volumes. Most of the characters reappear in *Masks,* but not, for the most part, in such a way as to become fully reintegrated into the plot. Korobkin's daughter has died of consumption, his son has become a guards officer and, we are told, is shortly to die in the war, while his wife and Zadopyatov are living together openly (the latter's wife has conveniently died). If *Moscow* hinted at a future spiritual transformation of these people, certainly nothing is to be seen of it now. The members of Korobkin's family have, indeed, no part to play in the plot of *Masks,* and are introduced, it seems, only because they are a part of the past life that the professor has to recall and reinterpret as he recovers from the madness into which he was plunged at the end of *Moscow.* However, a new family member appears, Korobkin's brother Nikanor, of whom nothing had previously been heard, except a single mention of his name at the beginning of *The Moscow Eccentric*.[20]

Bugaeva records in her memoirs how Bely's original ideas for the second volume changed between the completion of *Moscow,* in September 1925, and the beginning of work on *Masks,* in 1928. Certain minor characters that had been developed in *Moscow* beyond the needs of that novel, because he planned a more substantial role for them in the continuation, turned out not to be needed after all. The greatest change, however, was the reappearance of Mandro. At the end of *Moscow* he, too, went mad, and was said to have died in the prison hospital. But very much to his author's chagrin, he reappeared, and this seems to be the main reason why the novel changed its intended course and grew from two volumes to an envisaged four.[21] The direct consequence is that certain of the loose ends from *Moscow* are retrieved and developed. A dead Mandro could not be called a loose end; he might well have been left where he was had the character not forced itself back into Bely's imagination. But the character of Lizasha, whose development seemed bound either to be arrested or to take the political course sketched in at the end of *Moscow,* is able to play a much more substantial and integrated role in *Masks* with her father still alive. And in general the coherence of the two volumes in terms of plot seems to have been enhanced by Mandro's revival.

The main theme of *Masks* is Professor Korobkin's recovery from madness and amnesia, his reinterpretation of the earlier experience he recalls, and his attempt to put into practice the ethical convictions at which he finally arrives. His cure is due to another new character, the nurse Serafima Sergeevna. Once out of the hospital, he goes to live with Kierko and Lizasha, who are living incognito as Terenty and Eleonora Titelev, because they are involved in an underground political organization and are sought by the political police. Mandro, meanwhile, lives in the guise of a French journalist by the name of Drua-Domarden (Droit d'homme ardent). Korobkin's crucial act is to meet and forgive Mandro, then to bring him to Lizasha so that they, too, can be reconciled. The secondary strand of the plot involves the exposure of their pseudonyms and their consequent destruction. These two strands are woven together skillfully, and it is not easy to understand why the plot structure of *Masks* should have attracted so much adverse criticism.

In all, *Masks* has a cast of characters that runs into the hundreds, but many of them have no existence beyond a name and do not impinge

20. *Moskovskii chudak* (Moscow, 1926), p. 15. Further page references to the novel, reprinted in one volume with *Moskva pod udarom* (Munich, 1968), will be given in the text preceded by the roman numeral I.

21. See Bugaeva, *Vospominaniya o Belom,* pp. 142–46.

upon the plot. Those that do, apart from the distinct individuals already mentioned, tend to appear in groups, each group fulfilling a single function. The principal groups are the doctors and patients at the hospital, the associates of Titelev, and the army intelligence officers who have the task of unmasking and kidnapping Mandro. This last group has wide social connections in what is left of Moscow society, and a number of characters can be taken to represent that society. The political police, from whom the Titelevs are in hiding, also have a role in the novel, but they scarcely emerge as distinct characters. It is important to the structure of the novel, however, that none of these groups is hermetic; considerable cross-membership allows the secrets of each to be eventually exposed to the others. It is clear, for instance, that the doctors have connections with the intelligence service and that an ostensible medical commission to assess the professor's condition has in part the purpose of ascertaining whether he remembers his discovery. It is also crucial to the plot that the intelligence service has leaks to the political police. Nevertheless, the broad groups retain a clear independent identity, and are largely pursuing different and incompatible aims. Both at the individual level and at the group level, the characters of *Masks* are manifestly at cross-purposes, extracting from each other secrets that they either fail to understand or deliberately abuse.

This general bad faith is focused in the theme of revenge. Mandro becomes the hunted victim of the second volume. Lizasha desires revenge for the wrong he has done her, and consequently agrees to be hidden at a social gathering where he will appear and to confirm to the intelligence agents that their conjecture about his identity is correct. Korobkin offers the antidote to this cycle of reciprocal injury, but the practical consequences of his action are disastrous. Mandro, though identified, is safe in his hotel room because he is protected by British secret agents. Once removed from there to meet his daughter, he is exposed, and the Russian intelligence agents kidnap and kill him. When Nikanor discovers who it is that Korobkin has brought to the house, he attacks Mandro, and in the scuffle between the brothers Serafima receives an inadvertent blow. And lastly, the intelligence agents bring in their train the political police, who attack the house, whereupon the revolutionaries' stocks of ammunition in the basement are ignited, and the novel ends in a grandiose explosion.

3

All of Bely's earlier novels are composed of material that can to a very great extent be traced to his own life, and in most cases his memoirs are the principal documentary evidence for the establishment of prototypes and source materials. To some extent this is true of the Moscow novels as well, but the element of pure fiction is greater, particularly in *Masks*, and it is not without significance, perhaps, that the success of the plot structure is directly proportional to the fictionality of the material.

The domestic conflict to which Khodasevich drew attention as the essential subject of all Bely's novels is clearly in evidence in *Moscow*.[22] The early life of Professor Korobkin is almost identical to that of Bely's father, and the episode of Mitya's truancy corresponds to a story Bely tells about himself.[23] The professor's wife, however, bears little resemblance to Bely's mother as she is portrayed in other works, and the relations of the three of them are of quite minor importance. This is associated with the fact that the central character, whose point of view is most consistently shared by the narrator, is not the son but the father. Bugaeva has pointed out that it is only in externals that Professor Korobkin resembles Bely's father, while his inner experience is derived from Bely's own. She asserts, indeed, that no fictional character of Bely's was closer to its author than Professor Korobkin.[24] The novel's action is set in the decade after Professor Bugaev's death, and largely in a society with which Bely's father never interacted. Yet Bely had good reason to choose for a hero a character who so clearly resembles that other fictional depiction of his father, the Professor Letaev of the childhood novels. In both *Kotik Letaev* and *The Baptized Chinaman* Professor Letaev represents the life of pure reason, in antithesis to the mother's life of feelings and the senses, while the synthesis is enacted in the child. In the Moscow novels Professor Korobkin starts from a very similar position on his journey to regeneration.

We have no evidence of biographical sources for any of the characters beyond the family members. Mandro, Lizasha, Kierko, and particularly the minor and episodic characters seem to be pure creatures of the imagination. In *Masks* the only character for whom a prototype has been identified is the psychiatrist Pepesh-Dovliash, who, according to Bugaeva, is based on Nikolay Bazhenov.[25] However, in view of the role Bugaeva is known to have played in restoring Bely to mental equilibrium after his traumatic experiences in Berlin, it seems more than likely that she is herself the model for Serafima Sergeevna; modesty would have prevented her from suggesting such an identification. The one clear exception is the mysterious Dr. Donner in *Moscow*, Mandro's mentor, who, it is

22. Khodasevich, "Ableukhovy—Letaevy—Korobkiny."

23. A. Bely, *Na rubezhe dvukh stoletii*, izd. 2-oe (Moscow and Leningrad, 1931), pp. 26, 332–36.

24. Bugaeva, *Vospominaniya o Belom*, p. 148.

25. Ibid., p. 151. Bazhenov (1857–1923) was principal doctor of the first psychiatric hospital in Moscow. His name occurs several times in Bely's memoirs; see particularly *Mezhdu dvukh revolyutsii* (Leningrad, 1934). On p. 411 of the index to that volume (not included in all copies of the book) he is identified as the prototype of Pepesh-Dovliash.

suggested, may be no more than a figment of Mandro's imagination. The
evident similarity of this character to Dr. Steiner was one of the principal
pieces of evidence used by Mochul'sky and Stepun to confirm that Bely
was defiling his former idol in this novel. The resemblance is inescapable,
but the inference does not follow. Rather it seems that the figure of Dr.
Donner is a depiction of Steiner as Bely perceived him during the worst
period of his alienation from him in Berlin. The danger of confusion
between true spiritual knowledge and its demonic surrogate is a perennial
theme of Bely's and it is clear that Mandro has received some form of
satanic initiation; it may well be that Bely still vividly remembered seeing
Steiner in just such a light.[26]

Other tormenting recollections of Berlin also found their way into
Moscow. Bugaeva records a period in the summer of 1923 when Bely,
recently returned from the country and unable to find more congenial
accommodation, was living in a Berlin pension of a dubious character
near the Anhalter Bahnhof.[27] It seemed to consist of an endless maze of
corridors and to be inhabited by strange and hostile creatures who were
little in evidence by day but made weird and threatening noises most of
the night. On one occasion he discovered on the landing, right outside
the door of the pension, a patch of dried blood. The maze became the
source of several scenes in the novel in which characters undergo ver-
tiginous experiences related to the barbaric cultures that underlie the
present. The patch of blood grew into the separate theme of a dark-
skinned boy whom Mandro is rumored to have stabbed to death, who
then appears to Lizasha, provoking her to stab her father, and then
reappears in *Masks* as the son-brother born as a result of the rape, whom
Lizasha herself is at one time on the point of killing. Bely acknowledged
that the climactic scene of Professor Korobkin's torture was an exter-
nalization of a sense of suffering that had been with him for many years,
from childhood through to a climax in Berlin in 1922.[28]

In March 1913 Bely had written to Blok that he would never write a
novel called "Moscow" because he had "no words to portray the horror
of Moscow."[29] He was writing in a state of exhaustion from his work on
Petersburg and at a time when his relations with Asya Turgeneva were at

26. Most recently this question has been taken up again by Frédéric Kozlik, who argues
not only that Dr. Donner is based on Dr. Steiner, but that Professor Korobkin is a parody
of Dr. Steiner, while Mandro, Mitya, Lizasha, and the syphilitic dwarf Yasha Kaval'kas are
projections of different aspects of Bely himself in his relationship with Steiner (F. Kozlik,
L'Influence de l'anthroposophie sur l'oeuvre d'Andréi Biélyj [Frankfurt, 1981], III, 792–860).
This argument so disregards all the available evidence, both biographical and textual, that
it is difficult to subject it to serious criticism. In *Pochemu ya stal simvolistom*, p. 115, Bely
emphatically denied that Dr. Donner was a pastiche of Steiner.

27. Bugaeva, *Vospominaniya o Belom*, pp. 171–74.

28. *Pochemu ya stal simvolistom*, pp. 124–25.

29. Aleksandr Blok and Andrey Bely, *Perepiska* (Moscow, 1940), p. 325.

a point of crisis.[30] He had not in fact been living in Moscow for the best part of a year. His sense of its "horror" is attributable both to the gradual collapse, from the end of 1910 on, of his relations with most of the people to whom he had previously been close, and also to his increasing disaffection from the cultural life of Moscow. The setting of the novel on the eve of war is only approximate, for the purpose of identifying its outbreak with Korobkin's suffering; Bely and Asya were living in Germany and Switzerland in 1914, and he did not visit Russia that year. The atmosphere the novel evokes is a generalized atmosphere of the prewar period, when the high mystical hopes of the early years of the century had given way to vulgarity and disillusionment. Bely wrote to Blok that in writing *Petersburg* he had succeeded in overcoming his fatal connection with that city, but that Moscow still exercised an "accursed" hold upon him.[31] When he did take up the forsworn novel eleven years later, the horror of prewar Moscow was fused in his memory and imagination with the horror of postwar Berlin.

The sometimes vicious satire with which Moscow society is depicted is not, therefore, as surprising as some of Bely's early readers thought. That he should have used the names of real people, such as Valery Bryusov and Petr Struve (neither of whom he had forgiven for their refusal to publish *Petersburg* in *Russian Thought*), or such transparent pseudonyms as Balk, Buldyaev, and Bergakov (i.e., Blok, Nikolay Berdyaev, and Sergey Bulgakov), or unnamed but easily identifiable figures such as the lady poet who declared that "she disliked everything that existed, and liked everything that didn't, but even that—not entirely" ("ei ne nravitsya vse to, chto est', a ei nravitsya to, chego net; da i to—ne sovsem . . ." [I, 184])[32]—all these things could understandably be found offensive; but they are not evidence of a change of heart following Bely's return to Soviet Russia from Berlin in 1923.

Stepun took particular offense at Bely's depiction of prewar Moscow as a kind of prehistory.[33] Imagery of barbarism, of defunct or mythical civilizations, becomes increasingly evident as the two parts of *Moscow* develop. Just as the theme of paternity and parricide in *Petersburg* is subsumed in the overarching myth of Saturn, so in *Moscow* the theme of the collapse of culture is expressed in a series of references to Easter Island, the Aztecs of Mexico, and Atlantis. The city is depicted as a disorderly clutter of buildings from whose doors, which are "like fis-

30. It was in March 1913 that Asya told Bely that, as far as she was concerned, anthroposophy required asceticism, and sexual relations between them ceased (Bely, "Material k biografii [intimnyi], prednaznachennyi dlya izucheniya tol'ko posle smerti avtora," TsGALI, fond 53 [Bely], opis' 2, item 3).

31. Blok and Bely, *Perepiska*, p. 325.

32. The lady poet is Zinaida Gippius. Elsewhere Bely recalls her declaiming the line: "Mne nuzhno to, chego net na svete" (*Nachalo veka* [Moscow, 1933], p. 173).

33. Stepun, *Mystische Weltschau*, p. 350.

sures," monsters may emerge. The idea that European civilization was sinking into barbarism was not a new theme in Bely's work. It is clearly expressed in some of the articles he wrote for *The Stock Exchange Gazette* (*Birzhevye Vedomosti*) in the summer and autumn of 1916, and emerges with particular force in the brochure that he published in 1924, immediately on his return to Russia, called *One of the Mansions of the Kingdom of the Shades*.[34] The pamphlet evokes with horror the vulgarity and spiritual vacuity that he perceived in postwar Germany, and expresses them in similar terms of a descent into barbarism. It also contains passages from the second volume (never yet published in full) of the travel notes he wrote on his visit to North Africa in 1910–11. There he takes up, for instance, the topic of the French African colonies, twenty-two times the size of metropolitan France, and, in his perception, about to swamp French civilization. Unless these passages were deliberately revised before the pamphlet's publication in 1924—and there is no reason to assume they were—they show that the theme of barbarism was already present in Bely's thinking by 1911. When Stepun interprets the imagery of *Moscow* as an assertion by Bely the Bolshevik that history dawned only in October 1917, he is overlooking the long gestation these ideas had undergone.

Evidence of that long gestation is also contained in Bely's note to the effect that he had told Vyacheslav Ivanov about the hero Ivan Ivanovich Korobkin as early as 1909.[35] He later used the name for the hero of a short story, "The Yogi," written in August 1918; this character has been shown to be drawn in part from the philosopher Nikolay Fedorov.[36] Bely was not personally acquainted with the author of *The Philosophy of the Common Cause* (*Filosofiya obshchego dela* [1906]), who died in 1903, but he took a good deal of interest in his ideas, as did Vladimir Mayakovsky, Pasternak, and Nikolay Zabolotsky. At one time, in 1912, he even accepted a commission to write a monograph on Fedorov. At the core of Fedorov's thought is the idea of literal, physical resurrection through love. The Korobkin of the short story differs from the later professor in that he is given to exalted states of mind redolent of *Notes of an Eccentric*, though the two resemble each other in external details. The repeated use of the same name is clearly not accidental, and its derivation from *korobka* (box) indicates the linking theme. The box is both the isolated individual and the rational mind (*cherepnaya korobka*, cranium—literally

34. See, for instance, "Mertvye goroda," *Birzhevye Vedomosti*, no. 15745 (August 17, 1916); *Odna iz obitelei tsarstva tenei* (Leningrad, 1924).

35. *Kak my pishem* (Leningrad, 1930), p. 13.

36. "Iog (Rasskaz)," *Sirena*, no. 2–3 (Voronezh, 1918), pp. 17–30; S. S. Grechishkin and A. V. Lavrov, "Andrey Bely i N. F. Fedorov," in *Tvorchestvo A. A. Bloka i russkaya kul'tura dvadtsatogo veka*. Blokovskii sbornik III (Tartu, 1979), pp. 147–64.

skull box); true human love and community presuppose the overcoming of the rationalism of European culture.

The fact that contemporary culture is likened not to one but to several past civilizations is due to the theory of the cyclic succession of races and cultures which Steiner's anthroposophy shares with other branches of theosophy. Each race creates its own specific culture, adds its own contribution to the evolution of humankind and the universe, and makes way for the next. Each has an allotted role, a spiritual task to be accomplished, and it is the failure to carry out that task that creates evil. Some races, such as the Mongols, are believed to have failed in the past to fulfill their evolutionary task, and therefore to act as a retarding force, a force for evil, in the present world. This notion is the source of what sometimes strikes modern ears as an alarmingly racist tone in some of Bely's utterances. He insisted, however, that anthroposophy must be conceived as an all-embracing culture, not a doctrine of biological racial succession or racial supremacy.[37] It is also essential to this notion that every succeeding culture contains, in some sense, all preceding ones; every fresh stage of evolution recapitulates all past stages. Thus the collapsing civilization of *Moscow* also contains its predecessors.

On the level of individual experience this notion of cyclic repetition takes the form of the doctrine of reincarnation and karma. Into each successive existence the individual brings the fruit of former lives; evil in this life is the consequence of incorrectly lived former lives, and is to be overcome only by a future succession of lives lived correctly. Bely noted that *Moscow* had brought him face to face with the problem of karma,[38] and both volumes of the cycle contain numerous references to the idea. The clearest statement comes perhaps in *Masks*, when Lizasha, reflecting upon her affinity to her father, comes to the conclusion that "both he and she were guilty—before their birth—in a world already guilty—before creation" (251). At the climax of *Moscow in Jeopardy*, as Mandro tortures Korobkin, it appears that they are both the victims of Mandloppl, the "bloody and experienced priest" of ancient Aztec rites. Thus torturer and victim share the same karma, no one is innocent, and no one is exclusively guilty. The barbarism focused in Mandro and the rationalism represented by Korobkin are complementary aspects of a single, universal malady. A passage near the beginning of *The Moscow Eccentric* makes it clear that the professor's rationalism does violence to reality: "He feared incoherence: no sooner did he suspect incoherence in anything than he would rush to tear out its sting: decapitate it, squash it, bury it, and pave it over with a solid cobblestone; under the floor, imprisoned, the incoherence still sat there . . ." (I, 37).

37. See A. Bjely, "Die Anthroposophie und Russland," in *Die Drei*, 4 (1922), pp. 320–21.
38. *Pochemu ya stal simvolistom*, p. 95.

4

Moscow and *Masks* may surprise the reader familiar with *Petersburg*. The ingredients seem to be comparable—in each a great Russian city is the scene of an action that is set at a crisis point of recent history—yet the results are very different. Moscow does not have a function in these novels that can be compared with that of the northern capital in *Petersburg*. The urban imagery lacks the precision of the earlier novel, which incorporates Petersburg's geography into the map of its characters' minds. It is a matter of interest that, as Leonid Dolgopolov has shown, the journeys Bely's characters make through the city are physically impossible, but that judgment can be made only because the city is fundamentally recognizable.[39] No real geography is in evidence in *Moscow;* neither the familiar landmarks of the city nor the specific locale of the Arbat-Prechistenka region can be properly identified. The scenes with the greatest visual clarity are in fact those set on the outskirts of the city, and Bugaeva has pointed to some of them as derived directly from their house in Kuchino.[40] It is a weakness of the novels that the city is so anonymous, for along with geographical precision the sense of history is reduced. This is a surprising deficiency, since the changing face of Moscow was a topic dear to Bely, and one on which he had only shortly before published an essay of charm and precision.[41] No doubt part of the reason for it lies in the absence of a literary tradition for the depiction of Moscow to compare with that of Petersburg, which Bely had so successfully exploited before. Perhaps Bely felt that the patriarchial Moscow presented by Pushkin and Tolstoy or the commercial capital of Petr Boborykin was inappropriate to his purposes; whatever the reason, the complete absence of tradition and geographical verisimilitude robs Bely's Moscow of much of the demonic quality he meant to give it.

The 1905 Revolution and the echoes of the Russo-Japanese War came to life in *Petersburg* very largely because of the way they were linked to the city's geography. The workers in their Manchurian caps bustling across the bridges from the islands and the crowds demonstrating on the avenues are part of a clearly identifiable geographical and historical continuum. The historical background in *Moscow* and *Masks* is much more schematic. The ending of *Moscow in Jeopardy* is particularly weak in this respect. The outbreak of war is expressed in snatches of unattached dialogue and sketchily drawn military movements on the anonymous streets; the narrator's concluding summary is quite without concrete

39. L. K. Dolgopolov, "Obraz goroda v romane A. Belogo 'Peterburg,'" *Izvestiya Akademii Nauk, Seriya literatury i yazyka*, 34, no. 1 (1975), pp. 46–59.

40. Bugaeva, *Vospominaniya o Belom*, p. 194.

41. A. Bely, "Arbat," *Sovremennye Zapiski*, no. 17 (1923), pp. 156–82. This is a chapter from the third version of Bely's memoirs, the so-called Berlin redaction, which has never been published in full. See also A. Bely, "Otkliki prezhnei Moskvy," *Sovremennye Zapiski*, no. 16 (1923), pp. 190–209, particularly 190–92, 208–9.

reference: "The world-wide conflagration was beginning: somewhere lightning struck" (II, 248). In *Masks* the historical element is contained both in the frequent references to a military presence in the city—uniforms, marching platoons—and in sections that evoke fighting at the front. Extended networks of imagery connect the physical suffering of the soldiers with the suffering that Korobkin recalls during his recovery, but there is no historical precision. Given the ostensible dating of the action at the end of 1916, and by analogy with the ending of *Moscow*, the explosion with which *Masks* ends appears to represent in some sense the revolution of February 1917; though in the absence of any continuation it is not possible to be certain that it does. The identification of his own or his semifictional hero's inner experience with the external events of war and revolution was a constant theme of Bely's work between about 1916 and 1922. But it involved the premise that the revolution could be related to the war as resurrection to crucifixion. As Bely's confidence in that interpretation waned, the thematic identification lost its force. It sometimes seems that he maintained the historical parallel out of inertia rather than conviction.

According to the preface to *Masks*, the continuation of the novel would show how the half-mute "masks" that are its characters gain their true faces and voices in the revolution. Whether Bely could have redeemed that promise, had he lived, must remain very much a moot point. The promise seems to owe more to the demands of 1932 than to any genuine surviving belief. His disingenuous claim in the preface to *Moscow* that he was depicting the struggle between free science and the capitalist system is also a concession to the times. It is, moreover, a claim to a historicity that, as Khodasevich pointed out, is not there.[42] But if one takes that statement in the context of other attempts Bely made during this decade to assimilate his ideas to the official ideology,[43] it is possible to see it as genuinely indicating a central theme in the novel.

A topic that can be traced in practically all that Bely wrote in this period is the conflict between the free development of the human spirit and the dulling, inhibiting influence of static institutional forms. The revolution he imagined, and declared in 1924 had yet to come about, was the destruction of all such static forms forever.[44] His studies of verse rhythm and of the development of perspective in painting can be traced to the same concern.[45] Frequently in later years he expressed this idea

42. Khodasevich, "Ableukhovy—Letaevy—Korobkiny," pp. 191–93.
43. Such an attempt is perhaps best seen in *Ritm kak dialektika i "Mednyi vsadnik"* (Moscow, 1929), pp. 24–25, where Bely compares the history of the metrical forms of poetry with the Marxist concept of the succession of dominant social classes.
44. "Dnevnik pisatelya. 1. Ritm zhizni i sovremennost'," *Rossiya*, no. 2 (11) (1924), p. 140.
45. The theory of perspective is summarized in *Masterstvo Gogolya* (Moscow and Leningrad, 1934), pp. 115–19, but according to Bugaeva it was developed in greater detail in Bely's diary (*Vospominaniya o Belom*, p. 109).

through analogies with official doctrine, using "capitalism" as a kind of shorthand term to denote all such inhibiting forces, and asserting an identity between the strivings of the Symbolists in this direction and the political ambitions of the Marxists.

This is the theme of Evgeny Zamyatin's book *Robert Maier*, published in 1922.[46] Bugaeva has suggested that the torture scene in *Moscow* owes a direct debt to Zamyatin's scene in which Robert Mayer, the founder of modern theory about the nature of energy and matter, is "treated" for his madness by being confined in a straitjacket and strapped to a chair. His madness consists only in his insistence that his theories make sense and that they were originated by him and no one else. His commitment to a hospital has been instigated by his wife and her family, who lack all sympathy and understanding for his financially unrewarding pursuit of science and wish to turn him into a conventional provincial doctor. As Bugaeva also notes, the attitude of Professor Korobkin's family toward him in *Moscow*, though less actively malign, is not dissimilar, and the psychiatrist Pepesh-Dovliash in *Masks* treats his patients in a way Robert Mayer would have recognized. She recalls that when Bely read this short biography by Zamyatin he was moved to exclaim, "Such is the fate of genius!"[47] The depth of the impression it made on him is confirmed by an article written much later, in 1932, in which he compares the fact that Mayer was declared mad for his scientific discoveries with the charges of mysticism leveled at himself for his discoveries in the sphere of verse rhythms.[48]

"The innovator as heretic" would be a better definition of the theme than Bely's description in terms of the capitalist system. The theme makes another strong appearance in the scene of Korobkin's jubilee ceremony at the university, during which a newly discovered star is named after him, Kappa-Korobkin. The students' attempt to carry him shoulder-high down the stairs at the end of this ceremony is said to resemble the dragging of a heretic to the cliff from which he is to be thrown. The bust of Leibniz that adorns Korobkin's study has a bearing on this theme, too. Leibniz not only propounded the idea of "the best of all possible worlds," and thus is associated with the professor's complacent rationalism, but also discovered differential calculus, the significance of which his contemporaries quite misunderstood.[49] The innovator as heretic is a topic in which Bely had a deep personal involvement; it permits us to draw a parallel between the hero as misunderstood and

46. E. Zamyatin, *Robert Maier* (Berlin, Petersburg, Moscow, 1922); see also O. M. Cooke, "Bely's *Moscow* Novels and Zamyatin's *Robert Mayer*: A Literary Response to Thermodynamics," *Slavonic and East European Review*, 63, no. 2 (April 1985), pp. 194–209.

47. Bugaeva, *Vospominaniya o Belom*, p. 149.

48. "Poema o khlopke," *Novyi Mir*, no. 11 (1932), p. 245.

49. *Ritm kak dialektika*, p. 10.

abused scientist and the author as misunderstood and abused innovator in literary technique.[50]

Professor Korobkin, however, is not simply an innocent victim. As the rationalist and originator of the discovery, he bears responsibility for its possible consequences. What Bely says about the inability of Leibniz's contemporaries to understand the practical application of differential calculus is true initially of the professor himself. The two parts of *Moscow* reveal two processes taking place: the realization on the part of all concerned that domestic harmony is a fiction dependent upon the professor's absence at the university, and the professor's gradual understanding that his view of a static, rationally ordered universe is inadequate to the reality around him. These are the two poles of the professor's life. In his disordered domestic situation he is likened to his two-dimensional counterpart, the dog Tomochka, while his mathematical intellect, which inhabits a world of n dimensions, is identified with the star Kappa-Korobkin. From the synthesis of these two aspects a complete, three-dimensional man is to emerge.[51] The theme of such synthesis of opposites through a process likened to crucifixion is too familiar from Bely's earlier novels to require much comment.[52] What is new about the form it takes in the Moscow cycle is its specifically ethical character. In accepting the "crucifixion" that results from his refusal to part with his discovery, Korobkin is performing an ethical act that is available only to him, as possessor of it. The causal connection between the original discovery and the professor's suffering is a real one, requiring only the fact of his moral choice to be realized.

The theme of the discovery appears only in a somewhat attenuated form in *Masks*, where it is obscured by other, more prominent themes. It is present, however, in the fact that two of the conflicting groups have a clearly stated interest in its possession. The army officers infiltrate the hospital with a view to finding out whether the professor still remembers it; and the revolutionary Titelev (alias Kierko) attempts to persuade Korobkin that it is his moral duty to put it at the disposal of "the party." The professor declines to do so, refusing to connive at the murder that the surrender of his discovery would entail, and insists instead on his new doctrine of love. He then destroys the papers on which the calculations are written, and nothing more is heard about the discovery. The theme of the morality of knowledge is expressed in quite a different form in the therapeutic practice of Serafima Sergeevna, to which Korobkin owes his recovery. Her principal medicament is color; she

50. Bely addresses this issue in the preface to *Masks*, pp. 8–9.

51. Zh. [Yakov] El'sberg, "Tvorchestvo Andreya Belogo—prozaika," in his *Krizis poputchikov i nastroeniya intelligentsii* (Moscow and Leningrad, 1930), p. 212.

52. It provides the basic structure of *The Silver Dove*, *Kotik Letaev*, and *The Baptized Chinaman*, and is present in a parodic form in *Petersburg*.

teaches her patients to practice the concentrated perception of colors: "Collect them, examine them; the shades that are poured out into your eyes flow forth from your eyes as a science of seeing, so that without the history of painting you can learn for yourselves what is more important, so that you can understand exactly *for what purpose knowledge is needed*" (63). The identification of colors with moral and spiritual qualities is common to both theosophy and anthroposophy; in the case of Bely it was perhaps most decisively influenced by a reading of Goethe, whose *Farbenlehre* he had studied extensively.[53] What Serafima Sergeevna is propounding here is direct observation of nature in a way that immediately suffuses objective knowledge with moral significance, in direct contrast to the rationalism that has produced the destructive discovery. This route from morally neutral knowledge that can destroy the world to morally significant knowledge that can save it is Korobkin's route through the two volumes of the Moscow cycle.

Serafima Sergeevna, in her ministration to the professor, is likened to Cordelia with Lear. Korobkin, having lost the sight of one eye in the torture scene, has come, with Serafima-Cordelia's help, to see with clarity of a different order out of the other. This becomes a central image of *Masks*, and one that has been shown to contain echoes of Shakespeare's tragedy.[54] But the mad and solitary king is only one of Korobkin's aspects. Another is a clear affinity, in his impractical insistence upon simple truths that others ignore, to Don Quixote; and in the catastrophic ending that his action brings about, it is perhaps that latter-day reincarnation of Quixote, Prince Myshkin, who comes to mind. It is worth noting that Zamyatin makes much of Robert Mayer's apparent resemblance to Don Quixote in his tenacious defense of his discoveries against all the odds. It seems all the more likely that Zamyatin's book helped Bely to imagine the character of Korobkin as he reappears in *Masks*, a character who no longer bears much resemblance to Professor Letaev (or Professor Bugaev) or to the earlier incarnation of Korobkin in "The Yogi."

One thing the tragic Lear and the comic Quixote have in common, and share with such hounded geniuses as Robert Mayer, is isolation. Bely had always been preoccupied with the problem of isolation and community, of reconciling subjective and collective truths. His theory of Symbolism was, in an important respect, an attempt to show that the process of artistic creation was a way of overcoming that problem, of communicating to others the deepest subjective experience, which refer-

53. See Bely's *Rudol'f Shteiner i Gete v mirovozzrenii sovremennosti* (Moscow, 1917), chaps. 3 and 5.
54. See Olga Muller Cooke, "Moskovskii korol' Lir: Andrej Belyj's Debt to Shakespeare in his Moscow Novels," paper delivered to AATSEEL, Houston, 1980.

ential language cannot convey. The idea of the Symbolists as a community of individualists who had found a means of communication that resolved that paradox was inherent both in his championing of the Symbolist cause and in his immoderate disappointment each time his ecumenical ambitions collapsed. In Berlin he had even come to the conclusion that the Anthroposophical Society, that last repository of his hopes, was as stultifying and inimical to the spiritual development of the individual as any other social form.[55] The idea that an unrestricting, free community was still possible did not leave him, however. He mentions in *Why I Became a Symbolist* a conflict between a group of Moscow anthroposophists that took the name of Vladimir Solov'ev and another, named after Mikhail Lomonosov; his own sympathies lay with the latter group because of its commitment to the kind of community he had in mind, unlike the rigid structure into which the Anthroposophical Society in Germany had, in his view, degenerated.[56] This information makes possible the interpretation of a deliberately coded message in the dedication of *Moscow* to "the peasant from Arkhangelsk, Mikhail Lomonosov." Nothing in the text explains this dedication, and its seeming irrelevance has been remarked upon.[57] It is in fact a reference not only to the patron of the Moscow anthroposophists but also to one who (at least in their belief) was christened in honor of the Archangel Michael. The seven archangels, regarded as the spirits of nations, were believed to have successive periods of dominion over the world; the seventh and last such period is the dominion of Michael, the patron of Russia, who hands his authority over to the returning Messiah.[58] The task of men in the period of Michael's dominion is, then, to prepare the world for the second coming, to realize what Steiner called the "Christ impulse." It is worth noting in passing that Stepun remarked in his obituary of Bely that he had heard a rumor to the effect that Bely was working on a novel about the Archangel Michael; what Stepun did not realize was that he had already read it.[59]

This, in fact, is the deepest theme of the Moscow novels. In *Why I Became a Symbolist* Bely speaks of their theme as the development of the lower Ego (*Ya*) into the Ego proper.[60] In her memoirs Bugaeva describes the theme in terms of a theory he was developing in his unpublished study "The History of the Development of the Spiritual Soul," about the

55. *Pochemu ya stal simvolistom*, pp. 96–99.
56. Ibid., p. 106.
57. Khodasevich, "Ableukhovy—Letaevy—Korobkiny," pp. 190–91.
58. Margarita Woloschin, *Die grüne Schlange: Lebenserinnerungen* (Stuttgart, 1954), p. 276; A. Turgenieff, *Erinnerungen an Rudolf Steiner und die Arbeit am ersten Goetheanum* (Stuttgart, 1973), pp. 24–25; M. Chekhov, "Zhizn' i vstrechi," *Novyi Zhurnal*, no. 9 (1944), p. 13.
59. F. Stepun, *Vstrechi* (Munich, 1962), p. 160.
60. *Pochemu ya stal simvolistom*, p. 95.

growth of the "individuum" out of the "personality."[61] In contradistinc-
tion to the self-sufficient personality, which reached the apogee of its
development at the time of the Renaissance, the individuum, which is
developing at the present time, is conscious of itself as the unit of a
collective and at the same time represents the controlled harmony of the
various, possibly conflicting, potentialities of the personality. Bugaeva
describes this notion in purely psychological and historical terms, but it is
clear that to an anthroposophist an equally important feature of the
individuum must be his quality as the sum of incarnations in many
different personalities. This theme makes an appearance in *Notes of an
Eccentric,* where it is apparent that the organizing principle of the individuum is the awareness of the presence of Christ in every incarnation.
Christ is the "Ego proper."

This Ego proper is revealed in a process not of instruction or study or
even thought in the usual sense but of immersion in the contemplation
of that which is already contained in the ego. Much of the imagery of
Moscow shows Professor Korobkin undergoing such a process. It is because the appeal is to levels of the self which are normally beyond coherent expression and communication that Bely devised the stylistic and
linguistic innovations that made his own experience as author so similar
to that of his hero. Every level of Bely's text is affected by the philosophy
that his hero's fate embodies in action.

5

Bely's return to the novel form involved not only the restoration of the
plot element that had been largely absent from his autobiographical
novels but also a return to the third-person narrator, who had been
replaced after *Petersburg* by a narrator who spoke in the first person. In
reply to a questionnaire organized by an émigré journal in Berlin, he
had written of his conviction that literature was moving in the direction
of the "monumental poem," "whether in verse or prose I don't know."[62]
This meant that the narrative voice had also to be quite unlike the self-
conscious, Gogolian voice of *The Silver Dove* or the mélange of voices that
narrate *Petersburg.* Some of the stylistic peculiarities of the Moscow novels can be seen as ways of concealing the narrator, of reducing the
process of mediation through an ostensible narrator's consciousness.
These strategies are more highly developed in *Masks* than in the first
volume.

61. Bugaeva, *Vospominaniya o Belom,* pp. 155–59. The expression "Spiritual Soul" is the
accepted anthroposophical translation of Steiner's *Bewusstseins-seele.* A chapter of Bely's
study has been published by Julia Crookenden in *Andrey Bely: Centenary Papers,* ed. Boris
Christa (Amsterdam, 1980), pp. 39–51.
62. "My idem k predoshchushcheniyu novykh form," *Veretenysh,* no. 1 (1922), p. 2.

Bely's letters to the proofreader of *Masks* explain the significance of his arrangement of words on the page as a device for presenting graphically to the reader's imagination different levels of the characters' experience, and thus obviating explanatory remarks from the narrator. He uses indentation to differentiate between themes relating to the action of *Masks* and themes that show the professor's recollection of the action of the first volume; direct narrative on the order of "the professor remembered" is thus avoided. Indentation also serves to separate from a character's inner thoughts the distracting impressions received from the environment.[63] Bugaeva, describing his process of composition, notes that in the early stages his draft would often contain simple narrative passages of what he called a "fearless naïveté"; he would imagine the response of his critics: "There you are, I do know how to write simply. It's all comprehensible: 'he said,' 'she stood up,' 'the professor entered.' People should hear what Andrey Bely is capable of. There now—he's writing like a human being . . . Bravo! . . . He's come to his senses."[64] It is significant that the process of reworking the novel involved precisely the removal of such simple narrative passages; none are to be found in the published text.

Masks, in particular, contains an abundance of neologisms designed to replace the usual finite verb forms of direct narration. Actions are frequently rendered by what Vladimir Nabokov, in another context, has called the "interjectional" verb.[65] These are either monosyllabic words derived from the root of a verb (such as *torch, shamk, bod, bros, porkh*) or compounds derived from the addition of a prefix to such a root (such as *vstryas, vyyurk, nakhmur*). Many such words in Bely's language are neologisms, while others are standard nouns, such as *plesk i tresk*, pressed into service for this purpose. Others, again, appear at first sight to be neologisms, but turn out on examination to be attested by the dictionary of Vladimir Dal', which Bely greatly admired.

Nevertheless, despite such devices, a few instances of direct and sometimes quite startling narratorial interventions remain. In a few passages of *Moscow* the narrator inserts a comment on events belonging to a period later than the novel's action: "the house was taken apart for firewood" (I, 16). These passages are closely related to similar ones in *The Baptized Chinaman,* which also exploited Bely's recollections of the Moscow of his childhood and youth. In that novel they had a clear justification, in that they served to establish distance between the time of writing and the time of the action. Their effect in *Moscow* is similar; they appear to authenticate the historical aspect of the novel, to which Bely

63. Bely, "Pis'ma k A. M. Miskaryan," *Russkaya Literatura,* no. 1 (1973), p. 157.
64. Bugaeva, *Vospominaniya o Belom,* p. 206.
65. A. S. Pushkin, *Eugene Onegin: A Novel in Verse,* trans. and ed. V. Nabokov (London, 1964), II, 405.

draws attention in his preface.[66] In the absence of the first-person narrator and the autobiographical theme, however, that effect is harder to
understand as part of a coherent system. There remains a strong suspicion that such passages have crept in accidentally from another genre,
the memoirs. The other narratorial interventions in *Moscow* are of a
more traditional nature: ironic attempts to point a moral or deliberate
anticipations of future events. These are relics of the ironical narrator of
Bely's first two novels.

In his review of *Masks*, Leonid Timofeev wrote that only the clearly
present ironical narrator in *Moscow* provided a functional justification
for such stylistic devices as neologisms and rhythmic prose. That ironical
narrator was absent from *Masks*, and the devices consequently served no
purpose.[67] This is probably the only comment in the critical literature on
these novels that makes the essential connection between the stylistic
devices and the narrative voice. However, it appears to make it the
wrong way round. It is the development of the devices that makes possible the disappearance of the narrator. Nor is it in fact true that the
narrator entirely disappears from *Masks*, although Timofeev is surely
right in noting the absence of irony. (Perhaps the only exception is an
ironic question addressed to the architect responsible for Titelev's
house, on p. 41.) Apart from a couple of relatively unimportant antic-
ipatory comments, the narratorial interventions in *Masks* are of two
kinds. One involves the use of the first-person pronoun. A passage evok-
ing a windblown kaleidoscope of Moscow streets, for example, starts
with an address to a "blue-rumped birdie" (*sineguzaya ptashechka*): "Is it
of spring you will twitter to me?" (26). The first-person pronoun appears
again in an apostrophe to "my soul" that is unambiguously lyrical (38).
The other kind consists of a direct address either to the reader or to the
critics. The number of interventions of any kind in the four hundred
pages of *Masks* does not run into double figures, and it is not easy to see
them as forming any kind of system. The most feasible explanation of
their function is perhaps that they serve to remind the reader that concealed within the novel's text a narrator of a very specific kind is still to
be found.

6

The feature of Bely's prose in the Moscow novels which has attracted
perhaps the greatest volume of negative criticism is its insistent ternary
meter, which most critics have found irritating and tedious. Bely himself
drew attention to it in his preface to *Masks*, where he insisted that his

66. *Moskovskii chudak*, "Vmesto predisloviya" [p. 8].
67. Timofeev, op. cit., p. 214.

prose was not prose at all, but verse printed as prose simply for the purpose of economizing on paper. There has certainly been considerable doubt as to whether the language of these novels may properly be described as prose. Viktor Zhirmunsky, discussing the theoretical problem of rhythm in prose, excludes Bely's late prose from consideration on the grounds that it is a hybrid form.[68] Boris Tomashevsky argues that whereas the rhythm of prose is the result of the meaning and the expressive quality of the discourse, the rhythm of verse is itself the determining feature, within whose framework both meaning and expression have to be accommodated.[69] It is clear that rhythm in Bely's prose has much higher priority than this definition accords to prose rhythm; yet the language of the Moscow novels cannot well be defined as verse in these terms either. For the rhythmic patterns of verse comprise recurrent forms larger than the foot—the line and the stanza; these forms are not present here. The question of definition has been addressed in specific relation to Bely's prose by Mikhail Gasparov, who defines prose for this purpose as "a text that is not subject to extrasyntactic division into correlatable segments." He argues that in order to be sure that the language of *Masks* was not perceived as verse, it was necessary for Bely to make certain that the word boundaries could on no account be mistaken for line boundaries. He therefore increased both the number of dropped metrical stresses and the frequency of dactylic word boundaries at the expense of feminine ones, particularly at the ends of syntactic units where the suspicion of a line boundary is most likely to arise. As a result, Bely's text can never be divided into units resembling the lines of verse; any such identification is precluded either by a missed stress, by a dactylic word boundary, or by the unexpected ending of a sentence.[70]

In short, Bely's prose is prose in a real sense, because it specifically lacks the larger recurrent features of normal Russian verse in ternary meters. In the absence of these features the rhythm tends to be perceived as merely an accumulation of more and more of the same thing. Gasparov quotes Sergey Bondi as characterizing rhythmic prose with the help of an image from Vladimir Mayakovsky, who called the line of verse a burning fuse and the end rhyme a barrel of dynamite: in rhythmic prose the fuse burns on and on, but no explosion ensues.[71] However, Gasparov's consideration of the characteristics of this rhythmic prose in the context of an examination of the essential features of ternary verse is extremely helpful not only in settling the question of definition but also in providing an approach to the positive description of its rhyth-

68. V. Zhirmunsky, "O ritmicheskoi proze," *Russkaya Literatura*, no. 4 (1966), p. 105.
69. B. Tomashevsky, *Teoriya literatury. Poetika* (Moscow and Leningrad, 1928), p. 73.
70. M. L. Gasparov, *Sovremennyi russkii stikh: Metrika i ritmika* (Moscow, 1974), pp. 164–65.
71. Ibid., p. 164.

mic character. For clearly the disposition of word boundaries and dropped stresses is devised not simply with a view to the negative function of distinguishing the rhythmic prose from verse but also with a view to producing a specific aesthetic effect not achievable either by verse in the customary sense or by prose that is not metrical.

The difficulty critics have faced in coming to terms with the rhythmic character of this prose has lain partly in the relatively small amount of attention that has been paid to the analysis of the rhythm of ternary verse. The classical distinction between meter and rhythm, proposed by Bely himself in 1910 and resting upon the possibility of replacing any metrical stress except the last in the line by an unstressed syllable, operates only for binary meters, since the dropped metrical stress is virtually unknown in Russian ternary verse. Rhythmic variation within ternary meters is harder to perceive and depends, as Gasparov has pointed out, upon the positioning of word boundaries and upon the presence of hypermetrical stresses.[72] Within certain limits the methods Gasparov has now applied to ternary verse can also be used to show the rhythmic variability of Bely's prose, and in this case the additional feature of the dropped metrical stress has also to be included. The limits of the method's applicability are determined, self-evidently, by the absence of the longer recurrent units typical of verse. No comparisons are possible between "feet" on the basis of their position in the line or between "lines" on the basis of their position in the stanza. What is possible, however, is a broad analysis and description of the nature and extent of rhythmic variation in comparison with a hypothetical norm in which all metrical stresses would carry stress, and there would be no hypermetrical stresses. It is possible to describe the distribution of different types of word boundary relative to each other; the concentration of a single word-boundary type produces an effect in marked contrast to a passage in which the three types occur at random. A very clear example of the effect of concentration is to be found in the closing paragraph of the first section of the first chapter of *Masks*, where of twenty-three word boundaries, sixteen are dactylic, and the section ends with seven consecutive dactylic word boundaries. It is also worth noting, incidentally, that this rhythmic concentration is accompanied by dense alliteration:

> I—dom: tsveta pertsa; i—dom: tsveta persika; pepel'ny plevely; kleikogo berega krasnye gliny; zarechnye pesni; i vstrechnye vstrepety vetra.
> I—domik Kleokleva—
>   —v pepel'nykh plevelakh, pepel'no vleplennyi v pepel'nom vozdukhe! [16]

72. Ibid., pp. 27, 126.

And a house the hue of pepper; and a house the hue of peach; weeds—
ashen; red clay on the sticky riverbank; across the river—singing; and the
throbs of a head-on wind.
And Kleoklev's cottage—

—amongst ashen weeds, plonked down ashen in
the ashen air!

Dropped syllables are extremely unusual in the rhythmic pattern of
these novels. Indeed, they are virtually absent from *Masks*, where the
system is most fully developed. The natural breaks, which are perceived
exclusively on the basis of syntax, do not result in missing syllables, as
will happen in verse in any rhyme scheme with heterogeneous clausuli.
If a syntactic unit ends with a masculine word boundary, the following
unit will start with two unstressed syllables; if there is a feminine word
boundary at the end, the next segment will start with one unstressed
syllable. This is true even at the ends of the chapter sections, and includes the section titles. This unbroken continuity of the rhythmic outline is a major reason why the text cannot be perceived as verse. The
length of the perceived syntactic units becomes one of the elements
determining rhythmic variation, but it stands in an interdependent relationship with other sources of variability and cannot in itself be used to
define the rhythmic character. It appears to be the case that the longer
the syntactic units, the fewer other variations can be accommodated.
Certainly it is possible to point to passages in *Moscow* where a combination of long units and variations such as misplaced stresses or even
omitted syllables leads to a marked blurring of rhythmic outline. Given
the expectations that the general rhythmic pattern creates in the reader's
mind, the aesthetic effect of such passages appears aberrant and unpro-
ductive.

As a general rule, about half the syntactic units ("lines") into which the
text naturally divides contain rhythmic variations of one sort or another,
usually generated by dropped metrical stresses or hypermetrical stresses
(very rarely omitted syllables).[73] What matters, however, is not the average incidence of such features but the contrasts that can be created by
variations from the average. Such variations can be examined on different scales. An empirical examination on a small scale leaves the strong
impression that stress variations of these kinds occur much more frequently in passages of dialogue than in descriptive passages. A statistical
examination on a larger scale reveals considerable variations in chapter

73. A full rhythmic analysis would require an examination of the relative degree of stress
on the metrical stresses. If a satisfactory scheme could be devised for quantifying relative
degrees of metrical stress, it would be possible to demonstrate rhythmic variation over
longer segments of text.

sections. Three chapter sections of *Masks,* compared for the incidence of dropped metrical stresses and hypermetrical stresses as a percentage of total theoretical "feet," give the following variations:

Pages	Dropped stresses	Hypermetrical stresses
13–16	9.76	4.62
26–29	5.49	12.17
208–10	4.01	7.57

Clearly the simultaneous presence of these two features would lead, above some threshold of tolerance, to the perception of the hypermetrical stresses instead of the metrical ones, not as well as them, and thus destroy the perception of metrical form. It is therefore reasonable to suppose that there is a tendency toward an inverse relationship between them, although at relatively low percentage levels it probably does not operate. What these figures show, however, is that there is room for quite a substantial range of variation, and it is safe to say that the rhythmic characters of these three sections differ significantly.

Bely's last critical work on rhythm, *Rhythm as Dialectics,* falls in the period between *Moscow* and *Masks.* In that book he expounds arguments about the nature of rhythm in poetic language that he had been developing over many years. He had always considered that the rhythm of poetry contained the most direct expression of the poet's "creative agitation," and had stated in an earlier essay that of all the levels of poetic language, rhythm was the deepest.[74] All poets experience sound prior to image or idea; poetry is born from an original inchoate impulse that can be expressed only as the dim awareness of certain sounds. The final form of the poem, the images and ideas that are given body by the manipulation of those sounds, is never entirely adequate to the original impulse, and it follows that the reader who seeks the deepest meaning of the poem must delve beyond its semantics to its acoustic properties, and ultimately to its rhythm.

Bely presents the history of verse forms in terms of the relations of rhythm and meter. Rhythm has limitless possibilities, while meter consists in the canonization of certain limited forms. If rhythm is the genus, meter is the species. Each meter divides further into subspecies. As metrical forms become canonized, meter turns into a straitjacket from which true expression seeks to liberate itself.[75] His own empirical work on the rhythmic variability of the iambic tetrameter is the evidence on which this argument is based. The underlying assumption is that the more flexible the rhythmic form of the work can become, the more closely the final text can correspond to the original impulse.

74. "Zhezl Aarona," *Skify,* no. 1 (Petrograd, 1917), p. 200.
75. *Ritm kak dialektika,* pp. 20–29.

These arguments are important for perceiving the function of the rhythm in Bely's Moscow novels. The rhythm is an essential aspect of the narrative voice. As the semantically identifiable features of the narrator recede and the mediation of a conscious mind is maximally removed, so this essential function is transferred to that feature of the text which is held to express the deepest workings of the unconscious. The same concept of the personality that is embodied in the development of Professor Korobkin is also to be found in the replacement of a traditional third-person narrator by a narrative voice that functions not through semantics but through rhythm.

In the rhythmical analysis of *The Bronze Horseman* that provides the experimental material in *Rhythm as Dialectics*, Bely seeks to demonstrate the variations that can be perceived in the rhythmic character of the poem if different sections are compared with one another. He calculates a numerical average of deviation from absolute meter for the poem as a whole and then plots on a graph each section's deviation from that average. It then becomes possible to draw all kinds of parallels between sections that are found on this basis to be either similar or significantly dissimilar in terms of rhythm, and to use those findings about the "deepest" level of expression to modify the meaning of the more superficial level of semantics. What the words mean depends upon the rhythmic form in which the meaning is expressed. Bely justifies this notion by a concept of *"formo-soderzhanie,"* understood as a dialectical relationship between form and content, or specifically between rhythm and meaning. The same observations could be made in terms of an ironical relationship between two narrative voices, one that means what it says, as it were, and another that passes comment upon the ostensible meaning through the variations of rhythm. If one were to attempt a similarly detailed analysis of *Masks* (a formidable and daunting task), it would be possible likewise to draw connections between passages on the basis of rhythmic similarity or dissimilarity, and this exercise might reveal structural features not otherwise perceived. However, an ironical relationship between different narrative voices would not emerge from this process, because Bely's structure of rhythm is not imposed upon a text that can be read simply in a linear way. All the other compositional principles of these novels are also governed by the concern to replace the denotative character of conventional discourse by a language that allows maximum flexibility of interpretation.

7

Bugaeva's account of Bely's process of composition is an invaluable guide to the unraveling of the Moscow novels. The method she describes was the one he used in writing both *Moscow* and *Masks*, but never before; and she follows his own example in calling it a "mosaic" method. The first stage was a process of selection. For this purpose Bely compiled lists under a variety of headings on special strips of paper. The heading might be the name of a character, or it might be one of the novel's major themes, such as "Russia" or "War." The items in the list might then consist of particular characteristics, gestures, fragments of conversation, habits, ways of dressing, or specific landscape features, street scenes, or domestic trivia. Other headings might refer to larger or smaller units: the gestures of Nikanor might require a list to themselves; the relations of Kierko and the professor could become a separate section. But Bugaeva stresses that there was nothing stable or mechanical in this process; the lists could multiply and change character incessantly, some falling into disuse while others came into prominence. Bely gathered material at this level mainly while walking; he carried notebooks in which he would jot down anything that occurred to him, for transference to the official lists when he came home.

The development from this accumulation of raw material to the production of a finished text went through several stages of refinement, for each of which Bely had his own designation; but it was impossible for anyone else to know what exactly was the difference, for instance, between a "semilist" (*polu-rubrika*) and a "pre–rough copy" (*predchernovik*); and his nomenclature became much more complex than that. The general outline of the process, however, could be observed. Bely would go through his lists, or those of them that related to the themes to be touched upon in the section he was about to write, and would select the particular items that were needed at this point. Then began the gradual process, through anything up to six or more revisions, of turning that selection of material into a continuous text. As the writing of the novel progressed, the material on the lists would gradually be either exhausted or transferred elsewhere, and at the end of each major section Bely would "review his troops" and rearrange the remaining lists and items.[76]

In all Bely's novels, the basic structural unit is the two- or three-page subchapter, or section, into which the chapters are divided. The mosaic of these sections may be composed of a variety of elements taken from Bely's original lists. Easily recognizable are the leitmotifs and recurrent images that express the background reality: the demonic city in *Moscow*, the distant but ever-present war in *Masks*. In *Masks* an important role is played by the reappearance of images from *Moscow*, expressing the professor's gradual recovery from amnesia. But of great importance too are the elements that convey the characterization and the local atmosphere.

The characterization in the Moscow novels has been particularly se-

---

76. Bugaeva, *Vospominaniya o Belom*, pp. 186–91, 204–8.

verely criticized. In keeping with his maximal concealment of the narrator, Bely entirely avoids continuous description. The characters are represented by individual physical features that may recur as leitmotifs, by distinctive quirks of diction, which often help to identify the speaker in the absence of direct indication by the narrator, and to a very great extent by gestures. These are not the psychologically expressive gestures of, say, Tolstoy's characters, which reveal a level of inner experience that may be in conflict with their spoken words, or even not consciously perceived by the character, but which are usually relevant to the dramatic situation of the particular scene. Bely's gestures are thought of as revealing even deeper levels of experience and being essentially untranslatable into other terms. In the context of all the other patterns in the mosaic, the reader is meant to perceive them in such a way that he comes to participate in that which lies below conscious thought and analytic expression. But a dramatic relationship with the immediate action is usually hard to perceive, and the gestures themselves are often somewhat outré and tend toward caricature.

Local atmosphere is expressed above all through color. The color descriptions are a great deal more varied and complex in the Moscow novels than in Bely's earlier works. Their source is recorded in Bugaeva's memoirs. Starting in the summer of 1924, when he was just beginning work on *Moscow*, Bely began to collect pebbles of as many different shades as possible from the Black Sea beaches. He would then arrange them in trays, showing the minutest gradations of shade. At other times he did the same with autumn leaves. He would then use the colors from a particular tray, within a particular range of the spectrum, to describe the possessions or the environment of particular characters or situations.[77] This process entailed the coining of many neologisms, usually compound adjectives or compressed similes. The descriptions have a twofold purpose. On the one hand, the manner of their origin confirms that they are part of Bely's perennial concern to capture in language that which exists in nature but tends to slip through the gaps between established concepts. He had long held the view, entirely in agreement with Goethe's, that the colors of nature were infinite in number, while the notion of any color as an absolute hue was a mere abstraction.[78] On the other hand, the color descriptions express the moral quality of the character in question. Bely speaks of this in the preface to *Masks* (11). Goethe had argued that

> every colour produces a distinct impression on the mind, and thus addresses at once the eye and feelings. Hence it follows that colour may be employed for certain moral and aesthetic ends. Such an application, coinciding entirely with nature, might be called symbolical, since the colour

77. Ibid., pp. 178–86.
78. *Putevye zametki: Sitsiliya, Tunis* (Moscow and Berlin, 1922), pp. 147–49.

would be employed in conformity with its effect, and would at once express its meaning.[79]

Bely's use of color to convey his meaning to his readers is precisely the same device that Serafima Sergeevna uses in relation to her patients. Like the device of characterization through gesture, the device of scene setting and characterization through color is designed both to avoid narratorial intervention and to express that which lies beyond the customary domain of descriptive language.

If there is a single principle uniting the elements of the mosaic, it is the principle of synaesthesia. This is what Bely is referring to when he writes in the preface to *Masks* of his endeavor to suffuse meaning (*smysl*) with color and sound, so that color and sound may in their turn become "eloquent" (11). At work here, as elsewhere, is the anthroposophical tenet that abstract meaning is only a tiny fraction of the totality that is real meaning. Real meaning is grasped not simply with the mind but with all the faculties of perception. This becomes in the text an aesthetic principle: the correlation of moral qualities, as revealed in action, with the colors of the relevant settings and the sounds of the language in which it is expressed.[80]

The theory behind this method is developed in *Gogol's Craftsmanship*, on which Bely began work shortly after he completed *Masks*. The assertion of an affinity between particular colors and particular sounds was not new, of course, and Bely himself had argued it before, notably in *Glossolalia*. In *Gogol's Craftsmanship* he justifies such affinities in terms of natural synaesthesia. An expression such as "a warm color" is explicable by the fact that the range of visible colors is only one segment of known radiation; beyond visible red are the infrared rays, which consist precisely of warmth. Thus, it must be inferred, the phenomena perceived by the various senses differ only in degree, not in kind. As regards sound, Bely takes up again an idea expressed in his 1917 essay "Aaron's Rod," to the effect that the very phonetic elements of words are the roots of metaphor, and declares that "the acoustic metaphor posits color beyond the limits of the spectrum."[81] Radiation beyond the visible range can be perceived at the very edge of consciousness by means of "colored

79. Goethe, *Theory of Colours*, trans. Charles Lock Eastlake (London, 1840; reprinted 1967), p. 350.

80. The relation between sound and gesture is a further element of this synaesthesia, and one that underlies the development of the art of "eurhythmy," by which Steiner and some of his pupils sought to reveal the inner meanings of sounds in dance movements. Bely took a strong interest in this subject, as is witnessed by the diagrams of gestures relating to particular sounds in his *Glossolaliya* (Berlin, 1922), pp. 16–18. The possibility of connections between the gestures of the characters in the Moscow novels and phonetic features of their descriptions remains an unresearched topic.

81. *Masterstvo Gogolya* (Moscow and Leningrad, 1934), p. 116.

hearing," which in ordinary, everyday perception is obscured. Thus it is apparent that the euphonic patterns of a text may complement and supplement the sensory images created by the semantic meaning of the words. If color is inseparable from moral attributes, then so must be sound.[82]

The "acoustic metaphor" in its pure form, with its attached but untranslatable connotations of color and moral quality, can be seen to underlie the numerous instances, particularly in *Masks,* where phonetic elements clearly predominate over semantic meaning. Several characters make only a single appearance and consist, essentially, of nothing but the sounds of their names. There is, for instance, a rhyming list of schoolchildren taking part in a political demonstration, and an English baronet:

Ser Ranzher,—
        —s oranzhevoi bakoi,—
        v oranzhevom smokinge,—
                —orang-utangom
                otplyasyval tango . . . [112]

Sir Ranger—with orange sideburns—in an orange dinner jacket—like an orangutang—was dancing the tango!

Since such characters are nowhere incorporated into the plot, no further conclusions about them can be developed; and Bely described Sir Ranger as simply "a musical interlude between two chapters," inserted to give the reader a rest from the plot.[83] However, the example does provide a concise demonstration of how the principle operates. The dominant alliteration of *r, n,* and *zh* and the assonance on *a* are accompanied by the single color orange, while the gentleman who is the sentence's subject, himself a member of a decaying culture, dances a vulgar, barbaric dance in the manner of a subhuman animal. It is the pattern of alliteration and assonance, superimposed upon the basic skeleton of rhythm, that holds the sentence and its images together, exemplifying, it would seem, Bely's contention that poetry originates in the awareness of sound.

8

The dialectical concept of *"formo-soderzhanie"* which Bely posits in *Rhythm as Dialectics* can be extended beyond the specific relationship

82. Ada Steinberg has written at length on the moral significance of the acoustic patterns in Bely's novels in her *Word and Music in the Novels of Andrey Bely* (Cambridge, Eng., 1982).
83. Bely, "Pis'ma k A. M. Miskaryan," *Russkaya Literatura,* no. 1 (1973), p. 158.

between rhythm and meaning to a more comprehensive relationship between the content of his last novels, as expressed in characterization, description, and plot, and their form, understood as the totality of stylistic devices employed. Throughout the development of his aesthetic thinking, Bely can be seen to interpret formal classifications as movable points in an unbroken spectrum. In his argument about definition by genre in "The Forms of Art" (1902), he posits an unbroken spectrum between spatial and temporal forms, on which existent genres occupy certain given positions, but other positions can in principle be occupied by putative other genres.[84] His views on rhythm have the same characteristic, as he first demonstrates that the iambic tetrameter is in fact a number of substantially different forms, and later conceives of a range of possible rhythmic forms that removes the distinction of principle not only between different meters but between verse and prose. At the same time he develops with increasing definition his fundamental premise that style is not merely an accumulation of external features, but consists in the inner coherence of those features and is the most fundamental expression of an artist's outlook. Thus in the end no dividing line separates the content of a work of literary art from its form; a literary utterance has no meaning that can be perceived apart from its form. A formal feature such as a particular alliteration becomes, through the synaesthetic association among sound, color, and moral quality, an element of content as well. The meanings that can be contained in literary language understood in this way cannot be expressed in any other language. Any attempt to translate the relationships established in a literary text into analytical discourse is liable to render static and thus fundamentally distort that which has meaning only when it is perceived as part of a dynamic and fluid whole. The innovations of a morphological and syntactic nature in Bely's late prose are designed to facilitate the perception of dynamic meaning and to reduce tension between content, as conventionally understood, and that dynamic meaning of content and form fused together.

It was perfectly clear to Bely that he was making unprecedented demands upon his readers. They have indeed proved unwilling or unable to follow him into the arcane world that *Moscow* and *Masks* express. The voice crying in the wilderness, the unrecognized prophet preaching a new and unwelcome truth, is not only the theme embodied in the story of Professor Korobkin but also the inescapable import of the novels' style. And just as the plot shows the gradual emergence of the "higher Ego" in the hero, so it is the "higher Ego" of the reader that the whole novel as a complex of dynamic meaning is designed to appeal to and liberate from the tyranny of the status quo.

84. "Formy iskusstva," first published in *Mir Iskusstva*, no. 12 (1902), and reprinted in *Simvolizm* (Moscow, 1910).

The antipathy of critics and the indifference of readers to these novels has certainly been due in part to the fact that they have not fully perceived the works' aesthetic system, but it does not follow that the elucidation of that system must of necessity result in a reversal of the negative judgment. A reappraisal is clearly overdue, but a fresh assessment based on an interpretation of the aesthetic system, offered here, is bound nevertheless to remain somewhat tentative. *Moscow* has proved more accessible than *Masks* and has generally been more favorably received, perhaps because it is in fact both less innovative and less consistent than *Masks,* and because it contains often irrelevant thematic and stylistic echoes of Bely's earlier novels. *Masks* is arguably a much greater achievement, because of the consistency that runs throughout it, from the view of man and history and the ethical nature of knowledge that underlie the plot, through its narrative devices and the mosaic structure of its parts, down to the details of its linguistic texture, both its acoustic and semantic properties. Surely no other work in Russian literature proposes and executes so radical a redefinition of man's cognitive, ethical, and linguistic universe.

6

Bely's Memoirs

LAZAR FLEISHMAN

Throughout his career Andrey Bely drew on his own life for much of the material of his prose and verse. As Vladimir Alexandrov has shown in his essay in this volume, beginning with *Kotik Letaev* in 1915–16, the autobiographical stratum in Bely's work becomes more and more evident. Such works as *The Baptized Chinaman, Notes of an Eccentric,* and the long poem *The First Encounter* are often difficult to distinguish from autobiography or memoirs. One could point as well to specific memoir elements in Bely's portrait of cultural life in the Moscow novels. But beginning in the 1920s, Bely turned explicitly to the memoir, a form he had essayed very rarely before.[1] Of his works in this genre the best known are *Recollections of Blok* (*Vospominaniya o Bloke*, 1922–23), *On the Border of Two Centuries* (*Na rubezhe dvukh stoletii*, 1930), *The Beginning of the Century* (*Nachalo veka*, 1933), and *Between Two Revolutions* (*Mezhdu dvukh revolyutsii*, 1934). A few others have recently come to light, such as his memoirs of Rudolf Steiner. These works certainly testify to his attachment to the genre in the last half of his literary career.

Alexandrov has discussed in his essay the anthroposophical impulse underlying Bely's shift to a more overt autobiographical stance in his fiction. This shift had, of course, begun while Bely was residing in Switzerland, pursuing his studies with Rudolf Steiner and participating in the construction of the Goetheanum in Dornach. Bely's "retrospectivism" continued and even intensified after he returned to Russia in August 1916. With his renewed and increasingly active involvement in the quarrelsome and highly ideological literary life of Russia's two cap-

---

1. Bely's 1907 "silhouettes" of Jean-Léon Juarès, Dmitry Merezhkovsky, and Stanislaw Przybyszewski and his obituaries of Nikolay Storozhenko (1906), Lidiya Zinov'eva-Annibal (1907), and Valentin Serov (1916) must be regarded as appreciations rather than memoirs. The 1907 "Vladimir Solov'ev" falls into the same category, even though it is subtitled "Iz vospominanii"; it is the only work of Bely's before the 1920s so designated.

itals—a life he had thought long behind him when he settled abroad in 1913—Bely began to develop a new attitude toward his literary work, one that emphasized the "unsettled" nature of his professional image. "I am a writer by accident," he wrote in *Notes of an Eccentric*.[2] He struck the same note in 1928, in *Why I Became a Symbolist:*

> I see clearly that I could have become a philosopher, poet, prose writer, naturalist, critic, composer, theosophist, circus acrobat, circus rider, magician, actor, costumer or director; [. . .] having taken aim and having said firmly, *"I shall be a writer,"* I nevertheless consciously left for myself in the rear the possibility of tactical retreats [. . .]; possessing the resolution to execute my craft, I still had the will to fall back on the reserves—and if necessary to change my craft.[3]

In the last year of his life Bely wrote: "It is awkward and difficult to speak about myself as a writer. I am not a professional; I am simply a seeker; I could have become a scholar or a carpenter. I thought least of all about a career as a writer."[4] We can thus to some degree relate the intensified autobiographical orientation of Bely's work as a whole—one that erased the boundary between *Wahrheit* and *Dichtung*—to his awareness of and emphasis on the uncertainty, even contingency, of his calling.

A noteworthy feature of the memoirs proper is their striking heterogeneity both in style and in the ideological intentions that over many years impelled the author to persist in the genre. Often discrepancies, inconsistencies, and sharp contradictions emerge when accounts of the same events and portraits of the same people in various volumes of the memoirs are compared. Such inconsistencies raise the issue of the reliability of the memoirs as a historical source. Scholars have noted this aspect of the works and urged caution, while continually drawing on them for information. They have not, however, raised the question of the function of autobiography and memoirs both in Bely's own work and in the literary culture of his time. The present essay cannot fill this gap in Bely scholarship. Its goal is more modest: to describe in general terms the changing historico-literary context that prompted Bely to set down

2. *Zapiski chudaka* (Moscow and Berlin, 1922), I, 70. Compare the 1933 statement in "O sebe kak o pisatele" (see n. 4): "I became a writer only by accident."

3. *Pochemu ya stal simvolistom i pochemu ya ne perestal im byt' vo vsekh fazakh moego ideinogo i khudozhestvennogo razvitiya* (Ann Arbor, 1982), pp. 22–23. The manuscript is held by the Moscow Central State Archive of Literature and Art (hereafter TsGALI), fond 53 (Bely), opis' 1, item 74.

4. The opening sentences of "O sebe kak o pisatele," published in Polish translation in the journal *Wiadomości literackie*, no. 47 [518] (October 29, 1933). It appeared in full in Russian in the Soviet press only in 1972, in *Den' poezii*. The Russian text is reprinted in an appendix to K. N. Bugaeva, *Vospominaniya o Belom*, ed. John E. Malmstad (Berkeley, 1981), pp. 322–28.

his memoirs and determined the polemical orientation they took at a given time.

Such an inquiry is needed because memoirs in general have played a role in the study of Russian Symbolism quite disproportionate to their significance for researchers of other periods of Russian literature. Historians of the Pushkin period, for example, can rely in their investigations on a vast amount of published letters, diaries, and other personal papers. It is only very recently that such documentation has started to become available in any significant quantity for the decades in which Bely and his fellow Symbolists lived. We have had to rely heavily on memoirs instead, and no other published memoirs concerned with Russian literature in the modernist period can rival Bely's in the wealth of their information, the breadth of their panorama of literary life, or the contribution made by their author to the development of Russian Symbolism. Such leading figures of the movement as Valery Bryusov, Vyacheslav Ivanov, and Aleksandr Blok did not leave memoirs; those of such unquestionably influential figures as Zinaida Gippius and Georgy Chulkov and of more minor figures such as Petr Pertsov and Vladimir Pyast offer important details, but they cannot compete with Bely's in scope. The memoirs of Bely's other contemporaries—Aleksey Remizov and Marina Tsvetaeva, Osip Mandel'shtam and Boris Pasternak, and in particular Vladislav Khodasevich—contain invaluable insights and remarkable characterizations of the period, but none of these writers was among the founders of the Symbolist movement. None of them belonged to its organizational nucleus. It is Bely's memoirs that are still justly considered the major source on Russian Symbolism, but they present several problems.

The vagueness of the boundaries between Bely's memoir texts presents an immediate difficulty. We know that the death of Blok provided a direct impetus for the writing of the memoirs proper: Bely began them on August 11, the day following Blok's funeral.[5] He read them at two sessions of the Free Philosophical Association (Vol'fila) in Petersburg that autumn.[6] The full text (more than one hundred pages) of this initial version of the memoirs, devoted exclusively to Blok, was published in 1922 in the sixth and final issue of the journal *The Notes of Dreamers* (*Zapiski Mechtatelei*) as "Recollections of Aleksandr Aleksandrovich Blok."[7]

5. Bely's diary entries from August 8 to September 7, 1921, served as the basis of the work. They were recently published by S. S. Grechishkin and A. V. Lavrov in *Literaturnoe nasledstvo*, vol. 92, *Aleksandr Blok: Novye materialy i issledovaniya*, bk. 3 (Moscow, 1982), pp. 788–830.

6. M. A. Beketova, *Aleksandr Blok: Biograficheskii ocherk* (Petersburg, 1922), p. 305.

7. In 1964 the memoirs were reprinted as a separate book in England: Andrey Bely, *Vospominaniya ob Aleksandre Aleksandroviche Bloke*, Introduction by Georgette Donchin (Letchworth, 1964). All further references will be to this reprint, with its title given in quotation marks.

By this time Bely was no longer in Russia: in November 1921 he had settled in Berlin. Even before the publication of the Blok memoirs in *The Notes of Dreamers,* he had begun to expand them for *Epopee (Epopeya),* the journal he edited. Work on them occupied him almost exclusively during his first months in Berlin, and this new, expanded version, titled *Recollections of Blok,* took up the lion's share of the four volumes of *Epopee* that appeared between April 1922 and April 1923.[8] This text, however, in its turn formed only an insignificant fragment of an enormous three-volume memoir, "The Beginning of the Century" ("Nachalo veka"). This work was not published in Berlin, as planned, because of Bely's return to Soviet Russia in 1923 and the general decline in the publishing activities of Berlin's Russian émigré colony.[9]

It is to Marina Tsvetaeva that we owe the account of Bely's return to Moscow. She emphasizes the suddenness and spontaneity of Bely's act. In her literary portrait of Bely, "A Captive Spirit," she cites a letter he sent to her from Berlin in November 1923 in which he complained about Berlin and asked her to find him refuge in Prague, where Tsvetaeva was then living. Tsvetaeva asserts that this letter was sent on the very day that Bely set off for Moscow.[10] It would be difficult to find a more apt illustration of the impulsiveness, even rashness, of the poet's decision to return to his homeland and of the general chaotic state of his thoughts and actions.[11] John Malmstad was the first to suspect the accuracy of Tsvetaeva's testimony, for as he has shown, in November 1923 Bely was no longer in Berlin; he left there on October 23 and was in Moscow by October 26.[12] The supposition about the suddenness of Bely's decision to return to Soviet Russia also has no validity: in a letter written to Ivanov-Razumnik on March 1–3, 1927, Bely states that he had

8. *Epopeya,* no. 1 (1922), pp. 123–273, chaps. 1–3, dated "Petrograd–Berlin, 1921 goda"; no. 2, pp. 105–299, chaps. 4–5; no. 3, pp. 125–310, chaps. 6–7, dated "Zossen-Swinemünde, 22 g., May–June"; no. 4 (1923), pp. 61–305, chaps. 8–9, dated "Berlin, 1922 g. December." The title "Vospominaniya o Bloke" appears over the text, but the journal's table of contents lists "Vospominaniya o A. A. Bloke." I have chosen to use the first title (and to italicize it) to avoid confusion with the similarly titled text published in *Zapiski Mechtatelei.* The reprint of the four journal installments issued by Fink Verlag (Munich) in 1969 as *Vospominaniya o A. A. Bloke* makes a volume of 785 pages; all further references will be to this reprint and its new pagination.

9. Bely left the complete manuscript of the work in a large trunk, with other papers, in Berlin when he returned to Moscow. The trunk was for a time in the possession of his publisher, Solomon Kaplun-Sumsky, but then disappeared; see Nina Berberova, *Kursiv moi* (Munich, 1972), p. 466; Aleksandr Bakhrakh, "Po pamyati po zapisyam: Andrey Bely," *Kontinent,* no. 3 (1975), pp. 313–17. Bely apparently took with him a few portions of the third volume. At least that is all that is preserved now in Soviet archives in Moscow (TsGALI) and Leningrad (in the Saltykov-Shchedrin Library). This unpublished work should not be confused with the 1933 *Nachalo veka.*

10. Marina Tsvetaeva, *Izbrannaya proza v dvukh tomakh* (New York, 1979), II, 118–19.

11. See K. Mochul'sky, *Andrey Bely* (Paris, 1955), p. 239.

12. See his introduction to Bugaeva, *Vospominaniya o Belom,* p. 30.

already firmly made this decision in June 1923.[13] (This plan was also reported in the newspapers at the time.)[14] It is likely that the letter cited by Tsvetaeva was written not in 1923 but in November 1922, before the arrival in Berlin of Klavdiya Nikolaevna Vasil'eva (later Bely's second wife). In any case, Tsvetaeva's story is unsupported.

I would not linger over this question of chronology if it were not closely related to the writing of Bely's memoirs. In the letter to Ivanov-Razumnik of March 1927, Bely directly links his decision to leave for Moscow to the writing of the sketch "Moscow," a part of the third volume of the so-called Berlin redaction of "The Beginning of the Century."[15] Clearly, the memoir pieces on Moscow which Bely published in the émigré press in 1923 are fragments of that sketch.[16] In them the author described the Moscow of fifteen years earlier with a nostalgia so intense that his homesickness for Russia shows through on every page. Readers of the time could not have failed to see in them a kind of explanation of Bely's much-criticized decision to return to Russia and his farewell to the emigration. One could conclude that whereas Bely's memoirs originate with Blok's death, which occurred when Bely was preparing to leave Russia, the conclusion of this memoir cycle in 1923 is closely related to his decision (a far less spontaneous one than Tsvetaeva assumed) to return home.

The "Berlin redaction" (1921–23) of "The Beginning of the Century" remains unpublished as a whole. We are familiar with it only through the *Recollections of Blok,* which formed its core and appeared in the journal *Epopee,* and through several fragments in other publications.[17] We know, however, that while Bely further reworked the *Epopee* recollections, "Blok became," in his words, "only a pretext for my recollections. The entire revision moved in the direction of intimate recollections."[18] And a new work, "The Beginning of the Century," emerged. (Bely also considered but rejected the title "Blok and His Time" ["Blok i ego

13. See Georges Nivat, "Andrej Belyj: Lettre Autobiographique à Ivanov-Razumnik," *Cahiers du monde russe et soviétique,* 15, no. 1–2 (1974), p. 81.

14. "The poet Andrey Bely is going to return to Soviet Russia in August," wrote the critic Petr Pil'sky (under the pseudonym Pisatel') in a note in the "Literaturnyi kalendar'" of the Reval newspaper *Poslednie Izvestiya,* June 20, 1923.

15. Nivat, "Lettre autobiographique," p. 81.

16. See "Otkliki prezhnei Moskvy," *Sovremennye Zapiski,* no. 16; "Arbat," *Sovremennye Zapiski,* no. 17; and "Otkliki prezhnei Moskvy," in the Berlin newspaper *Dni,* July 1, 1923. "Arbat" was reprinted in the Moscow journal *Rossiya,* no. 1 (10) (1924).

17. In addition to the publications in the newspaper *Dni,* in the Paris journal *Sovremennye Zapiski,* and in *Rossiya* (see n. 16), see also "Iz knigi 'Nachalo veka,'" *Voprosy Literatury,* no. 6 (1974), pp. 214–45.

18. Quoted in K. N. Bugaeva, A. S. Petrovsky [and D. Pines], "Literaturnoe nasledstvo Andreya Belogo," *Literaturnoe nasledstvo,* no. 27–28 (Moscow, 1937), p. 614. One of the results of this revision are the memoir fragments telling of Bely and Asya Turgeneva's meeting in 1912 with Rudolf Steiner; see "Iz vospominanii," *Beseda,* no. 2–3 (1923), pp. 83–127.

vremya"].) In other words, already at this first stage of work on the memoirs (1921–23) there are seemingly three separate texts, successively growing out of and intersecting each other, each representing a different distance from its common source (Blok), and each further departing from that source in the direction of more general reminiscences. It should be borne in mind that Bely began his revisions even before the initial material had been published: we have already noted that he was writing that expanded Berlin version of the recollections of Blok before the short Petersburg original appeared, and he was engrossed in work on "The Beginning of the Century" before the expanded Blok memoirs were published in *Epopee*.

Of all of Bely's published works, the *Recollections* that appeared in *Epopee* afford the most complete, detailed, and objective—insofar as memoirs can be or ought to be objective—elucidation of events in the period 1900–1912. Although similar in initial impulse (the impact of Blok's death) to the version in *The Notes of Dreamers*, it elaborates on many incidents recorded there. Most important, because it is much longer than the Petersburg publication, it could cover events and years that fell outside the scope of the original version. Thus, here for the first time, Bely speaks in detail of the period of his differences with Blok and brings the narrative up to the time of the founding of the Musaget publishing house.[19] At the same time, the second version is not simply a memoir; it contains extensive passages giving detailed analyses of Blok's lyrics. Unrelated to the biographical "plot," these passages occur in the sections relating the two poets' disagreements and quarrels. Thus a kind of dialogue occurs between Bely's two different critical assessments of Blok's work, that of the first decade of the century (represented by long citations from Bely's old reviews of Blok's books) and that of 1922–23. These chronological shifts are intended to strengthen Bely's later anthroposophical interpretation of Blok's work and life. In resorting to such an interpretation, Bely would never have admitted that he was possibly falsifying his friend's image, despite Blok's patent alienation from the teachings of Rudolf Steiner. Rather, in 1922 Bely saw not only his whole personal life but everything of importance in it—and nothing was more important to him than Blok's art—in the "new light" of anthroposophy, as he put it in his 1927 letter to Ivanov-Razumnik.[20]

Both publications—the Petersburg one of 1922 and the Berlin one of 1922–23—helped establish an evaluation of the early Blok as a poet and mystic who unconsciously resonated with the "spiritual knowledge" of anthroposophy. At the same time, such a portrayal legitimized for Bely's

19. This borderline is important because, according to Bely, his break with Musaget in 1912 signaled his departure from literature (*Pochemu ya stal simvolistom*, p. 68).
20. Nivat, "Lettre autobiographique," p. 77.

contemporaries the notion, which persists to this day, of Blok and Bely as poet-twins, despite the differences in their lives. In the early 1920s such a notion appeared completely natural for the additional reason that in the years following the Revolution Blok and Bely, of all the poets of the Symbolist generation, were particularly close—in their acceptance of the October Revolution and attitude toward postrevolutionary conditions and in their participation in the Scythian group,[21] the Free Philosophical Association, and the journal *The Notes of Dreamers.*

Bely emphasizes his "brotherhood" with Blok both in the first decade of the century (Blok the "anthroposophist *avant la lettre*") and in the most recent past, when he gives glimpses of their shared experience of postrevolutionary Russia. This attitude should be seen in the light of Bely's Berlin experiences. He had looked upon his arrival in Europe as salvation, but he found himself under fire by opponents of various camps and abandoned both by his wife and by his former kindred spirits, the members of the Anthroposophical Society.[22] His attitude toward the Revolution became the focal point for many of the criticisms leveled at him, and he sometimes used the memoirs to defend himself against such attacks. He therefore deliberately violated chronology by including in his portraits of Dmitry Merezhkovsky and his wife, Zinaida Gippius, and of Bryusov sarcastic remarks implicitly contrasting their positions toward the Revolution—calling the Merezhkovskys "strikebreakers" who had abandoned the struggle against Bolshevism within Russia, Bryusov a "time server" of the new regime—with his own position and Blok's.[23] Similarly, negative remarks about the Anthroposophical Society at times find their way into discussions of Blok's works.[24] The memoirs thereby take on a doubly tendentious (the less favorably disposed would say biased) tone as they picture both the past and the present.

Bely's treatment of Berdyaev in the *Recollections* similarly reveals the close connection between the account of the past and the time at which the memoirs were written. In speaking of his philosophical acquaintances in Moscow in 1908, Bely singles out Berdyaev and, contrasting

21. See Stefani Hoffman, "Scythian Theory and Literature, 1917–1924," in *Art, Society, Revolution: Russia, 1917–1921,* ed. Nils Åke Nilsson (Stockholm, 1979).

22. Bely later spoke of this period as "the most difficult moments of my life," when "it seemed as if I had lost myself, my way, my friends 'of the right' and 'of the left,' when the anthroposophists (in Berlin, in Stuttgart) reviled me, the émigrés reviled me, as did the 'Soviets,' when they reviled me in Dornach and in Moscow ('aha—how he has FALLEN!')" (*Vospominaniya o Shteinere,* ed. Frédéric Kozlik [Paris, 1982], p. 173).

23. See *Vospominaniya o A. A. Bloke* (Fink ed.), pp. 351–53 on the Merezhkovskys and p. 143 on Bryusov: "At that time [1905–6] Bryusov was for all of us a 'figure' (not what he is now)." See also V. F. Asmus, "Filosofiya i estetika russkogo simvolizma," *Literaturnoe nasledstvo,* no. 27–28 (1937), p. 41.

24. See *Vospominaniya o A. A. Bloke* (Fink ed.), pp. 386–88, for example.

him to the Merezhkovskys, praises him with particular warmth and enthusiasm:

> At about the same time Nikolay Berdyaev entered my world of thought; truly, Berdyaev's personality, which was receptive to the vibrations of the time and understood the Symbolist psychology, really spoke to me; an original thinker who had gone through both the school of sociological thought and the school of Kant, he impressed me as a great man, filled with nobility; he impressed me as an independent man, who leaned neither toward the orthodox nor toward Merezhkovsky; at the same time his vitality was striking; I do not remember when I began dropping in on Berdyaev, who was then living [in Moscow] somewhere near Myasnitsky—but I remember: I was drawn ever more powerfully toward him; the atmosphere of his apartment prompted the liveliest intellectual exchange and a kind of coziness of conversation, unconstrained and sparkling; Berdyaev himself behind the tea table became dear to me; I liked his directness and the candor of his positions (I did not agree with him in particulars); and I liked the kindness that smiled out "from behind the dogmatism" of his maxims, and the always sad glance of his sparkling eyes, the Assyrian head; thus my sympathy for Berdyaev over the years naturally grew into a feeling of love, respect, and friendship.[25]

We hear in this description an echo of the enormous popularity that Berdyaev enjoyed on the wave of the religio-philosophical enthusiasm which gripped Moscow in the middle of 1922 and which was expressed, in particular, in the activity of the Free Academy of Spiritual Culture.[26] In his own memoirs, Fedor Stepun, for example, recalled: "Never before or after did I feel the volcanic nature of Berdyaev's spirit so strongly as in the last years of our life in Moscow."[27] The recent dramatic events in Berdyaev's life—in August 1922 he had been arrested in Moscow and a few weeks later he was exiled together with a large group of intellectuals—formed the direct background for Bely's praise of him in the *Recollections*. References to Berdyaev in Bely's later memoirs are less enthusiastic. And we might recall that soon after his arrival in Berlin in 1922, in a review of the first two issues of the journal *Epopee*, Berdyaev sharply criticized the *Recollections*. He accused both Bely and Blok of an inability to understand the Russian Revolution, a superficial attraction to its irrational and elemental nature, and a "passively feminine attitude" toward it. "Andrey Bely," he wrote, "constantly mixes up and equates 'the revolution of the spirit' with the external, sociopolitical revolution. Aleksandr Blok does the same thing. This is precisely the great lie and

25. Ibid., pp. 560–61.
26. See "Vol'naya Akademiya Dukhovnoi Kul'tury v Moskve," in *Sofiya: Problemy dukhovnoi kul'tury i religioznoi filosofii*, ed. N. A. Berdyaev (Berlin, 1923), I, 135–36.
27. Fedor Stepun, *Byvshee i nesbyvsheesya* (New York, 1965), II, 269.

temptation that must be exposed. This is the substitution of Anti-christ."[28]

No polemical tone colors the portrait of Blok in the memoirs in *The Notes of Dreamers,* where an elegiac-confessional note predominates, as it does for the most part also in *Epopee.* Blok's family members had warmly welcomed the poetic aura with which Bely surrounded Blok's youth in the funeral oration he delivered in Petersburg in August 1921 and in the "Recollections" in *The Notes of Dreamers.*[29] In *Epopee,* however, the narrative framework was expanded to encompass the period of disorder in the Symbolist camp, and could not avoid going beyond the "seraphic" Blok. An elucidation of the polemics in the Symbolist press—in which Bely was the fiercest participant and Blok, in Bely's words, was the only (although secret) topic[30]—demanded an accounting of the "shadowy" aspects of the past. Bely did not say a word here about his own unfortunate romance with Lyubov' Dmitrievna Blok; this story remained taboo until the last volume of his memoirs, *Between Two Revolutions,* which appeared posthumously (and even there Bely made every effort to conceal the identity of Lyubov' Dmitrievna). Cursory remarks about the Bloks' unsettled family life did, however, appear in the *Epopee* text.[31]

The last part of Bely's memoirs published in *Epopee*—the account of the years 1911–12—presents a counterpoint of two opposite fates or life courses: on the one hand, Bely's growing intimacy with Asya Turgeneva, their trip to Italy and northern Africa, return to Russia, and visit to Petersburg; and on the other, Blok's drunkenness, despair, and "gypsy abandon" (*tsyganshchina*). The poets' "last meeting" in February 1912 is described in a symbolist manner: Bely's account of their conversation touches lightly on an illness of Blok's which forces him to avoid the company of friends. The narrative hints at venereal disease, but the reader must make the assumption, and Bely passes on to other matters. The parting of the two friends is accompanied by a description of the street: "Pedestrians ran by, prostitutes were standing around; I thought: 'Perhaps that one right there will approach him. . . .' "[32] The veiled suggestion of disease later develops into the motif of Russia's sickness in the chapters that discuss Blok's late lyrics. Whatever Bely's motives for introducing such intimate hints, Bely depicted these shadowy moments in this version at least as forcefully as the glowing ones, if not in such detail. Therefore, his later assertion that he had given an overly idealized por-

28. Nikolay Berdyaev, "Mutnye liki," in *Sofiya,* p. 157.

29. Beketova, *Aleksandr Blok,* p. 305. Dmitry Maksimov describes Bely's oration in his memoir essay in this volume.

30. *Vospominaniya o A. A. Bloke* (Fink ed.), p. 490.

31. Readers of the time could also have obtained certain details about the Blok marriage from Beketova's *Aleksandr Blok,* which had just been published.

32. *Vospominaniya o A. A. Bloke* (Fink ed.), p. 718.

trait of Blok in 1922–23, that he had "overromanticized" him, has to be taken with serious reservations.[33] Because *Epopee* stopped publication with the fourth issue, the Blok reminiscences remained incomplete. It is difficult to judge what interpretation Bely might have given to the "gypsy" Blok in the later versions of the memoirs, since he did not reach this moment in them. But one can guess that in *Epopee*, Bely's own recent personal tragedy—his break with Asya Turgeneva—left its mark on his depiction of the "gypsy" Blok of 1912. It reflected his "universally homeless" situation in Berlin in 1922.

Upon his return to Russia, Bely tried to publish his Blok memoirs, but was thwarted by the censors. The situation in the country had changed decisively since 1921, when Bely had left for Berlin. The activities of the Russian Anthroposophical Society were forbidden, the Free Philosophical Association (Vol'fila, Bely's favorite "offspring") had been closed, and he felt himself isolated in the new literary world. Bely regarded Lev Trotsky's article about him, first printed in *Pravda* on October 1, 1922, when Bely was still in Berlin, as the "mark of Cain" casting him out of Soviet literature. He wrote in 1928: "I returned to my '*GRAVE*' in October 1923: to the 'grave' into which Trotsky had laid me, and after him his followers, and after them all the critics and '*truly vital*' writers [. . .]."[34] Like many others of Bely's complaints, this statement may now seem a paranoid exaggeration, but we can assume that his certainty in November 1922 that his "path [to Russia] was cut off"[35] and the letter written then to Marina Tsvetaeva were manifestations of the shock he experienced when Trotsky's article appeared.

In 1922, for the first time since the Revolution, Trotsky had appeared in print as a literary critic, and his critical feuilletons were the first public statements by one of the leaders of the Revolution on purely literary questions. (These articles were part of the "ideological offensive" then under way, which included the exiling of a group of academicians and philosophers, among them Berdyaev, to the West in the autumn of 1922.) Understandably, they carried the weight of a government edict. In his general survey of new Russian literature, Trotsky depicted Bely as the most important and typical figure of its extreme reactionary wing: "The individualistic, symbolist, mystical literature of the period between the revolutions [1905–1917], that literature which is decadent in mood and range and overrefined in technique, finds its most concentrated expression in Bely, and through Bely it collides with October most notoriously of all." The article ended with a devastating pronouncement to

33. *Nachalo veka* (Moscow and Leningrad, 1933), p. 472.

34. *Pochemu ya stal simvolistom*, p. 118.

35. See Bely's letter to N. O. Shchupak in Boris Sapir, "An Unknown Correspondent of Andrey Bely (Andrey Bely in Berlin, 1921–1923)," *Slavonic and East European Review*, 46, no. 116 (July 1971), p. 451.

which Bely alluded in 1928: "Bely is a corpse and he will not be resur-rected in any shape or form."[36]

In a letter to Stalin of August 31, 1931, Bely was to ascribe his isolation in Soviet letters to the "knockout blow" delivered by Trotsky, and add: "For two years after Trotsky's article I was, so to speak, beyond the threshold of literature."[37] It is noteworthy that Trotsky based his evalua-tion not on Bely's fictional works but almost exclusively on the "Recollec-tions of Aleksandr Aleksandrovich Blok" in *The Notes of Dreamers.* Trotsky's "death sentence" may explain why publication of that journal was halted in 1922, as well as why Bely was unable to publish "The Beginning of the Century" in the Soviet Union upon his return.

Bely's return to literature was signaled by the revision of the Moscow theme, not in memoirs but in the novel *Moscow (Moskva),* which he began in October 1924. But the stream of memoirs continued unchecked. Shortly after completing *Moscow,* Bely began to set down his recollec-tions of Rudolf Steiner. Obviously he knew that they were unpublishable in the Soviet Union of the late twenties; they were addressed to the narrowest circle of like-minded friends, his fellow anthroposophists, among whom copies circulated. Bely worked on them from 1926 to 1929.[38] They did not appear in the original Russian until 1982, and then, of course, only in the West. (A German translation was published in 1975.)[39] Their appearance in the West laid to rest once and for all the belief that Bely had not only left the Anthroposophical Society but bro-ken completely with Steiner's teachings after his return to Russia, a view given wide circulation by such writers as Mochul'sky and Stepun.[40] Bely scholars had long known this rumor to be false, and the publication in 1974 of the so-called autobiographical letter to Ivanov-Razumnik of March 1–3, 1927, offered positive proof. Nevertheless, the notion of Bely's rejection of anthroposophy persisted. It is now clear that despite the disappearance of open remarks about anthroposophy from Bely's public statements in the late 1920s and early 1930s, and the silence about

36. L. Trotsky, "Vneoktyabr'skaya literatura," *Pravda,* October 1, 1922; quoted from his *Literatura i revolyutsiya* (Moscow, 1923), pp. 37, 44. See Bely's *Pochemu ya stal simvolistom,* pp. 118–19.

37. Gleb Struve, "K biografii Andreya Belogo: Tri dokumenta," *Novyi Zhurnal,* no. 124 (1976), p. 159.

38. They are mentioned in the autobiographical letter of March 1–3, 1927, to Ivanov-Razumnik (see Nivat, "Lettre autobiographique"). Bely read parts of them to Mikhail Chekhov before Chekhov left the Soviet Union in 1928; see his "Zhizn' i vstrechi," *Novyi Zhurnal,* no. 9 (1944), p. 13.

39. Andrej Belyj, *Verwandeln des Lebens: Erinnerungen an Rudolf Steiner,* trans. Swetlana Geier (Basel, 1975). The manuscript of the Russian original is part of the Bely holdings of the Manuscript Division of the Lenin Library in Moscow. The text that reached the West was no doubt one of the several copies known to have been made by anthroposophists in the city.

40. See John Elsworth's essay, chap. 5 in this volume.

the issue in Klavdiya Nikolaevna Bugaeva's book on her husband, he had remained faithful to Steiner. This aspect of his intellectual life had simply gone underground, and the hidden references to anthroposophy in Bely's late works had been so well camouflaged that they remained undetected by readers for decades.[41]

Bely's works, the memoirs in particular, sometimes reveal a marked split between two worlds, one public, the other exclusively private. In the recollections of Steiner, intended for initiates only, the image of Steiner undergoes the same idealization as that of Blok in the published memoirs of 1921–23. But the memoirs about Steiner make no mention at all of Blok, as if the poet simply did not exist.[42] On the other hand, the passing references to Steiner in the Berlin reminiscences about Blok do not in the slightest presage the apologetics of the esoteric document of 1926–29. Despite the anthroposophical treatment of Blok's poetry in the Blok recollections, Steiner the man is absent, and the Steiner recollections were tightly closed to the "Blok world."

The explanation for this split in the memoirs can be found in one of the central ideas that Bely stressed in his later works, that of counterpoint. According to this idea, the concept of the personality is in opposition to that of the "individuum," which always represents a "collective of personalities." In Bely's words, at the age of seven he already sensed something that he was to realize fully at the age of seventeen: "the I [. . .] is expressed not in a personality but in a gradation of personalities, each of which has its own 'role.'" Therefore the principle of sequentiality, obligatory for the personality, is not applicable to the individuum, with its many personalities. Accordingly, Bely declared, his fundamental purpose was "to reveal polyphony [. . .] to find the dialectical rhythm of the movement of one method in another method; to see in the counterpoint of such movements the theme in variations."[43] He also wrote: "Don't pin me once and for all—you pinners, explainers, and popularizers—to Solov'ev, or to Nietzsche, or to whomever [a reference, no doubt, to Steiner]. I do not renounce them since I have learned from them, but to fuse 'my symbolism' with some other metaphysics is the height of stupidity [. . .]. My world view is the concept of counterpoint, the dialectics

---

41. See the essays by Alexandrov and Elsworth, chaps. 4 and 5 of this volume.

42. A quotation from Blok's poem "Rossiya" ("Opyat', kak v gody zolotye . . ."), cited without mention of the author's name in *Vospominaniya o Shteinere* (p. 226), therefore looks particularly odd. On the other hand, some people mentioned in the Blok reminiscences do make an appearance in the memoirs of Steiner. Berdyaev, who had heard Steiner lecture in Helsinki (see "Dva pis'ma N. A. Berdyaeva Andreyu Belomu," *Mosty*, no. 11 [1965], and "N. A. Berdyaev ob antroposofii: Dva pis'ma Andreyu Belomu," *Novyi Zhurnal*, no. 137 [1979]), is mentioned in passing, but the tone is always sarcastic, totally unlike the panegyric in *Epopee*.

43. *Pochemu ya stal simvolistom*, pp. 11, 42. See also Elsworth's essay, chap. 5 of this volume.

of the *n*th degree of methodological settings in the circle of the whole."
Movement—the "dance of thought," as he put it—is all.[44]

Why I Became a Symbolist, written in 1928 but published only in 1982, is
therefore noteworthy for its association of previously disparate, even
seemingly incompatible subjects—Steiner with Russian Symbolism and
Blok. For now both worlds are manifestly linked. Bely himself once
labeled the work an "article,"[45] but it can be considered an outline for an
autobiography. Several themes relate it to Bely's memoir volumes—the
origin of Symbolism in "play," the crucial role of Bely's father, the academic milieu of the Bugaev family, the influence of Bely's high school
years, and so on. All these themes reappear in *On the Border of Two
Centuries.* This book also contains a concise sketch of the history of Bely's
relations with Blok and the Merezhkovskys, speaks of "mystical anar-
chism" and the war against it in the Symbolist journals, and describes the
Moscow Symbolist publishing houses; that is, it treats many of the landmarks of Bely's literary biography and ideological struggles. All this
information appears through the prism of what is ostensibly a discussion
of Steiner and Bely's development of Symbolism and of his relations
with the Anthroposophical Society. Yet the account covers more of
Bely's life than any of his other published memoirs, taking events right
up to the moment of writing.[46] And it is far more outspoken. This
"article," which more closely resembles a confession than a memoir, was
clearly a turning point for Bely, and the leap from the Berlin to the
Moscow stage of Bely's memoirs (1929–33) is incomprehensible unless it
is taken into account.

Most striking in the work is the sharp change in Bely's attitude toward
Blok. "A symbolist who rejects the logical source of his experiments in
incoherence," Bely wrote, *"degenerates into a neurotic* if he is sincere
(Blok), or into an allegorizing stylist if he is not completely sincere
(Vyacheslav Ivanov)."[47] Although Bely's remark was designed to emphasize his own special mission in the Symbolist camp—the construction
of a rational theoretical foundation for Symbolism, an emphasis absent

---

44. *Na rubezhe dvukh stoletii* (Moscow and Leningrad, 1931), p. 187; see also *Nachalo veka,*
p. 267.
45. See Malmstad's commentary in Bugaeva, *Vospominaniya o Belom,* p. 360.
46. Only the unpublished "Material k biografii (intimnyi)," set down by Bely in Berlin in
1923 and now in the Bely holdings of TsGALI (fond 53 [Bely], opis' 2, item 3), is comparable in scope. It outlines Bely's life from the day of his birth, but it takes the story only up to
1915. It seems to have served Bely as a kind of aide-mémoire while he wrote the Berlin
reminiscences, but it also contains unusually candid descriptions of certain episodes in
Bely's life, such as his affair with Nina Petrovskaya, which helps explain the caveat that
appears beneath the title: "intended for study only after the author's death." Again we
have an example of a private memoir set down at the same time that Bely was at work on a
public document.
47. *Pochemu ya stal simvolistom,* p. 10; my italics.

from the earlier memoirs—such a contemptuous characterization would have been simply unthinkable seven years before. Then Bely wrote of Blok:

> To us who knew him closely, he was a beautiful puzzle, sometimes close, sometimes distant (always beautiful). We didn't know which he was more—a national poet or a sensitive, unique person, shielded by the purple robe of poetic glory [. . .] from whose folds at times appeared the features of a noble, omniscient, new, and beautiful being: *kalos k'agathos*. Thus one wants to define the combination of goodness, beauty, and integrity that marked with severity the soft image of a soul that could not bear rhetoric, affectation, poses, *"poetry,"* falseness, and other *"boom booms."*[48]

Now in 1928, Bely reconsidered his conflict with Blok in 1906 and his avoidance of it in the earlier memoirs: "Of the tragic collapse of my relations with the Bloks, on which I kept the curtain lowered in my recollections of Blok (*de mortuis aut bene, aut nihil*), I shall say only: In those recollections I diminished myself too much *'for the sake of'* a eulogy over the fresh grave. Now, I regret it, for I see that my restraint has given rise to all kinds of loose talk."[49]

What provoked this unexpected rebellion against Blok, "the only one who expressed our deepest thoughts: thoughts of sacred years," as Bely called him in 1921?[50] The revolution in Bely's attitude is clearly related to the marked tendency of Soviet literary criticism in the mid-twenties to contrast a Blok, "who went forth toward the Revolution," with a Bely, who remained "a captive of mysticism." An official cult of Blok began to form, while Bely's opponents kept harping on his "mysticism." Bely devoted several angry pages of his 1928 travel sketches *A Wind from the Caucasus* to this development.[51] But most provoking of all was the pub-

48. *Vospominaniya o A. A. Bloke* (Fink ed.), p. 10.
49. *Pochemu ya stal simvolistom*, p. 49.
50. *Vospominaniya o A. A. Bloke* (Fink ed.), p. 29.
51. *Veter s Kavkaza: Vpechatleniya* (Moscow, 1928), pp. 182–87. On p. 186 Bely traces the charges of mysticism back to Trotsky's 1922 attack in *Pravda*. He accuses Trotsky of deliberately distorting his views in the Berlin *Recollections*. There Bely had noted Blok's mystical "maximalism" and his own opposition to it. Trotsky, Bely continues, had translated "maximalism" into the realm of politics, equating it with Bolshevism and Bely's opposition with Menshevism. Bely slightly warps Trotsky's statement, just as Trotsky had misrepresented Bely's view, but it is true that Trotsky had used the word "Menshevik" in 1922. Bely well knew how dangerous this allusion had been in 1922, when the Mensheviks and the Social Revolutionaries were declared the most sinister enemies of the Soviet regime, and he knew too how open he was to accusations of ideological deviation, since prominent Mensheviks had been among his closest friends and publishers in the emigration (the Epokha publishing house belonged to S. G. Sumsky and D. Yu. Dalin), and his memoir sketch "During the Years of the Revolution" was scheduled to appear in the second volume of the Menshevik journal *Letopis' Revolyutsii*, which was not, however, published. (See the announcements in *Sotsialisticheskii Vestnik*, no. 2 [48] [Berlin, January 17, 1923], p. 20, and in *Letopis' Revolyutsii*, no. 1 [Berlin, 1923], p. 319.) Now, in 1928, Bely

lication in the winter of 1927–28 of Blok's letters to his family and selections from his diary.[52]

These two books marked a new stage in the posthumous "archival" struggle over Blok's legacy and reputation. With the disbanding in 1924 of the Free Philosophical Association (Vol'fila), which at first had monopolized Blok studies, the Blok archives fell outside the sphere of influence of Bely and his close friends. They were now controlled by the late poet's relatives—his aunt, Mariya Andreevna Beketova, and his wife, Lyubov' Dmitrievna, who not only did not share Bely's anthroposophical interpretation of Blok but had apparently been offended by other statements in the *Epopee* memoirs. The editors they selected chose entries from Blok's diary with the patent aim of disproving these statements.[53] The volume of Blok's letters, however, contained passages that were downright insulting to Bely. In particular, in a letter to his mother on April 21, 1908, Blok wrote the following about Bely and Sergey Solov'ev: "Moscow arrogance sickens me; they're obnoxious and crude; they're like tom turkeys. I keep wanting to spit, as if a bedbug had gotten into my mouth."[54] Since the publication of materials from Blok's archive had only just begun, Bely and others must have wondered what further surprises awaited them.

A leading Soviet Blok scholar has already speculated about the effect of the publication of such archival material on Bely's revaluation of his "twin," and Bely himself later alluded to the most offensive of Blok's statements.[55] But in view of the charges that Bely, unlike Blok, remained a captive of mysticism, it would obviously be an oversimplification to reduce everything to personal insult. Moreover, Blok's diary astounded many readers by the quotidian banalities in the life of the greatest poet of the Symbolist epoch.[56] As for his utterances on literary topics, they were totally unrelated to the question of symbolism as a theory or as a literary school. In one of his entries Blok had gone so far as to declare: "It is time to untie my hands. I am no longer a schoolboy. No more symbolisms—I shall answer for myself alone."[57] In Bely's eyes this new

does something similar to what he accuses Trotsky of having done in 1922. For by indirectly associating those who accused him of mysticism with Trotsky, he associated them with the favorite Soviet whipping boy of the time, who was shortly to be pronounced the most odious ideological enemy of the Soviet state.

52. *Pis'ma Aleksandra Bloka k rodnym*, with introduction and notes by M. A. Beketova (Leningrad, 1927); *Dnevnik Al. Bloka, 1911–1913*, ed. P. N. Medvedev (Leningrad, 1928).

53. Such as the note of January 20, 1913, about a conversation with E. K. Metner concerning Bely's anthroposophical pursuits. See *Dnevnik Al. Bloka*, p. 170.

54. *Pis'ma Aleksandra Bloka k rodnym*, p. 207.

55. Vladimir Orlov, "Aleksandr Blok v pamyati sovremennikov," in *Aleksandr Blok v vospominaniyakh sovremennikov* (Moscow, 1980), I, 24; *Nachalo veka*, pp. 297, 341–42, 345.

56. See B. Skvortsov, "Opustoshennaya dusha," *Novyi Mir*, no. 11 (1928), pp. 238–41; B. K., "Dnevnik opustoshennogo cheloveka," *Zhurnalist*, no. 4 (1928), pp. 49–50.

57. *Dnevnik Al. Bloka*, p. 177, entry for February 10, 1913.

picture of Blok, so different from the one he himself had drawn in his memoirs of 1921–23, coincided with the growing disparagement of the historic role and "social essence" of Russian Symbolism which began to dominate Soviet criticism after 1925. Hence the writing of *Why I Became a Symbolist*, in which Bely emphasized the continuing need to struggle "for a better memory of symbolism and symbolists" than was being fixed in the minds of a new generation.[58] It was this sense of urgency that fired the writing of the memoirs of 1929–33.

It is important to recognize how solitary Bely was in his mission. Not one of his former allies (or foes) among the Symbolists would have undertaken the thankless task of defending Symbolist ideals or of attempting to affirm the relevance of a movement considered long dead, its practitioners outdated, if not out-and-out reactionaries. It never occurred to Georgy Chulkov, Vladimir Pyast, or Maksimilian Voloshin in Soviet Russia or to Konstantin Bal'mont, Nikolay Minsky, or the Merezhkovskys in emigration to burden themselves with such anachronisms. (Vyacheslav Ivanov in those years took no part in public literary life.) It was the literary climate of the late twenties and the shock produced by Blok's "betrayal" from beyond the grave that forced Bely to undertake this quixotic struggle and publicly declare his fidelity to the Symbolist past and himself no less a Symbolist now than before.

In the summer of 1928, after finishing *A Wind from the Caucasus* in March and *Why I Became a Symbolist* in April, Bely began to prepare for the struggle by putting his voluminous autobiographical notes and diaries into order and by jotting down notes on his memories of his adolescence and of the various professors he had known as a child and young man. The careful preparations paid off in 1929, when in a matter of only two months he wrote *On the Border of Two Centuries* (he began it on February 6 and finished it on April 11).[59] Taking the course he had already suggested in the two earlier works of 1928—arguing that Blok's symbolism, not his own, lacked a rational foundation and challenging the charges of mysticism—Bely returned to his preliterary past, to his childhood and youth, to show how official critics had misconstrued the social roots of his generation because they were simply ignorant of his background. He portrayed himself as a child rebel against the "stagnation of the everyday" (*kosnyi byt*), and sought to prove that any thinking member of his "generation of the border" *had* to become a revolutionary and that Symbolism had been a truly revolutionary, not reactionary, force. Revolution, he argued, was as ingrained in his Symbolist milieu as mysticism was inherently alien to it. This point he insisted on. How, he

58. *Pochemu ya stal simvolistom*, p. 59.
59. "April 11, 1929," stands at the end of the volume. See also *Kak my pishem* (Leningrad, 1930), p. 10: "Last year I wrote 26 quires of my memoirs in two months." The first edition appeared in 1930, a second in 1931.

asked, could a generation imbued with an interest in the natural sciences from birth, as it were (in his own case by a mathematician father and the professor-scientists who figured in his upbringing), and trained in them, ground their revolt in anything but the rational? This background safeguarded them from religious obscurantism. There was no way he could have become a mystic. Blok had strayed, but never he. Critics were not impressed, and responded with skepticism and outright disbelief.[60]

In the fall of 1929 the literary situation in the Soviet Union changed abruptly. In August, Boris Pil'nyak and Evgeny Zamyatin, two of the most prominent "fellow travelers," became the targets of a vicious and unexpected campaign of slander. Both were forced to resign from the leadership of the All-Russian Union of Writers, the stronghold of the so-called fellow travelers. This campaign signaled the beginning of the total "reconstruction" of Soviet literature, with the goal of eliminating all nonaligned literary positions and of erasing all ideological differences. It became obvious that in the coming era independent literary and critical standards would no longer be respected or tolerated. The change in the ideological climate presented Bely with serious questions about his future: Could he adapt to the new demands? How would his past now be judged? His situation was the more precarious because Pil'nyak and Zamyatin, the two primary victims of the current purge, considered him their literary mentor.[61] With their overthrow, he found himself in a kind of vacuum.

These were the events that forced Bely in July 1930 to turn to a reworking of the Berlin version of "The Beginning of the Century." Publication of the work written in emigration was unthinkable not only from the external point of view—it completely contradicted the image Bely now needed to convey and could only compromise him—but also from the internal: it was in total disharmony with his new attitude toward Blok and with the new interpretation of Symbolism which he had developed in 1927–28. But it would not have been sufficient simply to revise the memoir to accord with his changed conception. Survival meant adaptation to the unpredictable shifts in the official line. And in the phantasmagorical atmosphere of 1929–31, an atmosphere of perpetual feverish reorganizations and crude directives bellowed from on high, it was impossible to predict which new slogan would replace the

60. See the review of the book by M. Rabinovich in *Novyi Mir*, no. 3 (1930), pp. 207–8. Compare the persistent emphasis on Bely's "mysticism" in the article about him by Aleksandr Voronsky in vol. 1 of *Literaturnaya Entsiklopediya* (1930), in particular: "In our literature Bely is the prophet of a particular symbolism. His symbolism is mystical symbolism. At its base lies a religious-moral world view."

61. Pil'nyak had helped Bely with the publication of the novel *Moskva*. See Malmstad's commentary in Bugaeva, *Vospominaniya o Belom*, p. 358. Viktor Shklovsky wrote of the direct dependence of the prose of Zamyatin and Pil'nyak on Bely's in "Andrey Bely," *Russkii Sovremennik*, no. 2 (1924), p. 239.

one in effect today, which new set of instructions would be released tomorrow, who would become the object of new badgering, which conception would take over as the next dogma among the authorities. The fall of 1930 was to see a wave of arrests directed against the scientific and engineering intelligentsia. The ferocious campaign against "bourgeois experts" and "right-wing communists" culminated in the widely publicized show trial of the "Industrial Party" in November 1930 and the Menshevik trial of March 1931. Bely had long been personally acquainted with two of the main figures in the trial of the Mensheviks—Vladimir Groman, a noted statistician and economist awarded the title "Honored Science Worker" only three years before, and Vladimir Ikov, an economist and literary historian (whom he had just mentioned in *On the Border of Two Centuries*). A natural science education and place in the scientific world, which Bely had just emphasized in *On the Border of Two Centuries* as central in his own biography, had ceased to be a guarantee of social reliability and fidelity to revolution. His association with the disgraced Zamyatin and Pil'nyak also continued to haunt him: in the winter of 1930–31 the three of them were singled out for abuse in articles about the collection *Kak my pishem* (*How We Write*), which had appeared in 1930.

Beginning in May 1931 the noose of terror began to tighten around Bely, too: at that time his closest friends—Klavdiya Nikolaevna Vasil'eva, his wife in all but legal name, her relatives, and Aleksey Petrovsky, one of his oldest and most trusted confidants—were arrested in connection with the mounting persecution of former members of the Anthroposophical Society. Bely, expecting arrest himself, immediately declared his own loyalty and that of his anthroposophical friends to the Revolution and the Soviet state. As a result, perhaps, Bely's friends were released from prison early in July, although several were exiled from Moscow. (Shortly thereafter, on July 18, Bely formally married Klavdiya Nikolaevna.) In August, Bely took an even more dramatic step—he wrote a letter to Stalin.[62] He detailed the difficulties of his personal situation and protested the obstacles that prevented him from demonstrating to all his commitment to the new state. The effectiveness of such an appeal to the leader had been convincingly demonstrated not long before that by Mikhail Bulgakov, Aleksandr Bezymensky, and Pil'nyak; in June 1931 (on Gorky's advice) Zamyatin also appealed to Stalin. Although Bely's letter apparently did not warrant a direct reply, it clearly brought about a similar miraculous turn in its author's fate. In the fall of 1931 unexpected signs of official goodwill toward Bely appeared, most notably the possibility of publishing the new, Soviet version of *The Begin-*

62. See Struve, "K biografii Andreya Belogo," pp. 158–61.

ning of the Century, which had been so hacked up by the censor that Bely regarded it as banned.[63]

One has to take these difficulties of 1930–31 into account in analyzing this text as we know it. (The book appeared for sale in the winter of 1933.) In particular, the metaphor of a "release from prison" that Bely uses in the volume to describe his mood in the spring of 1905 acquires psychological depth in connection with this whole recent background.[64]

Although the original Berlin version of "The Beginning of the Century" is not accessible to us, we can make several hypotheses about the kind of revisions Bely felt compelled to make.[65] Apparently the revision was carried out in two stages, as evidenced by a marked shift in narrative style. The first, basic stage extended over the second half of 1930 and represented a reaction to the specific current situation: the raging attacks against literary fellow travelers, the savage accusations against the technical intelligentsia, the complete unpredictability of official moods, and the necessity to break all ties with the emigration. Presumably this background explains the exceptional stylistic features of the new *Beginning of the Century* which sharply distinguish it from all of the author's other memoirs. Never before had the past become the object of such grotesque caricature and bitter derision. Interestingly, it was not so much philosophical or ideological positions that were ridiculed as microscopic aspects of gestures taken at random, accidental external features, seemingly meaningless details, such as Bal'mont's unbuttoned pants.[66] This satirical bias stunned his contemporaries. In a foreword to the book Lev Kamenev wrote:

> One would expect to learn at least something from Bely about the essence of intellectual life, about the struggle of ideas, about their development, even if only in the narrow stratum of the Russian prerevolutionary intelligentsia. But instead, you will find in the book a freak show, a wax museum, not the dynamics of ideas but the physiology of their bearers. Following his distinctive "creative method," Bely doesn't simply tell about people and their ideas, but "sculpts" ideas through noses, brows, teeth, saliva, gestures, interjections. As you read Bely's book, you will learn very little in essence about what particular thoughts, ideas, formulas, and slogans his comrades and opponents, companions and enemies—the Merezhkovskys, Rozanov, Blok, Bryusov, Bal'mont, Ellis, Metner, et al.—proposed and upheld. We know that all these people were able to express their thoughts

63. See a letter to A. S. Petrovsky of mid-March 1932 in Roger Keys, "Pis'ma Andreya Belogo k A. S. Petrovskomu i E. N. Kezel'man," *Novyi Zhurnal,* no. 122 (1976), p. 160.
64. *Nachalo veka,* p. 477.
65. Some notion of the extent of the revisions and cuts can be obtained from a comparison of the sketch "Arbat," *Sovremennye Zapiski,* no. 17 (1923), pp. 156–82, with the chapter "Staryi Arbat" in *Nachalo veka,* pp. 98–107. See also Shklovsky, "Andrey Bely," p. 245, for interesting remarks about the first "Arbat."
66. *Nachalo veka,* p. 219.

more or less articulately. In Bely's reminiscences, however, they are all tongue-tied to the point of complete nonsense. Bely forces them to express their world view not in words but through moustaches, warts, feet, and other equally unsuitable parts of their bodies. Bely's personages—no matter what occupied the center of their attention at a given moment: an appraisal of Goethe or the events of January 9, 1905, paintings by Botticelli or the feud between *Libra* and *The New Way*—miaow, lisp, sputter, grimace, grunt, chuckle, move hand, foot, and pelvis, but they don't speak.[67]

One of the leading literary critics of the emigration, Georgy Adamovich, agreed in part with this evaluation: "You read his reminiscences and willy-nilly you think: why, was this really all a comedy, a total farce, with the same intrigues and petty behind-the-scenes dirt as everywhere else, but without any internal foundation or justification?"[68]

Caricature is an integral feature of Bely's prose style, beginning with the symphonies, but until the Moscow edition of *The Beginning of the Century,* it had seemed uncharacteristic of his memoirs. The turn to the grotesque appears doubly surprising against the background of his lyrical outpourings in the Berlin *Recollections of Blok* or the relatively recent *Recollections of Steiner.* The spirit of grotesque nihilism touched even the sphere that was particularly dear to Bely, the group of "Argonauts," from which had sprung the impulse for many later Symbolist quests. Discussing the Argonauts in *Epopee* and relating his own early poetry to Blok's, Bely had used the motif there of "the dawn" (*zarya* or *zori*) and had asserted that the year 1901 was marked by an "intensely full awareness of the dawn." But in *The Beginning of the Century* no trace remained of the description of these youthful expectations, and only the title of the first chapter ("The Year of Dawns") serves as a reminder of what Bely was forced to strike out in the revision of the Berlin memoirs. This is how he himself explained the turn toward a new style of memoir narration:

In this volume I have adopted the style of humorous puns, grotesques, caricatures; but I am describing, you see, a circle of real eccentrics that grouped around me ("Argonauts"). Much in their style of addressing each other, in their style even of perceiving each other, may appear unnatural and stilted. Not I but the times are to blame: at present people don't talk or joke or perceive each other that way, but from 1902 to 1904 that is precisely the way they perceived each other in our circles and the way they joked.[69]

67. Lev Kamenev, "Predislovie," in *Nachalo veka,* p. iv. See also Kamenev's obituary, "Andrey Bely," in *Izvestiya,* January 10, 1934.

68. G. Adamovich, "Andrey Bely i ego vospominaniya," *Russkie Zapiski,* bk. 5 (Paris, May 1938), p. 138. Yu. Sazonova similarly appraised this book of Bely's in "Andrey Bely," *Sovremennye Zapiski,* no. 66 (1938), pp. 417–23.

69. Bely's introduction to *Nachalo veka,* p. 11.

This explanation cannot be accepted at face value. The Argonauts cannot be reduced to pranksters; their primary goal was a reworking of "myth" with the aim of a radical transformation of life.[70] Nor does it explain why non-Argonauts are also caricatured. Obviously Bely has hastened to mask himself as an eccentric (and blames "the times") precisely because in the circumstances of 1930–31 he was left with no alternative. Here it is worth noting his admission in the 1928 "confession" that "the image of the contemporary 'hero' is an image of humble caution in the conditions of seemingly routine trench warfare, not the image of tragic poses and saber rattling; by the rules of conduct of the contemporary hero, the ability to avoid wounds is as important as the ability to face them fearlessly."[71] With this in mind, a second aspect of Bely's "humble caution" in the memoir now comes into focus. For in equating his present grotesque "method" with the past norms of the Argonauts, Bely demonstrates his fidelity to those anachronistic standards that were unacceptable and incomprehensible in the contemporary world.

While satire predominates, it is not the only narrative style in *The Beginning of the Century*. It coexists with a more balanced, restrained, even sympathetic manner of talking about the past. This style appears, for example, in segments devoted to the philosopher Pavel Florensky or Fedor Sologub—that is, figures from the Symbolist era who did not emigrate yet retained their loyalty to former values in the new conditions. Although it is risky, given the present state of knowledge of Bely's manuscripts, to speculate on the relationship between the satiric and the more neutral descriptive manners in *The Beginning of the Century*, I shall venture the guess that the second manner was strengthened and the first deemphasized during Bely's *second stage* of work on the book. This stage dates from the winter of 1931–32, when Bely's prospects improved after his letter to Stalin and he returned to the memoirs. Now, with his situation apparently more stable, he had no need for extensive caricaturization. The decisive turning away from satire in the next book of memoirs, *Between Two Revolutions*, offers some confirmation of this hypothesis.

Thus Adamovich's interpretation of Bely's use of the grotesque in his memoirs as "masterful treachery" is unfounded.[72] It would be even less justifiable to view it as Bely's compliance with the "social command."[73] Literary officialdom expected not nasty caricature and ridiculing of de-

---

70. See A. V. Lavrov, "Mifotvorchestvo 'Argonavtov,'" in *Mif-fol'klor-literatura* (Leningrad, 1978).

71. *Pochemu ya stal simvolistom*, p. 70.

72. Adamovich, "Andrey Bely," p. 149.

73. This was how N. V. Valentinov viewed it in his *Dva goda s simvolistami* (Stanford, 1969). Bely preceded *Pochemu ya stal simvolistom* with a characteristic epigraph from Tolstoy's *Diary:* "People who adapt their striving toward truth to existing forms of society are like a being who is given wings in order to fly and who would use these wings to help himself walk."

tails but sincere repentance and a harsh exposé of figures and phenomena that history had left behind in its inexorable wake. In the context of Bely's general method of caricature, questions of ideological vices and reactionary positions or an analysis of "errors" did not figure. There were instead descriptions of physiological or psychological deformities so exaggerated that any suppositions about the ideological truth or falsehood of these artistic portraits (often brilliantly executed) simply could not even arise.

Bely had other choices: he could have rejected the memoir form entirely or limited himself to intimate confessions designed only for the desk drawer. This course would have removed him from the danger of "being wounded." But Bely deliberately chose to break his silence and offer his contemporaries his own version—albeit one complicated by caricature—of the Symbolist epoch and of its central figures. His insistence on this version derived, as we have noted, from the need for a struggle against Blok. In comparing Bely's memoirs of the thirties with the *Epopee* version, Vladimir Orlov asserts that the greatest change occurred in the treatment of Blok and the history of the two poets' relationship.[74]

The struggle with Blok became the central focus of Bely's last book of memoirs, *Between Two Revolutions*, which appeared only posthumously. Not only does Blok occupy proportionally more space here than in *The Beginning of the Century*, but more important, the relationship with Blok is constantly associated with Bely's attitude toward the revolution:

> In my fantasies the revolution and Blok are inversely proportional to each other; the more I withdrew from Blok, the more I was filled with social protest [. . .]. The revolution linked me to the Bloks no more than an apple to poetry; apples have inspired poets to write verse; and it was anger at Blok that inspired me to make attacks against the social order.[75]

This parallel reaches the absurd when Bely equates (not only as manifestations of the same historical order but also as inextricably linked events) the rebellion on the battleship *Potemkin* with his "first clash with Blok," the murder of Minister of the Interior Vyacheslav Plehve with the first "sparks of what led to the break with the poet." In contrast to the official Soviet portrait of the "revolutionary" Blok, Bely stresses the "vestiges of the nobility" in him and even draws a parallel between him and Nicholas II. He blends the dramatic history of his own romantic relations with Lyubov' Dmitrievna Blok with philippics against the Socialist Revolutionary leader Evno Azef, the "monster of capitalism," and

74. Orlov, "Aleksandr Blok," pp. 24–25.

75. *Mezhdu dvukh revolyutsii* (Leningrad, 1934), p. 6. The book actually came out in 1935 and included a largely sympathetic preface by the critic Tsezar' Vol'pe.

the repressive tsarist regime.[76] It might seem that Bely was darkening Blok's reputation because of his own tragic involvement with Lyubov' Dmitrievna in 1906. Both Bloks come off badly in Bely's depiction of this affair, particularly Lyubov' Dmitrievna, who at times is made to seem positively satanic. But such an interpretation inverts his true motivation: Blok and revolution are presented as antipodes not because of any lingering malice toward Blok's widow; on the contrary, because in the thirties Bely came to see Blok as his chief enemy, his animosity toward him colors his picture of her.

Behind the harshness of these attacks lay yet another oddity of the times. In 1932–33, when Bely was at work on *Between Two Revolutions*, his status in Soviet literature changed decisively. After the breakup of RAPP in April 1932 and the official rehabilitation of the fellow traveler writers, Bely suddenly found himself on the crest of the new wave of literary policy, in the confidence of officials, and generally respected. The euphoria produced by the sharp and unexpected "liberal" turn in Soviet culture is reflected in Bely's famous speech at the first plenum of the organizing committee of the newly formed Union of Soviet Writers in October 1932.[77] Bely again felt that he was not in isolation, but in a friendly collective: his immediate milieu was the editorial board of the journal *Novyi Mir*, headed by Ivan Gronsky, who then also chaired the organizing committee of the Writers' Union. At Gronsky's Bely met with such high-placed party officials as Mikhail Kalinin and Valerian Kuibyshev, who were considered patrons of literature.[78] For the first time since 1926 he was able to place articles (as opposed to travel pieces) in a journal: soon his reviews in praise and defense of Grigory Sannikov and Fedor Gladkov, both indisputably Soviet writers, appeared in *Novyi Mir*. In the winter of 1932–33 his series of public lectures in Moscow was a resounding success. The prominence given in the last volume of memoirs to Bely's public lectures in the years 1906–10 unconsciously reflects his pleasure in this new audience. In the summer of 1933, Aleksandr Fadeev, an influential writer personally close to Stalin, informed Bely of the regime's intention to involve him in the organization of the congress of Soviet writers planned for the following year.[79] (Bely died before it was convened.)

His exaltation at belonging at last to official literature forms the subtext of one of the central themes of *Between Two Revolutions*, that of his persecution by all literary factions during the *Libra* period and his exile

76. Ibid., pp. 81, 324. Compare the treatment of Blok's wife in the *Epopee* reminiscences: *Vospominaniya o A. A. Bloke* (Fink ed.), pp. 372–73.

77. See *Krasnaya Nov'*, no. 12 (1932), pp. 155–56.

78. Bely with pride tells of one such meeting in a letter to his sister-in-law, E. N. Kezel'man, who was then in exile. See Keys, "Pis'ma Belogo k Petrovskomu i Kezel'man." Pil'nyak also belonged to the *Novyi Mir* circle.

79. Fadeev's letter to Bely was published in A. Fadeev, *Sobranie sochinenii v semi tomakh*, vol. 7, *Izbrannye pis'ma* (Moscow, 1971), pp. 68–69.

from literature. His departure from the punning caricature method of *The Beginning of the Century* is related to this sudden and proud awareness of the solidity of his position in Soviet literature. Bely apparently did not realize the great distance between the objective situation and his reading of it. This is convincingly demonstrated by his discussion of realism in *Between Two Revolutions*. His arguments, based on quotations from his polemical articles of 1907–8, are obscure and chaotic, but their naïve intention is obvious: to prove the equivalence of Symbolism and realism.[80] The need for such an attempt is also clear: Stalin and Gronsky had just placed a new demand before Soviet literature, the adoption of a special approach—socialist realism, which neither they themselves nor the writers yet understood. Bely could hardly have been expected to comprehend the new concept, but one must appreciate his initiative in trying to get a head start on the discussion.

Bely bases his theoretical section on his old dispute with Vyacheslav Ivanov (who now lived in Italy) about the theory of Symbolism and on a 1930 article by Fedor Gladkov, his friend at *Novyi Mir*.[81] The first move was a safe one: there was no chance of finding a defender among Soviet writers for Ivanov's old articles on Symbolism. But Bely did not realize that the second gambit involved him in great risk. Gladkov's 1930 article, to which Bely appealed for unimpeachable Soviet support for his views, had called for dialectical materialism in literature, and belonged to a stage in the discussions about the need for a uniquely Soviet literary method which Stalin's call for socialist realism was designed to supersede. Bely, hoping to solidify his position in Soviet letters and unaware of this aspect of the discussion about socialist realism, had seized upon just those old slogans that were now to be discredited.

In 1922 Bely had attacked the Merezhkovskys in his *Recollections of Blok* for deserting the battle against Marxism by emigrating at a time when he and those around him who remained in Soviet Russia bore all the burden of this struggle. Exactly the same logic lies behind his posthumous polemic against Blok: how could one call Blok the "poet of the revolution" when not he but Bely knew the entire experience of Soviet postrevolutionary Russia—including the ordeal of emigration, isolation in literature, expectation of arrest, and constant fluctuations in the official line, of which socialist realism was only the most recent? It is noteworthy, therefore, that the joy of liberation expressed on the last page of *Between Two Revolutions* in connection with his flight with Asya Turgeneva to Venice in 1911[82] (but undoubtedly reflecting also the

---

80. See the fourth chapter, "Gody polemiki," especially the sections "Taktika" and "Platforma simvolizma 1907 goda," in *Mezhdu dvukh revolyutsii*.

81. Ibid., pp. 214–17.

82. Compare Pasternak's mention of Venice in *Okhrannaya gramota*, finished in 1931. Pasternak brought his book to Bely a few days before the latter completed *Mezhdu dvukh*

mood of the author's final year) blends with mention of the feeling of "imprisonment" which had appeared in the recent *Beginning of the Century*. Apparently doubts about the stability of the new situation gave Bely no peace.

In the last months of his life Bely worked on a sequel to *Between Two Revolutions*. This work was not completed, and is known to us only from the significantly abridged first two chapters that were published in 1937. In the "Introduction" Bely stated that the volume would deal with the period from 1910 to 1918. As in the earlier memoirs, Bely's political inclinations affect his presentation of the past. For example, he asserts that in 1911 he already discerned the "spirit of fascism" in Italy, and he depicts his journey from Italy to North Africa as an "escape from the bourgeois present into the patriarchal past."[83] A comparison of this remark with the two books of *Travel Notes* (*Putevye zametki*) published in 1921–22, containing a detailed description of this trip, demonstrates the great disparity between this interpretation and Bely's feelings and concerns in 1910–11.

Death abruptly ended Bely's work on this memoir before he could bring the narrative up to his meeting with Steiner in 1912 and his subsequent involvement in anthroposophy. He could not have avoided this topic, and clearly, a discussion of it would have created immense difficulties not only for himself but also for the literary circles now favorably disposed toward him. Indeed, any sympathetic mention of anthroposophy was impossible in the Soviet press. We thus lack the most telling indication of how far Bely was prepared to go in his desire "not to be wounded." We know how shocked the émigré literary community— Adamovich, Yuliya Sazonova, Stepun, Nikolay Valentinov, Mochul'sky— was by the transformation of Bely the memoirist. In particular, they viewed the new Soviet account of the beginning of the century as a frantic attempt at political self-rehabilitation and total moral surrender.

Yet one could argue that Bely's very fidelity to memoir writing indicates that he resisted the pressures of the times more stubbornly than many of his contemporaries. In the course of the thirties, the "literature of fact" so characteristic of the twenties, including memoirs with their potential for elaboration and justification, no longer found favor; indeed, by the end of the thirties it was virtually tabooed, and only with the thaw following Stalin's death would memoirs again become a prominent genre in Soviet literature. By late 1933, when *The Beginning of the Century* was published, the first signs of this bias were clearly to be seen: the

---

revolyutsii, and Bely singled out the segment on Venice. See my *Boris Pasternak v tridtsatye gody* (Jerusalem, 1984), pp. 118–19.

83. "Vospominaniya, tom III, chast' II (1910–1912)," *Literaturnoe nasledstvo*, no. 27–28 (1937), p. 414.

censor forbade a second edition of Pasternak's *Safe Conduct* (*Okhrannaya gramota*), and only Gorky's vigorous intervention made possible the publication of Benedikt Livshits's memoir of Futurism, *The One-and-a-Half-Eyed Archer* (*Polutoraglazyi strelets*). Soviet culture was beginning to show its unwillingness to tolerate ideological diversity of any kind. No invective against the tsarist regime and no revolutionary declarations could camouflage the fact that most of the people in Bely's memoirs belonged to a world that it was more and more inappropriate to recall. In a few years it could not be mentioned at all. Literary history was being rewritten, and name after name, especially of writers in the emigration, was disappearing from it. Others, such as Pavel Florensky and Sergey Solov'ev, whom Bely had imprudently described so warmly, had been removed from Soviet life by arrest and imprisonment. The same fate awaited many of the figures who appear on the pages of the three "Soviet" volumes. To this day they have not been republished in the Soviet Union. Bely may have caricatured his contemporaries, but at least a later generation could learn of their existence. In this perspective, Bely's memoirs stand as a unique witness to the Symbolist era in Russian cultural history.

7

Bely's Poetry and Verse Theory

G. S. SMITH

Introduction

It is a remarkable and suggestive fact that we do not seem to possess an extended analysis, a close reading, of any single one of the 500-odd lyric poems published by Andrey Bely. One of his two longer poems, *The First Encounter* (*Pervoe svidanie*, 1921), has received more adequate critical attention; the other, *Christ Is Risen* (*Khristos voskres*, 1918), has not. Circumstances have combined to foster either partial studies with a narrow thematic focus or generalizing works that wrench small quotations out of context and make broad summary judgments. The prose works have always been studied more than the works in verse, and never in conjunction with them.

It may well be that the generalizing approach is the most appropriate and the most adequate for the study of Bely's poetry, and that close reading would not necessarily reveal features more important than the generalizations. This would assuredly be the case if we were to accept an assertion made by Gerald Janecek in the concluding passage of one of the most incisive short treatments of Bely the poet:

> The fact is that Bely was basically not a miniaturist, not comfortable in a work of small compass. . . . Bely's fundamental compositional process is one of repetition of words and phrases and a building of complexities by developing associations with these units as they intertwine themselves in the fabric of a text. For this process to achieve its full effectiveness and depth of significance a certain amount of space is needed, more, certainly, than the length of a page-long lyric poem. . . . It has been pointed out [by J. E. Malmstad] that even Bely's books of verse are not intended to be read as collections of individual self-sufficient poems, but rather as carefully structured mosaics which form a total, unified picture in which each poem has its

particular place and function and is dependent on the whole for its full meaning.[1]

If the assertion in the last sentence of this passage is correct, then not only has Bely's poetry not been properly analyzed, but, more seriously, the proper analysis of it demands a technique that goes against the thrust of the most productive approaches of our time. It may be necessary to develop a specific analytical strategy for Bely's poetry, a strategy of macroanalysis rather than the microanalysis with which we are all familiar. How precisely we go about relating the individual lyric text to its context, even at the level of the lyric cycle, is an aspect of analysis that as far as I know has not been extensively discussed in modern poetics; the individual lyrics present enough problems to keep professional practitioners busy.

The problem of scale, though, is by no means the only one that has inhibited the discussion of Bely's poetry. Four other factors may be mentioned; they are all well known and have often been pointed out, though their ramifications have been examined but rarely. It is worth noting that in the context of the Russian critical tradition these factors are relatively benign, because they all tend to make for the intrinsic analysis of the text; that is, they tend to make for the study of the text as literature rather than any other kind of document (and this may be a reason for Bely's relative lack of impact as a poet—only rarely can he be read, for example, as a social critic). The four factors are, in descending order of nuisance value: Bely's compulsive revisions of his published texts; his activities as a theorist of verse rhythm and of rhythm as an aesthetic, philosophical, and psychological phenomenon (the three adjectives should perhaps be hyphenated); the sheer virtuosity and abundance of Bely's other writings; and, for the average reader, the forbidding obscurity of Bely's intellectual world. It hardly needs to be added that in addition to these difficulties, the manifestly idealistic, if not overtly religious, attitudes behind much of Bely's verse have discouraged serious discussion of it in the USSR.

Bely's habit of revision, much more pronounced in the verse than in the prose works, has simply made it extremely difficult to trust any of the verse texts. The frequent presence somewhere in the canon of more than one revision of a text has added an extra dimension of difficulty to any interpretation. For the critic, the effect is to reduce what one might call the specific gravity of the text by suggesting that these may not be the inevitable right words in the right order, but verbal clay that the

---

1. Gerald Janecek, "Introduction," in *Andrey Bely: A Critical Review*, ed. G. Janecek (Lexington, Ky., 1978), pp. 11–12 (hereafter cited as *Critical Review*).

author might cheerfully remodel whenever the whim took him. Again, for the average academic critic of lyric poetry, who counts the idea of inevitability and perhaps Yury Tynyanov's "density and unity of the verse series" (*tesnota i edinstvo stikhovogo ryada*) among his basic beliefs, this is an unsettling situation. This is to say nothing of the monstrous textological problem that has faced students of Bely's poetry. Until the Malmstad edition came to hand (and until one has learned one's way round in it) there has been nowhere that a textual problem could be reliably addressed without tedious and annoying spadework.[2] It remains to be seen now whether or not the Malmstad edition will provide that firm textological basis for studies of Bely's poetry that has been lacking so far. It should now be possible, for example, to investigate the contradiction that exists between the habit of revision and the "seamless garment" image of Bely's collections implied in Janecek's statement that was cited earlier: if each collection is indeed an artistic whole greater than the sum of its parts, how then can the author remove some of these parts and revise them, apparently without any notion of definitiveness?[3]

The second large problem that affects studies of Bely as a poet derives from his activities as a theorist. At this point it is important to say that Bely's contribution, while of immense significance as a catalyst, does not offer a basis on which to approach systematically either the work of other Russian poets or the work of Bely himself. For example, Bely's iambic tetrameter was studied in the light of the poet's theories by Kirill Taranovsky in one of the most valuable small-scale works we have on Bely's poetry.[4] But the fact is that iambic tetrameter is only one of the metrical resources that Bely employed, and his essays in rhythmical analysis have distorted its importance in his work in the minds of critics. In general, what Bely did not analyze is more important to an objective understanding of his poetic technique than what he did write about. But the aspects that Bely did not cover have hardly ever been discussed; the only real exception to this statement is an article by Ian K. Lilly, which shows that the rhyme technique used in Bely's first three books of verse, something the poet never touched on in his theoretical writings, is just as distinctive and innovatory as his "theoretically based" iambic tetrameter.[5] As John Elsworth has pointed out, "there is an immense gap to be filled between [Bely's] macrocosmic statements about the nature of

---

2. *Stikhotvoreniya*, ed. John E. Malmstad, 3 vols. (Munich, 1982–84).

3. There is no published study specifically devoted to Bely's revisions of his verse; the existing discussions are reviewed in "The Revisions," below.

4. K. F. Taranovsky, "Chetyrekhstopnyi yamb Andreya Belogo," *International Journal of Slavic Linguistics and Poetics* (hereafter cited as *IJSLP*), no. 10 (1966), pp. 127–47.

5. Ian K. Lilly, "On the Rhymes of Bely's First Three Books of Verse," *Slavonic and East European Review* (hereafter cited as *SEER*), 60, no. 2 (1982), pp. 379–89.

rhythm, and the analytical description of the individual poem."[6] Indeed there is such a gap. The intervening levels of description, and some of the many aspects of verse structure that Bely did not theorize about, will form one of the main emphases of the present study.[7]

The effect of Bely's other writings on the study of his poetry is a difficult thing to describe. Doubtless the main effect—though, of course, this assertion cannot be verified—has been to cause the poetry to be ignored, or at least relegated to a bad second place after the novels in critics' estimation. Perhaps the most intriguing formulation of the relative standing of Bely the poet and Bely the prose writer is that of D. S. Mirsky: "One usually thinks of Andrey Bely as primarily a poet, and this is, on the whole, true; but his writings in verse are less in volume and significance than his prose."[8] The opening phrase of this judgment suggests that Mirsky considers Bely to be in some sense a poet on a level that outranks genre, that is, whether Bely is writing something that is formally either verse or prose. This notion, we may note, has considerable implications with respect to the idea expressed by Janecek: artistic thinking on a large scale we would take to be one of the primary characteristics of the prose writer rather than the poet, and if we accept Janecek's assertion, we would be well advised to turn Mirsky's idea on its head and say that Bely is primarily a prose writer even when he is formally writing verse. The attitude toward revision would be more normal in a prose writer as well. Bely himself was once categorical: "Everything that I have written is a novel in verse: the content of this novel is *my search for truth*, in its achievements and shortcomings."[9]

We now understand something about the relationship between texts that are formally verse and those in which Bely writes metrical prose, although this question has by no means been exhausted.[10] But this is a relatively superficial aspect of a problem that goes near to the heart of

6. John Elsworth, "The Concept of Rhythm in Bely's Aesthetic Thought," in *Andrey Bely: Centenary Papers*, ed. Boris Christa (Amsterdam, 1980), p. 70 (hereafter cited as *Centenary Papers*).

7. The two existing general studies of Bely's versification are unhelpful, for different reasons. Boris Christa ignores the textual problems and uses a technique of analysis that obscures as much as it reveals and has very little in common with the standard procedures of professional metrists: "Bely's Poetry: A Metrical Profile," in *Centenary Papers*, pp. 57–117; P. A. Rudnev is concerned with Bely mainly as a source for contrastive material in a study devoted principally to Bryusov, and while his analysis is accurate and theoretically well founded, it does not give a clear picture of Bely's metrical development: P. A. Rudnev, "Metricheskii repertuar V. Bryusova," in *Bryusovskie chteniya 1971 goda*, ed. K. V. Aivazyan (Erevan, 1973), pp. 409–49.

8. D. S. Mirsky, *A History of Russian Literature* (London, 1949), p. 467.

9. Andrey Bely, "Vmesto predisloviya" (to the 1923 edition of the poems), in *Stikhotvoreniya*, ed. Malmstad, III, 424.

10. See, for example, Gerald Janecek, "Rhythm in Prose: The Special Case of Bely," in *Critical Review*, pp. 86–102.

understanding Bely as a writer. There is no possibility of saying with confidence that the superiority of Bely's best novels (*Petersburg*, *The Silver Dove*, *Kotik Letaev*) over all his poetry (except *The First Encounter*) is more than a temporary critical consensus. There is such a consensus, however, and the present essay will not attempt to argue otherwise. But it will leave aside, necessarily, discussion of the relationships—both formal and thematic—between Bely's prose and his poetry, after having noted the inhibiting effect that the weight of the novels seems to have had on serious consideration of the poetry.

The fourth factor that was alleged earlier to have held back the study of Bely's poetry is the obscurity of his intellectual world. This term should be qualified immediately. It would be absurd to claim that Bely's poetic world is inaccessible. Bely frequently advertised his intellectual connections. A complete description of his poetic style would have to take account of a very large number and range of influences. This is an aspect of Bely scholarship that has hardly begun; for example, we do not have adequate studies of things as salient in Bely's poetry as his use of the Bible, or the influence of any single one of the numerous pictorial artists who have been thought to affect his perception. But one's feeling is that these stimuli have been processed by a mind more complex than is usually found in a poet, especially a Russian poet. Some of Bely's poems, the *Star* (*Zvezda*) collection being the most obvious example, cannot be comprehended without the aid of interpretive tools derived from specialized sources, in this particular case from anthroposophy. But what I mean by "obscurity" is the feeling that Bely's poetry almost always requires such a key, much more than is the case with his contemporaries among Russian poets—Aleksandr Blok, Vladislav Khodasevich, Vladimir Mayakovsky, even Valery Bryusov and Velimir Khlebnikov, despite the fact that the latter two poets drew upon aspects of intellectual and physical experience quite as remote as Bely's. It may be, to phrase this problem in the simplest way, that the ratio of intellect to emotion in Bely's poetry is generally too high, the mind hermeticizing experience and removing it from the communality of the emotions. (But on some occasions the emotions paralyze the intellect.) It is undoubtedly this abstruseness that has led to some of the more damning judgments on Bely as a poet, such as Vladimir Markov's: "the fantastic visions of his early verse do not carry one away anymore, his bewailing of Russia in *Ashes* does not stun, and his later anthroposophic verse leaves one cold."[11] Even more crushing is an opinion passed in 1922 by Mirsky in an article that (like Bely's *Petersburg*) was rejected by P. B. Struve: "Reading Bely, you don't say 'There a man burned up.' Bely burns without

11. Vladimir Markov, "Preface," in *Modern Russian Poetry*, ed. Vladimir Markov and Merrill Sparks (London, 1966), p. lviii.

burning up, like a diamond sparkling in the sun. Therefore his cosmic flights take on the indecent appearance of buffoonery and acrobatic tricks."[12] "Burning without burning up" is perhaps the most devastating metaphor that has been applied to Bely's poetry and its effect on the modern reader; to define the causes of this effect is the most difficult challenge facing his critics.

Four major factors, then, have inhibited work on Bely's poetry. An enormous amount of basic work needs to be done before a really informed general study can be written. Only part of this groundwork will be supplied here. The main foundation on which the present essay will be based derives from the formal properties of Bely's lyric verse: an attempt will be made to describe these properties in their historical evolution. This study will incorporate the quantitative principle that Bely was the first to apply on a large scale to the study of Russian poetry, but will use it to describe structural features that Bely did not discuss. And, traducing the standpoint of its subject, this essay will use the quantitative principle without the philosophical superstructure it possesses in Bely's own theoretical work. For, in John Elsworth's words, "it is a premise that cannot well be verified outside the realm of occult meditation, and the assertions it leads to about the meaning of the poem are perhaps more striking than convincing. It only makes full sense in the context of Bely's anthroposophical *Weltanschauung*."[13] I would be inclined to omit the qualifying "well" from the opening phrase.

The remarks made so far have suggested some reasons why Bely's poetry has not been studied in detail. If we go back to Janecek's point about the essentially large-scale quality of Bely's poetry, though, we should expect that general studies rather than detailed studies will tend to be the most instructive. But the sad fact is that only two substantial general studies exist.[14] Boris Christa's monograph on Bely's poetry, while useful as a general introduction to the more obvious problems to which the subject gives rise, is marred by several major faults.[15] It was evidently not revised to take account of research published since its original date of writing as a thesis; besides the inadequate attention paid to the textual problem, the study suffers from a general lack of intellec-

12. D. S. Mirsky, "O sovremennoi sostoyanii russkoi poezii," *Novyi Zhurnal*, no. 131 (1978), pp. 94–95. This article may have benefited from a recent meeting between Bely and Mirsky in Berlin.

13. Elsworth, "Concept of Rhythm," pp. 77–78. Elsworth is discussing Bely's "premise of the dual nature of rhythm," but the observation is generally valid in regard to Bely's theories of poetics.

14. Konstantin Mochul'sky, *Andrey Bely* (Paris, 1955), contains a collection-by-collection summary of Bely's poetry; Oleg A. Maslenikov, *The Frenzied Poets: Andrey Biely and the Russian Symbolists* (Berkeley, 1952), contains very little comment not relating to the poet's biography. Neither Mochul'sky nor Maslenikov attempts a systematic analysis of individual texts.

15. Boris Christa, *The Poetic World of Andrey Bely* (Amsterdam, 1977).

tual and aesthetic sensitivity. By far the best general introduction to Bely
the poet is Tamara Khmel'nitskaya's essay in the 1966 Soviet edition of
the poetry.[16] This essay has been employed as the fundamental point of
orientation in the present essay; detailed acknowledgment of information deriving from it will not always be made, in the interests of economy
of space. The studies of Khmel'nitskaya and Christa have charted the
main stages in Bely's evolution as a poet. But of all the writings on Bely's
poetry, the most valuable from the point of view of interpretation remain Bely's own prefaces to and explanations of the various editions,
projected and realized, of his poetry.

The Lyric Poetry

The fundamental corpus of Andrey Bely's poetry consists of the original editions of the six books of lyrics that were published during his
lifetime and the two longer poems that were mentioned earlier. The
total number of lyric poems in the six books comes to just over 450. But
in addition to this corpus, there is a kind of shadow corpus that consists
of the uncollected lyrics and—much more substantially—the revised
versions of the published corpus. The question of whether or not the
revised versions of collections and individual texts constitute new and
separate items is, as I have said, one of the major factors that has inhibited discussion of Bely's poetry. I shall set the problem aside and begin
by looking at the six collections: *Gold in Azure* (*Zoloto v lazuri*, 1904), *Ashes*
(*Pepel*, 1909), *The Urn* (*Urna*, 1909), *The King's Daughter and Her Knights*
(*Korolevna i rytsari*, 1919), *Star* (*Zvezda*, 1922), and *After Parting* (*Posle
razluki*, 1922).[17]

One interesting feature of Bely's manner of presenting lyric poetry is
that he carefully supplied the date and place of writing for almost all his
works; he was anticipated in this diary-like concern by Zinaida Gippius
and succeeded by Marina Tsvetaeva. It is therefore possible to construct
a chronology of Bely's lyric poetry in much greater detail than is possible
for many modern Russian poets. The chronology is given in Table 1.

Naturally, this table may serve only as the crudest of guides to the
actual substance of what Bely was writing in verse at any given time,
since it gives no indication of the lengths of the texts concerned. The
numbers of pages in each collection is also the most approximate of

16. T. Yu. Khmel'nitskaya, "Poeziya Andreya Belogo," in Andrey Bely, *Stikhotvoreniya i
poemy* (Moscow and Leningrad, 1966), pp. 5–66.
17. All six collections are reprinted in vol. 1 (in two parts) of the Malmstad edition of the
Stikhotvoreniya. As the collections were photo-offset for this edition, their original pagination is preserved. Hereafter references will be given in the text proper with page numbers
following the title of each collection.

Table 1. Numbers of individual texts in Bely's collections of lyric poetry, by date of composition, 1900–1922[a]

Year	Gold in Azure	Ashes	The Urn	The King's Daughter	Star	After Parting	All collections
1900	12						12
1901	22						22
1902	25						25
1903	76						76
Before 1904[b]	7						7
1904	8	13	3				24
1905		11					11
1906		37					37
1907		17	22				39
1908		26	37				63
Before 1909[c]		5					5
1909			5	4			9
1910				1			1
1911				10			10
1912							0
1913					1		1
1914					8		8
1915					1		1
1916					17		17
1917					10		10
1918[d]					15		15
1919							0
1920							0
1921[e]						2	2
1922						57[f]	57
All years	150	109	67	15	52	59	452
Pages of text	266	247	139	56	72	125	905

[a]The individual constituents of cycles are counted as separate texts.

[b]Seven poems in *Gold in Azure* are undated.

[c]Five poems had not been previously published before they appeared in *Ashes* (published December 1908).

[d]April: *Christ Is Risen.*

[e]June: *The First Encounter.*

[f]Includes two texts revised from earlier lyrics.

guides, because of the vagaries of Bely's experimentation with typography. To take an extreme example, *After Parting* includes Bely's shortest lyric text:

Glukhi—
Dukhi! . .

Deaf—
Spirits! . .

which occupies a page to itself (*After Parting*, 104). Because of such experiments in typography, it is not really possible to make a useful computation of the lyrics in terms of verse lines without a tremendous amount of qualification.

Notwithstanding these caveats, Table 1 does make it possible to see clearly the location in time of Bely's most concerted efforts as a lyric poet. The year 1903 stands out as the time of most intensive work; there is another peak in 1908 and another in 1921–22. A long trough appears in the period 1910–15; 1919–20 is another fallow period. Bely was a lyric poet above all from 1903 to 1908, the period when something like 60 percent of all his collected lyrics were written. This most intense activity, therefore, *precedes* Bely's concern with verse theory.

The table also sheds some light on the problem of the separability of the six collections. It shows that *Gold in Azure, Star,* and *After Parting* form fairly well-detached chronological groups, but that *Ashes* and *The Urn* do not; the lyrics belonging to these two collections overlap in time, covering the same span (1904–9). The fact remains that in terms of the bulk of each book, *Ashes* precedes *The Urn*, but nevertheless, we should guard against the idea that they are successive. Bely spent a good deal of creative energy trying to separate these collections in order to give his poetic development the maximum appearance of consistency and progression. Finally, we should note that *After Parting* contains two texts that are reworkings of poems previously published in other forms; these revisions signal the end of Bely's career as a regular lyric poet. The energies that he devoted to poetry after *After Parting* went almost exclusively into the revision and rearrangement of the material whose original appearance is charted in Table 1.

Table 1 shows that *The King's Daughter* is a much slighter collection than the other five, hardly deserving consideration in the same terms as they, its appearance as a separate book probably due to external factors. If we also bear in mind that *After Parting* includes as separate items some texts that are very slight, we may observe in Bely's lyric poetry a consistent movement toward diminution in bulk. The real significance of this tendency, however, can only be estimated against the background of the totality of Bely's writings in all genres.

Criticism of Bely's poetry has tended to describe the six books in terms of a fairly ordered progression, with each successive collection taking the poet's development forward by one fairly clear and definable step; as I suggested earlier, Bely's copious explanations of his feelings about the collections have also fostered this tendency. I, too, will begin by summarizing the main points that have been made about each collection, and then I shall attempt to isolate some large-scale features of the whole.

Gold in Azure, Bely's first collection of verse, was published in Moscow in 1904. The book is divided into five principal sections, revealing at the very beginning of Bely's career as a poet that tendency to build toward larger, compound forms which is one of the major characteristics of his lyric style. In this respect, his manner resembles those of several of the Symbolists (Konstantin Bal'mont, for example) and of Tsvetaeva and Mayakovsky. The fourth of *Gold in Azure*'s five sections consists of a set of seven poems in prose. As far as I can ascertain, they have never been analyzed in detail either independently or in relation to the longer prose works.[18] Of the seven pieces, five date from 1900 and one from 1904; they cannot, therefore, be regarded as an early experiment that was superseded by composition in explicit verse forms. Bely himself omitted them from his principal discussions of his first collection.[19]

Almost all of the poems in *Gold in Azure* are dated in the original edition or have been supplied with dates in subsequent editions; only seven cannot be dated to within at least one year. The chronology of composition is not followed in the order of the poems in the original edition of the book. Just over one-half of the poems (76 of the 150) were written in 1903.[20] We may see, therefore, that Bely turned to composition in verse in a major way between the writing of the first two symphonies (*Northern*, 1900; *Dramatic*, 1901) and the publication of the third (*The Return*, 1905).

The leading stylistic and thematic characteristics of *Gold in Azure* have been described by Khmel'nitskaya, Konstantin Mochul'sky, and of course Bely himself in his various prefaces and in his memoirs. The book as a whole projects a mood of anticipation and hope, qualified by some elements of doubt and isolation. Bely presents himself as a lonely, misunderstood figure in a variety of guises. Some sections of the book draw heavily, and naively, on Greek and Teutonic mythology. The use of color imagery, especially in the descriptions of dawns and sunsets, is extravagant, self-consciously opulent. The recognition extended to Bely's mentors is in some cases explicit (Bryusov, Bal'mont, Vladimir Solov'ev); but some important intellectual and artistic influences, such as Schopenhauer and Arnold Böcklin, are not acknowledged in the text, and their precise contribution to Bely's thought and style in this collection still needs to be elucidated. The archetypal *Gold in Azure* lyric is perhaps "Expectation" ("Ozhidanie"), written in August 1901; dedicated to Sergey Solov'ev, it features holy anticipation, a spectacular sun-

---

18. They are dealt with summarily in Ronald E. Peterson, *Andrei Bely's Short Prose* (Birmingham, 1980), pp. 11–16. See, too, Roger Keys's essay in this volume, chap. 1.

19. See especially the prefaces to *Stikhotvoreniya* (1923), III, 425, and the recently published *Summonses of the Times* (*Zovy vremen* [1931]), III, 433–39.

20. In 1931 Bely stated that *Gold in Azure* was basically written in two months, something of an exaggeration (*Stikhotvoreniya*, ed. Malmstad, III, 433).

set, and an open-air setting whose denizens sympathetically echo the author's mood:

> Like an irrevocable dream,
> sparkles the gold of a leaf.
>
> My soul is full of familiar thoughts.
> Among the aroundflying avenues
> is a challengingly-melancholy, quiet sound
> about the nearness of sacred days. [. . .]
>
> Misty, redgold,
> upon us shone an evening ray
> in a nonearthly fiery stream
> from behind the autumnal, low clouds.
>
> Once more my soul regrets something.
> Like a damp mist night descends.
> A crimson maple, nodding into the distance,
> sadly wants to rush away from here.
>
> And once more there is the sound among the avenues
> about the nearness of sacred days.[21]

Bely's most cutting phrase among all the negative remarks he later heaped on his own first book of poems concerns the "I" figure; in the preface to the 1931 collection *The Summonses of the Times* (*Zovy vremen*), he describes himself as being "annoyed" by "the consumptive sniveling of this stooping *intelligent*" (III, 434–35). This is much too severe. The poems from *Gold in Azure* that have worn best are not the ones in which the imagery is at its most intense and the author's person disguised, but the ones in which a relatively direct, even naive mode is found to express the author's emotional state. The short lyric "Alone" ("Odin"), for example, finds the author indoors looking out, a moon instead of the persistent strong sun of *Gold in Azure,* and no dramatic projection of the author's "I" into the persona of Argonaut, centaur, Christ, or madman:

---

21. "Kak nevozvratnaya mechta, / sverkaet zoloto lista. / / Dusha polna znakomykh dum. / Mezh obletayushchikh allei / prizyvno-grustnyi, tikhii shum / o blizosti svyashchennykh dnei. [. . .] / / Tumannyi, krasnozolotoi / na nas blesnul vechernii luch / bezmirnoognennoi struei / iz-za osennikh, nizkikh tuch. / / Dushe opyat' chego-to zhal'. / Syrym tumanom skhodit noch'. / Bagryanyi klen, kivaya vdal', / s toskoi otsyuda rvetsya proch'. / / I snova shum sredi allei / o blizosti svyashchennykh dnei" (*Gold in Azure,* 221–22). The translations of verse texts here aim to be as literal as possible, reflecting Bely's neologisms and retaining as far as is consistent with English syntax the same disposition of matter to the line as in the original.

The windows have started sweating.
Outside is the moon.
And you are standing aimlessly
by the window.

Wind. Bowing down, arguing,
a row of grizzled birches.
There has been much grief . . .
Many tears . . .

And there rises up involuntarily
the tedious row of years.
My heart hurts, hurts . . .
I'm alone.[22]

This poem is placed toward the end of "Images" ("Obrazy"), the third section (*otdel*) of the five into which the book is divided. Its Russian-folkloric style and resigned, grieving tone contrast strongly with some of its companions in the section: they include the four centaur poems, the "Giant" cycle, and several other lyrics with which it has very little in common. There too, for example, we find the opening stanza of the flamboyant "In the Mountains" ("Na gorakh"):

The mountains wear wedding crowns.
I'm enraptured, I'm young.
I feel in the mountains
a cleansing cold.[23]

It is clear from these contrasts, which could easily be continued, that the problem of unity in Bely's larger-scale compositions is by no means a simple one. Evidently the author senses that some common element justifies the grouping of these poems together in his design; but this evidence does not point to an element centered in mood, imagery, or theme.

The examples that have been cited illustrate incidentally one of the most striking technical innovations made by Bely, namely, the printing of line-initial words with a lowercase first letter if they are not also the first word in a sentence. This device has now become so widespread that

22. "Okna zapoteli. / Na dvore luna. / I stoish' bez tseli / u okna. // Veter. Niknet, sporya, / ryad sedykh berez. / Mnogo bylo gorya . . . / Mnogo slez . . . // I vstaet nevol'no / skuchnyi ryad godin. / Serdtsu bol'no, bol'no . . . / Ya odin" (*Gold in Azure,* 170).
23. "Gory v brachnykh ventsakh. / Ya v vostorge, ya molod. / U menya na gorakh / ochistitel'nyi kholod" (*Gold in Azure,* 120). The entire poem is available in English in *Modern Russian Poetry,* ed. Markov and Sparks, pp. 184–87.

it takes some effort to see it as an innovation. As far as I am aware, the sources of this device have not been identified; it may, of course, have been an original idea of Bely's own. Remarkably, though, Bely abandoned it in his publications after *Gold in Azure*.

Another technical innovation appears in *Gold in Azure,* this time one that is more enduring and more striking than the lowercase initials. In 12 of the 150 texts we find that Bely breaks up the layout of the text in such a way that typographical units no longer correspond to the metrical units:

> Glittering
> for them, candles.
> Flitting by
> on the walls
> their farthingales
> and ringlets, and shoulders . . .[24]

This relatively simple example is from "The Ladies of Midnight" ("Polunoshchnitsy"), one of the eighteenth-century stylizations that make up the beginning part of the section "Then and Now" ("Prezhde i teper'"). All the examples in *Gold in Azure* are of this type, known nowadays in Russian as *stolbik* ("column arrangement"). The metrical lines, free amphibrachs in this case, are broken up so that typographical lines are shorter than metrical lines, and all lines are aligned at the left. Typography—the use of capital and lowercase initials—still indicates the metrical hierarchy, however. In this particular example, the result preserves the amphibrachic feet at line level; Bely's typography does not always do so.[25] It may be seen from this example that no single objective principle, such as integrity of rhyme or phrase, dictates the typographical arrangement.

The twelve poems in which *stolbik* is used are marked by no particular thematic or formal communality. And their metrical typology (two iambic and the remainder ternaries) and rhyme schemes reflect the overall norms of *Gold in Azure.* I will present the metrical typology of *Gold in Azure* after discussing some individual aspects of the next two collections.

In some important ways the construction of the next two collections, *Ashes* and *The Urn,* resembles that of *Gold in Azure.* In each of them, the

24. "Blistayut / im svechi. / Mel'kayut / na stenakh / ikh fizhmy / i bukli, i plechi . . ." (*Gold in Azure,* 73).

25. On the problem of Bely's experiments with typography, we have had only two very brief studies: Herbert Eagle, "Typographical Devices in the Poetry of Andrey Bely," in *Critical Review,* pp. 71–85; and Gerald Janecek, "Intonation and Layout in Bely's Poetry," in *Centenary Papers,* pp. 81–90. Janecek treats the question at length in the second chapter of his *Look of Russian Literature: Avant-Garde Visual Experiments, 1900–1930* (Princeton, 1984), pp. 25–67.

individual texts are arranged into cycles—seven in *Ashes*, eight in *The Urn*. The size of these groups ranges from two to twenty-four constituents; most of them include between twelve and eighteen texts. Some individual texts are further subdivided into sections, creating elaborate compositional hierarchies within the book as a whole. In both collections, the poems are supplied with the date and place of writing, but their order is not chronological either overall or within the groups; neither are poems written in the same place grouped together. These features of construction are found only in Bely's first three books of lyrics; division into subsections is found again in his revisions of the collections, but not in *The King's Daughter, Star,* or *After Parting*.

Both *Ashes* and *The Urn* carry the date 1909.[26] They are the easiest of Bely's books to sum up. In his preface to the 1923 edition of his poems, Bely characterized what he saw as the central significance of the two books in terms that have been echoed by all subsequent students of his work: "The poet collects into an urn the ashes of his burned-out rapture that had once blazed up as 'Gold' and 'Azure'" (III, 426). The "ashes" are the contents of *Ashes*, the earlier of the two collections (though not absolutely) in terms of time of writing. The book is dedicated to Nikolay Nekrasov and has a demonstrative epigraph from his work. The established interpretation of the collection sees it as marking a turn away from the solipsistic contemplation of *Gold in Azure* toward the specific social concerns of Russia at the time the book was written. The open-air settings for the philosophical musings of *Gold in Azure* turn into grieving laments over the poverty and backwardness of rural life. Mythological characters give place to beggars, convicts, and wandering hoboes. But the book does also deal with the city, used as the setting for grotesque vignettes of upper-class and intelligentsia life. Actually, it is easy to overestimate the degree of social concern in the book; an exaggeration of this element is one of the very few serious shortcomings of Khmel'nitskaya's preface to the 1966 edition. The dominant impression that *Ashes* leaves, if it is read independently rather than as a contrasting development from *Gold in Azure,* is of repugnance for the sordid brutality of social life. This repugnance is a reaction to sexual exploitation, death by violence, lust, drink, and crime, scenes of which occur throughout the book. This, of course, is just as much the legacy of Nekrasov as the social concern of the remorseful *intelligent*. But, though Nekrasov certainly has an element of prurience, it is not so strong as Bely's in *Ashes*. This element goes as far as necrophilia in several instances. However, the decadence of many poems in *Ashes* is rescued by the richness of the authorial attitudes in the book. The breast-beating tone of the famous "Despair" ("Otchayan'e"),

26. *Ashes* was actually published in December 1908; as was normal for books published in December, it carries the following year as its date of publication.

probably Bely's most frequently anthologized lyric, which opens *Ashes*, is
in fact not typical of the collection as a whole.[27] More characteristic is
either detachment—as in the series of lyrics, such as "The Priest's Wife"
("Popovna") and "The Ancient House" ("Starinnyi dom"), which are
ballad-like narratives—or resignation, as in the famous "To My Friends"
("Druz'yam"):

> Trusted the golden brilliance,
> But died from the sun's arrows.
> With thought measured the ages,
> But couldn't live through life.[28]

This summation, we should remember, was written at the age of twenty-
six.

Ashes also includes some texts that seem to fall between the manner of
Gold in Azure and that of the new social awareness. Among them is the
mysterious confessional lyric:

> Until above the dead
> Thou fall asleep alone, until such time
> Rattle thy rusty chains
> About liberty from the stone tower.
>
> May thy brow be covered,—
> Thy brow, with bloody sweat.
> Eyes through the turbid glass—
> Eyes—raised to the heights.
>
> Turquoise will flood the windows,
> Airy gold will flood.
> Day—a dull pearl—a tear—
> Flows from the sunrise to the sunset.
>
> A gray rain will seep through there,
> The sky show blue like the steppe.
> But here, imprisoned leader,
> Rattle thy rusted chain.
>
> Let morning, evening, day and night—
> Converge—the rays will stretch into the window:

27. "Dovol'no: ne zhdi, ne nadeisya . . . "; the poem is one of two by Bely included in *The
Penguin Book of Russian Verse*, ed. Dmitri Obolensky (Harmondsworth, 1962, and later
editions). It is also one of the eight poems by Bely in *Modern Russian Poetry*, ed. Markov and
Sparks, pp. 190–97.
28. "Zolotomu blesku veril, / A umer ot solnechnykh strel. / Dumoi veka izmeril, / A
zhizn' prozhit' ne sumel" (*Ashes*, 183). The poem is in *Modern Russian Poetry*, ed. Markov
and Sparks, pp. 188–89.

Converge—and glance: and rush away.
Will press against the window—and sink into eternity.

1907[29]

Here is a lyric that lacks specificity in time and place; it is also imperson-al, with no explicit identification of the "thou" who is addressed and counseled. It may, of course, be read in such a way as to identify the "thou, imprisoned leader" with Bely himself, and the poem as a projec-tion of his persecution complex. But the style of this lyric, as I shall assert later, is one of the central and abiding elements in Bely's verse, a com-promise between what may be polarized as the conceptual Symbolist abstraction of *Gold in Azure* and the historical specificity of *Ashes*.

The central situation of the addressee of "Until above the dead"—confined and, in this case, in bondage within an oppressive interior, with a window through which the subject views an obviously symbolic chang-ing natural scene—is one of the most persistent situations found in the lyrics of *The Urn*. In poem after poem of this collection, the lyric hero observes violent storms of rain and snow, is sucked into swirling sky-scapes, watches the night sky, and reads transcendental meaning into the stars and moon. The morbidity of *Ashes* is still present in *The Urn*, but in a much milder form. The most prominent motif in *The Urn*—though Christ himself is never mentioned in the text at all—is a kind of second coming that seems to promise the deliverance of the lyric hero from his captivity within the bounds of the physical and earthly realm. The "com-ing" takes the form of a descent of a mysterious figure—identified sometimes as a brother, sometimes as a demon (the latter, though, ap-parently benevolent)—from a sky full of stormy clouds. The sense of anticipation and the longing for delivery from captivity—

I am fettered
By the iron chain of fate,
Minutes, hours, and weeks.[30]

—is even stronger than in *Gold in Azure*, of which it is supposed to be the dominant element.

The Urn has sometimes been read as a poorly managed parody of early-nineteenth-century metaphysical poetry, especially as manifested

29. "Poka nad mertvymi lyud'mi / Odin ty ne usnul, dotole / Tsepyami rzhavymi gremi / Iz bashni kamennoi o vole. // Da pokryvaetsya chelo,— / Tvoe chelo, krovavym potom. / Glaza skvoz' mutnoe steklo— / Glaza—vozdetye k vysotam. // Nal'etsya v okna biryuza, / Vozdushnoe nal'etsya zlato. / Den'—zhemchug matovyi—sleza— / Techet s voskhoda do zakata. // To seryi seetsya tam dozhd', / To—nebo golubeet step'yu. / No zdes' ty, zaklyuchennyi vozhd', / Gremi zarzhavlennoyu tsep'yu. // Pust' utro, vecher, den' i noch'— / Soidut—luchi v okno protyanut: / Soidut—glyadyat: nesutsya proch'. / Pril'nut k oknu— i v vechnost' kanut" (*Ashes*, 147).

30. "Okovan ya / Zheleznoi tsep'yu roka / Minut, chasov, nedel'" (*The Urn*, 94).

in the lyrics of Fedor Tyutchev and Evgeny Baratynsky. This view is strongly argued by Mochul'sky; and without citing Mochul'sky's name, Khmel'nitskaya appears to be specifically refuting him in her argument for a higher evaluation of the book. To read the book purely as an exercise in stylization is seriously to underestimate it. As an illustration of the complexity of this issue, though, we may cite "Life" ("Zhizn'"):

> There rushes over the secret of life
> Of spaces and fatal times
> In the heavenly-blue fatherland
> A lightly flowing, smoky dream.
>
> The days ascend beneath the heavens,
> And fly above the heights
> Censed by the clouds,—
> Censed from time immemorial.
>
> Life is the depths,
> Spattered by a turquoise wave.
> With the foam of its days
> It obscures our eyes.
>
> But nonetheless, in transitory vanity,
> Prophetic dreams trouble us,
> When we stand before the universe
> Immersed, astounded,—
>
> And there opens out before us
> An unattainable homeland
> That has been revealed above the clouds
> By the azure depths.
>
> 1908[31]

The philosophical stance of this poem—the vision of a more real life glimpsed above and beyond the transitory vanity of "real" life—is central to Tyutchev, of course; but despite the classical form of the poem, which so upset Mochul'sky, its imagery is unmistakably Bely's. The color epithets, the aqueous dynamism of ethereal masses, the rapt contemplation of the skyscape—these are central elements of Bely's poetry from the very beginning.

31. "Pronositsya nad tainoi zhizni / Prostranstv i rokovykh vremen / V nebesno-goluboi otchizne / Legkotekushchii, dymnyi son. // Voznosyatsya pod nebesami, / Letyat nad vysotami dni / Voskurennymi oblakami,— / Voskurennymi iskoni. // Zhizn'—biryuzovoyu volnoyu / Razbryzgannaya glubina. / Svoeyu penoyu dnevnoyu / Nam ochi zadymit ona. // I vse zhe v suetnosti brennoi / Nas veshchie smushchayut sny, / Kogda stoim pered vselennoi / Uglubleny, potryaseny,— // I otverzaetsya nad nami / Nedostizhimyi krai rodnoi / Otkrytoyu nad oblakami / Lazurevoyu glubinoi" (The Urn, 107–8).

A countervailing force, however, opposes the metaphysical concerns that dominate *The Urn*. A number of poems—the most important of which are grouped in the sections "Philosophical Melancholy" ("Filosoficheskaya grust'") and "Dedications" ("Posvyashcheniya") and take their cue from the opening four lyrics of the book, which are dedicated to Bryusov—evince a detached and ironic attitude toward the kind of idealism that is embodied in "Life." This element is quite foreign to Tyutchev and Baratynsky; it is more akin, needless to say, to Pushkin. Several critics have pointed out that the poems in the sections just cited form the most substantial anticipation in Bely's lyrics of the tone of *The First Encounter*.

The poems included in *The King's Daughter and Her Knights* were, as we saw earlier, begun in the same year as the latest work in *The Urn*. But *The King's Daughter* stands with *After Parting* as the most self-contained and homogeneous of the collections. The poems are, of course, much shorter; their contents are comparable in size with the larger cycles of *Gold in Azure*, *Ashes*, and *The Urn*. *The King's Daughter* carries the generic subtitle "Fairy Tales" ("Skazki"). The sixteen poems in the collection (some of them compound in form, the longest, "The Clown" ["Shut"], a very substantial work) represent the most concentrated manifestation of the medieval element in Bely's poetic world. But some poems in *The King's Daughter*, most significantly "Evening" ("Vecher") and "You—dawns, you dawns! . ." ("Vy—zori, zori! . ."), take us straight back to the atmosphere of rapt expectation in a symbolic outdoor setting that dominates *Gold in Azure*. But in the *King's Daughter* poems, the hero is most often, as in *The Urn*, one who has suffered and has lost the cherished world of his past.

With *Star* we encounter a different kind of organization from the system used in the first three books. No longer are lyrics combined into cycles or groups. And it is even less possible here than in the other collections to point to a dominant single note; rather, we find—often in close succession—lyrics that seem to embody the supposedly antithetical tendencies represented in the first three collections. As an example, we may take the first few poems in the collection. "To Christian Morgenstern" ("Khristianu Morgenshternu") may be seen as a direct continuation of the "Dedications" cycle that comes near the end of *The Urn*. "The Star" ("Zvezda") and "Self-Awareness" ("Samosoznanie"), the second and third poems in the book, are copybook *Gold in Azure* lyrics in form, theme, and style; the first is in iambic pentameter, the second in *stolbik*-arranged mixed amphibrachs, and both poems sketch out visionary cosmic events splashed with the azure and turquoise hues of the first collection. Then comes the classical rigor of "Karma," a philosophical lyric in the iambic tetrameter quatrains of *The Urn*. The fifth lyric in the book is "To My Contemporaries" ("Sovremennikam"), which contains the agonized realization of tragic destiny that is strong in some poems in *Ashes*. It is true that the dominant note of *Ashes* is not reached until the sixteenth lyric in the book, "Russia" ("Rossiya"); here we have the lyric hero alone in a rural, desolate, and godforsaken Russia.

The most important new theme that is broached in *Star* is the love theme, specifically in the poems addressed to Asya Turgeneva. Seven such poems are scattered through the book in what seems to be a deliberate rejection of the relentless cyclization of the first three collections. None of the poems addressed to Turgeneva is in the historically specific mode: they all operate in terms of the abstract time-and-space imagery of *Gold in Azure*. One of them, "The Snowy Dew Glitters" ("Snegovaya blistaet rosa"), is the first example in Bely's lyrics of the explicit formal experiment: in this case, the text uses only two stressed vowels, *a* and *o*, and this fact is advertised under the poem's heading.[32] The other explicit formal experimentation in the collection is constituted by the series of five tankas. One of them, "Life" ("Zhizn' "), is among the most intriguing and successful of Bely's shorter lyrics; it is simultaneously both hermetic and instantaneously communicative because of the power of its principal image:

> Over the grass, a butterfly—
> A self-propelled flower . . .
> So I too: into the wind—death—
> Above myself—like a stem—
> I fly past like a butterfly.
>
> 1916[33]

Between *Star* and Bely's last collection of lyrics, *After Parting*, lies the monumental achievement of *The First Encounter* and the less impressive long poem *Christ Is Risen*. It is from the manner of the latter work that *After Parting* takes its lead; it has none of the controlled and yet passionate irony of *The First Encounter*. *After Parting* is the most extreme expression of the tendency in Bely's lyrics to destroy canonical verse forms as if in response to an uncontrollable emotional impulse. It is this naked display of emotion, the center of which is self-abasement (almost self-flagellation), and the apparently uncritical self-indulgence in capricious forms that have led to the almost universal condemnation of *After Parting*. This condemnation is quite justified. Of all Bely's works in verse, this is the one where the controlling and saving intellect has simply surrendered; the result is an almost arbitrary jumble of repetitive verbal gestures.

32. The poem is included in *Modern Russian Poetry*, ed. Markov and Sparks, pp. 192–93.
33. "Nad travoi motylek— / Samoletnyi tsvetok . . . / Tak i ya: v veter—smert'— / Nad soboi—stebel'kom— / Prolechu motyl'kom" (*Star*, 49).

Bely's six collections of lyric poetry, then, exhibit certain specific tendencies and developments. Fresh themes and emphases do emerge over time. The differences between the collections, however, are outweighed in importance by a small number of stylistic, thematic, and formal tendencies that are present in Bely's poetry almost from the beginning and persist throughout his lyric corpus. But before returning to this problem, let us survey the metrical characteristics of the six collections. In examining the metrical typology of Bely's lyrics I shall use categories of analysis that are now fairly standard in Russian metrics. I will make no attempt to compare Bely's practice with that of individual contemporaries; for the comparative material used here I am indebted to Mikhail Gasparov's concise history of the Russian metrical repertoire in his indispensable book of 1974.[34]

Table 2 presents a general typology of Bely's lyrics in three major metrical groups: iambic, trochaic, and ternary.[35] These three groups are usually referred to as the "classical" meters because the vast bulk of the Russian poetry written in the eighteenth and nineteenth century uses them in various permutations and combinations; to this day the "nonclassical" meters have not succeeded in seriously challenging their hegemony.

This is a very crude basis on which to make comparisons, but it is nevertheless indicative in many important respects. Mikhail Gasparov's figures for the three decades 1890–1924 provide a very broad indication of the general state of the metrical repertoire during the Symbolist period. On the basis of Table 2, we may see that Bely's work, compared with the norms of his time, favors the ternary group (about 20 percent over the norm); to supply the ternary group he takes away from the iambic group (almost 10 percent below the norm), the trochaic group (more than 7 percent below) and the nonclassical meters (about 5 percent below). Of these redistributions, the last is the most interesting when viewed in the context of what was happening in Bely's time in Russian versification. The major innovation made by the Symbolist poets was the use of the *dol'nik*.[36] For the decade immediately preceding the period 1890–1924, Gasparov's figure for the nonclassical meters is as low as 1

34. M. L. Gasparov, *Sovremennyi russkii stikh: Metrika i ritmika* (Moscow, 1974), pp. 29–75. Rudnev has compared Bely's works with those of Blok and Bryusov; see n. 7.

35. This conventional categorization of the meters distinguishes among the two binary groups, both of which have alternation of metrically strong and weak syllables, the strong syllables being the even-numbered ones in the iambic group and the odd-numbered ones in the trochaic group; and the ternary group, in which two metrically weak syllables occur between the strong syllables (there being three types: dactylic, where the strong syllables precede two weak ones; amphibrachic, where the strong syllables occur between two weak ones; and anapestic, where the strong syllables follow two weak ones, all counting from the opening of the line). The nonclassical meters are lumped together as "others."

36. The *dol'nik* is a meter in which there may be either one or two weak syllables between the strong ones; see Gasparov, *Sovremennyi russkii stikh*, pp. 220–93.

Table 2. Percentage of Bely's lyric texts and of selected Russian poetic texts, 1890–1924, in three metrical groups

	Iambic	Trochaic	Ternary	Others	All meters	Number of texts
Bely texts	40.5%	11.9%	35.9%	11.7%	100.0%	452
Selected texts	49.5	19.5	14.5	16.5	100.0	1,863

SOURCE: Figures for selected Russian texts are drawn from M. L. Gasparov, *Sovremennyi russkii stikh: Metrika i ritmika* (Moscow, 1974).

percent, and the rise to 16.5 percent is due principally to the arrival of the *dol'nik* as an accepted part of the metrical repertoire. The relatively modest figure of 11.7 percent in Bely's typology means that at the most general level of metrical analysis, his practice, contrary to all prevailing estimates, is actually conservative; at the highest level of generalization, his experimentation is within the bounds of the classical system rather than part of the contemporary revolt against them. At lower levels of structure, however, Bely does depart significantly from the norms of his contemporaries. (Unfortunately, these norms are much less easy to demonstrate than metrical typology at the level of the metrical group.)

We can investigate this aspect of Bely's versification further by breaking down the metrical typology into its components as represented by the various major collections. The figures are given in Table 3.

We see that the overall figures are masking some violent shifts in the distribution of Bely's metrical preferences through time. Each major collection has its own distinctive metrical profile. The overall figures are expounded most closely by *Gold in Azure,* and we may suspect that the bulk of this collection has had a strong influence on the overall figures. The figure for the ternaries in *Gold in Azure* is extraordinarily high in the history of Russian versification; it is matched to my knowledge only by Georgy Ivanov in his later émigré period, a phenomenon that is almost certainly unrelated to Bely's practice.[37] In *Ashes* we observe a distribution between the four metrical groups which is relatively even; and then in *The Urn* we have the domination of the iambic group to an extent unmatched by Bely's contemporaries—with the sole exception of Khodasevich, whose work in certain periods also exhibits this concentration on the iambic group.[38] *Star* gives evidence of a move back toward the distribution of *Gold in Azure,* with the bulk of the diminution of the iambic group going to the ternaries. And finally, *After Parting* evinces a distribution as odd as *The Urn* in terms of contemporary norms, but for the opposite

37. See G. S. Smith, "The Versification of Russian Emigré Poetry, 1920–1940," *SEER,* 56, no. 1 (1978), pp. 32–46.
38. See G. S. Smith, "The Versification of V. F. Xodasevič, 1915–1939," in *Russian Poetics,* ed. D. S. Worth and T. Eekman (Columbus, 1983), pp. 373–91.

Table 3. Percentage of Bely's lyrical texts represented in three metrical groups, by collection

Collection	Iambic	Trochaic	Ternary	Others	All meters	Number of texts
Gold in Azure	27.3%	4.7%	61.3%	6.7%	100.0%	150
Ashes	31.2	23.9	27.5	17.4	100.0	109
The Urn	92.5	1.5	4.5	1.5	100.0	67
Star	65.4	7.7	25.0	1.9	100.0	52
After Parting	8.5	25.4	39.0	27.1	100.0	59
All collections	40.3	12.1	36.8	10.8	100.0	437

reason: instead of the iambic group, the most traditional of the four, it is the nonclassical group that is salient, with the iambic group cut to below 10 percent.

An approach to the metrical repertoire that is less comprehensive than the approach through the four groups, but more sensitive in terms of individual meters, is to examine the major meters at line level. Gasparov's survey of the metrical repertoire reveals that at any given time, something like three-quarters of all texts use one or another of only seven meters. Table 4 sets out the seven most frequently encountered meters in the material presented in Table 2.

Quite surprisingly, the overall figure for iambic tetrameter in Bely's texts turns out to be very close to the overall average for the period. But in terms of other meters, he may be seen to be turning away from the staple repertoire. As I suggested before, the low figure for the *dol'nik* in Bely is particularly significant in view of the rising popularity of this meter during the period. Where is the remaining material in Bely's typology going? The answer is that Bely cultivated certain relatively rare meters to an extent unknown among his contemporaries. The second most common meter in his lyrics is amphibrachic trimeter, which accounts for 9.1 percent of all texts; this meter does not appear among the ten most popular in Gasparov's count. Then Bely has 5.5 percent of texts in each of mixed iambic meters and anapestic trimeter, which account respectively for 3.8 and 3.3 percent in the period averages. And Bely has 4.4 percent of texts in iambic trimeter (period average 2.1 percent). It is these and other less salient preferences that individualize Bely's metrical typology.

More significant than the overall figures for these individual meters, however, is their distribution among Bely's various collections. We saw some violent shifts in the distribution of metrical groups among the collections. The same is true of individual meters, as Table 5 shows.

The figures in Table 5 give us the most immediate pointers we have seen so far to the metrical makeup of Bely's major collections. The total percentage taken up by the major meters is one of the best indices of the

Table 4. Percentage of selected Russian poetic texts, 1890–1924, and of Bely's lyric texts written in seven major meters

	Iambic tetrameter	Iambic pentameter	Trochaic tetrameter	Free iambic	Dol'nik	Iambic hexameter	Trochaic pentameter	Others	All meters	Number of texts
Selected texts	18.9%	11.6%	8.0%	5.5%	8.7%	5.2%	4.5%	37.6%	100.0%	1,863
Bely texts	18.8	8.4	4.4	1.8	2.9	1.3	0.6	61.8	100.0	452

SOURCE: Figures for selected Russian texts are drawn from M. L. Gasparov, *Sovremennyi russkii stikh: Metrika i ritmika* (Moscow, 1974).

Table 5. Percentage of Bely's lyric poems written in eleven major meters, by collection

Collection	Iambic pentameter	Iambic tetrameter	Iambic trimeter	Mixed iambic	Free iambic	Trochaic tetrameter	Mixed trochaic	Amphibrachic trimeter	Free amphibrachic	Anapestic trimeter	Free anapestic	Others	All meters
Gold in Azure	10.0%	6.7%	0.7%	5.3%	4.0%	2.7%	0.7%	10.0%	10.0%	5.3%	11.3%	43.3%	100.0%
Ashes	2.7	21.1	3.7	0.9	0.0	6.4	14.7	10.1	0.9	8.3	1.8	29.4	100.0
The Urn	6.0	56.7	11.9	11.9	1.4	1.4	0.0	3.0	0.0	0.0	0.0	7.7	100.0
Star	11.5	26.9	3.8	15.4	1.9	1.9	1.9	5.8	1.9	1.9	0.0	27.1	100.0
After Parting	1.7	3.5	3.5	0.0	0.0	10.5	1.8	15.8	0.0	10.5	3.5	49.2	100.0

relative variety of the body of material. We see immediately that *The Urn* is the most homogeneous of the collections; well over half its contents are in iambic tetrameter, a figure not approached by any other individual meter in any of the collections. *After Parting* is the most varied of the collections; here Bely has moved outside the conventional repertoire to a large extent. *Gold in Azure* is also varied, with only one element, free anapestic, accounting for more than 10 percent, but the constituents are taken from within the conventional repertoire. Among other remarkable features, it is worth noting the high figures for mixed trochaic meters in *Ashes*, and the similar figure for mixed iambic meters in *Star*.

One of the many insensitive features of this (conventional) categorization of the metrical repertoire is that while some individual measures (such as iambic and trochaic tetrameter and pentameter) have headings of their own, the mixed and free meters are all grouped together under the heading appropriate to the metrical group. Thus the category designated as mixed iambic meters may subsume a greater or smaller variety of individual meters, all having in common the iambic line and the use of lines of different length in invariant order. It is therefore worthwhile to examine in greater detail the individual components of the mixed iambic and mixed trochaic categories in the collections where these categories are prominent. It turns out that there is in fact a considerable degree of homogeneity within the mixed categories. All of the sixteen poems in mixed trochaic meter included in *Ashes* have the same form, tetrameter-trimeter-tetrameter-trimeter, and nine of them are concentrated in the "Countryside" ("Derevnya") section of the book, creating a powerful association between this form and the rural setting. It is the only case in Bely's work where a direct association may be pointed out between metrical form and theme. The eight poems in mixed iambic meter that form an important component of *Star* are less homogeneous; they all have in common the alternation of longer and shorter lines, the longer lines being pentameters; but the poems are not placed together in the volume, as the mixed trochaic poems are in *Ashes*. Thematically, they display some polar oppositions of mood; for example, the despair of "Ruins" ("Razvaly") and the buoyant summons of "December 1916" ("Dekabr' 1916 goda").

Everything that has been said so far about Bely's versification has been derived from analysis at the level of the verse line. The data have been categorized according to the divisions that are now conventional in the description of the metrical repertoire of Russian poetry. It is worth making the point that Bely's own writings on versification make no mention of the categories and technique of analysis used here. Besides the level of the line, three other levels of structure have been studied by Russian metrists. The stanza and the associated level of rhyme have been relatively little studied; the bulk of our existing knowledge lies in the area that Bely pioneered, that of verse rhythm.

The most interesting and significant aspects of the rhythm of Bely's poetry have been adequately discussed. Kirill Taranovsky was attracted by the question of what Bely did in his own poetry that used the same meter he studied as a theoretician, namely, iambic tetrameter.[39] Taranovsky established that Bely switched from one rhythmical preference in iambic tetrameter to another in the course of his career as a lyric poet. He also showed that three distinct rhythmical types and two intermediary types could be closely associated with certain themes in Bely's lyrics. Most striking is the association between the historically most unusual type, with its relatively weak second ictus, and the theme of the grotesque, which is important in *Ashes* and *The Urn*. An example will be given of one stanza from "Melancholy" ("Melankholiya"), the poem Taranovsky cites in full to exemplify this rhythm; he describes it as "sharply asymmetrical, labored, stumbling, roughish":

> Nad górodom vstayút s zemlí,—
> Nad úlitsami klúby gári.
> Vdalí—nad golovoí—vdalí
> Obrývki bezotvétnykh árii.
>
> [*Ashes*, 127]

Bely avoids stressing the second ictus, which falls on the fourth syllable of the line; in Pushkin's iambic tetrameter, for example, the strength of this ictus is second only to the final one in the line (the eighth syllable). Taranovsky further shows that a number of other subtle links may be established between different rhythms in Bely's iambic tetrameter and various shades of the themes expressed by the relevant poems.

Of course, Taranovsky is dealing here with a unique historical example; no other Russian poet has written so extensively as Bely on the history and theory of verse rhythm. On the rhythms of other meters used by Bely, very little indeed has been written. The rhythms of Bely's preferred ternary meters have been discussed by Mikhail Gasparov in his pioneering examination of this rather neglected area in the history of Russian versification.[40] Gasparov's primary objective in this instance was to study the relationship between the rhythm of anapestic trimeter and amphibrachic trimeter and the rhythmical characteristics of nonverse language, rather than to elicit individual features of the rhythms used by the poets concerned, and he makes no attempt to relate rhythm to theme

---

39. See Taranovsky, "Chetyrekhstopnyi yamb Andreya Belogo," pp. 145–47.

40. M. L. Gasparov, "Trekhstopnyi amfibrakhii i trekhstopnyi anapest v XIX i XX v," in *Sovremennyi russkii stikh*, pp. 126–219.

in a way analogous to Taranovsky's work on the rhythms of Bely's iambic tetrameter. But Gasparov does here make some interesting remarks about the rhythm of Bely's binary meters and also of his prose. There is no doubt that in the latter area, the relationship between the rhythm of the ternary meters in Bely's verse and those of the prose texts in which he uses a ternary metrical base, lies the most promising and pressing field for further research. But without a preliminary study involving extensive statistical analysis, it is unwise to speculate on what a comparative rhythmical study would reveal.

Bely's versification at the level of the stanza has been discussed hardly at all; the most important exception to this statement is represented by the aspects of Bely's stanza preferences that are referred to in Ian K. Lilly's work on Bely's rhyme and in a note on Bely's stanza rhythm in iambic tetrameter that Gasparov appended to an article of my own.[41] Yet the stanza constitutes a very important formal level in Bely's work, as may be judged from the examples of his typographical experimentation that have been referred to earlier.

The statistical study of Bely's verse structures at levels higher than the line would demand, if it were to be carried out in complete detail, a larger apparatus of categorization even than the metrical typology at line level. I shall therefore restrict myself to some broad observations concerning the more salient features. We have seen that in twelve poems of *Gold in Azure*, regular stanzaic structure is broken, in this case by the use of *stolbik*. This kind of experimentation persists throughout Bely's work, but its relative extent is easy to overestimate. Eighteen of *Ashes'* poems have broken typographic structure (either *stolbik* or *lesenka*);[42] their structure is either those mixed ternaries whose first stage was seen in *Gold in Azure* or polymetric verse. They are found throughout *Ashes*, but disproportionately many, a total of six, are found in the "Russia" ("Rossiya") section of the book; "Merrymaking in Russia" ("Vesel'e na Rusi") is perhaps the most notable of them. It would seem that stanzaic regularity is one of the primary formal grounds on which Bely alotted material of the period to *The Urn*, which has only one poem, "Summers" ("Leta"), with anything but the most conventional quatrains or couplets. *The King's Daughter* and *Star* are similar; only two of *Star*'s poems use *stolbik:* "The Word" ("Slovo") and the ultimate *stolbik* poem, "A Joke" ("Shutka"), with its one-word lines. The stanza-breaking tendency reaches its apogee, of course, in *After Parting*. Here, apparently trying to reflect in a graphic way the emo-

---

41. See n. 5 and G. S. Smith, "Stanza Rhythm in the Iambic Tetrameter of Three Modern Russian Poets," *IJSLP*, no. 24 (1981), pp. 135–52.

42. In "stepladder form" (*lesenka*), segments are arranged in stepwise fashion, usually down the page from left to right, instead of all being aligned at the left, as in *stolbik*. On this device, see the articles by Eagle and Janecek cited in n. 25; no broad systematic study of the subject, however, has been undertaken.

tionally overwrought content of the collection, Bely destroys typographical conventionality and regularity, making the poems sprawl
over the page. Only seven of the fifty-seven poems in *After Parting* are set
in conventional stanzas.

Bely's use of *stolbik* and of the more broken typographical arrangements that culminate in *After Parting* need to be seen in the context of his
reluctance to abandon another formant higher than the line, namely, the
quatrainal rhyme scheme. Bely continues to use such rhyme schemes,
particularly favoring alternating rhyme, even in his most broken typographical design. In this respect, he is a clear predecessor of Mayakovsky.[43] While Bely's experiments with typography blur the visual outlines of the conventional stanzas, they certainly do not obliterate the
structural skeletons of those stanzas, at least in the collections before *After
Parting*. Of the 144 poems in *Gold in Azure* (that is, excluding the poems in
prose), only 19 are composed in anything other than quatrains.

This partiality to quatrains is not unusual among Russian poets; about
82 percent of Blok's poems, for example, are in this form.[44] The proportion for *Gold in Azure*, as was just indicated, is something like 85
percent. But what is unusual about Bely's quatrains—and here we have
one of the most distinctive elements of his versification—is the distribution of rhyme schemes among them. Of the 82 percent of Blok's poems
that are in quatrains, 54.3 percent have the rhyme scheme AbAb, 9.9
percent have the rhyme scheme aBaB, and no other schemes make a
significant showing. The characteristics of Blok's versification in this
respect are by and large typical of modern Russian versification as a
whole. With Bely, however, the situation is quite different. Among the
122 quatrainal poems in *Gold in Azure* we find the following proportions:
AbAb, 22.1 percent; aBaB, 32.8 percent; ABAB, 23.8 percent; abab,
11.5 percent; mixed, 4.9 percent; and others, 4.9 percent.

These figures provide an index to what is possibly the most original
and experimental feature of Bely's versification.[45] The prominence of
quatrains with a final feminine rhyme, as far as available data enable the
judgment to be made, is quite without parallel among Russian poets of

43. Gasparov, *Sovremennyi russkii stikh*, pp. 436–37, gives a general overview of the im-
pact that Bely's typographical experimentation probably had on Mayakovsky. See also
Gerald Janecek, "Belyi and Maiakovskii," *Russian Literature and American Critics: In Honor of
Deming Brown*, ed. Kenneth N. Brostrom (Ann Arbor, 1984), pp. 129–37.

44. This figure and the one below for rhyme scheme distribution have been extrapo-
lated from the data in Robin Kemball, *Alexander Blok: A Study in Rhythm and Meter* (The
Hague, 1965), pp. 484–86.

45. For a concise survey of experiments with stanza forms during the early twentieth
century, see M. L. Gasparov, *Ocherk istorii russkogo stikha* (Moscow, 1984), pp. 250–67.
Gasparov's conclusion is that experimentation with stanza forms was practically over by
about 1913, after which "the simplest quatrains dominate once more" (p. 256); most
regrettably, though, he gives no quantitative grounding for this statement and offers no
evidence about the relative distribution of rhyme schemes among quatrains.

any period. The significance of this feature is yet to be defined by metrists, however; at present we can only speculate in a vague way that Bely's preference for stanza-final feminine rhyme has some connection with a preferred intonation. But for our present purposes, it is sufficient to point out that Bely himself, as a theoretician, paid no attention to this feature, nor did he discuss it in any of his writings about his poetry. The innovation within conservatism that it presents is a feature that metrists do not yet know how to assess.

Innovation within conservatism is actually the fundamental feature that the present survey of Bely's versification has revealed. For example, Bely's persistent—but by no means dominant—experimentation with typographical presentation is found side by side with what is on the whole a retention of the basic structural features of nineteenth-century Russian versification. Bely did not even participate to any great extent in the major Symbolist contribution to the metrical repertoire, the development of the *dol'nik*.

Another aspect of Bely's lyric poetry that can only be pointed to here as an area for future study is the problem of his "orchestration," that is, his organization of phonetic material in addition to end rhyme; the latter aspect has been valuably illuminated in Lilly's work, but it is obvious to any reader of Bely's poetry that his phonetic awareness extends to all positions in the line, not just to its clausula. The study of Bely's orchestration would need to be intimately linked to the study of his neologisms, which are at least as abundant and persistent in his poetry as in his prose but have not been subjected to scholarly scrutiny. Neologism and phonetic organization go hand in hand in Bely's poetry; more than this we cannot say at the present state of research.

The Long Poems

The long or "longer" poem (*poema,* a term difficult to define in any case) is a category that cannot be clearly isolated in Bely's poetic work. We have seen that in three of the larger collections of lyrics (*Gold in Azure, Ashes,* and *The Urn*) Bely combined individual texts to form cycles; two other separately published collections, *The King's Daughter* and *After Parting,* may be regarded as attempts at longer unified compositions. And in his work of revision, especially for the Grzhebin edition of his poetry (1923), Bely regrouped some of his lyrics to form longer compositions. Specifically, three such compositions appear in the *Ashes* section of the book; and in the *Urn* section of the same edition there appears the longest verse composition Bely ever attempted, *The Tempter* (*Iskusitel'*), a twenty-six-part work stitched together from a number of previously independent lyrics. Conversely, some lyrics that were set out separately in the first edition of *Ashes* had previously been published as parts of a single long poem, *Funeral Service* (*Panikhida;* see III, 165–73). And we should not forget that Bely subtitled his treatise *Glossolaliya* (1917) "*poema.*" Clearly, we are here, as with so many other aspects of Bely's poetic work, faced with a set of critical and terminological problems that require extensive analysis at a level of detail that cannot be attempted in the present context. We will concentrate briefly on the two "explicit" longer poems, *Christ Is Risen* (*Khristos voskres*) and *The First Encounter* (*Pervoe svidanie*).[46]

The earlier of the two explicit longer poems is *Christ Is Risen,* written and published early in 1918. The poem has inevitably been compared with Blok's *Twelve* (*Dvenadtsat'*) by everyone who has ever discussed it, the main ground being that both are compound-structured lyric long poems that touch on revolution and Christ. The differences between the two works, though, are at least as substantial as the similarities; Khmel'-nitskaya has neatly pointed to some of them.[47] But her conclusion, the standard Soviet assertion that Bely's poem, like Blok's, is a gesture of acceptance of the October Revolution, tells us little about the poem itself. The text of the poem actually is a recapitulation of many familiar Bely *topoi.* The Revolution is much less substantive in Bely's poem than in Blok's, much less historically specific; and Bely's Christ, though by no means present throughout the poem, is considerably more central to it than is Blok's colophon to his. Bely's poem is essentially an expression of those hopes for some sort of saving apocalypse that had appeared in many of the lyrics from *Gold in Azure* on; and the event in *Christ Is Risen* takes place in the same swirling cosmos of colorful heavenly bodies that forms the setting of those lyrics. Also, the emotional tone of the work is that same exalted, near-hysterical transport of intellectual-emotional frenzy of those lyrics; the work has no restraining irony at all.

The text of *Christ Is Risen* is a twenty-four-part sprawl that anticipates the self-indulgence of *After Parting.* It has no narrative thread, no real development; both the first and last sections contain the proclamation that forms the poem's title. The poem has a first-person lyric hero who in the first part of the work speaks on behalf of a collective body of people; the presence of this "I" and the channeling of the poem's substance through his perception is actually the strongest point of difference between Bely's text and that of Blok. The resurrection of Christ is seen in terms of the destiny of Russia. In the first half of the text (up to the end of sec. 15) Russia is said to have transgressed in many ways and

46. The textual integrity of these two works is by no means absolute; *The First Encounter,* for example, was rewritten between its first and second publications (for the original text, see *Stikhotvoreniya,* ed. Malmstad, III, 324–50) and then split up into a kind of cycle for the Grzhebin edition.

47. Khmel'nitskaya, "Poeziya Andreya Belogo," pp. 54–57.

actually to have constituted the darkness that was the setting for the
Crucifixion and the subsequent period of hopelessness before the fact of
the Resurrection was known:

> My country
> Is
> A Grave
> That has held out
> A pale
> Cross—.[48]

After an interlude in which revolutionary events occur, central being
the murder of a railway worker (secs. 16–19), the resurrection of this
dead *Thing* that was Christ's body is asserted (secs. 18–21). And toward
the end of the poem, resurrected Russia is identified with one of Bely's
most cherished images:

> Russia,
> My country
>
> You are—that same
> Woman clothed in the sun [. . .].[49]

Christ Is Risen is essentially a private vision of resurrection, a vision that
was obviously central to Bely's spiritual experience, but one for which—
in verse at least—he did not always find adequate verbal expression.
That such expression *is* found is the main reason why the other explicit
long poem, *The First Encounter,* deserves its conventional esteem as Bely's
greatest work in verse. Throughout its four parts, amounting to a total
of more than 1,300 lines, Bely sustains his control of all aspects of the
text, whether he is dealing with the extremes of visionary experience (as
in *Christ Is Risen*) or the particular *realia* of the Moscow of his youth. The
poem is an evocation of Bely's spiritual autobiography in the Moscow of
1901, but it is also exactly what Gerald Janecek claimed it to be: "a
compendium of Bely's lifework in literature."[50]
Christ Is Risen and *The First Encounter* actually represent the ultimate
expression of the polarities toward which Bely's poetic work tends: the
Dionysian and the Apollonian, the self-indulgent and the controlled,
the naive and the ironic. The antitheses could be multiplied. The form

48. "Strana moya / Est' / Mogila, / Prostershaya / Blednyi / Krest,—" (II, 17).
49. "Rossiya, / Strana moya— / / Ty—ta samaya, / Oblechennaya solntsem Zhena" (II, 22).
50. Gerald Janecek, "Introduction," in Andrey Bely, *The First Encounter*, trans. Janecek (Princeton, 1979), pp. xi–xii. Nina Berberova's annotation to this text contains the only serious explication of any of Bely's poetry so far published, apart from the annotation in the 1966 Soviet edition.

of the two poems, as is the case with the lyrics that most forcefully express these tendencies, is an unmistakable index to these properties. *Christ Is Risen* is the most sustained example of those line-, stanza-, and graphic form-breaking impulses that lie behind Bely's experimentation with these features in the individual collections of lyrics. *The First Encounter*, composed throughout in iambic tetrameter with a strong quatrainal tendency and hardly a vestige of *lesenka*, is the culmination of the—for want of a better word—realistic Bely. Here mystical insights are achieved in a perfectly evoked historical setting; a deftly characterized dramatis personae counters the engulfing power of the author's own persona. The imaginative leaps, the abundant neologisms, the flights of intellect are ultimately held in check by a musical design that is much more palpable than that of any of the cycles and collections of lyrics.[51]

To trace the pedigrees of the two thematic and formal strains that lead up to the two explicit longer poems is a task for future research that may well hold the key to a broader understanding of the lyrics themselves and will certainly contribute to an understanding of Bely's technique of cyclization.

The Revisions

I mentioned earlier that Bely's habit of revision greatly complicates the study of his verse. This habit is not, of course, unique to Bely. Several other prominent Russian poets (Vasily Trediakovsky and Mikhail Lermontov among them) and many other major world poets (W. H. Auden above all in modern times) have shared this tendency. And many poets have with greater or lesser alacrity agreed to rewrite or repress their work under ideological pressure. Aside from Bely, though, probably only Auden and John Crowe Ransom have persisted with revision in the face of the cautions and condemnations of their peers. Khodasevich and Tsvetaeva were just two of many of Bely's contemporaries, poets of very different aesthetic persuasions, who warned him that his revisions diminished his work's artistic value.

Bely was not abashed by his compulsion to rewrite. And as in all matters, he rushed in with categorical justifications of the needs of the moment. He made many statements about the purposes and significance of the changes; for example, "A peculiarity of my verse is its looseness of texture [*rykhlost'*]; all the things I've written in verse from the viewpoint of the years look like drafts that I published prematurely [. . .]" (III, 433;

---

51. See Simon Karlinsky, "Symphonic Structure in Andrej Belyj's 'Pervoe svidanie,'" *California Slavic Studies*, 6 (1971), pp. 61–71.

1931). As I mentioned earlier, the notion of *rykhlost'* is in direct contradiction to Tynyanov's concept of "the compactness and unity of the verse series." But Bely's own statements about his revisions, while naturally of considerable interest as a key to his intentions, tend to be ad hoc, partial, subjective, and unsystematic.

The first careful and objective account of Bely's revisions to be published was that of Klavdiya Nikolaevna Bugaeva and Aleksey Petrovsky.[52] There is a concise account of them in Khmel'nitskaya's edition, and a discussion, with one telling example, in her preface.[53] But only with the publication of the Malmstad edition, with its long preface, has it become possible to study the textual reality of the revisions.[54] The revised texts occupy a substantial proportion of one volume of this edition (II, 95–351) and the less substantial variant readings make up a major part of the commentaries on the poems, which take almost the whole of the third volume (11–418). The revisions are so extensive and complex that a thorough discussion of them here is out of the question; I will give only the briefest of surveys, concentrating on one of the major collections, *Gold in Azure*.

Bely was dissatisfied with his existing texts from the very start of his writing career. Of the 150 poems in *Gold in Azure*, 96 had previously been published in various journals and collections, and nearly all of them were revised for their appearance in *Gold in Azure*.[55] The revisions, though, amount to no more than the normal, relatively minor stylistic alterations. But in the course of his life's work, Bely went back over *Gold in Azure* more often and more thoroughly than any other of his collections. Like Blok with his *Poems about the Beautiful Lady* (*Stixi o prekrasnoi dame*), though he repeatedly expressed dissatisfaction with the book, he never actually renounced it. Generally speaking, he felt its form to be inadequate to the value of its content. The content seemed to enshrine something precious from a time before his life's troubles began. Bely revised *Gold in Azure* to a greater or lesser extent no fewer than five times.

In 1913–14, for an edition of his verse proposed by Sirin (the publishing house of Mikhail Tereshchenko), Bely cut the number of poems in *Gold in Azure* by almost half and arranged them (as he did the rest of the contents of the book) in chronological order; this was the only time that he adopted this principle. He made few radical textual revisions to the

52. K. N. Bugaeva, A. S. Petrovsky [and D. M. Pines], "Literaturnoe nasledstvo Andreya Belogo," *Literaturnoe nasledstvo*, no. 27–28 (Moscow, 1937), pp. 575–638.

53. Khmel'nitskaya, "Poeziya Andreya Belogo," pp. 573–75, 50–54.

54. The fullest and clearest account of the revisions is contained in John Malmstad's "Introduction" to his edition of the poems (I, 11–62), on which this account is based.

55. For the publication of individual items during Bely's lifetime we may now consult, in addition to Malmstad's annotations in vol. 3 of the *Stikhotvoreniya*, "Andrey Bely," in *Russkie sovetskie pisateli: Poety; Biobibliograficheskii ukazatel'*, vol. 3, pt. 1 (Moscow, 1979), pp. 114–96.

poems he chose to preserve, but the changes were substantial. The edition, though, was not published. Bely next revised *Gold in Azure* in 1916–17 for an edition of the poetry proposed by the publisher Pashukanis; but as with the 1914 project, the political and economic situation prevented the book's appearance. The manuscript of this revision has not survived. A further edition of the poetry was prepared for the Shipovnik house in 1918, but once again publication was aborted, and the nature of Bely's revisions is unknown.

The one-volume edition published in Berlin by Zinovy Grzhebin in 1923 takes the Sirin text as its basis, but with further extensive revision. The poems were taken back out of chronological order; the *Gold in Azure* section was regrouped into three large cycles; some poems that had originally appeared in *Ashes* were added; and some poems that had originally appeared in *Gold in Azure* were transferred to *Ashes*. However, the changes made to *Gold in Azure* in this instance were less radical than certain others: *The First Encounter* was chopped into pieces, and a substantial number of lyrics that had originally appeared as independent units were combined to form compound-structured longer poems. The Grzhebin edition represents the most extreme of Bely's attempts to mold lyric texts into an entity larger than the single lyric. But the principle, if such a single guiding element does rule the revision, has never been satisfactorily explained, either by Bely or by any of his commentators. Such a principle is clearly incompatible with the chronological principle that governed the first major revision. But the revisions for Sirin and Grzhebin both operate primarily at levels higher than the individual text: they concern the rearrangement of complete texts relative to each other in the interest of higher objectives of composition.

Bely undertook a further revision of his poetry in 1925, but only the contents list of this projected edition survives (see III, 477–78). This so-called posthumous edition represents in essence an expanded version of the Grzhebin volume, with minor textual emendations and the restoration of *The First Encounter* as a separate entity. The list breaks off after spelling out ten additions to the *Gold in Azure* section, and it is impossible to make any really substantial observations about what the book might have been had it appeared.

Bely undertook the most radical revisions of the actual texts of the poetry in 1929–30, as part of his work on a projected two-volume edition of his poetry. He completed work only on the first volume, which bears the title "Summonses of the Times" ("Zovy vremen") and survives in manuscript; yet again, the edition never appeared. The complete text was published for the first time in the Malmstad edition (II, 143–351). The book returns to the compositional principles of the first three collections: it is made up of seven cycles of lyrics, and after them comes *Christ Is Risen*. Not only are the cycles completely new, not even reflecting the

arrangement of the Grzhebin edition: Bely reworked the actual texts to
such a degree that in some cases only Bugaeva's testimony can provide a
clue as to the source of the revised version. Bely regarded the 1929–30
revision as his final word as a poet; its results, he hoped, would cancel
out his earlier efforts. The text of *Summonses* is made up of 214 poems
(in addition to *Christ Is Risen*). To relate the shorter poems to previous
work is in many cases no simple matter. Besides the sheer degree of
dissimilarity I have already mentioned, some texts in *Summonses* are revisions not of texts in an original collection but of previously published
revisions, in most cases to be found in the Grzhebin edition. We also find
cases where one original poem engenders more than one new one, and
vice versa. These cases, however, are relatively marginal in the context of
the collection as a whole.

Of the 214 texts in *Summonses,* as many as 48 have no known source in
Bely's earlier work. It is obviously in a strict sense inappropriate to
discuss these poems in the context of Bely's revisions; but the fact is that
they actually represent nothing new in his work. They are all fairly
uniform in manner and relate to the themes and style of *Gold in Azure*
rather than to those of *Ashes* or *The Urn.* (The reason, as we shall see
shortly, is principally that Bely had already revised the latter collections
and in 1929–30 gave *Gold in Azure* priority.) The derivation of the identified revisions in *Summonses* is as follows: from *Gold in Azure,* 82; from
Ashes, 15; from *The Urn,* 7; from *The King's Daughter,* 16; from *Star,* 15;
and from *After Parting,* 31. The implications of this distribution are
reasonably clear: chronology, while not completely without significance,
has been a secondary factor in the shaping of the collection. The moods
and themes characteristic of *Gold in Azure* and dominant also in *The
King's Daughter* and *After Parting*—that is, the emotional, idealistic, egocentric manner—have been concentrated in this volume.

Khmel'nitskaya's illustration and discussion of a radically revised text
in *Summonses* compares "I Know" ("Znayu"), from *Gold in Azure,* with its
descendant of twenty years later, "The East that is now pale, the East
that is now silent" ("Vostok, poblednevshii,/Vostok onemevshii"). Her
conclusions are entirely justified in respect to Bely's radical revisions in
general. The shaping control of stricter, more traditional verse forms is
weakened; the proportion of neologisms increases markedly; only a single two-word phrase in the later poem corresponds exactly with the
source; "there is inventiveness in the selection of verbal resources, but
the inner meaning has been effaced."[56] A rather more generous estimate of a radical revision was arrived at by Herbert Eagle, who was
interested principally in its typographical aspect.[57] The detailed study of

56. Khmel'nitskaya, "Poeziya Andreya Belogo," p. 54.
57. Herbert Eagle, "Typographical Devices in the Poetry of Andrey Bely," in *Critical
Review,* esp. pp. 80–84.

the 1929–30 revisions is a matter for future work; it would be possible to devote a book-length study to the evolution of the *Gold in Azure* texts alone.

The revisions of *Ashes* and *The Urn* follow the pattern of the *Gold in Azure* revisions up to the Grzhebin edition. In it they too were reshuffled from the chronological order they had been given for the Sirin edition and arranged in large groups, of which the first *Ashes* group is the most extreme: called "Provincial Russia" ("Glukhaya Rossiya"), it is made up of a few short lyrics and three longer poems (all actually subtitled "*poema*") which have been compounded from *Ashes'* individual lyrics; their arrangement in the three longer poems does not necessarily reflect their placement in the cycles of the original publication. The Grzhebin edition's *Urn* consists of four large subsections, the third and fourth of which are multipart *poemy: The Tempter* (*Iskusitel'*), in twenty-six sections, and *The Dead Man* (*Mertvets*), in twelve. *The Tempter* actually includes some passages taken from *The First Encounter*. While the texts of *Gold in Azure* are left relatively untouched in the Grzhebin edition, except for their rearrangement, the *Ashes* texts bear the signs of Bely's first intensive bout of rewriting (we recall from Table 1 that two rewritten poems are to be found in *After Parting*, dating from about the time the Grzhebin edition was being prepared).

The Grzhebin text of *Ashes* is actually an intermediary stage between the two published editions of the collection as a separate work. But between the 1909 *Ashes* and Grzhebin's and between Grzhebin's and the 1929 "second edition" lie two further reworkings of the material, neither of which was published. The earlier dates from 1921 and the later from 1925, and their arrangement reflects essentially a cutting of the overall size of the book rather than rearrangement. The 1929 edition of *Ashes,* the second published edition, was rearranged yet again, and a substantial number of the texts were rewritten. The revision, however, was less extensive than the emendation to which *Gold in Azure* was subjected for *Summonses*. We may speculate that for the second volume of the set of which *Summonses* formed the first, Bely might well have gone back to the texts of *Ashes* and *The Urn* and reworked them just as radically. The only evidence we have, however, is the contents list of the projected second volume, which has the title "The Star over the Urn" ("Zvezda nad urnoi"). This list gives the titles of the poems with their sources; the *Ashes* material is divided into four subsections, some of whose contents differ from previous arrangements, though the earlier titles are retained. The list is prefaced by an author's note opening with the words "The second volume should be subjected to the same revision as the first" (II, 355), so it seems that Bely did have another capital revision in mind. The "Star over the Urn" list continues with material from *The Urn* and *Star* and closes with *The First Encounter*.

This account does no more than scratch the surface of an enormously complicated set of textual problems. The essence of Bely's revisions, however, may be sought along the following lines. The final sorting out of 1929–30 resulted in two large blocks. I have already characterized the first of them, enshrined in the "Summonses" manuscript, as emotional, idealistic, and egocentric, the style that leads from *Gold in Ashes* through *The King's Daughter* to *After Parting*. The style of the second is the hallmark of *Ashes, The Urn,* and *The First Encounter:* disillusioned, stylistically realistic, with an abundance of historically specific places, times, and persons. In the course of his development as a poet Bely found that these two styles appeared almost simultaneously, the one undercutting the other. His compulsive shuffling of his work and his eventual rewritings may be seen as attempts to compartmentalize the two styles.

The assertion that there are two styles, perhaps rather polarities, in Bely's poetic work is a very broad generalization that fails to cover a number of contradictory impulses that persist in the work and caused Bely constant anxiety. But it may at least serve as a point of orientation in further examination of this peculiar aspect of his work; no such guiding principle has previously been advanced.

The Verse Theory

Bely's writings in verse theory have never been brought together; none has ever been reprinted. And his work as a theorist of verse has never been studied comprehensively and objectively (the nearest approximation being the work of Sergey Grechishkin and Aleksandr Lavrov and of Boris Goncharov).[58] In his own time, his critics were either devotees who treated his method as gospel or proponents of rival theories who wished to denigrate Bely's work in favor of their own. Bely felt that in this area he was a prophet without honor, and the bitterness of this conviction was one of the things that clouded his last years.

Georges Nivat's list of the "polemical, critical, and journalistic works of Andrey Bely" is made up of 53 books and 328 articles dating from 1902 to 1934.[59] (The list includes the books of poetry, but not separate publications of individual poems and cycles.) Only four of the listed books

58. S. S. Grechishkin and A. V. Lavrov, "O stikhovedcheskom nasledii Andreya Belogo," in *Struktura i semiotika khudozhestvennogo teksta: Trudy po znakovym sistemam,* no. 12 (Tartu, 1981), pp. 97–111 (the article is an introduction to four previously unpublished texts on verse theory by Bely; as its title indicates, it deals only with Bely's work on versification); B. P. Goncharov, "Andrey Bely—stikhoved," *Filologicheskie Nauki,* no. 5 (119) (1980), pp. 20–27.

59. Georges Nivat, "L'Oeuvre polémique, critique et journalistique d'Andrej Belyj," *Cahiers du monde russe et soviétique,* 15, no. 1–2 (1974), pp. 22–39.

and about twenty-five of the articles are specifically concerned with poetry. Not mentioned in Nivat's list, for obvious reasons, are two kinds of item that form an important component of Bely's thinking about verse theory. The first is made up of the prefaces to the collections of poetry, published and unpublished in the poet's lifetime, of which seven are of major importance; the second is made up of works that for one reason or another were not published in Bely's lifetime and remained unpublished at the time Nivat compiled his list.

The hard core of Bely's writings on verse theory I take to be four articles included in *Symbolism* (*Simvolizm*, 1910), namely, "Lyric Poetry and Experiment" ("Lirika i eksperiment"); "Toward a Characterization of the Russian Iambic Tetrameter" ("Opyt kharakteristiki russkogo chetyrekhstopnogo yamba"); "Comparative Morphology of the Rhythm of Russian Lyric Poets in the Iambic Dimeter" ("Sravnitel'naya morfologiya ritma russkikh lirikov v yambicheskom dimetre"); and "Pushkin's 'Ne poi, krasavitsa, pri mne' (Toward a Description)" (" 'Ne poi, krasavitsa, pri mne . . .' A. S. Pushkina [Opyt opisaniya]"). Then there are the articles that arose from Bryusov's response to *Symbolism*, which remained unpublished until 1981;[60] "Aaron's Rod" ("Zhezl Aarona," 1917); "On Rhythm" ("O ritme," 1920); *The Poetry of the Word* (*Poeziya slova*, 1922); "Let Us Seek Melody" ("Budem iskat' melodii," the introductory article to *After Parting*, 1922); and *Rhythm as Dialectics and "The Bronze Horseman"* (*Ritm kak dialektika i "Mednyi vsadnik,"* 1929). All of these pieces deal with specific questions of verse structure. But, to state a truism, it is quite impossible to draw a hard-and-fast dividing line between Bely's writings on verse theory and those on other subjects. As John Elsworth in particular has shown, when Bely seems to be talking objectively about rhythm, he is also talking about the farthest reaches of his general world view. And conversely, when his autobiographical prose memoirs discuss poetry, as they often do, the theoretical statements are frequently as comprehensive as those in the writings explicitly devoted to verse theory. One could speculate endlessly on the question of whether or not the most notorious example of a *sui generis* work, *Glossolaliya* (1917), is actually a work of verse theory or something else.

But one point is worth making at the outset, because I believe that it underlies the way Bely's writings on verse have been received: what he wrote on this subject forms part of the Symbolist intellectual legacy, with its fundamentally idealist philosophical basis. However, the Russian tradition of inquiry into verse structure that emerged as a component of Formalism and has been of enduring importance had its intellectual origins in post-Symbolist currents, being especially close to Futurism, which had a strong (if not fundamental) element of positivism in its

60. See n. 58.

makeup. This is the basic reason for the fate of Bely's verse theory, both
the positive and the negative aspects of its reception.

Of all the writings on verse theory that were just named, the pieces
collected in *Symbolism*, and in particular the study of the rhythmic variations of iambic tetrameter, have had the strongest impact. The first
person to be vouchsafed a glimpse of what Bely accomplished in this
work was Vladislav Khodasevich. In the summer of 1909, Bely tele-
phoned him with an urgent summons to Moscow. When he reached
Bely's room, writes Khodasevich,

> on the table lay a gigantic heap of paper, ruled out in vertical columns. In
> the columns were dots that had been connected in eccentric-looking ways
> with straight lines. Bely smacked the paper with his heavy palm: "Here you
> have the iambic tetrameter. It's all here as plain as a pikestaff. Poems
> written in the same meter differ in terms of rhythm. The rhythm doesn't
> correspond to the meter, and it's determined by the omission of metrical
> stresses. 'Moi dyadya samykh chestnykh pravil' has four stresses, but 'I
> klyanyalsya neprinuzhdenno' has two: the rhythms are different, but the
> meter is the same, iambic tetrameter."

Khodasevich goes on to tell of his objection when Bely began to rewrite his
poetry in the light of his theoretical findings, and thereby, in
Khodasevich's view, ruined its sound: "It was then that I began to insist on
the necessity of conducting the study of rhythmical content only in
connection with the semantic content. . . . The study of rhythm outside
meaning seemed to me a false and harmful business."[61] (Despite
Khodasevich's objections to his method—or indeed, perhaps, because of
them—Bely included an analysis of Khodasevich's iambic tetrameter in
his review of the latter's *Heavy Lyre* [*Tyazhelaya lira*].)[62] Khodasevich's
statement that he could not agree with Bely's deliberately manipulative
attitude toward verse rhythm is somewhat disingenuous, for as Taranovsky has shown, Khodasevich in fact imitated the "forced" rhythm of
Bely's iambic tetrameter in the poem "Calico Kingdom" ("Sitsevoe
tsarstvo").[63] Bely's method of analysis involved essentially two stages: the
descriptive stage consisted of isolating the unstressed ictuses in a graphically presented model of iambic tetrameter; then, in a sense different
from what Khodasevich had in mind, an evaluative stage followed in
which the passages with the richest array of resulting figures were declared to be the most interesting or successful passages of poetry. (This, of
course, is a vastly condensed summary of a complex and very densely

61. V. F. Khodasevich, "Andrey Bely," in *Nekropol': Vospominaniya* (Brussels, 1939), pp.
78–79.

62. Andrey Bely, "'Tyazhelaya lira' i russkaya lirika," *Sovremennye Zapiski*, no. 15 (1923),
pp. 371–88.

63. See n. 4.

argued article.) Speaking very broadly, Bely's graphic demonstration of a method for charting rhythmical variation in iambic tetrameter and his arguments about which words should be considered stressed and which half-stressed have retained their authority among Russian poets. Bely's arguments appear in Nabokov's novel *The Gift (Dar)* as an explanation for the young poet's fascination with rhythm; they reappear in Nabokov's analysis of the rhythm of *Eugene Onegin;* and they appear again in Nina Berberova's introduction to her and Gerald Janecek's edition of Bely's *First Encounter.*[64]

The academic analysts of Russian verse rhythm have also recognized Bely's achievement, despite many polemical scuffles. Roman Jakobson paid tribute to the pioneering force of Bely's analysis, emphasizing particularly its contribution to the atmosphere of serious, enthusiastic inquiry that he encountered in Moscow intellectual circles in his early manhood. Jakobson's last statement about this part of his intellectual biography is interesting:

> A l'époque, autour de l'année 1910, j'étais un lecteur acharné des poètes et théoriciens symbolistes, surtout du grand poète russe Alexandre Blok et aussi d'Andrei Biély, auteur très intéressant dans sa poésie lyrique, dans sa prose et surtout dans ses recherches sur le vers et sur les problèmes de la structure poétique. Il y a eu, dans l'oeuvre de Biély, de ce point de vue, des intuitions vraiment géniales et à côté de cela parfois des pages très faibles, dues à un certain dilettantisme d'une part, à l'influence de certaines doctrines *a priori,* de l'autre.[65]

This generally positive but qualified assessment is echoed in the most substantial recent Soviet assessment of Bely's work in verse theory, by Boris Goncharov.[66] This scholar, whose animosity toward statistical metrics echoes the attitude of his senior colleague Leonid Timofeev, has used what he sees as Bely's concern for literary evaluation as a stick to beat the quantifiers. Until very recently, there has been a complete consensus about the pioneering value of Bely's work. A succinct formulation is that of Simon Karlinsky; the essays collected in *Symbolism* and *The Green Meadow (Lug zelenyi),* he asserts, "present pioneer methods of studying Russian metrics and versification, which have given rise to an entirely new scholarly discipline still thriving today."[67] Unfortunately, this assertion is rather misleading. To begin with, Bely was not the first

64. Vladimir Nabokov, "Notes on Prosody," in Aleksandr Pushkin, *Eugene Onegin,* trans. Nabokov (New York, 1964), III, 448–540, esp. 459–60; Nina Berberova, "Preliminary Remarks," in Bely, *First Encounter,* trans. Janecek, pp. xxiii–xxx.

65. Roman Jakobson, "Réponses," *Poétique,* no. 57 (1984), p. 8. See also his *Selected Writings* (The Hague, 1979), esp. V, 545, 568–69.

66. See n. 58.

67. Simon Karlinsky, "Andrey Bely," in *The Columbia Dictionary of Modern European Literature* (New York, 1980), p. 71.

scholar to use quantitative methods to study verse rhythm, either Russian or any other; the footnotes to *Symbolism* demonstrate his awareness of the work of his predecessors, mainly German students of the classics. Secondly, it is not Bely's work that has been productive, but rather that of Boris Tomashevsky, the true father of modern Russian quantitative metrics. And as Lazar Fleishman's publication of Tomashevsky's letters to Bryusov demonstrated, Tomashevsky developed his method independently of and if anything slightly prior to Bely.[68] The crucial difference between the theoretical approaches of Bely and Tomashevsky is that the latter's work rests on the theory of probabilities in spelling out the relationships between metrical and nonmetrical language and defining the special characteristics of the latter. It is to Tomashevsky's work that the post-1958 revival of quantitative metrics relates, and in a direct lineal way. Bely, it is true, was the first to quantify the major rhythmical types to be found in the historical development of Russian iambic tetrameter, the discovery that has been the cornerstone of the linguistic-statistical method. But for Bely himself this was not the most important insight his work yielded; rather, it was the relative richness of the graphic shapes he projected onto his charts of omitted metric stresses. Thirdly, Bely's work was confined to the level of rhythm, and he dealt in a substantial way with only one meter. The academic tradition of quantitative metrics has rested on the analysis of large samples of lines, many more than the 596 lines analyzed by Bely, and has also developed as an important aspect of the subject the investigation of metrical typology; contrasts at the level of meter have had almost as important a place in defining the individuality of poetic styles as have contrasts at the level of rhythm. The conclusion reached by Thomas Beyer from his survey of the polemic between Viktor Zhirmunsky and Bely, unfortunately written before Fleishman's publication of Tomashevsky's letters, cannot be supported: "He is still more highly regarded today than most Formalists were ever willing to admit."[69] More highly regarded in general, perhaps; and as a pioneer, but not as a theorist of verse rhythm.[70]

Later critics have all but ignored the works in which Bely used other than quantitative methods to deal with the theory of verse. This situation has come about because of the formidable obscurity of Bely's writing and the lack of any apparent congruence with any critical fashion or ortho-

68. B. V. Tomashevsky, "Pis'ma V. Ya. Bryusovu, 1910–1911 (vstupitel'naya stat'ya i publikatsiya L. S. Fleishmana)," *Uchenye Zapiski Tartuskogo gos. Universiteta,* vyp. 284 (1971), pp. 532–44.

69. Thomas Beyer, "The Bely–Zhirmunsky Polemic," in *Critical Review,* pp. 205–13.

70. The clearest statement of Bely's contribution to the development of Russian metrics, emphasizing his pioneering contribution but also its limited productivity, is contained in Gasparov's introductory chapter to *Sovremennyi russkii stikh,* pp. 18–38, translated as "Quantitative Methods in Russian Metrics: Achievements and Prospects," in *Metre, Rhythm, Stanza, Rhyme,* ed. G. S. Smith (Colchester, 1980), pp. 1–19.

doxy that has arisen since Bely's day. Only Georges Nivat has made an attempt to examine one of Bely's central theoretical concepts, that of rhythm.[71] His work, like that of Steven Cassedy in this volume, is of pioneering importance, pointing the way to the serious study of Bely as literary theorist.

Conclusions

This necessarily skeletal survey of Bely's work in verse and verse theory has reached certain conclusions and pointed to certain topics in need of further investigation.

We have seen that Bely's verse exhibits certain innovatory features, but that these innovations were the result of the redistribution of traditional elements of nineteenth-century resources rather than a departure from them; his very restricted use of the *dol'nik* in particular sets him apart from the most striking innovatory currents of the versification of his time. At the level of the stanza, Bely's experimentation is limited in terms of length but highly idiosyncratic in terms of rhyme schemes. Bely does show, however, a persistent if ultimately marginal tendency toward experimentation of a more radical kind, mainly in his departure from the typographical norms of his predecessors and contemporaries. This line-breaking tendency is anticipated in *Christ Is Risen* and reaches its climax in *After Parting*. But running counter to it is a tendency toward traditional strictness of form, expressed at its fullest in the use of iambic tetrameter and quatrainal stanza forms; this tendency is anticipated most forcefully in *The Urn* and reaches its apotheosis in *The First Encounter*. Now, the ultimate theme of verses that evidence both of these formal tendencies may be essentially the same visionary experience, but the greatest achievements of Bely the poet occur when he uses the traditional forms. These conclusions, however, have been asserted on the basis of very partial evidence, mainly on the study of verse structure at the level of the line. This is the level at which Bely's own pioneering theoretical contribution was made. Subsequent theorists, while almost unanimously concurring on Bely's importance as a pioneer have departed from his methods and his conclusions.

Greatly outweighing these conclusions is the number of topics for further study that this essay has indicated. At all levels of verse structure other than the line, much more work needs to be done before any well-based conclusions can be drawn. Stanza form, rhyme, and the entire area of phonetic organization in situations other than rhyme need de-

71. Georges Nivat, "Du rhythme chez Andrej Belyj," *Revue des études slaves*, no. 54 (1982), no. 1–2, pp. 171–76.

tailed investigation. No large-scale study has been undertaken of any single aspect of Bely's poetic style, of which neologism is possibly the aspect most in need of investigation. Apart from these problems, there remains the question of Bely's revisions and the status of the poetry he wrote after 1922. Study of this material, which has only recently become possible in a systematic way with the aid of the Malmstad edition, may force us to revise our estimate of the literary significance of the works Bely produced in the final decade of his life. It is doubtful that such a study will overturn the limiting judgments on Bely the poet by Mirsky and Markov that were cited near the beginning of this essay; but it will enable us to come nearer at least to a definition of the literary characteristics of this neglected side of Bely's creative activity.

8

Bely's Theory of Symbolism as a Formal Iconics of Meaning

STEVEN CASSEDY

If Bely had one çomplaint in life that overshadowed all others, it was that he was misunderstood. Entire sections of his memoirs are devoted to laments over the injustices he suffered at the hands of his contemporaries, including many of his closest friends, who stubbornly refused to accept what Bely took to be the patent validity of his latest ideas. In 1928, when he came to describe his career as a thinker in *Why I Became a Symbolist* (*Pochemu ya stal simvolistom*, published for the first time in 1982),[1] Bely devoted a major part of his book to expressions of self-righteous astonishment at the incomprehension and hostility that his theoretical work, particularly his theory of Symbolism as it evolved over the years, invariably encountered at each new stage in its development.

But when it comes right down to it, if anything is astonishing in all this, it is undoubtedly Bely's astonishment itself. After all, we must be fair both to Bely's contemporaries and to ourselves as readers of his work. From the beginning of his career as a published writer until the composition of *Why I Became a Symbolist*, Bely underwent so many apparently fundamental changes in philosophical outlook, attempted so valiantly to reconcile portions of his abandoned world views with his new ones, and as a consequence created such impossibly cumbersome syntheses of thought that it sometimes really is difficult to understand what he is up to.

The difficulty occurs not only because Bely's thought is intrinsically obscure. It is. But problems arise also because Bely is always challenging

This essay expands and adapts ideas that first appeared in my "Translator's Introduction" to *Selected Essays of Andrey Bely*, edited and translated by Steven Cassedy (Berkeley: University of California Press, 1985). Copyright © The Regents of the University of California.

1. Andrey Bely, *Pochemu ya stal simvolistom i pochemu ya ne perestal im byt' vo vsekh fazakh moego ideinogo i khudozhestvennogo razvitiya* (Ann Arbor, 1982).

his contemporary readers to deny the apparent contradictions between what he is saying today as a confirmed theosophist and what he was saying a few years ago as a confirmed Nietzschean . . . or Solov'evan, or Kantian, or Neo-Kantian, or Schopenhauerian, or natural scientist, or any of the many other things he was.

In fact, the problem presents itself even in shorter periods of Bely's career when he was presumably devoting himself to just one system. Bely's Symbolist period is customarily considered to extend from 1902 to 1910. This period alone saw a number of shifts in Bely's interests. The single year 1909, for example, shows an astonishing diversity of both subject and philosophical point of view in Bely's theoretical writings. There are the four essays on metrics and versification published in *Symbolism (Simvolizm)*, where Bely adopts the pose of a natural scientist and follows a strictly empirical, inductive method in investigating literary texts. There is "The Magic of Words" ("Magiya slov"), where Bely's concern is to show the connection of poetry with theurgy (the early pagan art of conjuring the presence of divinities through magic). And there is "The Emblematics of Meaning" ("Emblematika smysla"), a vast attempt at establishing a comprehensive world view on the basis of Bely's own theory of Symbolism.

Given the diversity of systems and methods that attracted Bely in the Symbolist phase of his development, the notion of a single, unified theory of Symbolism, even for this period, appears at first to be doubtful. The problem, then, is this: if one assumes that there *is* some degree of consistency in Bely's theory of Symbolism during the years 1902–10, then one of the most important questions that arise is whether or not this theory is ultimately metaphysical in its foundation. Does it, in other words, in its most comprehensive and far-reaching form, base its claim of universality, its claim to offer a real world view, on any belief in the existence of a being or realm of experience that transcends the limits of ordinary knowledge and to which conscious subjects have access only through means other than those of ordinary knowledge?

This question is important for several reasons. One is that so many of the systems that Bely and his theory of Symbolism passed through *were* metaphysical in nature: the Solov'evan Sophiology and the Theosophy of Helena Blavatsky are only two examples. Another reason is that, since Bely, like Vyacheslav Ivanov, always wanted Symbolism to be much more than just a theory of art, something that could define a whole world view, we need to know whether metaphysicality is an intrinsic attribute of Symbolism (as it was for Ivanov) or whether Symbolism is just something placed in the service of other philosophical systems that may or may not be metaphysical.

As it happens, *Why I Became a Symbolist* is extremely informative on this point. Bely's purpose in writing this brief memoir in 1928 was precisely to show that the theory of Symbolism was a constant throughout his entire career, despite the vagaries of his own intellectual and artistic development. The complete title, *Why I Became a Symbolist and Why I Never Ceased to Be One in All Phases of My Intellectual and Artistic Development,* is a clear indication of this purpose. And while it is easy to ridicule Bely's attempt in the final sections of the memoir to demonstrate that Symbolism and all the philosophical orientations he had adopted and abandoned represented a kind of irresistible movement toward Rudolf Steiner and anthroposophy, Bely is still completely persuasive in showing at least the formal constancy of the idea and logic of Symbolism. Persuasive enough, in fact, to lead one to conclude (1) that the theory of Symbolism *is* a constant throughout Bely's career and (2) that even though Symbolism has its formal origin in systems that are indeed metaphysical, even though it even at times masquerades as a metaphysical system in its own right, it is in fact a purely formal theory. Why? Because the purpose of Bely's theory of Symbolism differs from the purpose of any metaphysical system. In fact, in Bely's implicit view, it logically precedes any such system. The purpose of Bely's theory of Symbolism is to describe the *formal process by which conscious subjects universally produce meaning,* regardless of what that meaning may be.[2]

A word of clarification is in order concerning the relation between the present essay and "Bely the Thinker," Chapter 9 in this volume. The two essays belong together as discussions of Bely the theorist. This one treats only his theory of Symbolism, while the following one treats the general topic of Bely as a thinker. There is a logic in treating matters in this order. As I point out in "Bely the Thinker," Bely's thought broadly conceived shows a natural hierarchical order. His theory of Symbolism is the most far-reaching, the most universal area of his theoretical thought. It is the area that he hoped to make into a world view. As I shall argue, Symbolism for Bely is really a theory of meaning, and for Bely a theory of meaning is what a philosophy that pretends to be a world view must be. A theory of poetics and such related matters as the philosophy of language can consequently be only a subcategory under this larger heading. For this reason, these subjects are treated in "Bely the Thinker."

What Is a Symbol?

From 1902 until 1910 and 1911, when Bely's three collections of critical and theoretical essays, *Symbolism (Simvolizm), The Green Meadow (Lug zelenyi),* and *Arabesques (Arabeski),*[3] were published, the theory of Sym-

2. The first general study of Bely's theory of Symbolism, and the best of its kind to date, is John Elsworth, "Andrei Bely's Theory of Symbolism," *Forum for Modern Language Studies,* 11, no. 4 (1975), pp. 305–33.

3. *Simvolizm* (Moscow, 1910); *Lug zelenyi* (Moscow, 1910); *Arabeski* (Moscow, 1911).

bolism was certainly the most steady preoccupation of his intellectual and creative life. The number of writings from this period directly devoted to the idea of Symbolism or whose titles include the word "Symbolism" and its variants is testimony to the strength of this preoccupation. In addition to the collection of 1910, two essays bear the title "Symbolism," one written in 1908 and appearing in *The Green Meadow*, the other written in 1909 and appearing in *Arabesques*. There is also the early "Symbolism as a World View" (1903); "Criticism and Symbolism" (1904), written on the centennial of the death of Kant; "Symbolist Theater" (1907); "Symbolism and Contemporary Russian Art" (1908); and, of course, the massive "Emblematics of Meaning: Premises to a Theory of Symbolism" (1909).[4] But Bely's preoccupation was even more exclusive than this list suggests. The fact is that virtually every theoretical and critical article Bely wrote in this period is at least in part about the theory of Symbolism.

Still, the definition of a symbol that is at once the most succinct and the most clearly untainted by adventitious philosophical tendencies is undoubtedly the one in the opening pages of *Why I Became a Symbolist*, written almost two decades after the appearance of *Symbolism*, *The Green Meadow*, and *Arabesques*.

The idea of the symbol is inseparable from the process that produces a symbol, a process called symbolization. In order to demonstrate the truth of his assertion that he never *became* a Symbolist but had been one all along, Bely tells about a game he invented as a child, and shows that it consisted in performing the process of symbolization. This is how he describes the game:

> Wishing to reflect the essence of a state of consciousness (fear), I would take a crimson-colored cardboard box top, hide it in the shadows, so that I would see not the object but the color, and then walk by the crimson spot and exclaim to myself, "SOMETHING PURPLE." This "SOMETHING" was the experience. The purple spot was the form of expression. The two, taken together, constituted the symbol (in the process of symbolization). The "SOMETHING" was unidentified. The cardboard box top was an external object bearing no relation to the "SOMETHING." But this object, having been transformed by the shadows (the purple spot), was the end result of the merging of THAT (imageless) and THIS (objective) into something that is neither THIS nor THAT, but a THIRD. The symbol is this third. In constructing it I surmount

---

4. "Simvolizm," in *Lug zelenyi*, pp. 19–28; "Simvolizm," in *Arabeski*, pp. 241–48; "Simvolizm, kak miroponimanie," in *Arabeski*, pp. 220–38, translated as "Symbolism as a World View" in *Selected Essays of Andrey Bely*, ed. Steven Cassedy (Berkeley, 1985), pp. 73–92; "Krititsizm i simvolizm," in *Simvolizm*, pp. 20–30; "Simvolicheskii teatr," in *Arabeski*, pp. 299–313; "Simvolizm i sovremennoe russkoe iskusstvo," in *Lug zelenyi*, pp. 29–50; "Emblematika smysla: Predposylki k teorii simvolizma," in *Simvolizm*, pp. 49–143, translated as "The Emblematics of Meaning: Premises to a Theory of Symbolism" in *Selected Essays*, pp. 111–97.

two worlds (the chaotic state of fear and the object given from the external world). Neither of these worlds is real. But the THIRD world exists. And I found myself completely drawn into the cognition of this third world, which is given to neither the soul nor the external object. The creative act, this union, transforms cognition into a particular type of cognition. The result for cognition, articulated in the judgment "SOMETHING PURPLE," affirmed my move over into this THIRD world.[5]

As usual, Bely's exposition leaves much to be desired in the way of clarity and rigor. But several elements can be distinguished in this description. It is clear that the starting point is an internal experience (in this case, fear). An external object is then found that will somehow embody or express the internal experience. In this example, the external object is the cardboard box top. The final result is something that is not just the internal experience (what Bely here calls "THAT" or the "imageless"), not just the external object (what Bely here calls "THIS" or the "objective"), and not the mere sum of the two. It is a third element that is both greater than either of its constituent elements and greater than their sum. This is what Bely calls the symbol.

Two additional things are worth pointing out. The first is that the symbol cannot be understood apart from the process by which it comes into being, a process that Bely here and elsewhere calls "symbolization." The symbol, as Bely had pointed out in some detail in "The Emblematics of Meaning," is not only an ideal unity, it is also the end result of a unifying act. The very word "symbol," as Bely mentions in that essay, derives from a Greek verb meaning to throw together, to unite.[6]

The second point is that the creative act that produces the symbol makes for a new type of cognition. "The creative act," says Bely, "this union, transforms cognition into a particular *type* of cognition." Bely is resurrecting one of his favorite distinctions here, that between creation (*tvorchestvo*) and cognition (*poznanie*). Because of the nature of the creative act, the product of that act—namely, the symbol—imposes on the perceiving subject the necessity of apprehending it altogether differently from the way in which he apprehends the world of ordinary phenomena. At issue is a whole symbolic epistemology that is distinct from the epistemology of ordinary scientific understanding.

The true basis for the autonomy of this symbolic epistemology, for Bely's insistence on a "particular *type* of cognition," is only hinted at in the passage from *Why I Became a Symbolist*. It is the triadicity of the symbol, the incorporation into one signifying object of three components: the inner experience, the objective embodiment, and the overarching "symbol" itself. A full exposition of this fundamental principle is

5. *Pochemu ya stal simvolistom*, pp. 7–8.
6. *Simvolizm*, p. 67; *Selected Essays*, p. 128.

given in "The Emblematics of Meaning." There Bely shows how symbolic objects present the perceiving subject with a concrete facade behind which stands a transcendent essence of some sort, requiring him to apprehend that object by looking through and beyond it. I will discuss this essay later.

For the moment it is sufficient to point out the pervasiveness of the triadic concept in Bely's earlier writings on the theory of Symbolism. In the second of the essays titled "Symbolism" (in *Arabesques*) Bely discusses the "triple principle of the symbol" (*troistvennoe nachalo simvola*). "Every symbol," he says, "is a triad *abc*, where *a* is the indivisible creative unity in which the two constituents (*b*, the image from nature embodied in sound, color, words, and *c*, the experience that freely arranges the material—sounds, colors, and words—in such a way that this material completely expresses the experience) are combined."[7] Although Bely expresses himself rather oddly here, it is still clear that the same three elements are present as in the later passage from *Why I Became a Symbolist*. There is the experiential content (*c*), corresponding to fear in the example from *Why I Became a Symbolist;* there is what Bely here refers to as an "image from nature" (*b*), by which he means the external, objective form in which the experiential content is embodied; and there is the third element (*a*), the symbol itself. This third element consists in the combined unity of the two component elements but enjoys its own autonomous status as an overarching totality.

The image (*obraz*) to which Bely refers in this passage becomes one of the cornerstones of the theory of symbolic representation in "The Emblematics of Meaning." There it takes on a much more richly charged meaning than it has here, particularly in light of the dual meaning of *obraz* as "image" and "icon." But the idea of the image from nature as an embodying substance had been present in Bely's thinking for some time. Two years before the composition of the second "Symbolism" essay, in a piece titled "On the Results of the Development of the New Russian Art," Bely had said this of the Symbolist movement: "A characteristic trait of symbolism in art is the tendency to use an image from reality as a means of rendering an experienced content of consciousness." This image, he went on to say, "as a model of an experienced content of consciousness, is the symbol." And "the method of symbolization of experiences by means of images is symbolism."[8]

The notion of embodiment (*voploshchenie*) or incarnation, as the fundamental step in the process of symbol formation had also been a prime concern for Bely in his earlier writings. In the first "Symbolism" essay he had explored the theological dimension of this concept. His language

7. *Arabeski*, p. 245.
8. "Ob itogakh razvitiya novogo russkogo iskusstva" (1907), in *Arabeski*, p. 258.

seems designed to point up the analogy between the aesthetic philosophy of Symbolism and the Johannine logology. "The word of consciousness," he proclaims, "must have flesh. Flesh must have the gift of
speech." In Symbolist art, Bely continues, "the artist must become his
own form: his natural 'I' must fuse with his creation; his life must become art." The artist himself, then (by which Bely means the creative
persona of the artist, not the physical person), is "the word become
flesh."[9] All this is merely another way of describing the same process of
symbolization that Bely has described in a variety of other contexts. The
process starts with the artist, or creator, whose experience ("word of
consciousness" here) becomes flesh. To become flesh, of course, is the
same thing as to be embodied, since the Russian word for "embody"
(*voplotit'*) means literally "to render flesh" and contains the word for
flesh (*plot'*). Like God's world, then, the symbol is the word made flesh.

Here are the essential elements that have emerged so far in the definition of the symbol. Symbols are signifying objects. They may be traditional aesthetic objects (or parts of such objects), such as paintings, musical compositions, or poems. Or they may be external objects of any sort
("images from reality") that have been selected to perform the symbolic
function. Symbols come into being through the process of symbolization.
In this process a conscious subject takes a content of consciousness,
associates it with an external object, or image, and "embodies" that content in the image. The result is an object that bears the characteristics of
its physical, concrete dimension, the embodied content of consciousness,
and a third dimension as well. This third dimension is the unity of the
symbol. Thus for the perceiver symbolic objects are distinct from ordinary objects in the phenomenal world because they clearly present an
element of signification that would be lacking in any object in nature not
specifically chosen by a human consciousness as a vehicle for embodying
such an intention.

Our original question, however, remains. What precisely is the nature
of the content of consciousness that comes to be embodied in a symbol?
Is it really just that and no more, or does it have its source in some
deeper realm of being?

The examples we have just seen suggest that Bely's conception is entirely free of any metaphysical component at all. The whole thing appears to take place purely in accordance with the ordinary workings of
consciousness. The problem is that, as Bely elaborates his ideas, elements
of metaphysicality begin to insinuate their way into his conceptions.
They affect the notion of both the source and the process of symbolization. Since the theory of Symbolism reaches its culmination in 1909 with
the essays collected in *Symbolism,* we will turn to two crucial documents of

9. *Lug zelenyi,* p. 28.

that year: "The Magic of Words," in which Bely explores the theurgic properties of poetic creation, and "The Emblematics of Meaning," in which the general problem of symbolic meaning is treated in the context of a world view.

The "Magic" of Signification

Many of Bely's writings on the theory of Symbolism treat this theory in the abstract, without a primary emphasis on any specific area of creative endeavor, such as poetry, music, or painting. In "The Magic of Words," however, Bely is concerned with poetry alone, or, to be more exact, with poetic language.[10] Poetic language occupies a primary position in human experience, to judge by Bely's opening remarks in this essay. "Language is the most powerful instrument of creation," he begins. "When I name an object with a word I thereby assert its existence. Every act of cognition [*poznanie*] arises from a name. Cognition is impossible without words. The process of cognizing [*poznavanie*] is the establishing of relations between words, which only subsequently are related to objects corresponding to them" (429/93).

Bely spends a good deal of his essay on the distinction between poetic and ordinary language, a subject very much in vogue at the time, and one, incidentally, with its own indigenous source in Russia. In fact, Bely borrows so heavily from this source that those parts of his essay devoted to this subject contain scarcely anything original. The source I am speaking of is the nineteenth-century philologist Aleksandr Afanas'evich Potebnya (1835–91).

Potebnya had distinguished between poetic and prosaic discourse by referring to a vaguely defined "third" factor in poetic words, the first and second being the physical sound of the word and the meaning assigned (by convention) to that sound. The third element he called either the "representation" (*predstavlenie*) or the "image" (*obraz*), and its function is to impart vividness to the word, to give the word, through a certain newness and freshness, at least the appearance of bearing a connection with its signified object that is intimate and necessary rather than purely conventional and accidental.[11] This element in poetic words is what calls attention to those words *as words* and gives them a certain existential autonomy. In fact, it is the very concept that the Formalists will later elaborate into a whole aesthetic of automatization and de-

10. "Magiya slov," in *Simvolizm,* pp. 429–48; "The Magic of Words," in *Selected Essays,* pp. 93–110. All further references to this essay will be given in the text. The first number refers to *Simvolizm,* the second to *Selected Essays.*

11. Potebnya, *Iz lektsii po teorii slovesnosti* [Lectures in the theory of literature] (Kharkov, 1894), p. 123.

automatization. This is the concept that Bely develops in his critique of poetic language in "The Magic of Words."

But "The Magic of Words" is much more than a critique of poetic language through an extension of ideas shamelessly borrowed from Potebnya. It is also a genealogy of poetic creation and an ontology of poetic, which is to say symbolic, objects. For, once Bely has established the autonomy of poetic words, he goes on to endow them with the theurgic power to invoke presence and thereby to generate being. Poetic words have this power partly because, as virtual equivalents of their referents, they share a quality of existential autonomy with those referents. They are, in other words, as much a part of the objects they designate as are any of the physical determinants of those objects, and, what is more, they are just as much objects endowed with being as are the objects they designate. But the theurgic power of poetic words stems most of all from the creative act that generates them. This is really the supreme principle in "The Magic of Words."

In the following passages Bely distinguishes between creative, living words (that is, poetic words, or those possessing the theurgic powers that he calls our attention to) and dead words. Dead words are abstract concepts, or prosaic words, which signify by a purely conventional association with their meaning. The living word, Bely says,

> is the expression of the innermost essence of my nature, and, to the degree that my nature is the same thing as nature in general, the word is the expression of the innermost secrets of nature [. . .]. If words did not exist, then neither would the world itself. My ego, once detached from its surroundings, ceases to exist. By the same token, the world, if detached from me, also ceases to exist. "I" and the "world" arise only in the process of their union in sound. Supra-individual consciousness and supra-individual nature first meet and become joined in the process of naming. Thus consciousness, nature, and the world emerge for the cognizing subject only when he is able to create a designation. Outside of speech there is neither nature, world, nor cognizing subject. In the word is given the original act of creation. The word connects the speechless, invisible world swarming in the subconscious depths of my individual consciousness with the speechless, senseless world swarming outside my individual ego. The word creates a new, third world: a world of sound symbols by means of which both the secrets of a world located outside me and those imprisoned in a world inside me come to light [. . .]. In the word and only in the word do I recreate for myself what surrounds me from within and from without, for I *am* the word and only the word. [429–30/93–94]

Bely goes on to say that the poetic word is a *symbol*. What is curious about this passage is not only that it develops the idea of poetic genesis, the notion that naming things creates them or calls them into being, but also that it brings the creative genealogy of poetic creation into solidarity with the idea of symbolization as it appeared in Bely's earlier articles. When Bely refers to a "new, third world," when he says that the word "connects the speechless, invisible world swarming in the subconscious depths of my individual consciousness with the speechless, senseless world swarming outside my individual ego," he is referring to the same process that he describes in *Why I Became a Symbolist*. The new, third world is the world of the symbol, of the entity that connects consciousness with an external object but surpasses both and exists on its own.

In fact, Bely suggests, this is our supreme power as conscious beings. "The original victory of consciousness," he says, "lies in the creation of sound symbols. For in sound there is recreated a new world within whose boundaries I feel myself to be the creator of reality. Then I begin to name objects, that is, to create them a second time for myself [. . .]. The process of naming spatial and temporal phenomena with words is a process of invocation. Every word is a charm" (430–31/94).

If this is not a sufficiently forceful philosophical assertion of the autonomous mode of existence that poetic words both possess and invoke in the same way that a theurgist invokes or charms the presence of divine beings, Bely later formulates this thought in language that seems expressly designed to satisfy the needs of the philosophically oriented investigator. Speaking of metaphors and of the existence in them of the third element that distinguishes poetic from prosaic words, Bely says that poetic creation endows this element "with ontological being independently of our consciousness." He goes on to describe the process by which the very cornerstone of poetic language, what Bely calls the "metaphor-symbol," comes into being. "The goal (metaphor-symbol)," he says, "having received being, turns into a real, active cause (cause from creation); thus the symbol becomes incarnation [*voploshchenie*]. It comes to life and acts autonomously" (446/109).

What, then, is the "magic" of words? The idea of magic and theurgy serves Bely more as an analogy than as a literal description of poetic creation. The magic of poetic words is their ability to generate or, in a purely figurative sense, invoke a mode of being that is distinct from that of the phenomenal world, though just as autonomous. And the source of this autonomy is neither more nor less than the symbol, which is to say the transcendent unity that emerges from the combination of a content of consciousness with an objective image. But "transcendent" need not carry any metaphysical or even idealist sense here. The unity of the symbol is transcendent simply in the sense that it transcends the sum of its component parts, just as a phenomenologist would say, with no metaphysical implications whatsoever, that the constituted sense of an extended utterance transcends the sum of the senses of the individual words that utterance comprises.

Does poetry invoke being? Yes, but only in the sense that any signifying expression invokes being. Does it invoke it literally through magic?
No, the being that is invoked is simply that of a *meaning,* and to accord
meanings their own ontic status—as, incidentally, Edmund Husserl and
succeeding phenomenologists did in Bely's own age—does not of necessity imply any metaphysical assumptions. It simply enlarges the notion of
being in a way that is utterly consonant with currents in philosophical
thought that were contemporary to Bely and with which he was entirely
familiar. In fact, Bely later talks like a phenomenologist in his 1917 essay
"Aaron's Rod" ("Zhezl Aarona"), where he refers to meaning as an
object.[12] It is noteworthy that even in "The Magic of Words," where
Bely writes flamboyantly about the invocational and creative powers of
the poet, he never goes so far as to suggest that either the source or the
end product of this creative act is in any way metaphysical. The source is
the same as in the description of the childhood game he described in
Why I Became a Symbolist: a content of consciousness connected with an
external object or image. And the product, while perhaps more important than ordinary objects in the phenomenal world, is never said to be
literally from another realm of existence. It just has being, and that
appears to be all.

In "The Emblematics of Meaning" Bely makes his most prominent
effort to connect his symbolics with metaphysics. He does so by finally
committing himself to identifying a first principle, which he calls Value,
and by firmly establishing a theological system as the basis for his own
symbology. But here, too, as we will see, metaphysicality is a mere illusion, since the theological system provides a formal structure and no
more, and since the meaning that Bely has assigned to Value is completely devoid of any metaphysical connotation. Let us turn to that essay
now.

"The Emblematics of Meaning"

Earlier I said that it was Bely's fate to be perpetually misunderstood.
The incomprehension he so often encountered was not, however, always
a function of his abrupt changes in thinking. Of the many complaints
that appear in Bely's memoirs, second in frequency only to those regarding the failure of his public to understand him are those concerning the
objective reasons for his own shortcomings in getting his point across:
haste, hunger. cold, unsympathetic editors, and so on. It is truly a tragedy, then, that the fullest expression of Bely's entire theory of Sym-

---

12. "Zhezl Aarona (O slove v poezii)," *Skify,* 1 (1917), pp. 155–212. The idea of meaning
as object appears on p. 155.

bolism should have been the subject (the deserving subject, we might claim in an ungenerous moment) of one of those complaints. For if we are to believe Bely, "The Emblematics of Meaning," this central article that occupies close to a hundred pages of close print in *Symbolism*, was written in a single week without being corrected, and all because Bely's publisher could not wait.[13]

But "The Emblematics of Meaning" is certainly worth reading, despite its admittedly excessive length and its other shortcomings. It is the only theoretical essay in which Bely has given a fairly complete and detailed exposition of his theory. Its contribution to Bely's other theoretical writings lies in its systematic exposition of the logic of Symbolist thinking. It has another virtue as well: in it Bely's views are (with a little editorial help) presentable (if not always presented) in a philosophically rigorous form. And finally it should be said in Bely's favor that the problem he confronts in this essay is ultimately not a parochial one, of interest only to a particular literary and artistic movement in turn-of-the-century Russia. It is a philosophical problem of broad international interest, and Bely's approach to it, had his exposition been clearer, would certainly have placed him in the company of some of the recent and contemporary philosophers he esteemed most highly: Vladimir Solov'ev, Edmund Husserl, and such Neo-Kantians as Hermann Cohen, Paul Natorp, and Heinrich Rickert.[14]

Why All Meaning Is Emblematic

The subtitle to "The Emblematics of Meaning," "Premises to a Theory of Symbolism," suggests that the essay's real purpose is to point the way toward a fully elaborated, general theory of symbolism, something along the lines of what Bely apparently had set out to do in the earlier article "Symbolism as a World View." But in broadening the scope of his theory, Bely has at the same time narrowed his focus on the subject of that theory. The true subject of "The Emblematics of Meaning" is meaning, specifically emblematic meaning. Thus the title conveys two messages, which become clear only as one reads the essay. The first message is precisely that the real subject of a theory of symbolism, even when that theory is regarded ideally as an all-encompassing system of knowledge, is meaning. This is the true source for the universality of any theory of symbolism that might be successfully elaborated in the future (Bely

13. See *Mezhdu dvukh revolyutsii* (Leningrad, 1934), p. 377. See also n. 8 in Maria Carlson's essay, chap. 2 of this volume.

14. Bely gives a list of the philosophers most influential for him in a humorous passage of an article titled "Krugovoe dvizhenie," *Trudy i Dni*, no. 4–5 (1912), pp. 67–68. For a discussion of this article, see the essay by Robert A. Maguire and John E. Malmstad, chap. 3 of this volume.

claims in an introductory note to the essay that the time has not yet come for a truly definitive theory). The second message is the meaning of the title. Bely's title, "The Emblematics of Meaning," is an assertion that all meaning is emblematic, and his purpose in the essay is to show how and why.

What is "emblematic"? Like the concept of the symbol, the emblematic is a concept that can be understood only in light of the logical process by which it is derived.

"The Emblematics of Meaning" can best be explained by reference to the triangular diagram that accompanies it in *Symbolism* (reproduced here in figure 1).[15] For Bely, all activity designed to produce and organize meaning, activity that can be classified into the various sciences and other traditional fields of endeavor of the human spirit, can be divided into two categories: activity that is cognitive and activity that is creative. Bely has divided his triangular figure into smaller triangles and inscribed in them the names of these meaning-producing fields, as I will call them. The entire figure is bisected by an altitude line that is designed to separate the cognitive fields on the left from the creative fields on the right. Certain fields, it will be observed, such as theosophy, ethics, and customary morals, straddle this line. The inference to be drawn is that these fields are both cognitive and creative. The small triangle at the summit of the diagram bears the inscription "Value," which is clearly not the name of a field. I will return to this term and to those that label the points at the angles in a moment.

Cognitive fields, as Bely explains, are fields that produce meaning emblematically, that is, through the use of emblems. Creative fields are fields that produce meaning symbolically, or through the use of symbols. These terms, too, will be explained shortly.

By "cognition" (*poznanie*) Bely understands what might be called ordinary scientific understanding: the activity that Kant described in the *Critique of Pure Reason* as proceeding by means of the categories, or pure concepts of understanding. Its task is to organize and make sense of what would otherwise be for the conscious subject a mere rhapsody of sense impressions. This, in any case, is Bely's point of departure. But Bely adds a crucial element to the traditional Kantian epistemology, one that he had derived from his study of the Neo-Kantian Freiburg philosopher Heinrich Rickert (1863–1936).

Rickert's primary contribution to the late-nineteenth-century revision of critical philosophy was his effort to do away with Kant's sharp distinction between pure and practical reason and to introduce an ethical moment into the theory of knowledge. This effort is presented in *Der Gegen-*

---

15. The figure appears on an unnumbered page at the end of *Simvolizm* and in *Selected Essays*, p. 145.

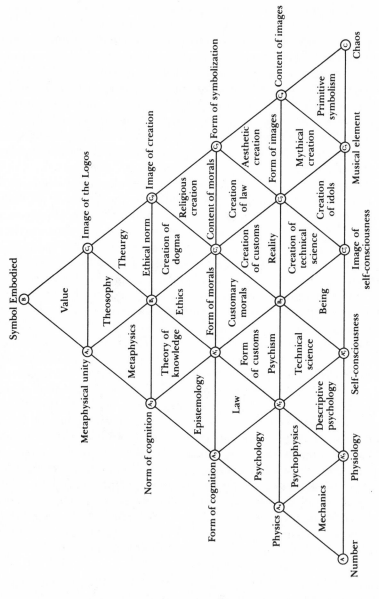

Figure 1

stand der Erkenntnis (*The Object of Cognition*), a work Bely cites frequently in "The Emblematics of Meaning." Rickert disputed the Kantian notion that the conscious subject simply absorbs sense impressions passively, and that these impressions are then organized in accordance with pre-established rules in a way that is effectively beyond the subject's control. Instead, Rickert says, the subject contributes an active element of *willing* to even ordinary acts of cognition. Every perception is in reality a judgment, Rickert maintains, and consists of an affirmation of a truth or a negation of a falsehood. Thus the simple observation that the sun is shining is equivalent to the judgment "The sun is shining." And the judgment "The sun is shining" is implicitly the same thing as the positive affirmation "Yes! The sun is shining."[16] Every act of simple cognition consequently represents the exercise of a kind of will to truth on the part of the subject.

The existence of an element of will in acts of what Kant would have called pure understanding implies for Rickert the presence of value (*Wert*), something, that is, whose worth the subject's practical judgment recognizes. The true object of knowledge in which truth is to be sought is not representations (*Vorstellungen*), as Kant had claimed. The true object of knowledge is value, says Rickert, and any act of ordinary theoretical knowledge is in actuality an act of "taking a position relative to a value."[17] Ordinary cognition is thus the re-cognition of the truth affirmed or denied in a judgment, and this truth is none other than a value. The truthfulness of ordinary cognitive judgments, the feeling of necessity that we experience in such judgments, is in reality an ethical necessity, what Rickert calls, borrowing the concept of the "ought" (*Sollen*) from Kant's practical philosophy, the "transcendent ought."[18] It is this supreme value-based concept, then, that is the ultimate object of all cognition for Rickert.

This is the position Bely adopts at the end of a lengthy and often rambling foray into epistemology early in "The Emblematics of Meaning." Why is it important? If we look at the right side of Bely's diagram, we see that the fields there, even in a purely Kantian scheme (that is, one that denies the operation of the faculty of judgment in ordinary, scientific cognition), all undeniably require the application of this faculty. They are, after all, the creative fields and thus lie outside the jurisdiction of pure understanding, or cognition, as Bely calls it. Bely holds it to be self-evident that the recognition of values is implicit in the application of

16. Heinrich Rickert, *Der Gegenstand der Erkenntnis: Einführung in die Transzenden-talphilosophie* (Tübingen and Leipzig, 1904), p. 98. Bely used the Russian translation published in Kiev the same year as the original: *Vvedenie v transtsendental'nuyu filosofiyu: Predmet poznaniya.*

17. Ibid., p. 105.

18. Ibid., pp. 125–32.

judgment, both what Kant would classify as moral judgment and what he would classify as aesthetic judgment. Thus all fields on the right side of the diagram can simply be assumed for this reason to be value-based without further discussion.

By adopting Rickert's purely epistemological position, however—the one that relates solely to ordinary acts of cognition—Bely has been able to show that both sides of the diagram, cognitive and creative, are value-based, and consequently that all activity related to meaning is founded on the existence of value and its recognition by a conscious subject. This is the reason that "Value" appears in the summit triangle of the diagram. Everything else appears beneath it, indeed is covered by it. Value is Bely's first principle, the essence from which all else is derived.

Now it is time to explain the logic of the diagram. In section 12 of "The Emblematics of Meaning" Bely explains the meaning of the hierarchic arrangement of fields in the triangle. Any small triangle on the diagram is said to govern the three triangles immediately beneath it, that is, to have a kind of logical priority over them. The example Bely uses is the most important one he could have chosen. If we take the triangle of Value at the top of the diagram and rearrange the three triangles beneath it—metaphysics, theosophy, and theurgy—so that they surround Value, then we can obtain a conceptual picture of the relation Bely has in mind. Bely in fact includes a diagram of this arrangement in *Symbolism* to accompany "The Emblematics of Meaning." These three fields are emanations of Value. In other words, our point of departure is Value itself, the undiluted quality from which all else is derived. As we pass from this undiluted essence outward to the three fields that are now placed in outlying positions relative to Value, we are passing from Value itself to, respectively, theosophical value, metaphysical value, and theurgic value. These subordinate fields are mere emanations of pure Value, having corrupted and concretized Value by infusing it with the elements peculiar to each of them.

Here is the essential point: the relation described by the move outward from Value to its three subordinate fields is one of symbolization. Bely puts it like this, using instead of "Value" the term "Symbol," which appears at the apex of the Value triangle: "The Symbol is expressed in symbolizations, and, in the present case, metaphysics, theosophy, and theurgy are such symbolizations."[19]

What is the meaning of "Symbol" (with a capital *S*) and what relation does it bear to Value? In section 16 of "The Emblematics of Meaning" it becomes clear that the terms that appear at the summit angles of the

---

19. "Emblematika smysla," in *Simvolizm*, p. 101; *Selected Essays*, p. 160. Hereafter references to this essay will be given in the text, the first page number referring to *Simvolizm*, the second to *Selected Essays*.

small triangles represent the norms, or points of highest striving, of the fields represented by those triangles. Thus the point of highest striving of epistemology is "norm of cognition," the norm of ethics is "ethical norm," and so on. The Symbol Embodied, or Symbol for short, would then be the norm of Value, and is consequently the highest goal of the supreme principle of the entire system. I will explain shortly how this notion is derived.

For now, however, another distinction should be pointed out, since it is crucial to an understanding of Bely's definition of symbols and symbolization. I have in mind the distinction Bely makes between Symbol and symbol. Bely says: "The Symbol cannot be given without symbolization. This is why we embody it in an image. The image, embodying the Symbol, is called a symbol only in a more general sense of the word" (105/164). What this means is that the process known as symbolization, the one that described the move from Value to subordinate fields, begins with a relatively pure quality (in the case of Value or the Symbol, it is not just relatively but also absolutely pure) and embodies that quality. The result of the process is a symbol. Thus for the moment it may be said that the Symbol is a kind of ideal purity from which embodied or concretized emanations may be produced by the process of symbolization.

But the use of the words "symbol" and "symbolization" gives us only half the picture. Earlier I mentioned that cognitive fields produce meaning through the intercession of emblems while creative fields produce meaning through the intercession of symbols. Bely does not present this distinction clearly in "The Emblematics of Meaning," although he continually refers to it and uses the terms "emblem" and "symbol" as though the difference between them were understood. Only later, in a passage in one of his memoirs, does he state succinctly what this difference is. There he says that "all our determinations [that is, of meaning] by means of concepts are emblems, while all our reflections of this reality by means of images are symbols."[20] In section 10 of "The Emblematics of Meaning" Bely defines emblematic concepts as those in which "the givenness of the world of reality and that of the world of consciousness combine to unite reality and consciousness into an image of immanent being" (90/150). Although the use of the word "image" in this passage is inconsistent, the point is still clear. Emblems and symbols are correlative notions: *an emblem is an embodiment of value through the use of (intellectual) concepts, and is thus the vehicle for the production of meaning in cognitive fields; a symbol is an embodiment of value through the use of images, and is thus the vehicle for the production of meaning in creative fields.*

Bely's triangular diagram is designed to show the overarching unity of meaning production. All meaning ultimately stems from Value and is

20. *Nachalo veka* (Moscow and Leningrad, 1933), p. 114.

produced through a process of embodiment. This process is called symbolization when (creative) images are used, and would be called, by
analogy, emblematization (Bely does not use the word) when (intellectual) concepts are used. Since Bely has not invented a generic term to
cover the analogous ideas of symbols and emblems, symbolization and
emblematization, he uses the word "emblematics" for this purpose. The
sense of the title can now be stated with more clarity. It is this: Why all
meaning, cognitive and creative, is emblematic. Or: Why all meaning is
produced through a process that embodies a higher principle of value in
a concrete form, through the use of either concepts (for cognitive fields)
or images (for creative fields).

The Derivation of the "Symbol Embodied"

In section 16 of "The Emblematics of Meaning" Bely gives a formal
derivation of the system represented in his diagram. He describes a
movement of ascent followed by a movement of descent along the triangular diagram, a kind of spiritual journey through the realm of meaning. It goes something like this: We begin at the bottom of one side of the
large triangle (Bely starts on the cognition side). We ascend step by step
through the various fields, aware that at each new stage we are approaching the purity of Value at the summit. The summit itself is
reached by a final leap of affirmation, by the proclamation "Yes!" This
assertive act lands us in the ideal purity of Value. At this point we
descend step by step, infusing the inferior fields with the transcendent
qualities of Value at the top. Bely describes the descent by referring to
the "norm" terms that appear at the summit angles of the small triangles. At this point in the essay he calls these terms "emblems of value."
Why? The norm of any field is the point of highest striving of that field,
as I have already mentioned. But the point of highest striving of any
field is the point closest to Value, or the particular form that Value,
through the process of symbolization described above, has assumed in
that field. This element may thus be described as the emblem of value
for that field, since it is an emblematic, that is to say concretized (embodied), version of Value itself. Thus in the field of metaphysics this element
will be "metaphysical unity," in the field of epistemology it will be the
"norm of cognition," and so on.

The descent begins from the norm of pure Value, or Symbol Embodied. We proceed downward, infusing the subordinate fields with increasingly small amounts of Value. As we proceed downward, each field
shows an increasingly large component of concretion and an increasingly small component of transcendence. Correlatively, as we proceed upward, each field shows an increasingly large component of transcendence and an increasingly small component of concretion.

We are now finally in a position to understand just how the notion of the supreme Symbol Embodied is derived. At the end of section 15 Bely had said: "The Symbol [Embodied] is the limit of all cognitive, creative, and ethical norms: the Symbol is, in this sense, the limit of limits" (111/168). This statement begins to make sense in light of the ascent–descent movement we have just examined. The movement of descent is clearly the movement of increasing symbolization, that is, of increasingly concrete, increasingly embodied symbolic or emblematic emanations of Value. Fields and norms of fields that appear lower on Bely's diagram will be more symbolic (or emblematic) than those that appear higher up. Now if we imagine a theoretical lower limit to the process of descent, it will be a field that is all concretion and contains no element of value at all. Perhaps this is the intended significance of the terms "chaos" (for the creative side) and "number" (for the cognitive side) which appear in the bottom corners of Bely's diagram.

But it is the other limit that interests us particularly. For if we imagine an ideal limit to the movement of ascent, yielding increasingly pure emblems of value, which is to say increasingly less symbolic or emblematic forms, this higher limit to the process of symbolization will be the point where all concretion disappears and Value alone remains. This higher limit to the process of symbolic embodiment is what Bely chooses to call the Symbol Embodied, capitalizing it to show that it represents the very idea of symbolic embodiment. The purest idea of symbolic embodiment will, at the limit, be a form that is devoid of embodiment altogether, and consequently is no longer a symbol at all but the very limit of limits. This is the Symbol Embodied.

Iconicity and the Status of Signifying Objects

Earlier I cited a passage in which Bely distinguished between symbols in general and the Symbol. He said: "The Symbol cannot be given without symbolization. This is why we embody it in an image. The image, embodying the Symbol, is called a symbol only in a more general sense of the word" (105/164). Bely follows this passage with an intriguing remark: "God, for example, is such a symbol, when seen as an existing something."

This statement must seem odd and puzzling, as there is little in the context to explain it. As it happens, however, it is motivated by a principle that lies at the very heart of Bely's system, and if Bely himself saw no need to explain his statement, it is undoubtedly because he assumed that virtually any Russian would understand it implicitly. I will call this principle "iconicity." My contention is that the formal principles of Bely's aesthetic symbology are actually those of the theology of icons in Russian Orthodoxy. Since the theology of icons is essentially derived from some of the fundamental principles of Russian Orthodox theology broadly conceived, and since statements like the one just cited presuppose a knowledge of those principles, it is not surprising that Bely should make such statements without further explanation.

In order to understand iconology, it is necessary first to understand the fundamental notion of kenosis and the kind of logic associated with this concept. *Kenosis* is Greek for "emptying," and refers to the act by which Christ emptied himself of divinity in order to appear on earth as a corporeal being. The Scriptural passage that describes this act and that serves as a source for the term "kenosis" is Philippians 2:7–8: "But [Christ] made himself of no reputation, and took upon him the form of a servant, and was made in the likeness of men: And being found in fashion as a man, he humbled himself, and became obedient unto death, even the death of the cross." The phrase "made himself of no reputa-tion" (*unichizhil Sebya Samogo* in Russian) translates the Greek verb from which the noun "kenosis" is derived.

The significance of this act for Russian Orthodox theology cannot be overstated. From it may be derived (at least logically, if not historically) the emphasis on suffering and humiliation (*unichizhit'* suggests humilia-tion or abnegation). But more important is the type of thinking to which the notion of kenosis gives rise. An example is the argument that derives the relative status of Christ and men. It runs something like this: Since Christ emptied himself of his divinity, he appeared on earth in a "humil-iated" form that allowed him to experience in the same way as men do, that is, corporeally. The most obvious measure of man's corporeality is his capacity to suffer. Christ was able to suffer, as is evident in his death on the cross. Consequently, it is possible for us, as corporeal beings, to partake to a limited extent in the experience of Christ. When we suffer we are sharing in the sole aspect of Christ's experience that is accessible to us, namely, the corporeal aspect. For we must bear in mind that even after the act of kenosis, Christ was still the God-man, not just a man. Even in his emptied or humiliated form as a corporeal being he retained a component of divinity, which, like God the Father, is never directly accessible to men. Suffering, that access to the purely corporeal aspect of Christ's person, is the closest we can come to the totality of his experi-ence.

What does all this have to do with icons? The important notion is the duality of Christ's nature, the coexistence in him of a transcendent (di-vine) component and an immanent (corporeal) component. As it hap-pens, icons enjoy the same status. When an icon painter paints an icon, or image (the Russian word *obraz*, as I have already mentioned, means both), of any of the traditional subjects—Christ, the Mother of God in any of various guises, a saint—he is meant to bear in mind and imitate an original image based on an actual, visual experience of that subject (for instance, Christ as he actually appeared when he lived on earth). The first icon image of any subject is made by a painter who saw the subject with his own eyes. The next generation of images must copy this first one. All succeeding images copy previous ones, and are thus meant to be ultimately an accurate reproduction of the original, free of any imaginative contribution by the painter.

But the icon is more than this. The true, ultimate original of any icon is not the physical person depicted but a far more abstract and transcendent quality, such as divine grace. The icon is thus meant to be appreciated not for the aesthetic pleasure it produces but for its concrete embodiment of the divine grace it represents. The icon stands in the same relation to divine grace as Christ the man stood in relation to God the Father: both are concrete, "humiliated" entities that also contain a component of transcendence and thus allow ordinary, corporeal beings to experience that transcendence in a limited way and through the only means available to them—that is, corporeally. Thus when we experience an icon we are experiencing divine grace in the same way that we experience divinity through Christlike suffering. In both cases we are coming as close as the intrinsic limitations of our corporeal natures allow to the actual experience of the divine, and in both cases we do so through objects that enjoy the dual status implicit in embodiment of transcendent qualities in concrete or (to use the theological term) humiliated form.

All this should sound familiar in light of our discussion of Bely's symbolism. As Bely's triangular diagram and his explanation of its principles show, the various meaning-producing fields, the objects they generate, and their norms, or "emblems of value," all have the same status as icons; that is, they all exist at a level of immanence but contain at the same time an embodied component of transcendence. The only difference is that, instead of God, Bely has chosen "Value" as the ultimate transcendent entity from which all else emanates. Otherwise, from a purely formal point of view, Bely's system is iconic through and through. Replace Value with God the Father and the Symbol Embodied with, say, divine grace, give the underlying fields a spiritual orientation, and you essentially have a Russian Orthodox theology of icons.

This is why Bely is able to make the otherwise baffling statement that "God, for example, is such a symbol, when seen as an existing something." What he means is that the conception we have of God is necessarily (in virtue of our own corporeal nature) a concretized one: we view him as an "existing something." But this "existing something," of course, bears only an iconic or symbolic relation to the original, since the original is not concrete at all, in fact is entirely inaccessible to our ordinary experience. Thus our ordinary conceptualization of God stands in relation to him as a symbol stands in relation to the Symbol Embodied.

There is more to it than this. Bely uses a whole range of terms taken from the vocabulary of Orthodox theology and iconology in "The Emblematics of Meaning," and all show the underlying iconic orientation of his thought. The following statement, for example, is comprehensible only in a theological context: "An Image [*Lik*] is a human image [*obraz*] that has become the emblem of a norm" (79/139). The word *Lik*, which turns up frequently in "The Emblematics of Meaning" and which I have translated as "Image" in *Selected Essays*, is used, among other things, for the image of a holy visage on an icon, and thus carries all the dualistic implications of icons in general. The sentence I have cited means that an iconic visage (of, say, a saint) is simply a concrete human image (that is, one that can be experienced by corporeal beings) that has come to serve as the embodiment of a norm, or ideal. If the norm is something like divine grace, then we can say that the Image (*Lik*) that represents it is the emblem of that norm. This emblem, then, is the humiliated or embodied representation of a transcendent quality not directly accessible to human experience.

Another concept that appears frequently in "The Emblematics of Meaning" is that of the divine Logos, or Word made flesh. The Johannine incarnation of the divine Word, as it happens, is also viewed as a kenotic idea in Russian Orthodoxy, since the making flesh, or incarnation (*voploshchenie*), of divinity is an example of the same kenosis or humiliation (*unichizhenie*) as that by which Christ became man. In this view, all creation is a humiliation, and has the same status as icons or the God-man. This is the sense of the language in section 12, where Bely uses both the concept of the Logos and that of the iconic Image. Here, after noting that the ideal unity that appears at the summit of his diagram appears to us in the "image [*obraz*] and likeness of man," Bely goes on to say: "To use the language of religion, creation leads us to an epiphany, or actual manifestation of the deity. The World Logos takes on the Image [*Lik*] of man [. . .]. In the language of icons this means: to transform the Word into Flesh" (94/153–54). Later, at the end of section 13, Bely shows even more clearly the connection between kenosis, iconicity, and his own concept of symbolization when he describes the "reality created by God" as a "symbolic reality" and distinguishes that reality from being. The implication there is, once again, that reality itself, the reality we experience, is the result of the Word's having been made flesh. Consequently, it is of a different nature from that of the Word itself (or true being), but gives us the closest possible approximation of the Word.

Metaphysical World View, or a Formal Iconics of Meaning?

Perhaps, then, Bely's world view could be provisionally defined in this way: The world for Bely, as for Hegel, is ultimately oriented toward and defined by the human spirit. It is seen as fundamentally the locus of the significations that the spirit generates. The world of our experience is the world of our meanings, and these meanings may for the sake of conceptual convenience be classified by the traditional names of disciplines of learning (fields, as I have called them).

Once this truth has been established, the next step is to find a way to organize and hierarchize the various types of meaning. This task, when it comes right down to it, is a simple one for Bely, and this is possibly where he most clearly betrays the essential Russianness of his outlook. For all he has really done is to take the iconic principles I have just explained and to found on them a system whose final concern is meaning rather than specifically divine truth. Perhaps it would not do too much violence to Bely's view to say that he has adopted an iconic system whose orientation is ultimately significative rather than theological. Bely, it seems, has "humiliated" the Word of God and replaced it with the word of signification, just as the Symbol in his own system becomes incarnate as a symbol. This is why iconics for him has become symbolics (or emblematics), and it is why God has become a quality called "Value."

But here we run into a problem, the final problem of this essay, and perhaps the most important. Is Bely's system metaphysical in the end? Does it imply or require as its source any entity, quality, or dimension of experience that transcends the limits of ordinary knowledge? In other words, is it necessary to import or include the notion of a supreme being, or any of the other notions that Bely's Kantian and Neo-Kantian schooling would have regarded as falling under the purview of metaphysics?

Many of Bely's critics automatically regard his philosophy as either mystical or metaphysical. A. L. Kazin, a Soviet scholar who has written a number of brief articles on Bely's theory and the philosophy of the Symbolist school, claims that Bely's system is "through and through metaphysical." His judgment is based largely on his perception that Bely's concept of the meaning of life differs from the Marxist one that he, Kazin, posits as axiomatic.[21] It is not difficult to understand this tendency among readers of Bely, even those for whom "metaphysical" is not necessarily a term of contempt. After all, the rhetoric, at least, of metaphysics and mysticism pervades Bely's work throughout his strictly Symbolist period. The novel *Petersburg* contains that well-known reference to "forces unknown to us," which make their incursion into the brain and serve as the source of human creation.[22] This idea suggests that creations of the human spirit, what Bely whimsically calls "idle cerebral play," are generated by some form of transcendent absolute outside the realm of ordinary human perception and experience.

21. A. L. Kazin, "Gnoseologicheskoe obosnovanie simvola Andreem Belym," *Voprosy Filosofii i Sotsiologii*, no. 3 (1971), pp. 71–75.

22. *Petersburg*, trans. Robert A. Maguire and John E. Malmstad (Bloomington, Ind., 1978), p. 35.

"The Emblematics of Meaning," too, is full of references to metaphysics. Admittedly, Bely often uses the word "metaphysics" in that essay to designate the traditional field of scholastic metaphysics. But he also says things that suggest an attempt to characterize his outlook as metaphysical. Toward the end of the essay, for instance, after having listed twenty-three "premises" to his theory of the Symbol and Symbolism, Bely says that "the Symbol is a criterion of Value for any metaphysics" (132/187). A page later he refers to "the metaphysical concept of the Symbol as unity" (133/188). Earlier in the same essay he had appeared to set up an equation between "metaphysical" and "emblematic" by claiming that when epistemological judgments are viewed as ontological judgments (as Bely says they should be), the epistemological judgment "is asserted as a metaphysical (i.e., *emblematic*) reality [*real'nost'*]" (124/181; my italics).

The real question, however, is not whether Bely's philosophy taken in its entirety is metaphysical. In at least one period of his life (his anthroposophical period, when *Petersburg* was written) it arguably was, and at other times it was not; and the mere fact that it changed so often makes it difficult to speak of a single philosophy, metaphysical or otherwise. The real question is whether Bely's theory of Symbolism is metaphysical. In other words, in the process by which we confer meaning on our experience and produce our own signifying objects, do we have access to a form of knowledge or experience that transcends the limits of ordinary understanding?

By the logic of Bely's triangular diagram, Value is the first principle from which all else is derived, and the Symbol Embodied is the norm of that principle. If there is any question of a transcendent essence whose existence underlies and logically precedes all signifying activity, then clearly these two ideas must be investigated. The Symbol Embodied presents its own problems, and I will return to them in a moment. For now, however, let us consider Value.

The problem is that Bely never gives a clear sense of just what he means by "Value." By all indications, he uses the term in the sense in which Rickert uses it, as something recognized by the will of the conscious subject. But this idea, of course, raises another problem. The whole point of Rickert's reformation of Kant's epistemology was to free knowledge from the severity of pure scientific rigor with which it is saddled in both Kant and a rival group of Neo-Kantians headed by Hermann Cohen (whom Bely humorously calls the High Priest of Epistemology at one point in "The Emblematics of Meaning" [142/196]). And the means by which Rickert hopes to breathe new life into ordinary knowledge, as I said earlier, is the introduction of an element of will into it. One is then tempted to say immediately, as far as Rickert alone is concerned, that this amounts to an introduction of a metaphysical element into ordinary theoretical cognition, the pure will in Kant being something beyond ordinary understanding. The only trouble is that Rickert himself is quite adamant in claiming that his own system is entirely free of any metaphysical implications whatsoever. Early in *Der Gegenstand der Erkenntnis* he speaks contemptuously of what he calls "metaphysical realism," by which he means any system in which the sensible world is viewed as a mere appearance (*Erscheinung*) of a metaphysical reality.[23] Even Kant was guilty of making this mistake, Rickert appears to be claiming.

Thus "metaphysical" becomes a dirty word early on in Rickert. Cognition, Rickert emphatically asserts, is never cognition of some reality existing in and for itself beyond the world of appearances. But the problem arises for Rickert when he finally tells us what the object of cognition really is. For truth, he then tells us, is a value concept (*Wertbegriff*), reality is something we *judge* to be such, and the ultimate object of our knowledge is the *transcendent* ought, itself a value concept. Thus the true end of all knowledge is not metaphysical in the sense of being a thing in itself lying behind the world of appearances, and yet it is, in Rickert's own words, transcendent. But if "transcendent" objects do not belong to the realm of metaphysics here, it can only be because Rickert has decided to give "metaphysics" a definition it never had for Kant: one, that is, that conveniently includes the thing in itself but excludes the pure will, judgment, and the whole realm of moral philosophy, and for no other reason, apparently, than that Rickert wishes to incorporate these things into his system while still reserving the right to call that system nonmetaphysical.

Is "Value," then, a metaphysical concept or not? All that can really be said about it is that, since it is a concept that Bely defined with Kant always in mind as a point of origin, and since the realm of ordinary, scientifically apprehended experience for Kant is not made accessible through the intercession of value, the will, or any sort of "ought," then *relative to this basis of comparison* Value is certainly a transcendent concept. And if this is so, then "ordinary" cognition for both Bely and Rickert contains a moment that is transcendent, relative to the same basis of comparison.

But it is one thing to say that the system is founded on a value concept that is transcendent relative to ordinary scientific understanding. It is another to say that the entire system posits or assumes the metaphysical possibility of contact with a transcendent or supernatural realm of experience. Although Bely's interest in experience of this sort was often keen and all-consuming, such experience is by no means intrinsically necessary to his theory of symbolism. The system stands on its own as long as

23. Rickert, *Gegenstand*, p. 73.

the iconic principle is followed, and this implies only that the transcendent principle must be *formally* recognized. The process of symbolic or emblematic activity requires us to act as if such a transcendent principle were objectively present, just as Kant's teleological judgment rests on a formal assumption of the presence of objective ends in nature. This is the reason, incidentally, why it is not really important for the *system* of Symbolism whether "Value" means the same thing as it does for Rickert or whether it is something entirely different, as, for instance, A. L. Kazin claims it is.[24]

But there is another, more compelling reason to regard Bely's system as ultimately formal or formalistic, and this has to do with the norm of the system, the Symbol Embodied. A moment ago I explained how this norm is derived from within the system, that it represents, to use Bely's own words, the "limit of limits" of the process of symbolization. The Symbol Embodied, as the extreme limit of symbolization in the direction of transcendent purity, is neither a symbol in the ordinary sense nor embodied in the ordinary sense. Being entirely free of any immanent component, it does not symbolize, that is, does not symbolically embody anything. It is simply the pure, limiting Idea of symbolic embodiment.

This is just the point. If Bely had constructed a system of iconics based on true principles of Orthodox theology, then the summit triangle in his diagram would probably have been God, and the norm of the whole system would probably have been something like divine grace. But God and divine grace are truly first principles, external to the entire system, and certainly metaphysical in any sense of the word. The Symbol Embodied, on the other hand, is generated from within the system itself. In fact, it is neither more nor less than the formal organizational principle of the system hypostasized and enthroned at the summit as if it were an absolute, metaphysical first principle. But this, of course, it clearly is not. It is as though one had constructed a system of religious belief starting with the principle by which divine truth is made manifest in that system and then called that principle God. If one were to perform a monstrous operation of this sort on Russian Orthodoxy, then the ultimate source of all truth in that religion would be not God but Iconicity or Kenosis.

Bely's system, seen in this light, is entirely self-contained and self-generating. The true first principle is not God or any other metaphysical entity, it is simply the formal principle of symbolization. Bely thus antici-

24. Kazin maintains that Bely "reworks the Rickertian concept of cognitive value within the spirit of symbolist irrationalism" to produce a concept of value as the "limit of the construction of [all] epistemological and metaphysical concepts." He goes on to say that Value for Bely is a symbol, and that the Symbol is "some sort of mystical principle of being from which creation and cognition arise." This, he says, is the concept by which Bely accomplishes his "cross-over from theory of knowledge to theory of creation, from epistemology to symbolic metaphysics, which in his system coincides with aesthetics" ("Gnoseologicheskoe obosnovanie simvola," p. 74).

pated the truth of *Why I Became a Symbolist* many years before that work was written. *Why I Became a Symbolist* is designed to show the primacy of the symbolization concept in its author's own life. The purpose of "The Emblematics of Meaning" is to show its constancy in all experience. But this really amounts to the same thing. After all, how better could one prove the constancy and invariability of Symbolism in all realms of human signifying activity than by showing its constancy and invariability in a philosophical career as inconstant and variable as Bely's?

But Bely seems to have been aware of the purely formal implications of his theory of Symbolism long before he wrote *Why I Became a Symbolist*. In "On the Results of the Development of the New Russian Art" ("Ob itogakh razvitiya novogo russkogo iskusstva," 1907), for instance, he says that "symbolist theory could not possibly be a form of dogmatism for art, but only a systematic listing of the means for functioning with images." He emphasizes the primacy of form and method of Symbolism over dogmatic truth by comparing his theory to Kantianism and economic materialism. "The hope of symbolism in aesthetics," he says, "is simply to give its method a theoretical foundation, in much the same way that Kantianism or economic materialism must be taken theoretically as methods of relations, [. . .] and not as truths in the form of dogma."[25] In "Theory or an Old Woman" ("Teoriya ili staraya baba," 1907) he again points to the logical primacy of methodology over dogmatic content. "The methodology and epistemology of symbolism," he says, "necessarily precede the construction of a theory of symbolism. And a theory of symbolism is the point of departure for all theoretical constructions. Theories of knowledge, religion, aesthetics, and science are but the particular objects of a theory of symbolism that has been formulated in a general form."[26]

Thus, in the end, the possibilities of the theory of Symbolism for a world view do not necessarily include any metaphysical implications or content at all. No, the theory of Symbolism simply has a different purpose from that of a system of metaphysics. It is meant to take logical precedence over all content of any sort.

How, then, can it ever pretend to any kind of universality? The answer to this question requires once more a clear understanding of the purpose of the system. The purpose of the system is not to give a philosophical world view in the sense of a system of ideas that gives the meaning of life or the meaning of the universe. The purpose is purely to describe the manner in which conscious subjects endow their experience with meaning. *This* is the source of the potential universality of the theory of Symbolism: what is held to be universal is the apparatus by which conscious subjects confer and produce meaning.

25. *Arabeski*, p. 259.
26. Ibid., pp. 269–70.

How do conscious subjects confer and produce meaning? The formal, logical properties of Bely's diagram suggest how they can do so. The fundamental principle is symbolization. Thus one starts with or assumes a value. Value can easily be understood here in the most ordinary sense as what the conscious subject, for whatever reasons he may have, esteems. If value comes to occupy a position of transcendent purity in Bely's diagram, it is more because this position suggests the importance we attach to it than because Bely necessarily believes in some absolute, metaphysical entity called Value. In fact, there is no necessity to regard this principle as in any way different from an idea like Kant's ends in nature: ideas in which we place our trust not because we know with certainty that they really exist objectively but because the mere fact of treating them as existing gives us a formal means for ordering experience.

So it is with Value for Bely. When we assign meaning to things, Bely believes, our innate tendency is to assume the existence of an absolute worth of which our meanings, our meaningful objects, and our meaningful disciplines are concrete emanations. And to understand the nature of these emanations, all we need to do is to use the formal analogy of iconicity; that is, the concrete embodiment of a quality that is not concrete, whether that quality is a true metaphysical absolute or simply, like Kant's ends in nature and like Bely's Value, a purely formal absolute.

9

Bely the Thinker

STEVEN CASSEDY

The Intellectual Tradition

If a glib formula were needed to define Bely's thought throughout his life, it would probably be accurate to say that he always hesitated between two conflicting world views, one metaphysical, the other secular and formalistic. As a metaphysician he was strictly an Orthodox thinker; that is, the logic of his thought followed the logic of Russian Orthodox theology. In his secular moments he was a Kantian.

This is not to say that Bely actually wrote theology, only that he had a strong penchant for the metaphysical, and in this sphere the structure of Orthodox theological thinking seems to have taken root early on in his way of seeing things. Nor did Bely embrace dogmatic critical philosophy at an early stage and remain committed to it for the rest of his life. But after a certain point, in the logic of Bely's thinking as well as in the logic of its development, Kantianism remained both the point of departure and the system in relation to which everything else was defined. The most confusing thing of all is that the metaphysician and the Kantian theorist of knowledge in Bely made frequent incursions into each other's territory.

In his memoir *The Beginning of the Century* (*Nachalo veka*) Bely relates that in 1901, before he was twenty-one, he had already come to be so closely associated with Kant that his friends used to form puns from the names Bely (as he had already come to be known) and Kant. Later he describes how even before he turned twenty-three his relation with Kantianism had become a struggle, but an unbalanced one that would

This essay expands and adapts ideas that first appeared in my "Translator's Introduction" to *Selected Essays of Andrey Bely,* edited and translated by Steven Cassedy (Berkeley: University of California Press, 1985). Copyright © 1985 The Regents of the University of California.

not allow him to escape the clutches of his foe. "In July 1903," he says, "in the guise of a struggle with Kantianism, I immersed myself in it thoroughly. And Kantianism, having become my very atmosphere, proceeded to poison me, as a lyric poem would."[1]

Bely's relationship with Kantianism is described most vividly in the memoirs of his widow, Klavdiya Nikolaevna Bugaeva. She devotes an entire chapter of her *Recollections of Bely* (*Vospominaniya o Belom*) to her late husband's thought (or, to put it more precisely, to the subject of thought in Bely's life), and here she puts the matter unequivocally. "He thought [*myslil*] elementally, like the wise men of ancient Greece; paradoxically, like Nietzsche; intuitively, like Goethe. But the *gesture* of his thought was tilled in the soil of Kant." Bugaeva is not implying that Bely's attitude toward the founder of critical philosophy was always (or ever) one of unqualified admiration. On the contrary, as the *Recollections* show, Bely was characteristically, obsessively hostile to Kant, but the very strength of his obsession demonstrates all too clearly that the need to reject Kant was founded on an implicit belief in the virtual impregnability of the edifice of critical thought. "His greatest enemy was always Kant," says Bely's widow. "But Kant was an enemy worth struggling with." In fact, he was so much worth struggling with that Bely "gave Kant almost all of his best years," breaking free only after he had forced the famous "corpse" to reveal his secrets.[2] The break came, not surprisingly, in the years 1913 to 1915; that is, at the time of Bely's conversion to anthroposophy.

But the best years of Bely's life, by this account, are the ones that precede anthroposophy (and also, oddly enough, Bely's marriage to Klavdiya Nikolaevna). They are the years when Bely was a true Symbolist. If Bely gave these years to Kant, he also gave them to Symbolism, and for this reason it is no surprise that he formulated his theory of Symbolism with the Königsberg philosopher always looking over his shoulder. In 1904, for instance, for the centennial of Kant's death, Bely wrote an article titled "Criticism and Symbolism" ("Krititsizm i simvolizm"), "criticism" meaning, of course (Kantian) critical philosophy. Here, in a burst of youthful enthusiasm, Bely shows how Kantian idealism serves as a philosophical foundation for the Symbolist movement in Russian letters. The article was included later in *Symbolism*, and there, in a note, Bely repudiated his earlier views on the significant role of critical philosophy in the Symbolist movement.[3] Even so, the article is

---

1. *Nachalo veka* (Moscow and Leningrad, 1933), pp. 18, 257.

2. K. N. Bugaeva, *Vospominaniya o Belom*, ed. John E. Malmstad (Berkeley, 1981), pp. 270, 272, 274.

3. *Simvolizm* (Moscow, 1910), p. 466. "Krititsizm i simvolizm" appears on pp. 20–30. It was first published in *Vesy*, no. 2 (1904).

revealing for its clear statement of a position that was not really abandoned but only modified later.

At this early date Bely's attitude toward critical philosophy is already ambivalent, for the chief value he sees in it is what might be described as the possibility it presents for its own destruction. Why? Kant's prime accomplishment was to discriminate between reason and what Bely calls "feeling" (*chuvstvo*). What critical philosophy and Symbolism have in common, says Bely, is their recognition first of this discrimination and second of the necessity for overcoming it, for annihilating the "schism between reason and feeling."[4] Perhaps in a muddled way Bely is alluding to Kant's claim that he wrote the *Critique of Pure Reason,* exposing the limits of scientific understanding, precisely to make room for what is left over after those limits have been reached; namely, faith, which bridges the epistemological gap in a way that scientific understanding cannot.[5] Bridging the gap, in any case, is clearly what Bely sees as the goal of Symbolism.

The analysis, even though it is flawed and even though Bely later rejected it, points up a concern that was to remain with him, certainly for the remainder of his period of overt interest in Kant and arguably until the end of his life. Bely always seems to seek a way of bridging the gap not only between scientific understanding and a faith that provides access to the transcendent but also between the concept-based scientific understanding and those areas of experience dominated by the will, namely, ethics and aesthetics. Bely seems to have wished above all to bridge the gap separating Kant's first *Critique* from his second and third, that is, separating ordinary reason from practical reason and judgment.

This is why the philosophy of the Neo-Kantian Heinrich Rickert (1863–1936) was so appealing to Bely in his Symbolist period. Rickert argued (not very persuasively) for the incorporation of a moment of ethical will into the "ordinary" process of scientific understanding. He maintained that ordinary perceptions are in actuality judgments, are based on acts of the ethical will (which expresses itself as a kind of affirmation of truth), and are consequently not as "ordinary" and "scientific" as Kant had claimed. In the passage I mentioned a moment ago from *The Beginning of the Century* Bely describes his Kantian period as including a six-year infatuation with the work of Rickert (from 1907 to 1913).[6] This is precisely the period when he wrote his most significant

4. Ibid., p. 24.
5. Immanuel Kant, *Kritik der reinen Vernunft,* "B" ed. (Riga, 1787), p. xxx; published in English as *Critique of Pure Reason,* trans. Norman Kemp Smith (New York, 1929), p. 29. The passage in question reads, in Kemp Smith's translation, "I have therefore found it necessary to deny *knowledge,* in order to make room for *faith.*"
6. *Nachalo veka,* p. 257.

Symbolist essays, and it is for this reason that Rickert figures so prominently in the most important of those essays, "The Emblematics of Meaning."[7]

A look at some of those essays will reveal another way in which Bely's Kantianism intruded into his Symbolist thinking, perhaps without his knowing it. Any reader of *Symbolism* cannot help being struck by the wide divergence in Bely's approaches to various topics in aesthetics and criticism. One's initial response is to wonder whether the author of these essays was the victim of some immense confusion. In sharp contrast to such an essay as "The Emblematics of Meaning," where Bely's purpose is to abandon science in favor of an apparently metaphysical world view, stand the essays on rhythm and metrics, where Bely overtly proposes an "exact" science of aesthetics.[8] But there is good reason to see the whole collection of articles as the expression of a single Kantian conflict. The articles on rhythm, on the one hand, propose a strictly empirical, scientific approach to the cognition of aesthetic objects. Such articles as "The Emblematics of Meaning" and "The Magic of Words," on the other hand, present fundamental challenges to the methods of exact sciences, asserting the superiority of man's creative faculties (those based on the will and the exercise of what Kant would call, depending on the case, judgment or practical reason) over his purely cognitive faculties. Thus the "scientific" essays taken together with the ostensibly metaphysical essays already present a contrast corresponding to the dualism between Kant's first *Critique* and his second and third.

Bely was not the first Russian thinker to attempt to integrate Orthodox theology with a Kantian critical system (or to integrate the Kantian critical philosophy with an Orthodox theological system). He had a model for such an integration in Vladimir Solov'ev (1853–1900), author of the *Lectures on Godmanhood,* proponent of Russian Orthodoxy as a model for a "Universal Church," and friend of Fedor Dostoevsky in the last years of the novelist's life. Solov'ev had an enormous impact on the thinking of the entire Symbolist movement of which Bely was a part.[9] But for Bely, who was personally acquainted with the philosopher, Solov'ev's importance went far beyond the merits and appeal of his ideas.

7. For the role of Rickertian epistemology in "The Emblematics of Meaning," see the "Translator's Introduction" to my *Selected Essays of Andrey Bely* (Berkeley, 1985) and chap. 8 of this volume.

8. I have discussed the apparent diversity of Bely's essays in "Toward a Unified Theory of the Aesthetic Object in Andrej Belyj," *Slavic and East European Journal,* 28 (1984), pp. 205–22.

9. For Solov'ev and the Russian Symbolist movement, see in particular James West, *Russian Symbolism: A Study of Vyacheslav Ivanov and the Russian Symbolist Aesthetic* (London, 1970), pp. 35–42. For Solov'ev and Bely, see Ekaterina Kuleshova, "O vliyanii Vladimira Solov'eva na Bloka i Belogo," *Polifoniya idei i simvolov* (Toronto, 1981), pp. 7–15. On Solov'ev in general, see Samuel D. Cioran, *Vladimir Solov'ev and the Knighthood of the Divine Sophia* (Waterloo, Ont., 1977).

Bely's memoirs are filled with accounts of the almost idolatrous awe in which he held the philosopher, particularly at a time when this attitude was shared by Solov'ev's nephew, who was a close friend of the young Bely.

Solov'ev was uncannily precocious as a thinker, and the essentials of his system were already in place when he was quite young. An early article titled "On the Reality of the External World and the Basis for a Metaphysical Cognition" (1875) develops the rudiments of an epistemology that is startling for the way it combines traditional Kantian dualism with a bold argument for a "metaphysical cognition."[10] Solov'ev accepts as undeniable that the conscious subject can know only appearances in the outside world, not essences. He departs from Kant, however, in his belief that we *can* know essences *in ourselves*, by means of what he calls "essential cognition" (*sushchestvennoe poznanie*). If we can know essence in ourselves, Solov'ev thinks, then we can know by analogy something of the essences of other beings, and consequently of metaphysical essences or the absolute first principle of the cosmos. This knowledge arises from what Solov'ev calls "metaphysical cognition."

Most startling is Solov'ev's claim to have a logical method for deducing this analogical metaphysical cognition. The argument goes like this: If there is a uniformity among external, independent appearances (and Kant would certainly say that there is, these appearances being subject to the rules of a logic intrinsic to the structure of our own mind), then the essences that stand behind appearances must have a similar, *internal* uniformity; thus the faculty by which we cognize these essences, while it does not "know" them in the same way that it "knows" appearances, must of necessity operate in a fashion analogous to the operation of ordinary cognition.

Several years later, in the *Lectures on Godmanhood* (1877–81), Solov'ev discussed the same distinction, but used the more traditional terms "knowledge" and "faith."[11] Here, too, he accepted as indisputable the Kantian account of ordinary knowledge and its limits, using terms and phrases that appear to have been lifted directly from the pages of the *Critique of Pure Reason*. But Solov'ev's interest was, of course, in the other side of ordinary knowledge, and so he combined his use of strictly critical analyses with an attempt to deduce rationally the existence of such transcendent objects as the Trinity and the world of ideas. The arguments on the transcendent are reminiscent of the analogy theory of Solov'ev's early essay, although they contain other analyses that sound more like Hegel than like Kant. But the point of the whole exercise was

10. "O deistvitel'nosti vneshnego mira i osnovanii metafizicheskogo poznaniya," in Vladimir Solov'ev, *Sobranie sochinenii* (Petersburg, 1911–13; reprinted Brussels, 1966), I, 216–26.

11. "Chteniya o Bogochelovechestve," in *Sobranie sochinenii*, III, 3–181.

to construct a purely Orthodox theology—with all of its characteristic emphasis on the radical separation of human and divine, immanent and transcendent, the Word as God and the Word made flesh—on a foundation of Kantian analysis. And while Kantian analysis, with its own divisions between the concrete world of appearances and a transcendent whose existence is knowable only through faith, is entirely compatible with Orthodox theology *as far as the establishing of limits to knowledge goes,* Solov'ev clearly wished to extend the analysis to the transcendent in a way that would at least begin to bridge the gap separating the poles of Kant's dualistic world view.

Solov'ev's desire to bridge the Kantian gap is clearest in his theories of beauty and art. He unabashedly proclaimed the objective existence of a supramaterial Idea that is embodied in nature in the form of beauty. Kant had wished to limit his assertions about the objective existence of beauty by claiming that beauty is the correlate of a purely formal type of judgment. In other words, if one follows the conclusions of the first *Critique,* one can make no absolute claim for the objective existence of the sublime or the beautiful, since our apprehension of these qualities is purely subjective. Our faculty of aesthetic judgment, however, operates *formally* in a way that supposes such an existence. Solov'ev did not agree, as the following passage from his article "Beauty in Nature" (1889) clearly demonstrates: "In truth, beauty is the idea actually [*deistvitel'no*] realized, incarnated in the world *before* the human spirit, and this incarnation of beauty is no less real and far more meaningful (in the cosmic sense) than the material elements in which it becomes incarnated."[12]

Especially significant for an understanding of Bely is the way Solov'ev carried his ideas on beauty in nature into the realm of art. Solov'ev not only refused to draw the line where Kant did in separating ordinary cognition from aesthetic judgment, but also refused to make the Kantian distinction between beauty in nature and beauty that is manmade. In an article titled "The General Meaning of Art" (1890) Solov'ev stresses the intrinsic connection between art and nature, art representing a continuation, not a duplication or imitation, of the work begun by nature. For art has a triple task, Solov'ev asserts: the direct objectification of the internal qualities of the living idea, the spiritualization of natural beauty, and the immortalization of nature's individual phenomena. Man alone, as the most conscious of nature's creatures, is capable of fulfilling these functions, since man alone, owing to the kind of metaphysical cognition whose existence Solov'ev has already proposed, is capable of apprehending the "living idea" and furthering nature's own purpose by actualizing, incarnating that idea in material form.[13]

---

12. "Krasota v prirode," in *Sobranie sochinenii,* VI, 33–74. The quotation is on p. 43.
13. "Obshchii smysl iskusstva," in *Sobranie sochinenii,* VI, 75–90.

Thus once again the objective existence of the metaphysical essence, in this case what Solov'ev calls the "living idea," is unhesitatingly asserted, and man's role is merely the apprehension and incarnation of that ideal. For Solov'ev, aesthetic judgment was no mere formal affair, as it had been for Kant. While Solov'ev was careful not to claim identical functions for scientific and aesthetic judgment, he still saw the two faculties as far more strictly analogous than Kant would ever have allowed.

An account of Bely's intellectual heritage certainly does not begin with Kant and end with Vladimir Solov'ev. There are other philosophers: the entire Neo-Kantian school, including Hermann Cohen, for whom Bely had an ambivalent mixture of admiration and scorn; Hegel, Schopenhauer, Nietzsche; Auguste Comte (whose last name in Russian looks and sounds enough like "Kant" for Bely to pun on the two names in *Petersburg* and even on occasion to overlook a misprint of one for the other in his own writings); Henri Bergson, who is mentioned in a few places; Edmund Husserl, to whose writings Bely was introduced by his friend Gustav Shpet; and many, many others. There are other systems and schools of thought: the theosophy of Helena Blavatsky and Annie Besant; Rudolf Steiner's anthroposophy; even the materialism that Bely adopted (or pretended to adopt) during the Stalin years.

In spite of the number and great diversity of systems that Bely passed through, the central principle remained in force, and that principle was the incorporation of Kantian criticism into Orthodox theology (or Orthodox theology into Kantian criticism) in a manner that resembles the structure of Solov'ev's thought. The difference is that, certainly until Bely's conversion to the anthroposophy of Steiner and arguably at certain moments thereafter, his theology remained at the level of pure, formal system. We find no act of faith by which Bely embraced the first principle of such a theology, namely, the divinity. And if Bely, after becoming an anthroposophist, accepted the notion of "knowing" the transcendent (because traditional distinctions between immanent and transcendent, "ordinary" knowledge and faith, epistemology and metaphysics are denied in the anthroposophical world view), he still did not adopt *as an act of faith* the theology that continued to inform the logic of his thinking. In fact, even the conversion to anthroposophy in its own terms cannot be taken as strictly religious or metaphysical, although Bely showed his strongest tendency toward unabashedly mystical assertions in this period. For one thing, anthroposophy by its very definition does not include a divinity. And for another, because the Steinerian system is predicated on the nonexistence of metaphysics (Steiner recognized no separate type of knowledge that would fall into the purview of "metaphysics"), one could argue that Bely came as close to genuine faith (or metaphysical understanding) as he did only by embracing a system of thought that officially authorized him to deny the existence of any such

distinct thing as faith. Bely was thus very much like Shatov in Dostoevsky's *Devils*, the character who professes a doctrinaire Slavophilism,
with its fanatical mixture of nationalism and Russian Orthodox Christianity, but who, when pressed to say whether he truly believes in God,
can only answer, "I—I shall believe."

This certainly describes Bely before anthroposophy. And afterward,
he believed—but there was no longer a God to believe in or any sort of
leap of faith (at least in the system's own terms). Perhaps it would be
most accurate to say that metaphysical understanding and strict formalism presented Bely with conflicting temptations that he never entirely resolved. The duality simply subsisted, and it continued to have
important consequences for the way he saw practically everything.

The Universality of Systems of Meaning

There is a constant in Bely's career, and that is the notion of symbolization. As I have suggested in "Bely's Theory of Symbolism as a
Formal Iconics of Meaning," symbolization is a formal, not a metaphysical, notion. The logic of the notion is derived from the logic of icon
theology, which is certainly a metaphysical system, but Bely replaced the
first principle of icon theology, the divinity, with the formal concept of
value. Thus any act of meaning creation or meaning apprehension is
accomplished only *as if* it were premised on the recognition of an absolute first principle.

Even though I believe this substitution shows that Bely's Symbolist
system is not strictly religious or metaphysical (in the sense of being
founded on faith or accepting the real existence of a transcendent that is
accessible—or even approachable—through the medium of symbols), it
shows that the analogy between religion and art as systems of meaning
was important to Bely. The big questions for him throughout his career
had to do with this analogy. Do art and religion have the same origin?
Are they expressions of the same underlying impulse in conscious
beings? Given that their objects (symbols and icons, respectively) demand that an observer take analogous cognitive stances, do they appeal
to some aspect of consciousness that is the same for both? These are the
things that concerned Bely the thinker above all else.

Bely's Symbolist period shows how keenly he felt these questions. In
his effort to build a system of symbolics on an iconic theology, Bely
exploited the overlapping terminology of the two systems in a way that
clearly points up the analogies between them. In fact, many of Bely's
favorite theological and iconic terms are precisely those that could easily
double as aesthetic terms, and specifically as poetic terms: *Slovo* (Word,
Logos), *lik* (image, iconic image), *obraz* (icon, image). And if Bely fre-

quently exploited the ambiguity that arises when such terms are used without a clear indication of the system from which they are derived, it is undoubtedly because he wished to show that it makes little difference: as far as the cognitive posture of the perceiving consciousness goes, both the theological and the aesthetic systems can be subsumed under something grander. This something grander is the formal structure of systems of meaning, a structure that Bely proposed as universal.

All of this brings us back to the duality I have been speaking of. The duality is most evident during Bely's Symbolist period. For it is clear that, in allowing his theological system and his symbolic system to overlap, Bely was showing his divided tendency toward the metaphysical on the one hand and the purely secular and scientific on the other. After all, even if it is true that he presented the theory of Symbolism during this period as something purely formal, even if it is true that the system's first principle (value) is present merely as the presumed correlate of a cognitive act, it is still undoubtedly no accident that the system Bely chose was a theological one.

It would probably be accurate to say that the Symbolist period shows Bely at his closest to a Solov'evan theory of meaning. But it is also the period of his strongest Kantian, which is ultimately to say secular, bias. For the theory of Symbolism is not itself premised on the existence of any true "metaphysical cognition" of the sort that Solov'ev proposed. To Bely's way of thinking, metaphysical cognition (the expression, as Solov'ev probably realized and as Bely could not have helped realizing, is an oxymoron in any idealist philosophy) could be nothing more than a formal model for the apprehension of objects of meaning, or symbols. And even though Bely never tired of railing against "cognition" in its Kantian sense as both dead and deadly (since it is the mode of apprehension whereby we acquire purely scientific truths), in the end, symbolic apprehension for him really was cognition, that is, a formal, categorial thought process. A moment ago I suggested that pure formalism and pure metaphysics represented twin, opposite temptations to Bely. Here the comparison with Dostoevsky's Shatov is especially apt. *The Devils* is about the dual temptations of faith and faithlessness—about the believer's temptation by atheism, about the atheist's temptation by faith, about the universality of man's position somewhere between the two unattainable ideals of pure atheism and pure faith. Substitute "formalism" for "atheism," substitute "metaphysics" for "faith," and you have Bely, the perfect, divided, Dostoevskian man.

The art-religion connection did not appear for the first time in the major writings that ended Bely's Symbolist period. In his early writings he had explored the mystical dimension of art by comparing it with the medieval mystery play. Nietzsche had been an attraction for Bely because he located the source of art in the same irrational realm of man's being (the "depths," as Bely calls it) that gives rise to the orgiastic rites of Dionysus. In fact, in the early "Symbolism as a World View," written six years before the culminating Symbolist essays of 1909, Bely had explicitly pointed up the connection between Nietzsche, Solov'ev, and the philosophy of Symbolism. And, as a glance at the two hundred pages of commentary to *Symbolism* will show, Bely's infatuation with theosophy had led him to speculate on art as an avenue to mystical truth.

Nor did Bely's interest in the connection end with the Symbolist period. It was during the anthroposophical period, at least until 1922, that Bely's writings came closest to a genuine mystical faith. One indication of this approach to faith is found in the implied theory of artistic creation in the novel *Petersburg* (written in this period), where the narrator refers to some sort of otherworldly force that exerts an influence on the writer and allows him to generate his novelistic world.[14] The other major indication is to be found in Bely's philosophy of language and the changes it underwent during the late teens and early twenties. Language is the signifying activity that Bely wrote about most. It thus serves as a gauge of the changes in his formalist philosophy.

Philosophy of Language

Is it proper to speak of Bely as having a philosophy of language? Perhaps not in the strict sense in which it is proper to speak of, say, Heidegger as having a philosophy of language. Bely produced no texts that can be said to have resulted from an avowed intention to present a philosophy of language in the traditional sense of this expression. What Bely really appears to have been interested in fundamentally was a theory of meaning. But a theory of meaning for Bely necessarily included a theory of verbal meaning, which is to say a theory of language. Plenty of his writings touch directly or indirectly on language, especially poetic language, and it is possible to discern in each of them a theoretical stance on certain crucial issues in language philosophy. I say "in each of them" because Bely always approaches things from a variety of perspectives and also because his thinking on this subject changed significantly at

14. The passage occurs in the final section of the novel's first chapter. (Bely did not make a single change in this section when he revised the 1916 text in 1922.) There the narrator speaks of "cerebral play," the creative mental force that generates being. He mentions the "incursion into the brain of forces unknown to us" (*vtorzhenie v mozg neizvestnykh nam sil*) and goes on to talk about the states of being that his character, Apollon Apollonovich, occupies. See *Peterburg* (Moscow, 1981), p. 56. In the Maguire and Malmstad translation the line reads: "Cerebral play is only a mask. Under way beneath this mask is the invasion of the brain by forces unknown to us" (*Petersburg*, trans. Robert A. Maguire and John E. Malmstad [Bloomington, Ind., 1978], p. 35). *Petersburg* is certainly not the first place where Bely played with the notion of an interpenetration of the transcendent and the real world. It can be found at least as far back as the *Second Symphony*.

least once. It becomes necessary to distinguish between two broad categories of theoretical stances on the issue of language.

What are the essential texts? The ones Bely wrote during his Symbolist period, particularly "The Magic of Words" and "The Emblematics of Meaning," suggest a clear, formalistic theory of meaning, which I have analyzed in "Bely's Theory of Symbolism as a Formal Iconics of Meaning." Of the texts written after Bely's conversion to anthroposophy, when his thinking on language took a turn toward the mystical, I will consider two, both written in 1917. The first is an essay called "Aaron's Rod (On the Word in Poetry)"; the second is the bizarre *Glossolalia: A Poem about Sound* (not published until 1922), a book-length fantasy about the origins and intrinsic meanings of the sounds of language.

Bely took the same position in the area of language philosophy as in virtually every other area of intellectual and creative activity to which he contributed. The contribution he made—at least in the Symbolist phase of his thinking—was substantial, and yet it was either not recognized or simply not widely known. Here as elsewhere Bely draws from a number of sources but leaves his own mark both by the combination of sources and by the direction he takes. Bely's thinking about language is peculiarly Russian and at the same time very cosmopolitan.

The Russian tradition in language philosophy was already eclectic before Bely came along to mix things up with his own brand of eclecticism. Naftali Prat has pointed out two philosophic lines that must be considered in Russian philosophy of language.[15] The first is Russian Orthodox theology, a largely indigenous tradition, though with foreign roots in Christian Platonism. The other is German idealism. This tradition is exclusively foreign, but its importance for the development of Russian thought in the nineteenth century is so profound and it was translated into a native Russian idiom so extensively that by the time Bely was writing, it, too, for all intents and purposes, might be considered indigenous.

The common element in both traditions is idealism. As Prat says, philosophy of language tends to merge with the Orthodox doctrine of the Logos, and in many works philosophical questions concerning the nature of words and meaning tend to look like theological questions concerning the relation between God and the Word, or God and his name. In fact, Prat points out, as late as 1912 (roughly the time when Bely was producing his most important statements of Symbolist philosophy) an entire group of Russian-language philosophers were engaged in a dispute on the question of *imyaslavie*, or "glorification of the name." The issue was whether God is immediately present in his name or

15. Naftali Prat, "Orthodox Philosophy of Language in Russia," *Studies in Soviet Thought*, no. 20 (1979), pp. 2–21.

whether he is transcendent over it. Given the strength of the religious tradition, it is no surprise that the philosophy of language in Russia should have turned on metaphysical or seemingly metaphysical questions, even when it was not set in a specifically theological context. The whole notion of the debasement of God's Word into material form and the question of the metaphysical status of God's Word are of paramount importance in Orthodox theology.

It is easy to see why Bely was attracted to this area of thought. The combination of native theological idealism and Western philosophical idealism was a perfect fit for Bely's mind. The work of the nineteenth-century Russian philologist Aleksandr Afanas'evich Potebnya (1835–91) provided a specific focus and point of departure for Bely's musings in the philosophy of language. Potebnya wrote a great many books and articles on language, specifically on literary language, but the fundamental principles of his theory were worked out in his first major work, *Thought and Language*, which was published in 1862.[16] Bely wrote a critique of this work in an article published in 1910 in the short-lived Russian journal *Logos*.[17] The article is an immensely important document though it is seldom referred to, undoubtedly because very few copies of the journal found their way to the West. It is as informative about Bely's own philosophy of language as it is about Potebnya, and for that reason it bears close examination here.

Bely's critique of Potebnya turns on a debate that Potebnya had taken up from the German philologist Wilhelm von Humboldt (1767–1835), who was as influential for Potebnya as Potebnya was for Bely. The debate was between the "nativist" view of language on the one hand, according to which words are naturally generated by a necessary connection with the things they designate, and a "geneticist" view on the other hand, according to which words are creatively generated by the individual speaker or by an entire nation. Humboldt subscribed to the geneticist point of view. In his posthumously published introduction to a work (never completed) on Kavi, the ancient language of Java, Humboldt distinguished between the notion of language as *ergon*, or finished product, and language as *energeia*, or activity, holding that only the *energeia* view is correct.[18] The *ergon* view of language is a nativist one, since according to it language is already complete, having been generated by necessary and intrinsic connections between words and things. The *energeia* view, on the other hand, is geneticist, since according to it language

16. Potebnya, *Mysl' i yazyk* (Kharkov, 1862).
17. "Mysl' i yazyk: Filosofiya yazyka A. A. Potebni," *Logos*, no. 2 (1910), pp. 240–58.
18. Wilhelm von Humboldt, *Über die Verschiedenheit des menschlichen Sprachbaues und ihren Einfluss auf die geistige Entwicklung des Menschengeschlechts*, in *Wilhelm von Humboldts gesammelte Schriften*, ed. Albert Leitzmann (Berlin, 1907; reprinted Berlin, 1968), VII, 1–344. The *ergon–energeia* distinction occurs on pp. 44–46.

is creatively generated. Humboldt's fundamental conviction was that language is a continuing creative activity in which all the members of a community of speakers, or nation, participate. He rejected the mystical laws of correspondence, by which certain traditional views of language account for the connections between words and things, in favor of an ineffable notion of necessity, by which language organically expresses national character. In the nativist view the creation of language has already taken place in some mythical past; in the Humboldtian view the process is always going on in the present.

Potebnya, as Bely shows, came down on the side of the geneticists. For Humboldt, the *energeia* conception of language meant that language production stemmed from unconscious impulses in the speaker. Potebnya, however, was a modern scientist and psychologist, Bely says, and was thus inclined to be a bit less vague than Humboldt, asserting a precise connection between language production and psychophysiological phenomena.

But Bely shrewdly and rightly saw that the great Russian linguist was really far less of a geneticist than he held himself to be. One of the continuing themes of Potebnya's work, from the early *Thought and Language* to his posthumously published works on the theory of literature, was the notion of "inner form." Humboldt had used the term *innere Sprachform* to refer to the principle by which the creative production of language works harmoniously with the actual sounds of language so as to produce a kind of necessary fit between the two.[19] The term is not defined with great scientific precision, but it is certainly used in a way that is consistent with Humboldt's geneticist concept of language. Potebnya unwittingly abandoned the geneticist stance, Bely shows, by insisting on a new view of inner form that placed language back in the old static, nativist conception. Inner form for Potebnya has to do with the inseparability of idea and image, or concept and sound. In fact, in passages that Bely does not mention, Potebnya explains that the vividness of a word, its fidelity to its own inner form, is a function of its closeness to its etymological root, as if the etymological root represented a state of prehistoric linguistic purity in which words were endowed by nature with the power to signify exactly what they signified.[20] Bely calls Potebnya's revised doctrine a "mysticism of the word itself," remarking also that Potebnya, strangely enough, arrived at this most unscientific aspect of his theory from a purely scientific point of departure in linguistics, grammar, and psychology.[21]

By reviving the old myth of a necessary correspondence between the sign and the signified, Potebnya flew in the face of his mentor, Hum-

19. Ibid., pp. 86–94.
20. Potebnya, *Mysl' i yazyk*, 5th ed. (Kiev, 1926), pp. 77–78.
21. Bely, "Mysl' i yazyk," p. 251.

boldt, and his ideas had lasting consequences in language philosophy over the next few generations. The characteristic late nineteenth- and early twentieth-century distinction between poetry and prose in all likelihood has its origin right here in Potebnya's theory of inner form. The idea is that there is an intrinsic difference between the language of poetry and the language of prose. The distinction rests on the feeling that poetic words of necessity signify their objects with a freshness that brings the objects to perception with extreme clarity and also calls attention to the words themselves. Prosaic words, on the other hand, owing to frequent use in ordinary conversation and to the consequent loss of freshness that habitual use entails, signify their objects purely by an automatic, conventional association between word sound and object.

The notion of a specific difference between poetic language and prosaic language was by no means new in Potebnya's or Bely's era; it goes back at least as far as Aristotle and was an article of faith in Romantic poetics. Humboldt had argued for a distinction between poetry and prose, claiming that poetic language is by nature similar to music and is capable of apprehending reality directly in its sensible appearances. Prose, in Humboldt's estimation, is better suited to the expression of scientific truths and the truths of everyday life. Humboldt even anticipated the modern theory of poetic language, referring to the phenomenon whereby metaphors gradually lose their vividness and autonomy through repeated use until they become mere conventional signs.[22]

But for Humboldt the myth of language was consistently an organic one, the myth that the speakers of a nation are always creating language as part of some vaguely defined vital process. The creative impulse is always there in the present, and it is ultimately the source of the poeticity of poetic language. Potebnya, however, returned to an older myth, the myth of origin, according to which the act of creation has already taken place in an ideal past. The inner form of a word, that vivid image to which the word owes its poetic qualities (if it is a poetic word), is directly linked with the word's earliest known etymological root, and the unwritten assumption is that this root has an inarguable conceptual purity about it.

It is likely that Potebnya's regressive reinterpretation of Humboldt decisively affected the theory of language adopted by the next generation or two of literary theorists in Russia. It is just as likely that Bely had something to do with the trend. Bely's "Magic of Words" is in large part a set of variations on Potebnya, and among its most prominent ideas is the distinction between poetic words as "living" vehicles of signification and prose words as "dead" abstractions. Viktor Shklovsky's early writings reflect the same concerns as we find in "The Magic of Words." His

22. Humboldt, *Gesammelte Schriften*, VII, 193–96, 93–94.

"Resurrection of the Word" (1914) is devoted to exactly the same distinction between vivid poetic words and dead prosaic words that we find in Bely.[23] And in an early critique of Potebnya (1916), Shklovsky attempts to refine Potebnya's account of the poetry–prose distinction by claiming that the true distinguishing quality of the poetic word is not its symbolism or "imaginality" (*obraznost'*) but its "palpability" (*oshchutimost'*).[24] But of course, as Shklovsky's earlier article shows, the palpability of a word derives from the very same semimystical qualities as the ones on which Potebnya had based his theory. The strangely nonformalistic orientation of Shklovsky's early writings represents an early attempt in Russian Formalism to provide an account of the specificity of poetic language, something that later writers, such as Roman Jakobson, would attempt to do with a greater semblance of scientific rigor.

The visionary writings of such Russian Futurists as Velimir Khlebnikov and Aleksey Kruchenykh give a similar view of language, beginning at roughly the same time that Bely wrote "The Magic of Words." Their theory of an ideal *zaum'*, or "transrational" language (to which, incidentally, Shklovsky devoted another of his early writings),[25] a language capable of speaking the world in a direct and immediate fashion or creating worlds by means of the immediate signifying power of transrational words, arises from the assumption that the words of contemporary language have been bled of their intrinsic signifying powers. When Khlebnikov and Kruchenykh were not simply inventing sound combinations out of caprice, they, like Potebnya, equated linguistic purity with etymological archetypes, finding their own state of Edenic perfection in specifically Slavic rather than Indo-European roots.[26]

In charging Potebnya with espousing a "mysticism of the word itself," Bely appears perhaps to open himself to the charge of hypocrisy. Isn't this, after all, his own position in "The Magic of Words"? There is no doubt that Bely believed strongly in the specificity of poetic language. But he stopped short of declaring that poetic words "have" magic, as the title of his essay might lead us to think. "Magic" for Bely merely described the ability of words, particularly poetic words, to conjure up existence in the form of meanings. I have argued this point in "Bely's Theory of Symbolism as a Formal Iconics of Meaning." Nonetheless, Bely's role in formulating the terms of the poetry–prose polarity in the

23. Viktor Shklovsky, "Voskreshenie slova," in *Texte der russischen Formalisten*, ed. Jurij Striedter (Munich, 1969–72), II, 2–17.

24. Viktor Shklovsky, "Potebnya," in *Poetika: Sborniki po teorii poeticheskogo yazyka* (Petrograd, 1919), pp. 3–6.

25. Shklovsky, "O poezii i zaumnom yazyke," in *Poetika*, pp. 13–26.

26. See, for example, Aleksey Kruchenykh and Velimir Khlebnikov, "Slovo kak takovoe," and Kruchenykh, "Deklaratsiya slova kak takovogo" and "Novye puti slova," all in *Manifesty i programmy russkikh futuristov*, ed. Vladimir Markov (Munich, 1967), pp. 53–58, 63–64, 64–73.

early twentieth century—seeing it, that is, as a distinction between words that call attention to themselves as words and words that simply stand in place of a concept—must be recognized.

If Potebnya was less of a geneticist than he thought, he still strongly endorsed the Humboldtian notion of language as *energeia*, feeling that language and poetry both stem from some undefinable creative source. This is the subject of another of Bely's insightful historical comments, one that sheds light on both Potebnya and Bely himself. Potebnya's adoption of the *energeia* concept, Bely felt, led him to anticipate some of the most important trends in modern criticism. Why? The logical consequence of the *energeia* concept, which stresses the creative capacity of the speaker and of language itself, is a view of language as autonomous and objective. If language is, as Bely expresses the Humboldtian conception, "living, ceaseless activity" with its own dynamic force, then to a certain extent it escapes both the world to which it refers and the speaker who generates it. And, once again, while this view is supported in part by the least scientific aspect of Potebnya's theory—namely, his assertion that language and poetry stem from the same vaguely defined creative source—still, Potebnya's point of departure was scientific. For this reason he was a modernist *avant la lettre*.

Here is how Bely says it: "Long before contemporary criticism, [Potebnya] had already erected a bridge joining the investigations of science with the ardent preaching of the independent status of artistic creation by contemporary innovators in art—and all because he unified the production of the activity of language with the production of poetry, seeing both as the products of a single creative urge [*tvorchestvo*]." Potebnya had thus anticipated all modern criticism by proclaiming the autonomy of the poetic word, just as Stéphane Mallarmé had done (Bely mentions Mallarmé in this article), just as Bely had done, and just as the Futurists and the Formalists would do after him. Moreover, as Bely points out, the specific reason for the autonomy of the poetic word, the reason it may be justifiably called "the word as such" (*slovo kak takovoe*— Bely uses the same term that the Futurists were to canonize in subsequent years) is precisely the "inseparability of idea and image," that is, the almost mystical correspondence between the inner form of a word and the concept with which it is associated (since in Potebnya's theory words stand for concepts, not for things).[27]

Bely is pointing to something that emerges in "The Magic of Words," something that truly is modern in literary theory and aesthetics. It is an ontological interest in language. Any assertion of the autonomy of the poetic word already implies a way of thinking about language that calls into question language's peculiar mode of being. "The Magic of Words"

27. "Mysl' i yazyk," pp. 245, 252.

is concerned somewhat less with the mode of being of language than with the mode of being of the meanings of language. Toward the end of the essay Bely refers to the power of literary creation to generate "ontological being independently of our consciousness."[28] But the orientation of the inquiry is ontological, and Bely's identification of Potebnya as a precursor in this trend is an important contribution to our understanding of both the history of modernism and Bely's position in that history.

The part of Bely's article that reveals the most about Bely himself, in addition to providing an astute commentary on Potebnya, is the part that discusses Potebnya's psychologism. Potebnya had attempted to base his linguistic theories on a notion of psychophysiological parallelism, according to which a necessary, physiologically based response to the sensual perception of language is responsible for actualizing meaning. Bely, of course, does not agree, and so he offers first a patronizing explanation for Potebnya's misconception and then an equally patronizing correction. Potebnya simply had the misfortune to live in an age heavily inclined toward psychologism and its excesses. What is the truth that Potebnya was missing?

> The "psychic" life of the word, the laws of this life may be established only formally, and are, moreover, outside the boundaries of psychology as a science. The psychology of literary art [slovesnost'] is in essence a theory of values of the word, considered from the point of view of its [the word's] irrational content. Such a theory requires no psychological foundation. The systematizing of this content is the domain of aesthetics. And Potebnya in fact was inclined in this direction, but became entangled in the psychological theories of his day. Indeed, the problem of values, seen as an epistemological problem, had not yet been distinctly advanced in Potebnya's time in quite the way that it is advanced, for example, in the Freiburg school.[29]

In other words, Bely is defending Potebnya's psychologistic tendencies by pointing out that the great linguist did not have the benefit of Neo-Kantian value philosophy. Bely had already introduced his readers to the problem of values in "The Emblematics of Meaning." There he refers repeatedly to Heinrich Rickert, the Freiburg Neo-Kantian whose name is most closely associated with the notion of values. Rickert's theory was that acts of value recognition form an integral part of ordinary, scientific understanding, which, Rickert believed (in defiance of Kant), contained an element of willing (since values are established and recognized by the will). In "The Emblematics of Meaning" Bely establishes the idea of value as a formal first principle, arguing for a type of meaning

28. Cassedy, Selected Essays, p. 109.
29. Bely, "Mysl' i yazyk," p. 249.

apprehension that *formally* recognizes value as if it were the metaphysical source of all signifying objects (such as artworks, words, icons).

Bely never explicitly states in his essay that his own theory of Symbolism is purely formalistic, but the conclusion is inescapable. In the passage I just quoted from the Potebnya essay, it is clear that Bely is making this claim for philosophy of language in general. For, by saying that the laws of the psychic life of the word lie outside psychology and may be established only *formally*, by adding that problems of this sort belong properly to aesthetics and epistemology, Bely is really arguing for a nonempirical ("presuppositionless," as Edmund Husserl, a contemporary antipsychologistic thinker, would say), strictly formal and logical approach to the problem of meaning.

The very cornerstone of Bely's Symbolist theory of meaning is the idea that signifying objects invite from the perceiver the same cognitive stance as religious objects, with the difference that, in the case of non-religious signifying objects, the cognitive stance is a purely formal, "as if" sort of stance. One confronts a signifying object *as if* it were a hypostatic emanation of a metaphysical essence, even though one may not assume on faith the actual existence of such an essence. And one thus confronts a (poetic) word *as if* it bore a necessary, mystical connection with its referent, even though one may not actually believe this (on faith) to be the case.

This brings us right back to Bely's dual pull toward the strict logic of epistemology on the one hand and theology on the other. The formalistic approach to meaning theory already shows the two tendencies all by itself. But in this case it is probably sufficient to say simply that Bely's approach is Kantian, pure and simple. The model of a cognitive stance operating *in a purely formal manner*, like the sort of superhuman knowledge that could have the transcendent as an object, is entirely analogous to Kant's faculties of judgment, whose task it is to bridge a gap left in ordinary knowledge by operating under the purely formal presupposition of such unknowables as purpose and beauty in nature.

All of this applies to Bely's language theory as it stood during his Symbolist period. A crucial change occurs, however, in his next phase of pronouncements on language, the one that includes "Aaron's Rod" and *Glossolalia*. As I mentioned earlier, both pieces were written in 1917, when Bely was a devout anthroposophist. While Bely is said to have remained a faithful anthroposophist until his death, this is the period when anthroposophical thought finds its most unmistakable expression in his writings.

Perhaps the most amazing thing about "Aaron's Rod" is Bely's mystifying failure to exploit the metaphorical possibilities of his title. The essay is about the signifying powers of language, and Bely has chosen for his title an allusion to an Old Testament story that is precisely about language, signifying, and revealed truth. Aaron is the elder brother of Moses, and, because he is the more eloquent of the two brothers, God appoints him to be Moses' spokesman before Pharoah. God gives Moses a rod that has the magical power to turn into a serpent. This instrument of divine revelation will help to convince the Egyptians that, in seeking the release of the Israelites from bondage, the wielder of the rod speaks with the authority of God. Since it is Aaron who will be doing the talking, the rod is given to him, to enhance his already formidable native eloquence—a perfect central image for an essay by a thinker who customarily exploits the analogy between the language of poetry and the language of divine revelation. But for some strange reason Bely uses the image of Aaron's rod to describe one of his pet bugbears, abstract words. Such words, instead of being wise and living serpents, are mere lifeless rods, says Bely in a metaphor as wooden as its own object of comparison.

In any case, toward the end of "Aaron's Rod" Bely returns to the problem of sound and thought, the same problem he had addressed in the Potebnya essay (which was a critique of Potebnya's book on this problem). He points out the difficulties that arise if one adheres to either of two extreme points of view on the subject: the aestheticist view, which insists on a literal identity between sound and thought, and the rationalist view, which denies any such identity. Each of these positions, Bely maintains, results in an impasse.

How do we escape the impasse and resolve the patent contradiction between sound and thought in language as we know it? Here is where Bely strikes out most unabashedly in favor of a metaphysically grounded philosophy. The solution, he says, lies "in the creation of a new world of verbal speech and meaning in the image and likeness of the past: in the act of creation. About this past," he continues, "we already know: it is the word that was with God."[30]

The entire essay is full of linguistic mysticism of the type that Bely only seven years earlier had accused Potebnya of practicing. Bely seems aware of some of the latest developments in the philosophy of meaning. He begins his essay, for example, with an apparent nod to Husserl (and mentions him by name later on in the essay), asserting that meaning can be defined as an "object." But he then spends his time developing a notion of language entirely incompatible with the rarefied logical purity of Husserl.

Language is clearly assigned a position of logical priority over all existence in "Aaron's Rod." Meaning and consciousness themselves come into being only with language. Reality derives from cognition, a perfectly acceptable idealist view, but cognition in turn derives from poetic language (*slovesnost'*—a word roughly comparable to the German *Dichtung*,

30. "Zhezl Aarona (O slove v poezii)," *Skify*, no. 1 (1917), p. 205.

meaning something like "artistic verbal creation"). Indeed, Bely claims at one point, the root of a word is equivalent to the beginning of the emergence of reality itself. The essence of a word is its creative mythical power and may be "fully expressed only in myth." Bely speaks unhesitatingly of a "faith" in *slovesnost'* that accepts the existence of an ideal Word underlying all words. To bolster this position of faith, Bely has recourse to much of the same Johannine theological vocabulary he had exploited in "The Emblematics of Meaning." Here, however, Bely appears to expect his readers to take the use of such vocabulary seriously. "The new poetry," he says at one point, referring to the type of literary creation practiced by those with the "faith" I have just mentioned, "arises on the lips of those who have in truth seen the Image [*Lik*] of the living Word, who raise and nourish It as their own secret word, with all the enthusiasm of a true life's exploit."[31] The final sentence of the book refers to the "Second Coming of the Word."

Glossolalia, written in the same year as "Aaron's Rod," shows the same kind of thinking.[32] In fact, the very choice of a subject for this book already indicates the mystical bent in Bely's thinking. Bely's purpose is to investigate the intrinsic meanings of sounds, which he sees as intimately connected with gestures, these gestures being, in turn, intimately attuned to our cognitive processes. If we read *Glossolalia* as an exposition of linguistic theory, we are likely to be struck primarily by its utter madness. But Bely subtitles his work *A Poem about Sound* (*Poema o zvuke*), suggesting that we are dealing not with a theoretical work at all but with some sort of long narrative poem and consequently must not look for the kind of philosophical positions we would expect to find in an overtly theoretical work. Either way, it is clear that Bely has, at least for the moment, gone over to an attitude of mystical faith in his approach to language.

It would be wrong to describe Bely's language philosophy during his anthroposophical period as being continuous with the formalistic tendency that had been there from the beginning and through his Symbolist period, especially if we define "anthroposophical period" as the time from Bely's conversion until his death. After *Glossolalia* the picture is at best confused. Bely wrote little that is even indirectly concerned with a theory of language. The most one can do is attempt to discern an implicit theory in his subsequent writings on literary subjects. The two significant remaining works are *Rhythm as Dialectics and "The Bronze Horseman"* (1929), which modifies Bely's earlier theories of rhythm by tortuously superimposing upon them an absurd left-Hegelian theory of

31. Ibid., pp. 166, 177, 190.
32. *Glossolaliya: Poema o zvuke* (Berlin, 1922). The book's title was mistakenly printed *Glossaloliya,* but the error was not Bely's, and it is customary now to cite the book with the title corrected.

dialectical materialism, and the posthumously published *Gogol's Crafts-manship* (1934).[33] But neither of these works is much help in pointing toward anything like a philosophy of language. *Rhythm as Dialectics*, in its nondogmatic passages, is an exercise in numerical analysis, like the studies of rhythm published in *Symbolism,* and *Gogol's Craftsmanship* is largely a work of descriptive criticism (though a brilliant one).

The confusion is not restricted to Bely's theory of language. An attempt to characterize Bely's thought in general from the early twenties until his death encounters enormous difficulties. On the one hand, we have all the biographical and autobiographical evidence that Bely remained a confirmed anthroposophist until the very end, despite his break with the official organization in the early twenties. On the other hand, we have Bely's admittedly disingenuous claims in the late twenties and early thirties that he had become a materialist and left-Hegelian. Either way, Bely's ideas about language in the twenties veered sharply from the mystically oriented positions of his 1917 writings, as the two works of criticism I have just mentioned clearly indicate.

Placing Bely

Any final assessment of Bely's place in modern thought will reflect positively on his modernity. In view of the ideological confusion in Bely's later writings, it would be safe to say that, with one or two exceptions, only his writings of the Symbolist period are worth considering in this historical perspective. And it would be safe to characterize Bely's contribution to modern thought by saying that it covers three closely related areas: poetics, philosophy of language, and general philosophy of meaning.

Bely was also an enormously gifted critic, as *Gogol's Craftsmanship* clearly shows, and his contribution in this area is substantial. But I regard this as a separate subject, and not because criticism is implicitly distinct from (or inferior to) thought. Literary criticism and scholarship always imply an underlying theory. The odd thing about Bely, however, is that his practical criticism, of the sort that we see in *Gogol's Craftsmanship,* never appears to bear any relation to what he is saying in his more purely (and abstractly) theoretical writings. Pure theory and practice just seem to be separate.

Placing Bely in the history of poetics is a fairly simple matter, because the task has already been done by other figures in that same history. Bely's essential contribution here was the method of rhythmic analysis

33. *Ritm kak dialektika i "Mednyi vsadnik"* (Moscow, 1929); *Masterstvo Gogolya* (Moscow and Leningrad, 1934).

he proposed in "Lyric Poetry and Experiment" and the three accompanying essays published in *Symbolism*. Roman Jakobson assigns these essays a seminal role in the development of modern metrical analysis,[34] and many subsequent writers, from Viktor Zhirmunsky to Vladimir Nabokov, have agreed with this view.

In the areas of language philosophy and theory of meaning, Bely's contribution is less obvious, and it has gone relatively unnoticed. One can assign Bely a place and compare him with other thinkers, but always with the awareness that important contacts that could have taken place never did. But the time has come to recognize that contribution as the formidable intellectual accomplishment it is. The most striking thing about the Symbolist theory of meaning is that Bely, whose contemporaries (especially the Formalists) were so eager to assail the metaphysical leanings of his Symbolist writings and the insufficient scientific rigor of his metrical studies, should be the one figure in the line extending from Potebnya to the Formalists whose philosophy of meaning actually manages a theoretically plausible, logically defensible accommodation of a traditional mystical view of signifying objects and the sort of scientific conventionalism that Ferdinand de Saussure and his legacy would canonize in the twentieth century. Bely's idea of signifying objects as symbols that human perception regards *as if* they bore a necessary, direct connection to some independent realm of being (truth, the transcendent, ordinary reality), but without making a firm claim *on faith* either for the existence of that connection or for its actual accessibility through symbolic objects, incorporates both views without losing itself in mystical speculation.

When Bely turns specifically to language, the mark of his modernity is his stress on both the creative aspect of language and its objectivity and autonomy. One of the might-have-beens of Bely scholarship is Bely's connection with the phenomenological movement that followed him. Bely knew some of the early works of Husserl. But Husserl knew nothing of Bely, and there is certainly no evidence that later phenomenologists who wrote on the philosophy of language, such as Roman Ingarden and Maurice Merleau-Ponty, knew the first thing about him, either. And yet Bely's value-based theory of language anticipates the phenomenological theories in a most important respect. Ingarden, for one, insisted on the creative aspect of language, on the gap that exists between a speaker's intent in composing discourse and the final meaning of that discourse. The point for Ingarden was that the meaning of a discourse, owing to the dynamic, generative capacity of language, will surpass the speaker, whose job, especially if he is a literary artist, is to make his intent conform to what his discourse (or artwork) has revealed

34. Roman Jakobson, *Selected Writings* (The Hague, 1979), V, 569–70.

itself—even to him, the speaker—to mean.[35] Ingarden, too, proposed a formalistic theory of value in his investigation of the cognition of literary artworks. The ultimate object of literary cognition for Ingarden is something defined as "value," just as it is for Bely.[36]

Merleau-Ponty stressed the dynamic power of language, which allows meaning at the level of an utterance to transcend the mere syntactic summation of the meanings of the individual words that make up that utterance. There is a leap, in other words, from the constituent words of an utterance to the moment when "something has been said."[37] In both views, precisely because it has a creative power of its own, language comes to occupy a position that is autonomous and objective relative to the speaker-creator.

For Bely, too, language is a dynamic and creative medium. His comments on Potebnya's modernism show complete solidarity with the use of Humboldt's *energeia* model and with the consequences that the use of this model leads to. For Bely just as for Potebnya, the creativity of language is what renders its ultimate meaning autonomous and objective. His ontological arguments in "The Magic of Words" are ample testimony to this tenet.

Still, there is no denying that Bely's philosophy of language presents confusions that his successors were able to escape. I have already discussed many of them. But the fundamental confusion is the one that arises from the dualistic tendency that is the theme of this essay. The pull toward the metaphysical always remained strong for Bely. So strong, in fact, that the characterization of him as a formalist has to be made in spite of him, for he would have been unlikely to agree. But we should not let Bely's confusion become ours, because in the end the picture that emerges, the reconciliation of the logical and the metaphysical that Bely has effected, really is singular in his age and really almost works. Succeeding generations would have had much to learn from him had he been luckier—and had he written more coherently.

35. On this point, see William S. Hamrick, "Ingarden and Artistic Creativity," *Dialectics and Humanism*, 2, no. 4 (1975), pp. 39–49. On the ability of language to surpass its creator's intention, see especially pp. 46–48.

36. See Roman Ingarden, *Vom Erkennen des literarischen Kunstwerks* (Darmstadt, 1968), sec. 24, "Das ästhetische Erlebnis und der ästhetische Gegenstand," pp. 181–226; published in English as *The Cognition of the Literary Work of Art*, trans. Ruth Ann Crowley and Kenneth R. Olson (Evanston, Ill., 1973), sec. 24, "The Aesthetic Experience and the Aesthetic Object," pp. 175–218.

37. On the question of how an utterance can "suddenly contract into a single signification," see Merleau-Ponty, "On the Phenomenology of Language," in *Signs*, trans. Richard C. McCleary (Evanston, Ill., 1964), pp. 84–97, especially p. 91.

10

Seeing and Hearing Andrey Bely:
Sketches from Afar

Dmitry Maksimov

These are random sketches that do not add up to a general picture. I do not have sufficient material for that. I do not even have the right to call myself an acquaintance of Andrey Bely, as there were no long-standing ties between us. I was born a quarter of a century after him; therefore I can regard myself as his contemporary only with considerable reservation. When all is said and done, I observed him from a distance: as a very unprepared young man I attended several of his public lectures in the 1920s. I had occasion to speak with him only once, although I must say that our long conversation had a great deal of substance to it.

All the same, it seems to me that I do have the right to offer such a profile. If we wish to show a writer as he was in life, like any other man, as well as in his art, it helps to look at him from various angles and perspectives, close and distant.

Where should I begin?

If I am to be faithful to the sequence of my impressions, I must first recall the time when the image of Bely arose from a book, as a printed text, a disembodied author.

The first work of his I happened to read was the novel *Kotik Letaev*, published in the miscellany *The Scythians* (*Skify*). I read it in 1919 or 1920, when I was no more than fifteen. I had grown up in a family with populist traditions, and I took a dilettantish interest in the "exact sciences." I was completely unprepared to read Bely. Moreover, hearsay had inclined me to approach Bely and the Symbolists in general warily,

Translated by Robert A. Maguire and John E. Malmstad. The text first appeared under the title "O tom, kak ya videl i slyshal Andreya Belogo," in *Zvezda*, no. 7 (1982). It was revised and shortened by the author for this translation.

to see them as "twisted little lordlings," decadents, and "individualists" who were sacrilegiously ignoring social issues.

But to my surprise, I found *Kotik Letaev* gripping. To help myself understand the novel, I even wrote out a rather long analysis based on my first impressions. As I remember, my composition reflected many of my earlier prejudices toward the "decadents," which ultimately derived from articles by Nikolay Mikhailovsky and those who thought like him. Surprisingly enough, however, something else besides a modicum of grumbling was present in my "opus": my naïve astonishment at the new and hitherto unsuspected image of the world that unfolded in the novel, and at the hitherto unknown verbal forms that registered this perception.

What I found most gripping about my discovery was the sense the author managed to convey of the connection between human consciousness (the infant Kotik), as it was in the process of being born and imagining itself, and that which was fathomless and strange, the whole of the universe, images of the chaos of the universe as it seethed in turbulent and menacing whirlwinds. (When I think of this now I recall Mikhail Vrubel's picture of a child in a baby carriage with eyes wide open, eyes blank or wild, and filled with an immense superhuman thought—an image that seems to anticipate the world of *Kotik Letaev*.) My perception of this association shattered some of my youthful prejudices against Bely, and I now think it may have been possible because I was still an adolescent with a living memory of a childhood that antedated memory and time, and had not yet suppressed those preexperiences of infancy which linked me to Bely's hero. They were more authentic for me than for the adults in my family.

I now wonder if this was mysticism. Probably not, or at least only a shadow of it. Do we need this weighty word here? If we try to get at the origins of what we see in *Kotik Letaev*, we find that it is a mysterious realm unilluminated by consciousness, unnamed by human language, a flickering indication of the homeland we all share—the universe. It is a mystery inseparable from life itself, from science, philosophy, and poetry, an intuitive, irresistibly attractive image of existence in the process of being generated. What good here is a label that would seem to define the indefinable? The word "mysticism" does not suffice to cover a mystery best regarded pristinely and in silence. Mysticism, as I understand it, consists in thinking through to the end that which is inexpressible, in arbitrary attempts to decipher and solve it. In *Kotik Letaev* we find instead confirmation of the existence of an immense, unfathomable, and formless mystery, an attempt to convey it in images or intuitions that seem neither real nor wholly conventional, and most important, with no crude demands for acknowledgment of their adequacy to that which lies beyond them.

Perhaps, in simpler form, that was also the case with such Romantic writers as Vasily Zhukovsky. Zhukovsky (or Robert Southey, whom he translated) was hardly so naive as to believe in the "real," earthly or semi-earthly existence of his corpses that galloped on horseback, witches, and devils with claws, but undoubtedly he believed in what lay behind these images and peered out—the reality of mysterious evil forces that do exist in the world.

Be that as it may, while I was reading *Kotik Letaev,* I too wanted to believe that the author, when he looked at the world through the eyes of a child, was not mistaken in saying that "the armchairs wearing grayish, severe dustcovers and thrusting forth in the deaf-mute darkness" of the empty rooms had some relation to eternity. Like the hero of the novel and its creator, I too was still capable of feeling that the cry "Lion's coming," which Kotik often heard and which announced the appearance of a real Saint Bernard named Lion (Leo) somewhere between the Arbat and Sobach'ya (Dog) Square, could and did summon out of the darkness of the subconscious the image of an immense shaggy lion's muzzle in "the yellowgens of sands," and immediately thereafter unfathomable premythological images of some kind—"memory about memory"—images of a certain unimaginably solemn event in a dark antiquity that was inaccessible to human thought.

Convincing and gripping too were those images of the real, everyday world that surrounded Kotik as he grew up and were the opposite of the deliriums of his earliest childhood. These images were light- and warmth-filled impressions of the material world, nature and people, such as his governess and friend Raisa Ivanovna. She was a young girl who was comfortable to be with, and the epithet "nice" accompanied her as a leitmotif.

As I look back now, I come to the following conclusion: *Kotik Letaev* and the poetry of Blok, which completely bowled me over at almost the same time, proved decisive in the formation of my literary inclinations and ultimately brought me to the study of Symbolism. It was Bely and Blok themselves, as creative artists—not any of the people in their circles—who gave me the necessary push to embark on this difficult and lonely journey that by no means met with everyone's approval. I am glad that when I met Andrey Bely as an adult I did not neglect to tell him what *Kotik Letaev* had meant to me and what role it had played in my life.

I read *Kotik Letaev* and, shortly thereafter, *Petersburg,* Bely's most significant work and the best Russian novel of the twentieth century. It was not long before I saw the author himself with my own eyes.

Those were difficult times. The Civil War was still in progress, NEP was just getting under way, Russia and its two capitals were starving. But intellectual and artistic life in Russia's large cities had not ceased and in fact was reaching levels of rare intensity and great energy. Andrey Bely was also caught in this vortex. He froze in unheated rooms and stood in lines to buy cabbage, but he never lost his potential for spiritual and creative work, and he continued to do a great deal of writing and lecturing. He had yet to experience the breach with his surroundings that became all too apparent only a few years later.

Though a native of Moscow, Bely lived in Petrograd in 1920–21. I did not know him by sight and would not have recognized him had I encountered him on the street or in the House of Writers on Basseinaya (now Nekrasov) Street. There of an evening Petersburg intellectuals, hungry but yearning for impressions of a life far removed from their surroundings, would gather to listen to regularly scheduled lectures, chat, or buy a little collection of new poems and *The Herald of Literature* (*Vestnik Literatury*), a slim journal produced on newsprint.

But finally Bely appeared before me as a living person. As I observed in one of the notebooks I kept then, this event took place on May 20, 1921, at an open evening session of Vol'fila (The Free Philosophical Association), which I had the temerity to visit now and then, even though I was more or less underage. At that time Vol'fila was located on the Fontanka, in house no. 50, on the corner of Grafsky Lane, now Mariya Ul'yanova Street. The particular session that I attended was devoted to a report by Ol'ga Forsh, who was not yet famous, on *Petersburg*.

I remember her low-pitched voice as she read. I could not fully take in what she was saying: it was too difficult for me. "Miss Forsh" (that is the old-fashioned way I jotted it down) made no attempt at popularization. Later on her article "The Sung Herbarium" ("Propetyi Gerbarii"), published in the 1925 miscellany *Contemporary Literature* (*Sovremennaya Literatura*), helped me to make sense of what I had heard. It grew out of the lecture and no doubt had much in common with it. As I now read the article and look through the brief notes I made on the lecture, I must admit that the lecture—though intelligent and interesting, like the article itself—was meandering and overcomplicated and did not provide a very precise evaluation of the novel. Forsh had a great deal to say about the way in which the characters created by Bely, Pushkin, and Dostoevsky were related, but she detected in *Petersburg* a departure from an earlier "carnally spiritual literature" and the achievement of a new, purely spiritual art through which the life of the universe could be perceived. (This had a different ring to it in the article.)

It seemed to me then that there was a great distance between the text of the novel and the lecturer's interpretation, that she did not find everything in the novel congenial, and that the audience, made up largely of admirers of *Petersburg*, understood that and was therefore on its guard.

Bely himself was in the small audience—someone pointed him out to me. I made the following simpleminded note about him immediately after coming home from Vol'fila. It indicates how childishly naïve I was then. But I was also capable of noticing something objectively, albeit naïvely. "Bely is about thirty-five to forty (hard to tell his age, because he's clean-shaven). Not good-looking [so for some reason it seemed to me then!]. Smiles a lot. Small eyes, sort of dove-colored. Undoubtedly either very nervous or maybe even mentally unbalanced."

After the lecture was over, during the break before the discussion, Bely came up to the person sitting next to me, a lady I did not know.

"I'm terribly tired today," he said, bending down. "And I understood nothing in the lecture."

The only thing I remember of the discussion is the comments made by Nina Gagen-Torn, perhaps the youngest of the Vol'filites and later a professional ethnographer. In a fit of temper she accused the lecturer of failing to understand the novel. But everything—Gagen-Torn's impertinent attack, the lecture itself, everything else—was eclipsed by the statement Bely made.

In a brief, impetuous, and heated speech he touched not so much on what Forsh had said as on the novel itself. I am unable to reconstruct the contents of the speech in any coherent fashion, but I distinctly remember Bely's impassioned outburst about the "sardine tin of horrible contents," the bomb with the ticking clockwork mechanism, which found its way into Senator Ableukhov's study.

"And this bomb," Bely exclaimed, "is in each of us! And it must explode. . . ."

I have no clear picture now of Bely's face as it was that day. What remains in my memory differs slightly from those gauche adolescent notes I have just quoted. But I do distinctly remember Bely's slender, elastic, and unusually agile figure. I remember his quick and very fluid movements, the excitement emanating from him in waves, and that cry, full of pathos, almost a shriek, about the metaphorical bomb within each of us, ready to blow us to bits.

I had another chance to hear Bely that same spring of 1921. Once again I was at a meeting of Vol'fila, which was held to commemorate the hundredth anniversary of Napoleon's death. My notes on that meeting are skimpy and not very revealing. But they do exist and they correspond to what I remember. I see that Bely, in his remarks on that occasion, came right out and called himself an anthroposophist. In addition, he took great exception to the lecture on Napoleon by another Vol'filite, Lev Pumpyansky (later a well-known literary scholar), and he attempted to refute his conclusion that Napoleon was the "culmination of history." He also spoke of the need to keep politics and history separate, as well as of the reconciliation of beauty and physical labor, which must be united in the future by a common creative rhythm. I liked what Bely said, particularly this idea, inasmuch as it opened into the realm of social life. The following note, almost as naïve as the previous one, appears in my notebook: "I find both him [Bely] and his words profoundly congenial."

Soon afterward a shattering event occurred. Even at a time that was rife with tragedies, misfortunes, and losses that stunned and dulled the senses, it shook the Petersburg intelligentsia: the death of Aleksandr Blok. As Marina Tsvetaeva has said, this was a "thunderclap that struck the heart." For many, the death of Blok became a boundary marker that divided their lives into two vitally significant periods: before and after. I still did not know Blok's poetry very well, but something illuminating and powerful in it pulled at me and somehow compelled me to join the crowd of mourners that followed his body to the Smolensky Cemetery. And in the procession, moving with the crowd through the sun-drenched, hot August streets empty of trolleys, I later learned that I had been very close to Bely. He was unkempt, wearing a soldier's greatcoat and leg wrappings, his head drooping, and he wept as he and others carried the open coffin on their shoulders. I did not recognize him in the throng, or did not notice him; I heard of his presence and his appearance only later, from third parties.

Yet the death of Blok bound me to Andrey Bely even more tightly than before. Beyond that, it gave me the opportunity to see Bely at full stature, in all his brilliant and hypnotic charm and talent.

I saw him on a truly memorable day—August 28, 1921. It was a morning meeting of Vol'fila dedicated to the memory of Blok, and it was packed. It seems to me it was not simply a memorial meeting, but an event in the spiritual life of many of those present.

The meeting was held in the great hall of the Russian Geographical Society on Demidov (now Grivtsov) Lane, near the former Haymarket. Throngs of people milled about on the sidewalk in front of the building, in the entryways, on the staircase, all trying to get in. I abandoned all hope of making my way through the front door and upstairs, and quietly joined the others who were standing there. I thought it was hopeless. But before long, something happened which to this day seems incredible to me; the superstitious would perhaps call it providential.

Suddenly a tall lady, no longer young, graying and completely unknown to me, emerged from the entryway, which I had been unable to reach because of the crowd. Skirting the jostling crowd, she walked right up to me, a most ordinary and unremarkable adolescent. Without explanation she told me to follow her. The dense crowd in the vestibule and on the staircase parted before us, impressed, no doubt, by the vigorous stride of the lady, who may have been one of the organizers of the meeting, though possibly I am mistaken. We entered a hall that was filled to overflowing. The intellectual elite were in the majority, the Petrograd intelligentsia that had not yet been sorted out by the Revolution.

"Sit here," my guide said to me.

She indicated an empty place in the front row and, to put it grandly, forever vanished from my life.

It so happened that I was sitting directly opposite the podium. I was surrounded by adults, all highly respectable people, not very far from two women dressed in mourning—Blok's mother and wife, whom I had seen earlier at the Smolensky Cemetery.

Present were friends and acquaintances of the deceased, writers, theater folk, scholars—everyone, young or old, who loved Blok—the cream of the Petersburg intelligentsia of 1921, as well as devotees of the poet from all levels of society, down to his casual admirers who had read only one of his works: *The Twelve* (*Dvenadtsat'*).

Andrey Bely opened the meeting with a few brief words of introduction and then gave a long lecture on Blok. In the second and final part of the meeting, Ivanov-Razumnik and Aaron Steinberg, the philosopher and Vol'filite, shared their reminiscences. The texts of all these speeches were published in Vol'fila's well-known *In Memoriam: Aleksandr Blok* (*Pamyati Aleksandra Bloka* [Petersburg, 1922]). The printed word, however, cannot capture the agitation of the speakers on that occasion and the extraordinary mood which bound them together spiritually.

This meeting, in all its solemn and sad atmosphere, produced an enormous impression on me at age sixteen and forever imprinted itself on my memory. Then and now it seemed to me that the unification that had come about in the hall, the unification of people who were like a family in their sense of a common wound and a common grief, was unique, unprecedented, and very likely possible only at that particular time, when the loss of Blok had just been sustained, when the grave was still fresh, when the wound had not yet begun to heal. Even more, it seemed to me, dimly then, more distinctly now, that the thought shared by all about Blok, sorrowful yet revealing, was so concentrated and was reaching such an intensity during those minutes and hours that the very experience of his death was illuminated and transfigured by this thought, and took on a different quality.

The leading voice in this chorus was Andrey Bely. He was the soul, the spiritual center, the inspiration of this wake, which was attended by so many. If I could have found the appropriate words, I would have said that on that day I saw Andrey Bely not only as an orator and a man but as a *phenomenon*.

He began his introductory remarks by saying that Russia had lost its beloved poet, and, for many of those present, a friend. From that moment the very sound of his ardent voice cast a spell over the hall. He concluded with words full of pathos. They seemed to lift what was taking place out of the ordinary order of things.

"Let those who have come here out of curiosity," Bely proclaimed, "let all those 'alien' to Blok understand that they have no place here. I would ask such people to get up and leave the hall." (Now, when I recall this, I think of the exhortation by the priest which shook the souls of worshipers in early Christian communities and which is preserved to this day in the liturgy: "Catechumens depart!")

A pause followed, a brief moment of anticipation, and something like embarrassment. Of course, no one left the hall, but the tone of the meeting had been established.

I listened to Bely's introductory remarks and the lecture that followed from a seat opposite the podium, as close to him as possible. I was enthralled by his unusual manner as poet-orator and by the powerful lyricism of his words.

Marina Tsvetaeva always maintained that every time Bely appeared he was accompanied by a luminescence, a "delicate flame," as she expresses it in one of her poems. She did not put the word "luminescence" in quotation marks and did not suggest that it should be understood metaphorically. It seems to me that Tsvetaeva's intuition and her talent for seeing, "seeing and nothing more," did not deceive her. It is hard to come up with an explanation for the way she saw him. Was this effect produced by the silver of the hair that still remained at his temples and flew in all directions? Or was it, in fact, some glowing emanation of his spirit, or the luminiferous image of the speaker that arose by association in the minds of the listeners? Or was it all these things? I will not venture to decide. But in all likelihood the phenomenon of luminescence on this memorable day may well have seemed real to others besides Tsvetaeva.

When I now read Bely's words about Blok as published in the Vol'fila volume, they fail to produce the dazzling effect they once did. Much in them looks old-fashioned today; some things, especially in the introductory remarks, seem cerebral, even mannered, full of jargon, and tinged with an anthroposophical symbolism hardly necessary for understanding Blok. But even now I must acknowledge the synthesizing power of Bely's insights and the depth of his perspective on Blok's art. The death of Blok made Bely forget their old feuds and fallings out. In this lecture he created a comprehensive picture of Blok's poetry and made his listeners feel both its breadth and its depth. He especially brought out its all-or-nothing quality, the boundless demands it made on life. Bely spoke of Blok without qualification, lovingly and insightfully, as a Russian national poet who was comparable to the giants of world literature, who stood at the same level as Dante, Goethe, and Pushkin.

It still seems to me that Bely's speech was superior to any I have ever heard for élan, deep spirituality, and power of delivery. Nothing recalled the manner of his "chamber" improvisations, about which memoirists have written, performances accompanied by special gesticulations and pliés, almost dances on a stage. On such occasions Bely was speaking to a select few, sometimes standing at a blackboard, chalk in hand. Now he was in the capacious hall of the Geographical Society, where every-thing worked to produce a different manner: the restraining influence of the large space filled with people, the uniqueness of the moment, the lofty subject matter. This was a ringing oration, laden with pathos, pro-phetic in tone, truly musical, yet utterly devoid of diffuse lyricism and empty rhetoric, an oration that combined emotion and intensity of thought as it soared. Unlike Blok, who was no orator and who delivered his speeches from a prepared text, Bely of course spoke without notes or outlines of any kind, or at least made no use of them as he spoke.

Quotations from Blok's poems punctuated the flow of words. Bely recited them in a loud and melodious voice, bringing out their music without destroying the shifts and subtleties of meaning. All in all, this was a reading full of energy and temperament in which music and meaning were fused. Many quotations did not find their way into the printed text, perhaps for lack of space. But Blok's poem about Russia—"the mare of the steppes"—from the "Kulikovo" cycle especially sticks in my mind. If I am not mistaken, Bely chanted it in its entirety. In any event, I remember it as the musical center of the entire speech.

Everything in this speech—text and verse citations—merged into an organic whole. But above it all stood the image, equally whole, integral, and incongruous with the surroundings, of Bely as ecstatic poet-thinker. Later, when I was developing a passion for poetry, I happened across some lines of Bely's that fit this image, although he had not written them about himself:

> Your speech—prophetic explosions.
> And your eyes—hidden prospiciences:
> Blue, immense breaches
> Into blue, immense expanses.
>   ["To Karl Bauer"]

These lines really seemed to be a portrait that captured the ideal image of Bely as orator, although even then, when I had not completely outgrown my romantic phase, it bothered me a bit to apply them to the actual man who had stood on the podium in a suit coat. It was not something I could talk about with others; it remained private, mine and mine alone.

Only one thing was wrong: the eyes of the poet who spoke that day were not blue, as the verse has it, but light blue, almost white, bluish-white (to some at times they looked mad). But that was the first time I had ever seen them at such close quarters, burning with inspiration, looming over me from the podium, aimed at me and the hall. Those eyes, filled with a bluish-white fire, the silvery halo-like hair at the temples, the little black silk cap, a skullcap like those worn by aged academicians and at one time by medieval alchemists—all that I remember distinctly.

As I left the meeting in Demidov Lane I did not know that it would be quite a while before I saw and heard Bely again. Shortly thereafter he left Russia for several years.

I saw and heard him again at the beginning of 1924. By the time I attended his public lecture at the Petrograd Capella, I was a first-year university student. Shortly before that, Bely had returned from Berlin, where he had witnessed a great deal and had grown thoroughly sick of it. This was the topic of his lecture. I believe this lecture served as the basis for his pamphlet titled *One of the Mansions of the Kingdom of the Shades* (*Odna iz obitelei tsarstva tenei*), dated March 1924.

Bely improvised as he moved from one side of the stage to another, now quickening his pace, now stopping altogether. The very theme of the lecture—his impressions of the chaos and sickness of life in Berlin—and perhaps his subdued mood as well contributed to the diffuseness of his speech and robbed it of the overpowering and inspiring unity that had so gripped me at the Vol'fila memorial service for Blok. His speech did not flow, and he seemed gloomy or preoccupied. On this occasion there was good reason to doubt Tsvetaeva's words about the radiance that accompanied him. In retrospect, I suppose that the labored and uneven quality of his speech came from within—from his preoccupation with the difficult business of adjusting and revaluating his position vis-à-vis the new order of things in Russia.

My impressions of that lecture and of the pamphlet that followed (I recently reread it) make clear that a shift in Bely's outlook had occurred. He perceived "dun-colored" postwar bourgeois Berlin as a kingdom of foxtrotting specters, the pathetic graveyard of a once great German culture. The Russian emigration, which had found a haven in Berlin, seemed to him just as wretched, spiritually bankrupt and creatively impotent. Obviously all Bely's observations and conclusions had been sharpened to the extreme by a blow of exceptional severity—the break with the woman he loved to the point of sheer torment, his wife, Asya.

As far back as 1907–8, while still a young man, Bely had heaped invective on Russian decadence of the garden and literary variety in his columns in *Libra* (*Vesy*). He saw the October Revolution as the spiritual renewal of the world. He accepted the Revolution and moved as close to it as his own outlook permitted. In postwar Berlin his savage contempt for the "bourgeois Sodom," the brutalization of people, the disintegration of the soul, the "tedious boredom," the "organized madness" (terms taken from his own pamphlet) flared up in all its old intensity. Yet when I compare my memory of Bely's lecture with the pamphlet, I am certain that his criticism of the emigration, especially its literary wing, was more extreme in the lecture. (As I recall, he spoke favorably of only one émigré, Sasha Cherny.) And against this "kingdom of the shades" Bely set his faith in revolutionary Russia, its spiritual health, and its drive toward genuine culture.

It was not yet entirely clear to everyone at the time that this lecture reflected Bely's desire to forge firmer links with Soviet life. (People who were ill disposed toward Bely called him a conformist.) Here Bely set out on the journey that eventually led to the book *A Wind from the Caucasus* (*Veter s Kavkaza*) and the three volumes of his memoirs, all of which were written from this new standpoint.

The public that filled the Capella was anything but homogeneous. It is not surprising, therefore, that they listened to Bely intently and reacted in contradictory ways—some with understanding, others with censure. The majority were sympathetic to Bely's new position. But those who were unhappy with it made their attitude known.

I distinctly remember the text of one of the notes (evidently unsigned) which someone sent up after the lecture. Bely read it to the audience with a trembling voice:

"As I listen to you I am ashamed for mankind."

Bely was profoundly agitated and upset by the note, and could not hide his feelings. He seemed disarmed, almost pathetic.

Shortly thereafter, I witnessed a similar incident at one of Mayakovsky's public appearances. After reading aloud an anonymous and truly insulting note, he flew into a rage. He literally began to roar and was ready to smash his invisible enemy right then and there. Bely reacted altogether differently. His gestures and his face showed that pain was greater than rage. I have already noted that he was capable of fierce polemics, impassioned ripostes, and violent attacks, but on this occasion there was something helpless about him. He tried somehow to answer the note—how, exactly, I do not recall (probably no one could recall his half-intelligible words). The only thing that sticks in my memory is his total confusion and the way his tangled reply simply broke off when he invited his unnamed opponent to stop by the greenroom after the lecture to talk things out. That did not happen, and Bely apparently never learned that the note had been written by Anna Akhmatova. (She told me much later.)

Six years passed. During that time Bely published his book of travel sketches, *A Wind from the Caucasus*, the two parts of the novel *Moscow* (*Moskva*), and the book *Rhythm as Dialectics* (*Ritm kak dialektika*). He adapted *Petersburg* for the stage, and it was performed by the Second Moscow Art Theater. A goodly number of works. But interest in their author had noticeably declined. Fewer and fewer of his former readers were left, while the new generation was either unable to accept him or simply could not grasp what he was up to. Bely rarely gave public lectures any more and none at all, it would seem, in Leningrad. I had no occasion to see him again until 1930, when I met and talked with him.

If the reader is to understand what this meeting meant to me, I must say a few words about myself.

I had graduated from Leningrad University. At first I was scraping by on the barest minimum, as they say, doing work that was remote from my main interest. But little by little I was preparing myself for the study of literature, and I never lost sight of my old special interest—Russian Symbolism. This subject was disliked in literary circles and in institutions involved in philological studies. The study of Symbolism was permitted only in bite-sized portions, and on condition that one adopted a harsh attitude toward it. Such an attitude was not to my liking, although, I am sorry to say, that did not prevent a certain sociological bias, albeit quite sincere, from creeping into what I wrote. The bias against Symbolism grew stronger in the mid-thirties. But my situation did not change. When all is said and done, my subject was not quite legitimate, and I found it uncomfortable to carry on my weak shoulders. On those rare occasions when I gave a talk, I was not always treated kindly in the discussion that followed.

All the same, I made my way, slowly and with difficulty, into the subject that exerted such a pull on me and was unknown to the younger generation. Russian Symbolism enticed me with its many riches—its universality, the spirit of world culture that had penetrated to its very depths and had become its flesh. At first I singled out an area that provided a broad background and served as an introduction to the study of the core of Symbolist culture, its poetry. I mean the periodicals of Russian Symbolism. At some point in the future I wanted to write a large monograph based on my work. Naturally, my hopes proved utopian and vain. I had to be satisfied that I managed to write and publish two essays on Symbolist journals—one on *The Northern Messenger* (*Severnyi Vestnik*) and another on *The New Way* (*Novyi Put'*). Then I was faced with the most important part of my plan: the study and description of the most influential and militant organ of the Symbolist press, the journal *Libra*.

I familiarized myself with all the essential materials, first of all with *Libra* itself. I worked in archives and, as far as possible, met with people who had been part of the literary movement at the beginning of the century. Those still alive and accessible could and did provide necessary information. With some of them I established firm and long-lasting ties after these meetings. I talked with Sergey Polyakov, the editor and publisher of *Libra;* with Zhanna Bryusova, wife of the poet; with Petr Pertsov, Korney Chukovsky, Georgy Chulkov, Ivanov-Razumnik, Mikhail Kuzmin, Lyubov' Gurevich, and Konstantin Erberg.

My meeting with Andrey Bely falls into this category. (Of course, the "lyrical" quality of this particular meeting excluded it from all categories and comparisons.) It took place outside Moscow, in the small community of Kuchino, where Boris Nikolaevich, unable to find an apartment in Moscow, had been living for five years.

No one had provided me with an introduction. I was therefore in a state of great agitation as I boarded the train at the Kursk Station, as I made the journey itself, and as I got off at Kuchino and approached the small wooden house that served as Andrey Bely's lodgings. Would I be received, or would I have to return empty-handed? And in part my apprehensions proved to be well founded.

At my knock a middle-aged woman opened the door (the "mistress of the house," the "Cerberus," I thought) and promptly devastated me by announcing: "Boris Nikolaevich is not at home."

I expressed my disappointment, but decided to persist. I did not go away, but seated myself on a nearby bench and said that I would wait. It was summer, and the prospect of waiting did not daunt me.

I whiled away the time by surveying the small yard that adjoined the house. Aside from the house itself, it contained a few trees, a turf-covered ice cellar, and a shed. Next to the yard was a vegetable garden. A quiet, modest, ordinary bit of Moscow suburb! Not far off was a stretch of grass, a wood, and a clearing where Boris Nikolaevich took his daily walks (I learned about them later).

I was correct in surmising that the Cerberus' words—"not at home"—were actually a white lie, a generally accepted tactic, old as the hills, to ward off sudden invasions. I had been waiting less than an hour when the front door flew open and out came Andrey Bely at a brisk clip. He was wearing an overcoat and a hat pulled down over his forehead. Without so much as a greeting, and scarcely looking at me, he began to talk without pause, all in one breath, his voice astonishingly melodious and full of suffering:

"I receive no one, no one, and I cannot receive you. I am busy, busy, extremely busy and have no time at all. . . . And it's hard for me to . . ."

By way of reply I tried to explain that my business with him was quite specific—namely, questions about the history of Symbolism—that I had come from Leningrad specially to talk with him, and finally, that Ivanov-Razumnik had suggested that I turn to him.

When Bely heard all this, he immediately relented and adopted a different tone. His melodious aggressiveness turned to a melodious gentleness that was almost affectionate.

"Please excuse me, *my dear young man,* but I really cannot meet with you today. Would it be convenient for you . . ."

He suggested that I come to see him in a few days, late in the morning. And his farewell was very gentle and kind.

All the way back I was accompanied by his voice, and particularly by "*my dear young man.*" In this expression I seemed to detect a nice old-fashioned Muscovite note that was virtually out of the question in the speech of the Petersburg intelligentsia, such as Blok. And of course it had no trace of condescension about it.

The appointed meeting took place on June 5, 1930. It lasted no less than six hours, and remains in my memory as an immense monologue by Bely, or more precisely, a series of monologues. My contribution consisted of putting questions that got him going, making brief responses, but most of all, listening.

I made two sets of notes on this conversation. One was in a notebook and consisted of a brief account of Bely's answers to my questions about the history of *Libra*. This notebook still exists, and I partially drew on it for one of my published works. Therefore I will not discuss it here. The other reflected my general impressions of the conversation with him, and has long since been lost (rather, it was confiscated during a search in the 1940s). Yet the fact that it *was* made and that I had occasion to tell others of my conversation with Bely before it was lost helped me to preserve some fragments of it in my memory—and I take responsibility for them.

As I have already noted, the house where Bely lived was small, made of wood, and more like a cottage, but winterized. Boris Nikolaevich led me through a small room that looked like a dining room into another, also small, which served as his bedroom and where he evidently worked. It was in this second room that our conversation took place. It was virtually bare, and ascetic as a monk's cell. It contained a table, two or three chairs, and a very simple, neatly made bed. (I later learned that Boris Nikolaevich had still another room in this house where his wife, Klavdiya Nikolaevna, lived. I did not meet her on that occasion, but got to know her and became good friends with her after his death.) There were no bookcases, no piles of books, no pictures you would notice, no comfortable furniture in the room. Tacked to the wall above the head of the bed—for some reason my eyes fastened on it—was a small piece of paper: a laundry list. Only one subject stood out sharply and immediately attracted attention: a large picture of Rudolf Steiner that hung above the bed. The eyes—enormous, intent, burning-black, piercing, hypnotic—instantly fixed on anyone who entered the room and continued to stare, commanding and enigmatic.

When Boris Nikolaevich and I sat down, he began by half apologizing and explaining why he had been unable to receive me the last time. The situation had indeed been unusual. By some strange coincidence (the second miracle that occurred on my journey to Bely), just when I had previously appeared in Kuchino, Bely was being visited by his closest friend and confidant, Ivanov-Razumnik, with whom I too was well acquainted.

"Razumnik Vasil'evich and I talked all night," Bely said. "He was very tired. He lay down to rest and fell asleep, and I didn't want to wake him up when you came. . . . He told me about you in detail."

Then Bely turned to the topic of the conversation at hand. "I have heard that you are interested in Symbolism, its theory. What exactly interests you about it, and from what angle do you want to approach it?"

And the monologue began. Bely sat opposite me, but frequently got up and walked around the room in quick, light movements. There was no "dancing" or "gesticulating" or "radiance." But his speech flowed irrepressibly.

I will not venture to reproduce the exact contents of Bely's monologue. I remember only that it began with an enumeration of the names of the philosophers who were significant for the theory of Symbolism. "According to Kant," "according to Wundt," "according to Rickert," "according to Solov'ev," "Schopenhauer," "Nietzsche," and still more and more names, less renowned, yet well known.

This display of fireworks seemed a bit strange, almost ostentatious, hardly necessary to our conversation, and designed less "for the good of the cause" than for the purpose of dazzling the young man who sat politely on the chair, and who, as it was, had entered this house filled with the highest respect for the authority of the host. "Isn't he overcompensating for having been abandoned, forgotten, deserted by his readers, for having been forced into semisilence, for the bare walls, for having to live in a godforsaken suburb of Moscow?" I assure you that these thoughts, justified or not, came to mind precisely as I was listening to Bely. And now, besides respectful attention and interest, I felt a tinge of sympathy for him (I hesitate to say compassion).

Naturally, Boris Nikolaevich's monologue abruptly ceased when I reached into my briefcase and produced a letter written by Bryusov, as well as several sheets of paper in his handwriting. (They had been given to me by his widow, Zhanna Matveevna.)

"A familiar handwriting—Bryusov's!" Bely exclaimed, scarcely glancing (or not glancing? seeming not to glance!) at the sheets from the other end of the room. I was struck by the unexpected, almost casual sharpness of his eye, by his ability to take note, all unwittingly, of his surroundings, of externals that seemingly did not exist for him.

Now we began to talk about the topic that had brought me to Kuchino—*Libra*, Bryusov, Polyakov, the Merezhkovskys, the alignment of forces on the journal's editorial board, and even its financial situation. I put the questions and Boris Nikolaevich answered them simply, precisely, and in detail. It was evident, however—indeed, one might have guessed it beforehand—that the practical, business side of editorial life interested him far less than the people, the human and ideological relationships.

"Boris Nikolaevich, your signature is among those at the end of this document. Look! Do you remember it? In his diary Bryusov calls it the 'constitution' of *Libra*."

Bely replied: "I have absolutely no memory of such a paper! No doubt it was handed to me, and I signed it without looking. But I think that everything in it was carried out to the letter."

And so on and so forth. About *Libra* and Symbolism.

But the greater part of the conversation had no direct bearing on my subject. My subject was sending out shoots, branching forth, and becoming overgrown with related subjects that finally pushed it out altogether.

As before, Bely more or less did all the talking, while I kept interposing brief phrases into his vast, inexhaustible monologue.

Of course, such a ritual performance made it impossible for the speaker to probe the personality of the individual sitting before him. But the presence of that individual was nonetheless acknowledged by the speaker. (That is not always the case.) Bely's manner of speaking had none of the hermetic, self-sufficient quality of prophetic utterance. It was lively, impetuous, vibrant, open to give and take, and sensitively responsive to the reactions of the other person.

"You understand? You understand?" He kept addressing this phrase to me over and over with a kind of neurotic persistence. It literally peppered and permeated his speech and passed into the "trans-sense" realm: "Yyy . . . unnn?? Yyy . . . unnn?"

Evidently, Boris Nikolaevich had often had to address people who did not understand him, had become used to a lack of understanding in his listeners and took it for granted.

What, then, remains in my memory and in my notes of all that he said on that occasion?

Not very much, just snatches, but all the same . . .

He talked about his solitary life in Kuchino, about solitude in general as a necessary condition for the writer, and in this connection he mentioned Tolstoy's Yasnaya Polyana and Chekhov's Yalta. A parallel with Kuchino emerged by itself, as did an implicit analogy to the people who lived in those other places.

When the conversation touched on Steiner, Boris Nikolaevich looked at the picture and heatedly disputed the common opinion that he, Bely, had disavowed anthroposophy and its founder. Bely asserted that even now he remained true to anthroposophical teaching, and that there were people in Moscow who shared this faith with him. One could only conclude that his irritation with Steiner—of which many people spoke—had been short-lived, and that he had regained his former respect for the Doctor, as Steiner was called in anthroposophical circles.

I was well aware of Bely's stature as an artist, and naturally did not wish to irritate him with inept remarks or a show of independent-mindedness. But neither did I want to deceive him by maintaining a silence that he might have misconstrued as sympathy.

"Boris Nikolaevich, I have recently read several books by Steiner and, forgive me, but in many respects [I said "in many respects" to soften it]

they seemed dead. There's something unattractive about them, an unpleasant underside to them. When material, even anatomical comparisons are made with the spiritual world, I get a bit queasy. I just can't
believe that there are astral 'lotus flowers' whirling about in certain
specific parts of the human body. There's something all wrong about
that!"

Bely did not get angry, and he looked at me without a trace of ire. "I
understand. Steiner's power is not to be found in his books, but in direct
personal contact."

He may have phrased this last sentence somewhat differently, but I
am rendering its meaning exactly.

I can add that Klavdiya Nikolaevna Bugaeva was of precisely the same
opinion as Bely. She regarded Steiner as her teacher, and revered him.
Many years later, when I told her what Bely had said, she wholeheartedly agreed: "The Doctor didn't know how to write. All his power really lay
in his lectures and talks."

The explanation given by Bely and Klavdiya Nikolaevna helps us understand why Steiner's followers were so exceptionally devoted to him.
But it is impossible to defend or condemn anthroposophy as a teaching
on the basis of such opinions. And I have clung to my old position.
Anthroposophical doctrine as a whole has always seemed to me eclectic
and based on arbitrary and fantastical assumptions, although I feel that
something worthy of attention might certainly be found in the theory
and practice of the Steinerians.

Andrey Bely, an ardent believer in anthroposophy, received the impulses that emanated from it and incorporated them into his writings.
But in so doing, he consciously or unconsciously cleansed them of mystical doctrinairism, and in fact created entirely new structures on their
foundation. The logic of his art and his artistic tact ensured that what
was unwarranted speculation in Steiner's "science of the spirit" actually
became, in his own works—as I have already remarked in connection
with *Kotik Letaev*—lyrical and psychologically motivated variants that
merely hinted at more, but did not contain the conclusions that were
obligatory for Steiner.

I arrived at all this much later, but the seeds were already beginning to
germinate within me even then.

At any rate, Boris Nikolaevich and I did not return to the topic of
anthroposophy again.

A confessional note gradually crept in as Bely talked that day. (Subsequently I learned that he could converse on personal, even intimate
subjects with people he had never met before.)

Then he talked of how his view of the world had always been constant,
and of how he still remained himself even in present-day conditions,
with his "former self," the experience of his entire life, intact. There had

been no retreat. Yet he was connecting this "former self" with the "new" one that had matured within him over the past few years and was drawing him closer to his surroundings, to contemporary life. And he showed me the typescript of his book *On the Border of Two Centuries* (*Na rubezhe dvukh stoletii*), which was lying on the table. And he said, with naïve pride, that he had succeeded in making such a connection in this book, and that the publishers were pleased.

I remember that our conversation shifted to the theory of ethics. It was clear that Boris Nikolaevich was violently opposed to Kant's notion of the categorical imperative. Unfortunately, I am unable—as in several other instances—to reconstruct everything he said on the subject, but I was able to grasp his general idea. Bely considered that the ultimate source of man's conscience lay in the depths of the unconscious. He believed that morality was a form of the imagination, "moral imagination," that is, a manifestation of human creativity—free, nondogmatic, yet possessed of value. (Klavdiya Nikolaevna later explained that this idea had come to Bely from the anthroposophical Mecca, Dornach. Needless to say, she did not use the word "Mecca.")

I also remember some of the judgments that he made—either in passing or at length—during the course of our conversation. For instance, I cannot forget his enthusiasm and delight when he spoke of the production of *Hamlet* at the Second Moscow Art Theater, with the brilliant Mikhail Chekhov in the leading role. Bely regarded this production—which really was remarkable—as an anthroposophical mystery play. (As a matter of fact, Chekhov was an anthroposophist, and when I saw it, I too sensed its mystery-play quality.)

"Now Lunacharsky," Bely exclaimed, "didn't even notice that. He sat there in the theater and applauded. And Lunacharsky was not the only one in ecstasy. You unnn . . . [understand]? Even the trolley conductresses wept when they talked about it."

On that occasion I also heard Bely make other appreciative remarks about the Second Moscow Art Theater. He compared it to the Kamerny Theater, of which he had a negative opinion. It was only many years later that I learned from Klavdiya Nikolaevna that Boris Nikolaevich had not always approved of the productions of the Second Moscow Art Theater either. She had in mind his opinion of their production of his own play *Petersburg*. Despite the presence of Mikhail Chekhov (in the role of Apollon Apollonovich), Bely considered it a failure, owing to the clash of directorial styles. The result, as Bely put it, was the same as in Ivan Krylov's fable about the swan, the crayfish, and the pike. (The directors had been Serafima Birman, Vladimir Tatarinov, and Aleksandr Cheban. I hope this neat symmetry does not lead the reader to think that *I* allowed myself such personal zoological comparisons!)

I find it difficult to recall the logical order of the conversation that followed. We talked about Pavel Florensky's book *The Pillar and Affirmation of Truth* (*Stolp i utverzhdenie istiny*), which Bely called rationalistic. And about Nikolay Berdyaev, whom he accused of dogmatism, about Vladimir Solov'ev, whom he accused of nothing, as I recall, but about whom he seemed to speak with no trace of his old enthusiasm.

Toward the end of the conversation, with a trustfulness that was touching, Bely unexpectedly paused to remark on the fate of the Russian countryside, its complete remaking that was under way in those days of collectivization. And I saw that he was profoundly agitated. He even spoke of the "failure of the rural experiment."

For some time I had been concerned about tiring my host, and now I got up. Boris Nikolaevich saw me out and bade me a hearty farewell. When we were almost at the door, he responded to one of my remarks by starting to talk about truthfulness.

"Truth above all. Truth is the most important, the most important thing. To be truthful in everything, only truthful. . ."

When I recalled these words of Bely's many years later, I thought: Years before we met, Bely had written about truth in a lengthy cycle of highly subtle aphorisms, where the notion of truth was examined, as it were, in a long series of mirrors and refracting prisms (see *The Notes of Dreamers* [*Zapiski Mechtatelei*], no. 5 [1922]). That series, however, contained none of those starkly simple, seemingly banal, but decisive words I had heard from him that day. But he was capable of them, they were in him, and with their bright light, they could have illuminated the fine speculative fabric of his symbolic constructs on the subject of truth. "To be truthful in everything, only truthful . . ."

These were the last words of importance I ever heard from Andrey Bely. I met him once more in Tsarskoe Selo, on the steps of Ivanov-Razumnik's house, but our meeting did not last very long, and there is nothing to say about it.

When I left Bely's, it was beginning to grow dark in Kuchino. Filled with impressions, I walked to the station. Small squat wooden houses, roofed with shingles and iron, their windows faintly gleaming in the already wan light, cracked gray fences, trees with laundry hanging on the branches, a solitary nanny goat in the street—everything around me on that summer evening seemed melancholy and forlorn. "Dear, melancholy, eternal"—Bely returned to that theme and that formula many times over. And here, on this street in Kuchino, there was the "dear" and even the "eternal," but the "melancholy" predominated. Everything I had seen and heard but not yet fully comprehended in the modest (painfully modest) dwelling of the hermit of Kuchino was backlighted by this melancholy.

Yes, I well remember the complexity of my feelings, my desire to grasp and understand what I had experienced. The lonely aging man with the incredible white eyes (and they had been blue!), the almost incorporeal bearer and seer of the spirit, endowed with a dazzling, stunning gift but already showing signs of creative exhaustion, highly wrought, vibrating like a taut string, straining to transcend the confined space of the room, thrashing about in that space, condemned by the times and by himself, as well as by the whole makeup of his personality, which was incompatible with the times. Power and—forgive me again for the sacrilegious words that perhaps I should not even utter—the power to arouse sympathy and pity.

> I believed in golden radiance,
> But died from the sun's arrows.
> I measured the ages with my thought,
> But did not know how to live my life.
>   ["To My Friends"]

It seems that these lines have been recalled and written about by everyone who has not merely been interested in the formal aspects of Bely's works or in his theory of rhythm, but wanted to fathom his personality and art as an organically whole phenomenon. The motif of suffering and human pain ran through his entire life and all his works. "O my soul" welled up from the heart of one of the characters (Dudkin) in Bely's most important novel, *Petersburg:* "O my soul . . . I am so wretched. . . ."

Yet I know that not everyone had forgotten Andrey Bely, despite the oblivion washing over him. Even at that time there were people who continued to take an interest in him, most often people of the older generation, but also those of the younger, and even of my generation. They were not numerous (even before there had been few, yet more than now), but they were faithful admirers who forgave the abrupt changes in his position and conduct, who forgave the isolated instances of creative fatigue, people who remembered him not as the author of the labored *Moscow* and the overworked *Masks* (*Maski*), but as the creator of *Petersburg,* which was immeasurably more powerful. And most of all, people who remembered him as a *figure,* a personality who could not be contained within any prescribed framework, rank, or hierarchy.

Boris Pasternak questioned me about Bely with great interest. I visited him several days after the meeting at Kuchino that I have described.

Lyubov' Dmitrievna Blok reacted differently to the news of my meeting with Bely (my conversation with her took place much later). She showed no desire to inquire about his life, and confined herself to one drawled and utterly indifferent question, to which, of course, she expected no reply: "Is he still as crazy as ever?"

The forced nonchalance of her tone, if in fact it was present in this casual query, did not alter the contents. Her attitude toward Bely came out fully and unmistakably.

And then, without the slightest provocation on my part, Lyubov' Dmitrievna told me—with simplifications and retouchings—about Bely's love for her and her tempestuous reaction (as she put it) to the letter in which he asked her to become his wife.

"I was very angry and ripped up his letter," she said by way of finishing her brief and not very accurate tale.

Zhanna Matveevna Bryusova, a simple and levelheaded woman of whom I saw a great deal at that time, proved to be more fair-minded.

"I know him well," she said, after hearing my story about Bely. "He can be a genuine human being. . . ."

She did not elaborate on the meaning of her words, but I sensed that they were tacitly aimed at those admirers of Bely who were carried away by his eccentricity, and at those countless enemies who took umbrage at it. Both overlooked his human qualities: his love of people, the pain he felt for his fellow man and for his country.

Now, when we are apparently beginning to take Bely's measure and even to study him after a fashion, we should return to what Zhanna Matveevna said and complete it in our own words.

Yes, Andrey Bely was a uniquely original individual, a superb writer, an intensely spiritual man with a tragic experience of the world and a complex and tragic destiny. He was endowed with great strength and great weakness. He was a Russian pilgrim, unencumbered by the things of this world, homeless, a restless wanderer, as were Velimir Khlebnikov, Marina Tsvetaeva, and Vladimir Solov'ev.

Almost everything important that we know of Bely has come to us from his works and from reminiscences, his own and others', all of which reflect his extraordinary personality. But certain traits that explain the phenomenon of Andrey Bely, certain emanations of his individuality, even I grasped when I looked at and listened to the living man himself. I had the chance to see Andrey Bely as he was in life. To be sure, it was only a side view, but even the little bit I did see and have related on these pages has left a deep mark on my memory.

Bibliography

Works of Andrey Bely Cited
(Exclusive of individual articles and poems)

Arabeski: Kniga statei. Moscow, 1911. Reprinted Munich, 1969.

Chetyre simfonii. Munich, 1971.

The Dramatic Symphony and The Forms of Art. Translated by Roger Keys, Angela Keys, and John Elsworth. Edinburgh, 1986.

The First Encounter. Translated and introduced by Gerald Janecek, with preliminary remarks, notes, and comments by Nina Berberova. Princeton, 1979.

Glossolaliya: Poema o zvuke. Berlin, 1922 (misprinted as *Glossaloliya*). Reprinted Munich, 1971.

Khristos voskres. Petersburg, 1918. Reprinted in *Stikhotvoreniya,* vol. II. Munich, 1982.

Korolevna i rytsari: Skazki. Petersburg, 1919. Reprinted *Stikhotvoreniya,* vol. I, pt. 2. Munich, 1984.

Kotik Letaev. Petersburg, 1922. Reprinted Munich, 1964.

Kotik Letaev. Translated by Gerald Janecek. Ann Arbor, 1971.

Kreshchenyi kitaets. Moscow, 1927. Reprinted Munich, 1969.

Krizis kul'tury (Na perevale III). Petersburg, 1920.

Krizis mysli (Na perevale II). Petersburg, 1918.

Krizis zhizni (Na perevale I). Petersburg, 1918.

Kubok metelei: Chetvertaya simfoniya. Moscow, 1908. Reprinted in *Chetyre simfonii.* Munich, 1971.

Lug zelenyi: Kniga statei. Moscow, 1910. Reprinted New York and London, 1967.

Maski. Moscow, 1932. Reprinted Munich, 1969.

Masterstvo Gogolya. Moscow and Leningrad, 1934. Reprinted Ann Arbor, 1982.

Mezhdu dvukh revolyutsii. Leningrad, 1934. Reprinted Chicago, 1966.

Moskovskii chudak. Moscow, 1926. 2d ed. Moscow, 1927. Reprinted as *Moskva* I and II, Munich, 1968.

Moskva pod udarom. Moscow, 1926. 2d ed. Moscow, 1927. Reprinted as *Moskva* I and II, Munich, 1968.

Nachalo veka. Moscow and Leningrad, 1933. Reprinted Chicago, 1966.

Na rubezhe dvukh stoletii. Moscow and Leningrad, 1930. 2d ed. Moscow and Leningrad, 1931. Reprinted Letchworth, 1966.

Odna iz obitelei tsarstva tenei. Leningrad, 1924. Reprinted Letchworth, 1971.

O smysle poznaniya. Petersburg, 1922. Reprinted Chicago, 1965.

Pepel. Petersburg, 1909. 2d rev. ed. Moscow, 1929. 1st ed. reprinted in *Stikhotvoreniya*, vol. I, pt. 2. Munich, 1984.

Perepiska. By Aleksandr Blok and Andrey Bely. Ed. V. N. Orlov. Moscow, 1940. Reprinted Munich, 1969.

Pervoe svidanie. Petersburg, 1921. 2d ed. Berlin, 1922. Reprinted in *Stikhotvoreniya*, vol. II. Munich, 1982.

Peterburg. Petersburg, 1916. Reprinted Letchworth, 1967, and Moscow and Leningrad, 1981 ("Literaturnye pamyatniki").

Peterburg. Berlin, 1922. 2d, censored ed. Moscow, 1928. 2d ed. reprinted Moscow, 1935; Munich, 1967; and Moscow, 1978.

Petersburg. Translated, annotated, and introduced by R. A. Maguire and J. E. Malmstad. Bloomington, Ind., 1978; Hassocks, Sussex, 1979.

Pochemu ya stal simvolistom i pochemu ya ne perestal im byt' vo vsekh fazakh moego ideinogo i khudozhestvennogo razvitiya. Ann Arbor, 1982.

Poeziya slova. Petersburg, 1922. Reprinted Chicago, 1965.

Posle razluki: Berlinskii pesennik. Petersburg and Berlin, 1922. Reprinted in *Stikhotvoreniya*, vol. I, pt. 2. Munich, 1984.

Putevye zametki: Sitsiliya, Tunis. Moscow and Berlin, 1922.

Rasskazy. Munich, 1979. Published in English as *Complete Short Stories*, translated by Ronald Peterson. Ann Arbor, 1979.

Ritm kak dialektika i "Mednyi vsadnik": Issledovanie. Moscow, 1929.

Rudol'f Shteiner i Gete v mirovozzrenii sovremennosti. Moscow, 1917.

Selected Essays of Andrey Bely. Edited, translated, and with an introduction by Steven Cassedy. Berkeley and Los Angeles, 1985.

Serebryanyi golub'. Moscow, 1910. 2d ed. Berlin, 1922. 2d ed. reprinted Munich, 1967, and Ann Arbor, 1980.

Severnaya simfoniya (1-aya, geroicheskaya). Moscow, 1904. Reprinted in *Chetyre simfonii.* Munich, 1971.

The Silver Dove. Translated by George Reavey. New York, 1974.

Simfoniya (2-aya, dramaticheskaya). Moscow, 1902. Reprinted in *Chetyre simfonii.* Munich, 1971.

Simvolizm: Kniga statei. Moscow, 1910. Reprinted Munich, 1969.

Stikhi o Rossii. Berlin, 1922. Reprinted New York, 1978.

Stikhotvoreniya. Berlin, Petersburg, and Moscow, 1923.

Stikhotvoreniya. 3 vols. (vol. I in 2 parts). Variorum edition, edited and annotated by John E. Malmstad. Munich, 1982–84.

Stikhotvoreniya i poemy. Biblioteka poeta, bol'shaya seriya. Moscow and Leningrad, 1966.

Tragediya tvorchestva: Dostoevsky i Tolstoy. Moscow, 1911. Reprinted Letchworth, 1971.

Urna. Moscow, 1909. Reprinted in *Stikhotvoreniya*, vol. I, pt. 2. Munich, 1984.

Veter s Kavkaza: Vpechatleniya. Moscow, 1928.

"Vospominaniya, tom III, chast' II, 1910–1912." *Literaturnoe nasledstvo*, no. 27–28 (Moscow, 1937).

"Vospominaniya ob A. A. Bloke." *Zapiski Mechtatelei*, no. 6, 1922. Reprinted as *Vospominaniya ob Aleksandre Aleksandroviche Bloke.* Letchworth, 1964.

"Vospominaniya o Bloke." *Epopeya*, nos. 1–4 (1922–23). Reprinted as *Vospominaniya o A. A. Bloke.* Munich, 1969.

Vospominaniya o Shteinere. Paris, 1982. First published in German translation as *Verwandeln des Lebens: Erinnerungen an Rudolf Steiner.* Basel, 1975.

Vozvrat: III['ya] simfoniya. Moscow, 1905. Reprinted in *Chetyre simfonii.* Munich, 1971.

Zapiski chudaka. 2 vols. Moscow and Berlin, 1922. Reprinted Lausanne, 1973.

Zoloto v lazuri. Moscow, 1904. Reprinted in *Stikhotvoreniya*, vol. I, pt. 1. Munich, 1984.

Zvezda: Novye stikhi. Petersburg, 1922. Reprinted in *Stikhotvoreniya*, vol. I, pt. 2. Munich, 1984.

Works about Andrey Bely Cited

Adamovich, Georgy. "Andrey Bely i ego vospominaniya." *Russkie Zapiski*, bk. 5. May 1938.

Alexandrov, Vladimir E. *Andrei Bely: The Major Symbolist Fiction.* Cambridge, Mass., and London, 1985.

———. "Unicorn Impaling a Knight: The Transcendent and Man in Andrei Belyi's *Petersburg.*" *Canadian-American Slavic Studies*, 16, no. 1 (Spring 1982).

Anschuetz, Carol. "Bely's *Petersburg* and the End of the Russian Novel." In *The Russian Novel from Pushkin to Pasternak*, edited by John Garrard. New Haven, 1983.

———. "Recollection as Metaphor in *Kotik Letaev.*" *Russian Literature*, no. 4 (1976).

Askol'dov, S. A. "Tvorchestvo Andreya Belogo." *Literaturnaya Mysl'*, Al'manakh 1 (Petrograd, 1923).

Asmus, V. F. "Filosofiya i estetika russkogo simvolizma." *Literaturnoe nasledstvo*, no. 27–28 (Moscow, 1937).

Bakhrakh, Aleksandr. "Po pamyati, po zapisyam: Andrey Bely." *Kontinent*, no. 3 (1975).

Beketova, M. A. *Aleksandr Blok: Biograficheskii ocherk.* Petersburg, 1922.

Bennett, Virginia. "Echoes of Friedrich Nietzsche's *The Birth of Tragedy* in Andrej Belyj's *Petersburg.*" *Germano-Slavica*, 3, no. 4 (Fall 1980).

Berberova, Nina. *Kursiv moi.* Munich, 1971. Published in English as *The Italics Are Mine*, translated by Philippe Radley. New York, 1969.

———. "Preliminary Remarks." In Andrey Bely, *The First Encounter*, translated and introduced by Gerald Janecek. Princeton, 1979.

Berdyaev, Nikolay. "Mutnye liki." In *Sofiya: Problemy dukhovnoi kul'tury i religioznoi filosofii*, vol. I. Berlin, 1923.

———. "Russkii soblazn: po povodu *Serebryanogo golubya.*" *Russkaya Mysl'*, no. 11 (1910).

Beyer, Thomas. "The Bely-Zhirmunsky Polemic." In *Andrey Bely: A Critical Review*, edited by G. Janecek. Lexington, Ky., 1978.

Bolotnikov, A. "Neudavshiisya maskarad." *Literaturnyi Kritik*, no. 2 (1933).

Bugaeva, K. N. *Vospominaniya o Belom*. Edited, annotated, and with an introduction by John E. Malmstad. Berkeley, 1981.

——, A. S. Petrovsky [and D. M. Pines]. "Literaturnoe nasledstvo Andreya Belogo." *Literaturnoe nasledstvo*, no. 27–28 (Moscow, 1937).

Burkhart, Dagmar. "Leitmotivik und Symbolik in Andrej Belyjs Roman *Peterburg*." *Welt der Slaven*, December 1964.

Cassedy, Steven. "Toward a Unified Theory of the Aesthetic Object in Andrej Belyj." *Slavic and East European Journal* 28 (1984).

——. "Translator's Introduction." In *Selected Essays of Andrey Bely*. Berkeley and Los Angeles, 1985.

Chekhov, Mikhail. "Zhizn' i vstrechi." *Novyi Zhurnal*, no. 9 (1944).

Christa, Boris. "Bely's Poetry: A Metrical Profile." In *Andrey Bely: Centenary Papers*, edited by Boris Christa. Amsterdam, 1980.

——. *The Poetic World of Andrey Bely*. Amsterdam, 1977.

Cioran, Samuel. *The Apocalyptic Symbolism of Andrej Belyj*. The Hague, 1973.

Crone, Anna Lisa. "Gnostic Elements in Bely's *Kotik Letaev*." *Russian Language Journal*, no. 36 (1982).

Dolgopolov, L. K. "Obraz goroda v romane A. Belogo 'Peterburg.'" *Izvestiya Akademii Nauk, Seriya literatury i yazyka*, 34, no. 1 (1975).

——. "Simvolika lichnykh imen v proizvedeniyakh Andreya Belogo." In *Kul'turnoe nasledie drevnei Rusi: Istoki, Stanovlenie, Traditsii*, edited by V. G. Bazanov. Moscow, 1976.

——. "Tvorcheskaya istoriya i istoriko-literaturnoe znachenie romana A. Belogo 'Peterburg.'" In A. Bely, *Peterburg*, edited by L. K. Dolgopolov. Moscow and Leningrad, 1981.

——. "V poiskakh samogo sebya (K 100-letiyu so dnya rozhdeniya Andreya Belogo)." *Izvestiya Akademii Nauk, Seriya literatury i yazyka*, 39, no. 6 (1980).

Eagle, Herbert. "Typographical Devices in the Poetry of Andrey Bely." In *Andrey Bely: A Critical Review*, edited by G. Janecek. Lexington, Ky., 1978.

El'sberg, Zh. [Yakov]. "Tvorchestvo Andreya Belogo-prozaika." In *Krizis poputchikov i nastroeniya intelligentsii*. Moscow and Leningrad, 1930.

Elsworth, J. D. "Andrei Bely's Theory of Symbolism." *Forum for Modern Language Studies*, 11, no. 4 (1975).

——. *Andrey Bely*. Letchworth, 1972.

——. *Andrey Bely: A Critical Study of the Novels*. Cambridge, Eng., 1983.

——. "The Concept of Rhythm in Bely's Aesthetic Thought." In *Andrey Bely: Centenary Papers*, edited by Boris Christa. Amsterdam, 1980.

Fasting, S. "Andrej Belyj's *Simfoniya, 2-aja dramatičeskaja*." *Scando-Slavica*, no. 25 (1979).

Fleishman, Lazar. *Boris Pasternak v tridtsatye gody*. Jerusalem, 1984.

Foster, John. *Heirs to Dionysus: A Nietzschean Current in Literary Modernism*. Princeton, 1981.

Gasparov, Mikhail. *Ocherk istorii russkogo stikha: Metrika, ritmika, rifma, strofika*. Moscow, 1984.

———. "Quantitative Methods in Russian Metrics: Achievements and Prospects." In *Metre, Rhythm, Stanza, Rhyme*, edited by G. S. Smith. Colchester, 1980.

———. *Sovremennyi russkii stikh: Metrika i ritmika*. Moscow, 1974.

Gerigk, H. J. "Belyjs *Petersburg* und Nietzsches *Geburt der Tragödie*." *Nietzsche Studien: Internationales Jahrbuch für die Nietzsche-Forschung*, no. 9 (1980).

Goncharov, B. P. "Andrey Bely—stikhoved." *Filologicheskie Nauki*, no. 5 (119) (1980).

———. "Russkoe stikhovedenie nachala XX v.: Stikhovedcheskie vzglyady A. Belogo." In *Russkaya nauka o literature v kontse XIX-nachala XX v.*, edited by P. A. Nikolev. Moscow, 1982.

Grechishkin, S. S., and A. V. Lavrov. "Andrey Bely i N. F. Fedorov." In *Tvorchestvo A. A. Bloka i russkaya kul'tura dvadtsatogo veka*. Blokovskii sbornik III. Tartu, 1979.

——— and ———. "O stikhovedcheskom nasledii Andreya Belogo." *Struktura i semiotika khudozhestvennogo teksta: Trudy po znakovym sistemam*, no. 12 (Tartu, 1981).

Hoffman, Stefani. "Scythian Theory and Literature, 1917–1924." In *Art, Society, Revolution: Russia, 1917–1921*, edited by Nils Åke Nilsson. Stockholm, 1979.

Holthusen, Johannes. "Andrej Belyj und sein Roman 'Peterburg.'" In *Studien zur Ästhetik und Poetik des russischen Symbolismus*. Göttingen, 1957.

Ivanov-Razumnik, R. *Aleksandr Blok, Andrey Bely*. Petersburg, 1919. Reprinted Letchworth, 1971.

———. "Andrey Bely." In *Russkaya literatura XX veka*, edited by S. A. Vengerov, vol. III, pt. 2. Moscow, 1916.

———. *Vershiny: A. Blok, A. Bely*. Petersburg, 1923.

Jakobson, Roman. "Réponses." *Poétique*, no. 57 (1984).

———. *Selected Writings*, vol. V. *On Verse, Its Masters and Explorers*. The Hague, 1979.

Janecek, Gerald. "Andrey Bely." In *The Look of Russian Literature: Avant-Garde Visual Experiments, 1900–1930*. Princeton, 1984.

———. "Anthroposophy in *Kotik Letaev*." *Orbis Litterarum*, no. 29 (1974).

———. "Intonation and Layout in Bely's Poetry." In *Andrey Bely: Centenary Papers*, ed. Boris Christa. Amsterdam, 1980.

———. "Introduction." In *Andrey Bely: A Critical Review*, edited by G. Janecek. Lexington, Ky., 1978.

———. "Introduction." In Andrey Bely, *The First Encounter*, translated by G. Janecek. Princeton, 1979.

———. "Literature as Music: Symphonic Form in Andrei Belyi's *Fourth Symphony*." *Canadian-American Slavic Studies*, no. 8 (1974).

———. "Rhythm in Prose: The Special Case of Bely." In *Andrey Bely: A Critical Review*, edited by G. Janecek. Lexington, Ky., 1978.

———. "The Spiral as Image and Structural Principle in Andrej Belyj's *Kotik Letaev*." *Russian Literature*, no. 4 (1976).

Kalbouss, George. "Andrey Bely and the Modernist Movement in Russian Drama." In *Andrey Bely: A Critical Review*, edited by G. Janecek. Lexington, Ky., 1978.

Kamenev, Lev. "Andrey Bely" (obituary), *Izvestiya*, January 10, 1934.

———. "Predislovie." In Andrey Bely, *Nachalo veka*. Moscow and Leningrad, 1933.

Karlinsky, Simon. "Andrey Bely." In *The Columbia Dictionary of Modern European Literature.* New York, 1980.

——. "Symphonic Structure in Andrej Belyj's 'Pervoe svidanie.'" *California Slavic Studies,* 6 (1971).

Kazin, A. L. "Gnoseologicheskoe obosnovanie simvola Andreem Belym." *Voprosy Filosofii i Sotsiologii,* no. 3 (1971).

Keys, R. J. "Andrey Bely and the Development of Russian Fiction." *Essays in Poetics,* 8, no. 1 (1983).

——. "The Bely–Ivanov-Razumnik Correspondence." In *Andrey Bely: A Critical Review,* edited by G. Janecek. Lexington, Ky., 1978.

Khmel'nitskaya, Tamara. "Poeziya Andreya Belogo." In Andrey Bely, *Stikhotvoreniya i poemy.* Moscow and Leningrad, 1966.

Khodasevich, V. F. "Ableukhovy—Letaevy—Korobkiny." *Sovremennye Zapiski,* no. 31 (1927). Reprinted in *Literaturnye stat'i i vospominaniya.* New York, 1954.

——. "Andrey Bely." In *Nekropol': Vospominaniya.* Brussels, 1939.

——. "Andrey Bely: *Kreshchenyi kitaets.*" *Sovremennye Zapiski,* no. 32 (1927).

Kovač, Anton. *Andrej Belyj: The "Symphonies" (1899–1908). A Re-evaluation of the Aesthetic-Philosophical Heritage.* Bern, Frankfurt am Main, Munich, 1976.

Kozlik, Frédéric C. *L'Influence de l'anthroposophie sur l'oeuvre d'Andréi Biélyi.* 3 vols. Frankfurt am Main, 1981.

Kuleshova, Ekaterina. *Polifoniya idei i simvolov: Stat'i o Belom, Bloke, Bryusove i Sologube.* Toronto, 1981.

Kuznetsov, Mikhail. *Sovetskii roman.* Moscow, 1963.

Lavrov, A. V. "Mifotvorchestvo 'Argonavtov.'" In *Mif-fol'klor-literatura,* edited by V. G. Bazanov. Leningrad, 1978.

——. "Yunosheskaya khudozhestvennaya proza Andreya Belogo." In *Pamyatniki kul'tury: Novye otkrytiya, ezhegodnik 1980.* Leningrad, 1981.

——. "Yunosheskie dnevnikovye zametki Andreya Belogo." In *Pamyatniki kul'tury: Novye otkrytiya, ezhegodnik 1979.* Leningrad, 1980.

Lilly, Ian. K. "On the Rhymes of Bely's First Three Books of Verse." *Slavonic and East European Review,* 60, no. 2 (1982).

Ljunggren, Magnus. *The Dream of Rebirth: A Study of Andrej Belyj's Novel "Peterburg."* Stockholm Studies in Russian Literature 15. Stockholm, 1982.

Loks, Konstantin. "O spornom i besspornom." *Krasnaya Nov',* no. 11 (1926).

L'vov-Rogachevsky, V. L. See V. L.

Malmstad, John E. "Introduction." In Andrey Bely, *Stikhotvoreniya,* vol. I, pt. 1. Munich, 1984.

——. "Introduction." In K. N. Bugaeva, *Vospominaniya o Belom.* Berkeley, 1981.

Markov, Vladimir. "Preface." In *Modern Russian Poetry,* edited by Vladimir Markov and Merrill Sparks. London, 1966.

Maslenikov, O. A. "Andrej Belyj's Third 'Symphony.'" *American Slavic and East European Review,* 7 (1948).

——. *The Frenzied Poets: Andrey Biely and the Russian Symbolists.* Berkeley, 1952.

Metner, E. K. "Boris Bugaev protiv muzyki." *Zolotoe Runo,* no. 5 (1907).

——. "Simfonii Andreya Belogo." *Pridneprovskii Krai,* December 15 and 16, 1903.

Mirsky, D. S. *A History of Russian Literature.* London, 1949.

——. "O sovremennoi sostoyanii russkoi poezii." *Novyi Zhurnal,* no. 131 (1978).

Mochul'sky, Konstantin. *Andrey Bely*. Paris, 1955. Published in English as *Andrei Bely: His Life and Works*, translated by N. Szalavitz. Ann Arbor, 1977.

Nabokov, Vladimir. "Notes on Prosody." In Aleksandr Pushkin, *Eugene Onegin*, translated and with commentary by Vladimir Nabokov, vol. III. New York, 1964.

Nivat, Georges. "Du rhythme chez Andrej Belyj." *Revue des études slaves*, no. 54, no. 1–2 (1982).

———. "L'Oeuvre polémique, critique et journalistique d'Andrej Belyj" [bibliography]. *Cahiers du monde russe et soviétique*, 15, no. 1–2 (1974).

———. "Le Palimpseste de l'enfance." In *Kotik Letaiev*. Lausanne, 1973.

Orlov, Vladimir. "Aleksandr Blok v pamyati sovremennikov." In *Aleksandr Blok v vospominaniyakh sovremennikov*, vol. I. Moscow, 1980.

Paperny, V. M. "Andrey Bely i Gogol': Stat'ya I." *Uchenye Zapiski Tartuskogo gos. universiteta*, vyp. 604 (1982); "Stat'ya II," vyp. 620 (1983).

Peterson, Ronald E. *Andrei Bely's Short Prose*. Birmingham, 1980.

———. "Andrey Belyi's Third Symphony: Return or Demented Demise?" In *Russian Literature and Criticism: Selected Papers from the Second World Congress for Soviet and East European Studies*, edited by E. Bristol. Berkeley, 1982.

Prat, Naftali. "Orthodox Philosophy of Language in Russia." *Studies in Soviet Thought*, no. 20 (1979).

Pustygina, N. "Tsitatnost' v romane Andreya Belogo *Peterburg*." *Uchenye Zapiski Tartuskogo gos. universiteta*, vyp. 414. *Trudy po russkoi i slavyanskoi filologii* XXVIII, 1977; vyp. 513, XXXII (1981).

Rudnev, P. A. "Metricheskii repertuar V. Bryusova." In *Bryusovskie chteniya 1971 goda*, edited by K. V. Aivazyan. Erevan, 1973.

Sazonova, Yuliya. "Andrey Bely." *Sovremennye Zapiski*, no. 66 (1938).

Shklovsky, Viktor. "Andrey Bely." *Russkii Sovremennik*, no. 2 (1924).

———. *O teorii prozy*. Moscow, 1925. 2d ed. Moscow, 1929.

Smith, G. S. "Stanza Rhythm in the Iambic Tetrameter of Three Modern Russian Poets." *International Journal of Slavic Linguistics and Poetics*, no. 24 (1981).

———. "The Versification of V. F. Xodasevič, 1915–1939." In *Russian Poetics*, edited by D. S. Worth and T. Eekman. Columbus, 1983.

Starikova, E. "Realizm i simvolizm." In *Razvitie realizma v russkoi literature*, edited by U. R. Fokht et al., vol. III. Moscow, 1974.

Steinberg, Ada. *Word and Music in the Novels of Andrey Bely*. Cambridge, Eng., 1982.

Stepun, Fedor. *Mystische Weltschau*. Munich, 1964.

———. *Vstrechi*. Munich, 1962.

Struve, G. P. "Andrej Belyj's Experiments with Novel Technique." In *Stil- und Formprobleme in der Literatur*, edited by P. Böckmann. Heidelberg, 1959.

———. "Andrey Bely redivivus." In *Andrey Bely: A Critical Review*, edited by G. Janecek. Lexington, Ky., 1978.

Szilard, E. "O strukture Vtoroi simfonii A. Belogo." *Studia Slavica Hungarica*, no. 13 (1967).

Taranovsky, K. F. "Chetyrekhstopnyi yamb Andreya Belogo." *International Journal of Slavic Linguistics and Poetics*, no. 10 (1966).

Tarasenkov, A. "Tema voiny v romane A. Belogo 'Moskva.'" *LOKAF (Znamya)*, no. 10 (1932).

Timofeev, Leonid. "O 'Maskakh' A. Belogo." *Oktyabr'*, no. 6 (1933).

Tomashevsky, B. V. "Pis'ma V. Ya. Bryusovu, 1910–1911 (vstupitel'naya stat'ya i publikatsiya L. S. Fleishmana)." *Uchenye Zapiski Tartuskogo gos. universiteta*, vyp. 284 (1971).

Trotsky, Lev. *Literatura i revolyutsiya.* Moscow, 1923. 2d ed. 1924. Published in English as *Literature and Revolution.* New York, 1957.

Tschiževskij, Dmitrij. "Andrej Belyjs 'Symphonien.'" In Andrey Bely, *Chetyre simfonii.* Munich, 1971.

—— and A. Hönig. "Einleitung." In *Kreshchenyi kitaets.* Munich, 1969.

Tsvetaeva, Marina. "Plennyi dukh." In *Izbrannaya proza v dvukh tomakh,* vol. II. New York, 1979. Published in English as "A Captive Spirit," in *A Captive Spirit: Selected Prose,* translated by J. Marin King. Ann Arbor, 1980.

Turgenieff, A. *Erinnerungen an Rudolf Steiner und die Arbeit am ersten Goetheanum.* Stuttgart, 1973.

V. L. [L'vov-Rogachevsky]. "Andrey Bely: *Serebryanyi golub'.*" *Sovremennyi Mir,* no. 9 (1910) (2d pagination).

Valentinov, N. V. *Dva goda s simvolistami.* Stanford, 1969.

Voronsky, Aleksandr. "Andrey Bely." In *Literaturnaya entsiklopediya,* vol. I. Moscow, 1930.

Woloschin, Margarita. *Die grüne Schlange: Lebenserinnerungen.* Stuttgart, 1954.

Yurieff, Zoya. "'Prishedshii': A. Bely and A. Chekhov." In *Andrey Bely: Critical Review,* edited by G. Janecek. Lexington, 1978.

Zakharenko, N. G., and V. V. Serebryakova. "Andrey Bely." In *Russkie sovetskie pisateli: Poety, Biobibliograficheskii ukazatel',* vol. III, pt. 1: *Bezymensky-Blagov,* edited by O. D. Golubeva et al. Moscow, 1979.

Zamyatin, Evgeny. "Andrey Bely." In *Litsa.* New York, 1955.

Zavalishin, Vyacheslav. *Early Soviet Writers.* New York, 1958.

Zhirmunsky, Viktor. "O ritmicheskoi proze." *Russkaya Literatura,* no. 4 (1966).

Contributors

JOHN E. MALMSTAD   Professor of Slavic Languages and Literatures, Harvard University

VLADIMIR E. ALEXANDROV   Associate Professor of Russian Literature, Yale University

MARIA CARLSON   Ph.D., Indiana University

STEVEN CASSEDY   Associate Professor of Slavic and Comparative Literature, University of California, San Diego

JOHN ELSWORTH   Senior Lecturer, School of Modern Languages and European History, University of East Anglia

LAZAR FLEISHMAN   Professor of Slavic Languages and Literatures, Stanford University

ROGER KEYS   Lecturer in Russian Language and Literature, University of St. Andrews

ROBERT A. MAGUIRE   Professor of Russian Language and Literature, Columbia University

DMITRY MAKSIMOV   Professor of Russian Literature, Emeritus, Leningrad University

G. S. SMITH   Professor of Russian Language and Literature, University of Oxford, and Fellow of New College

Index

Titles of Bely's works appear in English translation among the alphabetical listings, without attribution. Titles of works by other writers appear under the names of their authors.

Studies of the Harriman Institute

This book forms part of the Studies of the Harriman Institute, successor to:

STUDIES OF THE RUSSIAN INSTITUTE

Abram Bergson, *Soviet National Income in 1937* (1953)

Ernest J. Simmons, Jr., ed., *Through the Glass of Soviet Literature: Views of Russian Society* (1953)

Thad Paul Alton, *Polish Postwar Economy* (1954)

David Granick, *Management of the Industrial Firm in the USSR: A Study in Soviet Economic Planning* (1954)

Allen S. Whiting, *Soviet Policies in China, 1917–1924* (1954)

George S. N. Luckyj, *Literary Politics in the Soviet Ukraine, 1917–1934* (1956)

Michael Boro Petrovich, *The Emergence of Russian Panslavism, 1856–1870* (1956)

Thomas Taylor Hammond, *Lenin on Trade Unions and Revolution, 1893–1917* (1956)

David Marshall Lang, *The Last Years of the Georgian Monarchy, 1658–1832* (1957)

James William Morley, *The Japanese Thrust into Siberia, 1918* (1957)

Alexander G. Park, *Bolshevism in Turkestan, 1917–1927* (1957)

Herbert Marcuse, *Soviet Marxism: A Critical Analysis* (1958)

Charles B. McLane, *Soviet Policy and the Chinese Communists, 1931–1946* (1958)

Oliver H. Radkey, *The Agrarian Foes of Bolshevism: Promise and Defeat of the Russian Socialist Revolutionaries, February to October 1917* (1958)

Ralph Talcott Fisher, Jr., *Pattern for Soviet Youth: A Study of the Congresses of the Komsomol, 1918–1954* (1959)

Alfred Erich Senn, *The Emergence of Modern Lithuania* (1959)

Elliot R. Goodman, *The Soviet Design for a World State* (1960)

John N. Hazard, *Settling Disputes in Soviet Society: The Formative Years of Legal Institutions* (1960)

David Joravsky, *Soviet Marxism and Natural Science, 1917–1932* (1961)

Maurice Friedberg, *Russian Classics in Soviet Jackets* (1962)

Alfred J. Rieber, *Stalin and the French Communist Party, 1941–1947* (1962)

Theodore K. Von Laue, *Sergei Witte and the Industrialization of Russia* (1962)

John A. Armstrong, *Ukrainian Nationalism* (1963)

Oliver H. Radkey, *The Sickle under the Hammer: The Russian Socialist Revolutionaries in the Early Months of Soviet Rule* (1963)

Kermit E. McKenzie, *Comintern and World Revolution, 1928–1943: The Shaping of Doctrine* (1964)

Harvey L. Dyck, *Weimar Germany and Soviet Russia, 1926–1933: A Study in Diplomatic Instability* (1966)

(Above titles published by Columbia University Press.)

Harold J. Noah, *Financing Soviet Schools* (Teachers College, 1966)

John M. Thompson, *Russia, Bolshevism, and the Versailles Peace* (Princeton, 1966)

Paul Avrich, *The Russian Anarchists* (Princeton, 1967)

Loren R. Graham, *The Soviet Academy of Sciences and the Communist Party, 1927–1932* (Princeton, 1967)

Robert A. Maguire, *Red Virgin Soil: Soviet Literature in the 1920s* (Princeton, 1968; Cornell, 1987)

Studies of the Harriman Institute

T. H. Rigby, *Communist Party Membership in the U.S.S.R., 1917–1967* (Princeton, 1968)

Richard T. DeGeorge, *Soviet Ethics and Morality* (University of Michigan, 1969)

Jonathan Frankel, *Vladimir Akimov on the Dilemmas of Russian Marxism, 1895–1903* (Cambridge, 1969)

William Zimmerman, *Soviet Perspectives on International Relations, 1956–1967* (Princeton, 1969)

Paul Avrich, *Kronstadt, 1921* (Princeton, 1970)

Ezra Mendelsohn, *Class Struggle in the Pale: The Formative Years of the Jewish Workers' Movement in Tsarist Russia* (Cambridge, 1970)

Edward J. Brown, *The Proletarian Episode in Russian Literature* (Columbia, 1971)

Reginald E. Zelnik, *Labor and Society in Tsarist Russia: The Factory Workers of St. Petersburg, 1855–1870* (Stanford, 1971)

Patricia K. Grimsted, *Archives and Manuscript Repositories in the USSR: Moscow and Leningrad* (Princeton, 1972)

Ronald G. Suny, *The Baku Commune, 1917–1918* (Princeton, 1972)

Edward J. Brown, *Mayakovsky: A Poet in the Revolution* (Princeton, 1973)

Milton Ehre, *Oblomov and His Creator: The Life and Art of Ivan Goncharov* (Princeton, 1973)

Henry Krisch, *German Politics under Soviet Occupation* (Columbia, 1974)

Henry W. Morton and Rudolph L. Tökés, eds., *Soviet Politics and Society in the 1970s* (Free Press, 1974)

William G. Rosenberg, *Liberals in the Russian Revolution* (Princeton, 1974)

Richard G. Robbins, Jr., *Famine in Russia, 1891–1892* (Columbia, 1975)

Vera Dunham, *In Stalin's Time: Middle-class Values in Soviet Fiction* (Cambridge, 1976)

Walter Sablinsky, *The Road to Bloody Sunday* (Princeton, 1976)

William Mills Todd III, *The Familiar Letter as a Literary Genre in the Age of Pushkin* (Princeton, 1976)

Elizabeth Valkenier, *Russian Realist Art. The State and Society: The Peredvizhniki and Their Tradition* (Ardis, 1977)

Susan Solomon, *The Soviet Agrarian Debate* (Westview, 1978)

Sheila Fitzpatrick, ed., *Cultural Revolution in Russia, 1928–1931* (Indiana, 1978)

Peter Solomon, *Soviet Criminologists and Criminal Policy: Specialists in Policy-Making* (Columbia, 1978)

Kendall E. Bailes, *Technology and Society under Lenin and Stalin: Origins of the Soviet Technical Intelligentsia, 1917–1941* (Princeton, 1978)

Leopold H. Haimson, ed., *The Politics of Rural Russia, 1905–1914* (Indiana, 1979)

Theodore H. Friedgut, *Political Participation in the USSR* (Princeton, 1979)

Sheila Fitzpatrick, *Education and Social Mobility in the Soviet Union, 1921–1934* (Cambridge, 1979)

Wesley Andrew Fisher, *The Soviet Marriage Market: Mate-Selection in Russia and the USSR* (Praeger, 1980)

Jonathan Frankel, *Prophecy and Politics: Socialism, Nationalism, and the Russian Jews, 1862–1917* (Cambridge, 1981)

Robin Feuer Miller, *Dostoevsky and "The Idiot": Author, Narrator, and Reader* (Harvard, 1981)

Diane Koenker, *Moscow Workers and the 1917 Revolution* (Princeton, 1981)

Patricia K. Grimsted, *Archives and Manuscript Repositories in the USSR: Estonia, Latvia, Lithuania, and Belorussia* (Princeton, 1981)

Library of Congress Cataloging-in-Publication Data

Andrey Bely : spirit of symbolism.

(Studies of the Harriman Institute)
Bibliography: p.
Includes index.
Contents: Bely's symphonies / Roger Keys—The silver dove / Maria Carlson—
Petersburg / Robert A. Maguire and John E. Malmstad—[etc.]
1. Bely, Andrey, 1880–1934—Criticism and interpretation—Congresses. 2.
Symbolism (Literary movement)—Soviet Union—Congresses. I. Malmstad,
John E. II. Series.
PG3453.B84Z55 1987   891.78'309   86-29095
ISBN 0-8014-1984-0 (alk. paper)